Whispering Death
"Our journey with the Hmong in the Secret War in Laos"

ROBERT CURRY

Table of Contents

Forewords:

By Harry C Aderholt, Brigadier General USAF, retired

The book entitled "Whispering Death, Our Journey with the Hmong in the Secret War of Laos" by Robert Curry are true facts of the Hmong and their more than 15 years of fighting the Vietnamese to relieve the pressure in South Viet Nam and to interdict the Ho Chi Minh Trail. In this book, he gives an account of his combat missions in the OV-1 Mohawk, and how he learned the reason for being in that war. This is a book that must be read to understand what our country owes the Hmong Tribesmen.

In this operation, the Hmong were betrayed by the U.S. Government, and the Hmong lost their homeland, tens of thousands of their young men, a generation; and many to this day are still being chased in the jungles of Laos by the North Vietnamese and Laos communists.

In 2004, after more than thirty years, those in Thailand refugee camps, some fifteen thousand, were screened and transferred to the United States. They finally have a chance for a new life. This comes after living for many years in squalid refugee camps in Thailand. Thirty-five thousand will still be left behind after the fifteen thousand are admitted.

I highly recommend this book to be read for knowledge of how the Secret War in Laos was fought and why we owe the Hmong so much. There are chapters that have been written by Hmong men who fought this clandestine war.

By Larry Sanborn, RAVEN FAC, Call-sign: Sandy

"Trail of the Mohawk … land of the Hmong" by Robert Curry, describes the fascinating tour of duty of a young U.S. Army aviator in Southeast Asia in 1971. He takes you into the cockpit with him as you experience his combat missions in the OV-1 Mohawk. As a fellow aviator of the same period, I felt the thrill of combat flying he describes so vividly – the sights and sounds of the flight line and the tenseness resulting from anti-aircraft fire, pursuing MiG fighters, and the constant struggle with weather, aircraft malfunctions, and fatigue. This book put me back in the cockpit again flying in slow propeller-driven aircraft on classified missions.

The author meets the Hmong after moving from his base at Phu Bai, South Vietnam to the large American installation at Udorn, Thailand. Here he begins flying the Barrel Roll mission in northern Laos. With the Mohawk providing night surveillance using side-looking radar, visual and infrared sensors, he locates trucks, armor, and large guns for destruction by fighters or gunships with devastating results. This night mission over the famous Plaines des Jarres was an effective companion to the daylight mission led by the airborne Forward Air Controllers, the Ravens living in Laos. This airpower advantage combined to offset the North Vietnamese Army superiority in weapons and personnel - for a while.

The story woven here casts a compassionate eye for the beautiful, but battle hardened Hmong people. It is interwoven with chapters written by Hmong men who fought this clandestine war with their American allies. It tells of America losing the will to continue the fight and the resulting consequences when the war comes to an abrupt end and America abandons its Hmong ally. Perhaps this book will motivate the reader to realize that war does not end merely with the stroke of a pen.

This Raven finds the book a compelling story of combat aviation. It is an excellent description of the little known, but courageous mission of the Mohawk and its skilled operating teams. My hand comes up in salute to our professional brothers in arms, the Army Mohawk aviators, as we did the best we could for the Hmong in Laos.

Forward by Yang Chee, President Lao-Hmong American Coalition

The Hmong, which means "free people or freedom loving people," are fiercely independent Laotian hill tribesmen, noted for their warrior tradition, loyalty, and bravery. In early 1961, President John F. Kennedy initiated the ultimate American-Hmong connection to fight a "secret" war against communism. Freedom, democracy and justice were principally the core factors in the formation of a profound alliance between the two distinctively different people. With a common belief, their minds and hearts were bound together as eternal brothers and sisters. They fought side-by-side in guerrilla and conventional warfare both in the air and on the ground against communist tyranny not only to protect their own freedom and the sovereignty of the country of Laos, but also to defend the U.S. policy and to protect its interests in Southeast Asia during the Vietnam War. And, they did it so willingly with great risks, often taking the journey of no return together.

In early 1961, President John F. Kennedy initiated the ultimate American-Hmong connection to fight a "secret" war against communism. Freedom, democracy and justice were principally the core factors in the formation of a profound alliance between the two distinctively different people. With a common belief, their minds and hearts were bound together as eternal brothers and sisters. They fought side-by-side in guerrilla and conventional warfare both in the air and on the ground against communist tyranny not only to protect their own freedom and the sovereignty of the country of Laos, but also to defend the U.S. policy and to protect its interests in Southeast Asia during the Vietnam War. And, they did it so willingly with great risks, often taking the journey of no return together.

As the war escalated, the Air and Ground War intensified. More airplanes and more pilots were needed. The Hmong called those airplanes "Dav Lhau," meaning "Iron Eagles." And all American and Lao-Hmong pilots were called, "Tub Tsav Dav Lhau," meaning "Masters of the Iron Eagles." Those key Hmong allies of the air included the Ravens, Air America, T-28, Bird Air, the United States Air Force pilots, and these Army Mohawk aviators.

The author of this book, *Whispering Death . . . Our Journey with the Hmong in the Secret War of Laos*, was one of America's youngest honorable "Masters of the Iron Eagles" with the Hmong. And, he was a Master of the Mohawk himself. Along with their American counterparts, Hmong pilots flew thousands of dangerous sorties bombing enemy positions and supply lines. Half of the Hmong pilots were killed in action. American and Hmong back-seaters, Forward Air Control/Forward Air Guide (FAC/FAG) officers, CIA Case officers, Air Commando, Special Forces, Air America, Bird Air and USAID officers/personnel all undertook crucial roles in the co-ordinations of this "undeclared" war.

As a consequence, Laos became the most bombed country on earth. Over thirty-five thousand Hmong and over seven hundred Americans lost their lives in the defense of freedom. Then, in May of 1975, the United States pulled its armed forces and withdrew its support from the region, leaving its staunchest ally - the Hmong Special Guerrilla Units (SGU) and their families at the mercy of their archenemies.

Whispering Death . . . Our Journey with the Hmong in the Secret War of Laos is one of the most comprehensive and fascinating books ever written to catch your attention. The title itself is compelling enough to touch many people's hearts. The heroic stories of these valiant men reflect fresh memories of their faithful past in the U.S most covert and longest over-sea war in history. Their patriotic service remains a living legacy that will forever stand tall with dignity. Their noble acts of bravery, personal sacrifices and historic contributions to the free world should be recognized, and their unparalleled acts of patriotism need to be told, so all generations can learn from, and appreciate the price of freedom.

Dedication

This book is dedicated to my three girls, June, Amy, and Kristy who I love from the bottom of my heart. Who stood by me when the full effect of this conflict destroyed their lives; whose unwavering love saved mine. Their strength and love is the key to my heart and soul.

It is dedicated to the over eighty Mohawk aviators who lost their lives, became POW's, or are still MIA from the wars in Southeast Asia. Who flew where no one dared, often alone and unarmed to the home of the enemy. Whose missions were always classified and whose stories have never been told. To those who crewed, supported, and maintained these aircraft under the most trying of wartime conditions. Knowing it was often only through their efforts that brought us back from places where there was no friendly, no chance for failure.

To those unsung heroes who served in this Secret War in Laos; those of the US Military, Air America, Continental Air Services, Bird, USAID, the CIA, Air Commando's, the Butterflies and the Ravens. To Major General Richard Secord, Brigadier General Heine Aderholt, Bill Lair, Charlie Jones, Jim Stanford, and those others who selflessly gave everything they had for our country and the Hmong people. A special thanks to a Raven FAC friend, Larry (Sandy) Sanborn who truly made this work a better book.

To our Lao-Hmong brothers and sisters, who stood by the Americans to the bitter end, who fought for home and family, and lost both. Whose story of courage and tragedy of an unprecedented scale that has been hidden and ignored for decades. To all my Hmong family including Neng Naopao Lee, Robert Lohr, Xia Vue Yang, Yang Chee, Colonel Xay Dang Xiong, Chue Lee and Maika Lee. For Lieng Lee, the Hmong Flying Ace who won the respect of every American Airman who knew of his feats. To the Hmong women who fully lived and bore the wrath of this war and to the children who struggle to understand their silence and pain.

Preface to Betrayal

We returned one by one, from the most horrid place our minds and bodies had ever experienced. We brought with us memories of our brothers who died, and the brutal way in which they left. We returned to find peace, and instead we found hate. We did not choose our path, for that was the peruse of the politicians and its people. Now we would endure all the hate and scorn for a war a nation had grown tired of.

And a people would start on a new odyssey, and thousands more would die and suffer. They, the Lao-Hmong, would be left to die by these same politicians that declared peace. The lucky ones would be torn from their homes, and placed in squalid camps for years as Washington covered its ears to what it had set in motion. The lucky ones would make it to France or the US to start a new life in the most foreign of lands. Then there would be the less lucky, thousands who were forced by gunpoint back into their country to be killed or hunted in the jungles. And the shots still ring out today.

While the battle over Vietnam loomed in the American political boxing ring, another war was fought in the hills, jungles, and villages of Laos. War in Asia was not unique to the US; it had gone on for centuries as differing cultures and people fought to expand the same, or to survive. While a number of Americans took up the political banner of supporting the people's movement of Ho Chi Minh, a very different side of this same populist. North Vietnam at great human cost, expended huge military efforts to drive the Hmong hill people of Laos from their homeland. All to instill a like-minded regime in Laos that supported its ideology, and it wasn't the first time.

Unlike Vietnam, where the communists until the very end fought a guerilla war against the US, in Laos these roles were reversed. It was the North Vietnamese who fought with large standing military units including artillery, tanks, planes, etc.

The Lao-Hmong had lived for over a hundred fifty years on the high grounds and mountains of Laos, having moved south from China over a century ago to escape persecution. In Laos, they had known war for decades. First, they would find survival by fighting alongside the French to protect their villages, and then both would turn the fight against the Japanese invaders during World War II.

___

10

After Japan's defeat, France would return to Indochina, attempting to return to the days of their earlier colonial empire. But the various peoples' movements of the region would find them on the wrong end of another bitter war they would soon withdraw from. After France withdrew from Indochina, the Hmong found they were now being hunted again, payback for allying with the French. They were also tremendous soldiers, so it would be in the interest of the communists to eliminate any potential source of conflict in the future.

By this time, the spread of communism had drawn the attention of the United States to this little country. Laos would fill the news headlines well before the word Vietnam would etch itself forever in the American soul. Russia and the US would find themselves heading to a political crisis over a beautiful and tiny nation tucked in the teaming jungles and mountains of Southeast Asia far off the beaten path of world events, until now. History would not choose Laos for the battleground of the superpowers, at least not openly. Talks were hastily established in Geneva, and by 1955 an agreement was reached by all parties involved, agreeing that they would respect Laos' neutrality. Barred from the Geneva Agreements against formally placing troops into Laos, the US had decided on fighting the growing war in Laos with clandestine forces under direction of the CIA. The North Vietnamese were less formal; they just denied having any forces in Laos. The war would continue, now under the covers.

So, the Hmong followed the suggestion of their parting French allies, and continued their war of survival by fighting alongside the Americans. Only they'd be fighting a war with the shadowy side of the US, fighting a guerilla war against the expanding North Vietnamese and their Pathet Lao brothers. The Hmong subsequently carried out the most dangerous missions, to rescue downed US pilots, provide intelligence about enemy operations, attack the heavily defended Ho Chi Minh Trail, guard US strategic installations and direct an increasing amount of US airpower against all of the above. They fought a war with their families and children alongside them on the battlefield and in their villages. Their war was one of bitter survival; they were fighting and dying in order to hold on to their homeland, villages, and culture. Lao-Hmong pilots flew thousands of missions alongside the US Air Force & Army. These Lao-Hmong pilots conducted deadly bombing raids using old World War II slow flying aircraft supplied by the US onto enemy positions and supply lines where more than half of them never returned. As a result of battles raging year after year against forces that far out numbered them, a generation of Hmong men were decimated, eventually replaced with

Hmong boy soldiers, some as young as ten years old. They suffered the greatest casualties, out of a population of three hundred fifty thousand people; over thirty five thousand Lao-Hmong men & women lost their lives in the defense of living as the Hmong only knew, free. Proportionally, their causality rate was more than one hundred times higher than that of the United States in Vietnam. They threw their allegiance and trust to the American soldiers and aviators that would grow to admire their courage and skill. These Americans and Hmong would quickly come to know each other as brothers and family.

Laos would become the most bombed country in history during the Vietnam War. There were more bombs dropped on Laos than were dropped in all of World War II, including Europe and the Pacific. An average of over two thousand pounds of bombs were dropped for every man, woman, and child living in Laos. This brutal conflict by both sides would totally decimate their lives, villages, farms, livestock and way of life. With the US hastily withdrawing in 1975, the communists would quickly sweep through Laos and seek a brutal revenge on a people who had valiantly fought them to a stand still during this long war. The Hmong would become victims of some of the most brutal atrocities and persecutions the world has seen. Only like the secret war before it, this wanton bloodshed would occur far away from a world that had grown tired of another war called Vietnam. And the politicians, who sacrificed these Hmong like pawns to get the agreement they wanted, would never allow this struggle to become public. Least this Hmong blood cast a shadow of guilt and shame on their newfound claim as peacemakers.

Several thousands of this faithful ally fled the country in chaos to refugee or internment camps in Thailand, languishing for years. Thousands more would escape to the jungles, to be hunted for decades. Many survived only because of the valiant efforts of the local US forces who scraped together planes and pilots to ferry whole families and villages out of the path of the murder that had just started. These Americans found that the US government had made no plans of helping their longtime allies escape the bloodshed. The American government had closed shop, literally.

Betrayal is seldom a term that invokes a sense of political impartiality. But then, the Vietnam era betrayed all normal political definition and predictability. No matter what side of the political spectrum, this sense of betrayal was rampant. Liberals felt betrayed by a government that they felt decades earlier endorsed the wrong freedom movement in Vietnam. Americans, always ready to spill their sons and daughters

12

blood to help freedom in some far-flung corner of the world, had their morals as a nation questioned. The military could no longer trust Washington, who gave no clear purpose, but daily inflicted new rules that cost thousands of lives. A Washington who tried to mandate what regimes would rule, all in the struggle to let the people decide? Except they never would decide in the ballot box, only on the battlefield. And when Washington grew tired and confused, the lofty goals of freedom and self-determination turned to political survival. While people died on the battlefield, in the villages, their next journey would be decided in conference rooms and hallways a million miles away.

And a group of beautiful hill people in a little country who's name would pass in the night that had decided decades earlier they would fight their own war of freedom alongside the US, would be betrayed.

And on that fateful day, January 23, 1973 the politicians would betray them. The American government would sell them out for a peace of paper that let us extradite ourselves from the "other" war we grew tired of, no longer understood.

In 1969, an eighteen year old steeped in the belief that his duty was to follow the call of a nation, went to war. I believed in mom, apple pie, that our cause was always just, but more than anything I wanted to fly. My journey took me into places I still struggle with today. I would find everything I had been led to believe questioned on the battlefields, the villages, the roads, and skies of this place called Vietnam, of a country called Laos, and a people called the Hmong. The news would leak to us that those brothers returning stateside from this horror of places were being spit on in the streets, being blamed for all that went wrong. The arguments for our involvement were batted around between the missions or the small pieces of sleep. But we could do nothing about the politics a million miles away. Someone very seriously wanted to kill us here, every day. Survival was the priority, and that meant killing; it was a simple choice.

So our war was fought on the ground and over the jungles. Instead of trip wires, we feared anti-aircraft fire, and around any corner might come streaking that SAM missile guided by radar. Death was different, many times death came at a distance, watching an explosion, and a brother was forever gone. Or right in our face, strapped into a cockpit that we were entombed in until we ejected or made our way home. What animalistic satisfaction one took in seeing the enemy that hunted you die, we imagined, as trucks burst in flames below us. And when we returned, death visited us in our huts and bunkers as we slept, ate, or awaited an enemy always close by.

The planes we flew were unique, so unique most history books fail to mention the Mohawk or its role. Our missions touched every facet of the war. One day we hunted Vietcong for a Marine ground unit outside Khe Sanh, the next day we hunted trucks with the Air Force in Laos. And one moonlit evening a lonely unarmed Mohawk flew at tree top level in a field outside Hanoi searching for a suspected camp holding our POW's. The far ranging capabilities of the plane embroiled the Army and Air Force in a fight over whose control they should be in. The Mohawk was always "on point" in this air war. Like it's grunt brothers on the ground, point was up front, alone, trying to find the enemy, often the first to be found, to die. Except these two warriors flew alone and unarmed with no force behind to call upon.

And flying in places the government repeatedly denied we ventured. It was a thought one tried to keep far back in one's mind that we were alone hunting for an elusive enemy in his backyard. And when we met trouble, only luck and this ever more elusive God above was the only hope we had to bring us back.

And when the enemy didn't have us in their sites, our own government was taking pot shots. Rules of war did not allow attacking a Sam missile site or an anti-aircraft gun battery while it was under construction. We'd be gentlemen and wait till they were done and fired the first shot. We could fly far into Laos or China, but the Air Force brass didn't feel it was the mission of the Army Mohawk to be armed. But while the brass back home fought, Army Mohawks worked tightly with Air Force and Navy fighters and gunships in destroying large amounts of supplies and men moving from the North into South Vietnam through this land called Laos.

I would soon find out there was another war here, hidden from most. While it was an integral part of what was going on in Vietnam, it defied the conventional wisdom of all the confusion going on in Vietnam. And when the government began the secret air war in Laos, it enlisted the Mohawk and their pilots, crews that would fly under the direct control of the Air Force and the CIA. A small unit of Mohawks, this "rat patrol" would be detached, to fly classified missions in the north of Laos and Vietnam; and the South of China in this secret war. This conflict called Vietnam was a piece of a larger puzzle, the War of Southeast Asia.

———

14

These conflicts were grossly intertwined and at the same time very different.

This book contains a sliver of my journey there. There is much more I've yet to deal with even today. Some of the names of those I've been unable to talk with, I've changed to protect the self-imposed anonymity of many a Vietnam Vet. It's set against the backdrop of a beautiful people, the Lao-Hmong, who allied with America to fight a common enemy. Hmong stands for free people, the freedom to live as they had tried for centuries, amongst their families high in the mountains. It was this freedom that was a threat to all those who ruled by dictate, and Asia was full of these. The Hmong would find themselves hunted for this simplest of human desire; they would ally with a country whose foundation was built on similar ideals. And then we abandoned them to die in the jungles with the signing of a piece of paper.

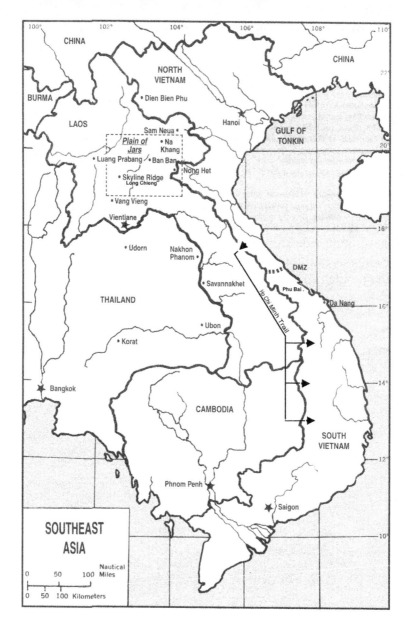

SOUTHEAST ASIA

0   50   100   Nautical Miles

0   50   100   Kilometers

16

Ornaments in the Trees
Chapter One

"Curry, they want you down at intel," came a voice through the screen door of my hootch. Then it quickly disappeared until I heard the voice and footsteps at the hootch next store requesting someone else's attention. It was dark inside here as I was playing some reel-to-reel music attempting to let time move on. Shit, nothing good ever came when someone arrived unannounced yelling out your name. But at least I'd have company in a shit storm whose name I didn't yet know. I quickly threw on my jungle fatigue top, my baseball cap, and headed out for the intelligence shack. At least if I was going to be yelled at, it would be in the frigid hundred degree air conditioning of the intelligence room where numerous men or boys were peering over film with magnifying glasses trying to make out a gun, truck; or that ever elusive NVA Popsicle stand on the Ho Chi Minh Trail; shit they had to have one, this heat was brutal.

It took me the full walk up to the shack for my eyes to adjust to the blazing intense sunlight of midday. Outside the Intel shack was Sarah, my pup's mother lying in the puddle of water draining out of the air conditioner that was loudly straining to squeeze the moisture out of the hot air inside the intel shack. Sarah looked like a beached whale in that puddle appearing in the middle of this endless sandbox called Phu Bai. She was oblivious to anything around here, I found myself jealous of that.

Curry, glad you could get your ass down here," boomed Thud, "didn't break up your siesta did I?"

"Nope, I guess I can put off my scholarly reading of the Old Testament for another day," I quipped back. "How's your war going today?"

Thud glared at me with his shiny red face. I was never sure if it was a reflection off the numerous film and light tables, or from an artery on the verge of exploding. "Funny you should bring that up, it's about to get real interesting and we need you to tell us how good. Tonight we are putting in an arch light on route nine north of Tchepone. We got a lot of movers heading south we think to reinforce the staging areas on the trail. We'll put an infrared mission in after sunset to confirm the positions. We'll want you and Jack to be there at dawn and get us some film and visuals on what we got after the B-52's go in. Think you can fuck that up?"

I was staring at the map of Laos trying to imagine the monstrous jungle leaping up at you from the mountains and valleys. It was tough seeing a lot out there on the ground. I was already thinking of the streams or hilltops I'd have to use to plan out the correct film runs to get everything covered. "Sure, but I got the SLAR mission up north by Dong Hoa tomorrow."

"No sweat, you'll have time after you get back from this one to clean out your pants and digest some of Kaminski's grub. You'll fly with Jack, check back here after the infrared mission returns about twenty one hundred and plot your runs out. I want you two in the air no later then zero four hundred," Thud finished, walking off to pounce on Jim who just walked through the door.

"Arch-light" I sputtered to myself. That was a B-52 strike coming in on something big or important, or both. I've seen the arch lights at night dropping a carpet of bombs screaming at the ground in unison; it lit up the night sky as bright as day, hell . . . brighter. We'd bounce in the air miles away from the onslaught as these five hundred pounders hit in a ballet of incredible death and destruction. I couldn't imagine being anywhere on the ground close to that rain of hell. If you survived, you certainly would lose your hearing and be a basket case for the rest of your life. Now we'd get to see the damage first hand, never a dull day at the office.

By the late sixties there were four Mohawk units still stationed in Vietnam. Several units had left earlier or evolved into one of the remaining units. The units still flying included the 73rd Aviation Company located at Vung Tau, later moving to Long Thanh. Can Tho was home to the 244th Aviation Company. Both these units flew similar missions. There was Market Time, the radar surveillance of the coastal waters. Here the Mohawks would fly the coastal waters off South Vietnam, once the radar detected a "mover" or boat was tracked, the Mohawk would hand over the attack to the Navy. Game Warden had the same mission, only targeted on the inland Mekong waterways. Operation Firefly or Lightning Bug utilized B or C model Mohawks working with Hueys armed with searchlights and weapon systems to take out the enemy moving under the curtain of darkness they had previously enjoyed. The 225th Aviation Company was based at Phu Hiep, then on to Tuy Hoa in 1970. They flew border patrol, infiltration

18

routes, coastal patrol, and missions for the Republic of Korea units. And my home, the 131st Aviation Company was way up north, on a small airstrip outside Hue called Phu Bai. Every unit had a unique set of missions it was responsible for. Many involved flying recon mission for various Army and Marine units in its area of responsibility. Many missions were unique to the territory it flew.

The 131st was charged with three basic missions, all classified. The first was to fly recon mission for area ground units, including but not limited to the various Army and the Marines units up in I Corps. These missions included daytime visual and photo recon and nighttime with infrared sensing equipment on suspected enemy positions. Many recon missions found the enemy out in the open and exposed, allowing those Mohawks with armament to take them out before they blended back into the jungle. Whether the Mohawks were armed depended on the current state of the cat and mouse game the Army and Air Force brass were playing back home. The Air Force saw the Mohawk as a direct threat to its mission. The Army wanted the Mohawk for both its instant battlefield intelligence and with its ability to sneak up on an enemy in the open. They wanted the Mohawk to take out the enemy before they ran and hid again. Too many times the Air Force won, requiring the Mohawks to perform their missions unarmed. That was until a company commander with balls found a way to rearm them at least for a while.

The second set of missions were the round the clock SLAR or radar flights into North Vietnam. This radar film, which detected vehicular traffic, was analyzed immediately after each flight returned by the military intelligence crew located directly next to the flight line and sent directly to MACV headquarters in Saigon. These flights took the two man Mohawk crew far north over North Vietnam alone and unarmed. The North Vietnamese tried various games to take down or capture a Mohawk. The intelligence electronics would be a gold mine for their Russian and Chinese partners, pay back for their investment of the tools of war. Tired of watching these Mohawks constantly scanning their country from head to foot, the North Vietnamese once built a fake navigation site to capture one. Flying in total VFR conditions during the endless monsoons, a crew would routinely look for Channel sixty-nine at Phu Bai to direct it back home. The rumor we heard never knowing if it was true had a fake station sixty nine set up years earlier by the North Vietnamese to direct and talk a Mohawk crew into landing in bad weather on what they thought was Phu Bai, only after they landed would they realize they were in North Vietnam.

The third focus were the Laos missions, mission twenty would fly every night into Laos flying the breath of the Ho Chi Minh trail from the Cambodian border to the Mia Gia pass where most of the supplies entered Laos from North Vietnam on its journey south. The Air Force called the operations in southern Laos Steel Tiger. Here the Mohawk would fly under direct Air Force control, coordinating its flight with the orbiting command ship Moonbeam each evening. Take off times varied to not offer a pattern or time line for the NVA to work with. Once the Mohawk crew detected targets or movers in almost real time, they plotted the positions on maps and fed the coordinates to Moonbeam who reached into its bag of available strike aircraft to take out the targets. Truck kills improved over sixty per cent when the Mohawks flew in Hunter-Killer teams with the AC-119 or C-130 gunships. Unlike the missions in North Vietnam where bombing pauses more than not curtailed attacking the enemy, Laos was open season over the trail. It also included the largest concentration of anti-aircraft guns the world had ever seen. From 37mm to 100mm, they had every available gun the communist countries could build and field. In 1970, SAM missiles sites were being constructed for the first time in Laos. Radar controlled guns were beginning to appear and set the notch for death up one for the enemy. They were deadly serious about protecting their vital artery to South Vietnam in order to press the war forward.

The crews flying mission twenty would for the most part specialize on flying this mission. Every night out there made one more familiar with the hidden trails under the jungle, coordination with the Air Force, and tricks of the trade in finding and destroying trucks and truck parks. Once you proved yourself on the trail, you were ready for the 131st's classified missions flying out of country. While still assigned to Phu Bai where all your mail came and went, those selected would fly directly for the CIA and Air Force on missions flying in Northern Laos known as Barrel Roll. This rat patrol of Mohawks was based out of the Royal Thai Air Force and Air America base at Udorn Thailand just across the Mekong River from the Laotian capital of Vientiane. This theater of operation was largely centered on the Plain of Jars, home of the Hmong allies who took the fight to the NVA and Pathet Lao on the ground. As they had done with the French, the Hmong proved above all to be America's strongest ally. There was never a doubt when going into a fight with a Hmong soldier; he had your back all the way. For those who had the honor to serve multiple tours, some a good piece of their career with these incredible people, there developed a bond that was closer than family.

Then there were the oddities, the missions needed for a special project, a new campaign or to follow on a hunch by someone with enough clout to pull strings and redirect missions on an already over worked Mohawk unit. Lamson 719 was all of the above, the invasion of Laos by the South Vietnamese Army. For years the arguments had continued over how to stop the flow of materials down the now infamous Ho Chi Minh Trail. The US had stayed clear of placing US troops in a country whose neutrality it agreed to honor along with the Russians in the Geneva Accords on Laos. In the late fifties the US and Russia almost went to war over Laos well before Vietnam entered the daily news. They both backed away from the brink by agreeing to honor the neutrality agreement hastily reached in Geneva. With the outbreak of war between North Vietnam and the United States, Russia could then hide behind a North Vietnamese army now in place in Laos. The Vietnamese routinely justified its position or denied their existence. While no longer at the brink of war with Russia, the US was reeling politically from its recent invasion of Cambodia. Tactically they had destroyed tons of material ready to be used in South Vietnam that until then was safely out of harms way across the border in Cambodia. Politically they had added gasoline to the protest fires around the world violently opposed to any expansion of the war in Vietnam. But these wars had decades earlier expanded to most of South East Asia, only the Americans at home were unaware of it.

With Kissinger pressing for an end to the war, the pressure to buy South Vietnam time from the anvil hanging over its head from the North increased the pressure to do something about the North Vietnamese pipeline of supplies to the south. To hit it and cut off the trail would buy the south another year with limited NVA activity due to the tourniquet applied against its trail of supply and men. Numerous military leaders argued against the plan, some held it was too late in coming, most predicted defeat when Washington dictated the rules and played armchair quarterback a world away especially without US troops leading the way. But the rules of this invasion dictated that South Vietnamese ARVN forces alone would be involved in the invasion with only air and artillery support from the US. The idea was to skirt a public relations backlash by not introducing US ground troops in Laos. Once the dust settled the invasion was on and we'd be busy as hell and soon we'd be minus some more fine men . . . such is war.

It was called Lamson 719, to commemorate a Vietnamese battle over China centuries ago. The goal was to move several ARVN battalions of troops from the northeast corner of South Vietnam near the old Khe

Sanh base into Laos moving north and west with the end target being the crossroad town of Tchepone. While the ground forces moved west along the roads, more troops would be inserted by helicopter at strategic locations to take out strong enemy positions, to catch them in a leapfrog move. Further north and west of Tchepone, Air America or the Air Force would drop in some Hmong units to block any exit by the NVA that way. Tchepone was at the cross roads of several main trail roads bringing supplies into the southern reaches of the trail. It was indeed a key city. We flew it every night on our missions; it was always ripe with movers and intense anti aircraft fire. The North Vietnamese knew its value well.

So the word came down in January they'd need all kinds of intelligence quickly. We were loaned several aircraft from other Mohawk units to give us the physical resources we were out of. As far as the crews, who needed sleep? During the day we flew photo recon in teams of two for each flight to map every piece of ground between Khe Sanh and Tchepone and beyond. Multiple flights would be required every day to get the job done. Once the MI boys found targets on the film, we'd have to re-fly the area to keep track of any movement in or out. At night the infrared missions flew the same ground hoping to pick up the activity or clues in the darkness only nighttime brings on the trail. These flights always flew at treetop level in order to gain the best intelligence and give the gunners below less time to aim and shoot . . . hopefully.

Activity all around us picked up tremendously, now there were C-130's landing supplies every ten minutes out on the airstrip. Phu Bai was soon to become a major staging area for the invasion. A chimp could have figured out something big was up, and soon almost everyone would know.

Jim caught up with me by the time I got back to the hootch. "Hey Bob, lets head down to the 101st, I hear they got some more Sterno in their PX."

"I'm with you buddy, my war starts later," I replied, and with that we were off. We grabbed some M-16's, couple ammo clips, and jumped into the trusty mail jeep. Amazing what trading some sausages from back home will get you.

We raced down the dirt road off our small airstrip here west of Hue and drove through the dusty village of Phu Bai. Most of the traffic was military today clogging this part of old highway one. We bull shitted

22

about news from back home, rumors of war, what was being concocted in the mess hall this evening. You know, everything and nothing of substance.

We hit the PX at Camp Eagle that looked like any metal storage building back home. Jim ran off to grab little cans of cooking sterno so he could cook up his canned spaghetti. We went though great lengths to eat anything but what was served us. I cruised the aisles taking in the values sitting here today, certainly gone by tomorrow. My eyes focused on a gun belt, you know the old western style gun belt they wore at the OK Corral; from what I hear that is. That was too much to pass over, I snatched it up and pushed my way upfront to find Jim balancing cans of sterno and beans and franks. This would go down as a successful day in-country.

As we drove back I found myself buffing the leather gun belt while we took in the scenes along highway one. The gun belt would allow me to put the .38 handgun and shells the Army had given all its flight crews to carry somewhere other then in my shirt breast pocket. The term half-ass precedes everything they do here, but I guess it keeps us natives busy.

Yup, just as I figured, the mess hall was shoveling chemically enhanced leather strips with that awesome gravy that gives off that pretty rainbow under the harsh mess hall lighting. So bad, the starving dogs that stand outside of the mess hall begging for scraps smell this and run away. Thank god Jim got the franks and beans.

A quick sterno enhanced dinner and I hit the bunk early, as I'd need to be on the flight line at three am for the surrey into Laos. We wanted to be on target at sunrise.

Three a.m. came, as it always does, never pretty. I dragged myself to the ops hootch and guzzled some hot black mud to attempt to break the coma. By the time I had the plane prepped, Jack was there giving Spud one-seven its preflight inspection. No problems and we were airborne streaking west before most peoples work day started.

As we crossed the border into Laos, I put the call into Moonbeam advising them of our presence in their control space in and over the Ho Chi Minh Trail. Moonbeam was a flying C-130 cargo plane with a tailor full of electronics, radios and men slid in its cargo bay. They would keep control of every plane flying in its sectors; here it would be the whole of the Ho Chi Minh Trail that snaked west of the Vietnam border. Their job was to coordinate this strange chess game of aircraft, each with different moves, speeds, missions, all trying to achieve one goal, kill the supplies heading to the war in South Vietnam. In addition to the aircraft, it would also handle all the radio traffic from various ground units; Thai, Lao and the CIA sponsored indigenous forces fighting in Laos, along with Special Forces road spotter teams who called in visual targets from their hiding places.

When targets were found, or ground forces needed fighter or bomber support, Moonbeam would reach into its grab bag of available strike aircraft and select the best match for the job needed. Nothing required more focus then a downed pilot or crew. Every asset in the air or available off the ground or a ship would be diverted to this rescue operation. Even now, the word was out if you were shot down in Laos, the chances of making it north to the POW camps and perhaps freedom when and if the war ever ended were minuscule. If you were unfortunate enough to be captured by the Pathet Lao, the results were guaranteed torture and death.

It was still dark as we streaked over the skies heading north and west to Tchepone, the crossroads city of the Ho Chi Minh Trail. A NVA unit had been moving near the position of the Hmong blocking force Air America had inserted earlier to assist the South Vietnamese forces hoping to scare the NVA into the trap. But this unit's movements so near the Hmong SGU or special guerilla unit had not been predicted. They might have sensed the SGU unit or just happen to be in the area unknown of their presence. Either way, they moved themselves to the top of the hit parade and earned themselves a deadly serenade from several flights of B-52's just hours ago. We were to see how they liked the concert, and see if there were any traffic problems leaving the concert area with anyone still capable of driving.

"Moonbeam, Spud one-seven diverting north for assigned run. Notify if any friendlies expected in mission area?" The last thing we wanted was a late arrival dropping their load of bombs on us as we take pictures.

"Negative Spud one-seven, you are cleared in" crackled the response.

The cameras were fired up ready to roll. As I spread the maps out over my lap, I dug out the sheet detailing the coordinates to make our runs with. This A model Mohawk had both front & belly mounted cameras that would take a film mosaic of any area we wanted. The night before I laid out all the separate runs we'd need to allow for the width of ground each film run would take. To cover the large area they wanted would require over twenty separate runs to give them enough film to put together the giant mosaic. The intel guys would piece this jigsaw of film together and with huge magnifying glasses over light tables explore for any person, soldier, weapon, gun, etc. Flying these paths requires exact precision, but as we were flying down on the deck right over the treetops, it also meant we'd be a predicable target for any NVA with half a brain and a gun, or was it the other way around?

We had the first element of surprise, as you couldn't hear the Mohawk coming, but once we were there flying our straight lines for the camera all hell could break out. So we tried to mix the sequence of the runs up as much as possible, couldn't make it too easy for these guys. Jack had already been dropping altitude as we headed north and west. We wanted to have the sun behind us on at least half of the runs to blind anyone on the ground willing to fire off some rounds. If there were anti aircraft guns here it would get real interesting real fast.

When we skirted the town of Tchepone the sun was rising from behind us allowing us to verify our flight path with some visuals on the ground, several road bends and rivers. As we came up on the target area the ground fog was dissipating, allowing the rich green of the jungle to streak underneath us.

"One minute to first run" I keyed the intercom.

Jack gave me the thumbs up as he read the coordinates attempting to line us up. I turned on the cameras having learned it was always better to have too much then not enough. We settled into our altitude and stared ahead as the jungle rushed underneath us. The sun was now partially up and glissioning off the water beads and the little ground fog that still covered the now quiet jungles. It was as if someone had placed a National Geographic magazine in front of us and we were flying through it. It took our breath away.

"Curry, what in the hell is that?" the headset barked.

Jack was staring way ahead of us now not sure what he was seeing. I strained to make sense. It was as if the tips of the trees were sparkling, like ornaments on Christmas trees.
I continued to stare as we raced at over two hundred miles an hour toward it, until.

"Holy shit"

It was body parts, strewn across any trees still standing. Arms, torso's, legs, it was as if your dog went crazy in your daughter's doll collection. The brain was still trying to take in what we were seeing until the smell hit.

The B-52 strike had been a surprise and on target. Its load of five hundred pound bombs had blanketed what had been the staging area of an NVA regiment. They never had time to run or hide. There was no hole deep enough for this type of destruction. Destruction that rained earth and bodies back down on what had been a beautiful sea of green.

The smell then hit like someone punched me in the chest, grabbing every once of air out of my lungs and replaced it with the potent acid rotting smell of death. I started hyperventilating but the carnage continued to roll in front of us. How Jack kept the plane in the air was amazing. We said nothing, there were no words, the impenetrable smell of death said all that needed to be said.

On our second path, the carnage and winds of death engulfed us again; I vomited over my microphone until every spec of fluid in my stomach was gone. My eyes burned and teared, everything moved fast, but at the same time appeared strange, weird, as if certain items were in slow motion. As we continued our camera runs with only the conversation of coordinates to plot our next run, my mind began to fixate on various pieces. A mid section there, partially wrapped in its uniform, an arm bend backwards hanging in a ruptured tree almost like a Christmas hook over there. Heads with no bodies, their eyes open, staring into the air as if trying to see what had engulfed them.

For forty-five minutes we flew only feet above this torrent of pieces glissioning like ornaments on the trees or scattered across the ground, filming this one success of war. It had been the ultimate mission where not one of our soldiers or airmen died. Somehow it seemed meaningless right now.

And sometime that hour or day or year we were finished, flying east to deliver the canisters of film people were waiting on. There was no need to radio ahead with the results, they'd see it soon enough. While we streaked east back into Vietnam the smell of that day never left. If only I could let someone smell it when they asked me how it was, only then would they know, comprehend the insanity of it all.

Someone created this mess called Vietnam, a country, a war, an era, a feeling, or all of it? In the end, it was a beast that ravaged Southeast Asia and almost brought America to its political knees. It killed in a place called Phu Bai, in a secret mountain base called Long Chieng, and on a college campus called Kent Michigan. Eighteen years old and the insanity was amongst us, it was every place we went, in everything we did.

Remember what you were doing when you where eighteen; graduating, starting that first real job, taking the summer off? A sense of freedom, of excitement, and some trepidation in the new found freedom that eighteen brings.

Eighteen years old, and lined up in my shiny new jungle fatigues and boots, I waited with dozens of other teenagers for the word to board our plane. It was a beautiful Sunday morning in Oakland, California. The kind of morning one would spend in shorts and a T-shirt loading your car for an afternoon out on the water. Instead, one hundred and twenty-eight boys in soldiers' uniforms were heading off to a place we'd only seen in short bursts on the evening news. We all chatted amongst ourselves until the word came filtering down to begin boarding the golden DC-8 sitting on the runway tarmac.

If not for the fact that all the passengers on the plane were wearing jungle fatigues, we could have passed for being on a vacation trip to anywhere in the world. Anywhere else that is, except Southeast Asia. The plane was filled with noise and excitement as the young passengers found their seats and introduced themselves to those around them. Somehow I had expected more. Perhaps a large, darkly camouflaged Air Force troop transport boarding solemn troops at some out of the way military base in the dead of night. Yet, here we were, leaving from Oakland on a commercial jet, complete with stewardesses, pillows, playing cards, Newsweek and Time. The shock would be delayed, occurring some twenty-three hours later when the flight ended.

Sitting down and buckling in for the long flight we quickly became acquainted with the guys sitting around us. As one learns in the military early on, you build friendships that last a day, a week, or months and then end as fast as they had begun. Even though we had never met, here we all had a common bond, that we were scared shitless, and we weren't exactly sure what about. We had watched the war nightly from our living room or the dinner table. Brief minutes of helicopters kicking up dust and disgorging soldiers into rice paddies or jungle clearings. The sounds were helicopters and explosions of a battle close at hand. Then the pictures of men running, carrying their bloodied buddies back to the choppers, yelling amid all these sounds of confusion for help. The enemy was always out there, beyond the camera lens. It reinforced the mystique of a silent deadly enemy you could certainly feel, but seemingly impossible to find. Then as quickly as it had begun, the news report ended. The routine was built and reinforced; we accepted it as part of our life, a half a world away.

As time continued, the protests grew. First it consisted of students, intellectuals, artists and authors. Segments of society that Middle America had a hard time relating to, much less seeing as influential leaders they would follow. But the protests grew, gnawing away at those ideals that had been hammered at us since our youth. Those noble ideals that we as a nation carry the fight for those less fortunate around the world. But as the protests grew, so did its leaders. Political leaders from both parties began to question our direction. And America began to listen, to think, and to question.

For an eighteen year old it all appeared as confusion. What I had been taught to believe was being called into question. Sitting on this plane I remembered those moments of confusion and death we had watched on TV. The youth that tells you life is forever was beginning to come to grips with a reality, however unreal, just twenty-three hours away.

I was interrupted by a huge blond kid tripping over my body trying to get to the seat next to me.

"Sorry buddy, these aisles get a little small when they rush ya."

"That's OK, the name's Curry, how 'bout you?"

"Taylor, Don, straight from Georgia to get these goddamn chinks on their feet, so I can get back home quick."

Taylor was a grunt, a foot soldier. The soldier all those news reports centered on. I had the deepest respect for these grunts, as he was the one that would carry the war personally beyond the camera lens to the enemy we couldn't see; and the one I was sure that would most often pay the price. Little did I know there was no front line, no safe place? Oh, some were safer then others. Being a grunt was a hell of a lot riskier then being a supply clerk back in Cam Ranh Bay, but then that's the they made mortars for. I'd soon realize I'd be flying alone over some god-forsaken jungle over North Vietnam or Laos, a perfect target for any number of guns and itchy fingers. But then, I didn't know a whole hell of a lot.

Don was a cracker jack on the plane, talking the whole time. I'd never know if he was always this talkative or if it was the nervousness of the moment.

Across from me sat a young black helicopter crew chief going by the name of Jess McGee. We immediately jumped into conversations about our flying. Jess was about nineteen years old and spoke with a southern accent. His dad was a career military man in the Air Force and had spent several tours in Da Nang and Thailand. Jess wanted to go on to college, but family money problems prevented that. Then the draft caught him and he was off to infantry or what we affectionately referred to as grunt training. Somewhere in this confusion he volunteered for the crew chief program, as he always loved aircraft. Unfortunately, being a crew chief was not the safest profession in a war.

Vietnams was America's poor mans war as they drafted the poor and minorities off the streets of America, while the middle class and the rich kids filled the college campuses. You could avoid the military if you were middle class enough to get into college and stay there as long as you could, on what was called a college deferment. Or if your family was rich and well connected, you could get into one of the Military Reserve or National Guard Units where positions were very limited, given Johnson and later Nixon pledged they would not be used in the war.

We talked fondly of the solitude that flying gave us when you were floating high over the landscape. And the adrenalin rush one feels when watching treetops and phone poles skimming past us at several hundred miles an hour. It was total freedom, no one yelling over your shoulder telling you what to do. You were free, yet totally aware what a mistake would cost. Over the length of the trip, I watched both our realities sink in slowly, as we began to realize this part of the game was for keeps, there was no way out.

I was on my way to fly right seat in a Grumman OV-1 Mohawk aircraft. Over forty feet long and powered by two large turboprop engines, this plane was designed to fly recon or close air support missions, finding out where the enemy was or where he was moving to. Due to the limited number of Mohawk aircraft, McGee still wasn't sure what I flew in or what I did. No one ever did.

Taxiing to the runway, the chatter and noise on the plane settled down. Conversations were more immediate and hushed. I looked over at Jess and noticed a sense of nervousness.

Tauntingly I looked at him, "Scared of take-offs, could be a bitch in your business."

His southern accent disappeared, "Shit Curry, I just never trust anything that flies with wings, just helicopters that can go anywhere and land anywhere."

Finally airborne, we all settled in for the long trip. Conversations broke out again all over the plane. Don and Jess were both from Atlanta, although from very different sides of the track. A planeload of total strangers began to act as if they had been together for months. The first leg of our trip took us to Anchorage, Alaska for a fuel stop and a chance to stretch our legs. We arrived on a rather cold night with a howling wind and snow on the ground at Anchorage International Airport. I'm not sure if it was by design or accident that we arrived at a deserted airport at eleven in the evening. While the plane refueled we wandered around the airport. I had a chance to buy a postcard, quickly fill it out, and mail home to my fiancée'. We must have looked like a strange invasion force . . . in this airport that jetted off normally dressed families and business people during the day. One hundred twenty-eight men dressed in green jungle fatigues had taken over the airport for a short period of time this evening. As we left, we left American soil, some for their last time.

The call came to re-board and all of us settled in for our long haul to Japan for another refueling stop and leg stretcher. The initial "excitement" had kept everyone awake, talking and joking from Oakland to Anchorage. Now the plane turned quiet as most turned off their lights and fell in and out of sleep. I would awake after numerous short naps to engage in conversations around me.

Up ahead of me and across the aisle sat John. John was a supply clerk, or at least that's what they trained him for. The Army had congratulated him upon graduation, with orders for Vietnam. He was hoping to get assigned to some huge warehouse in the middle of the large U.S base at Cam Ranh Bay. Here he could live out his year in the relative obscurity of the largest military base in Vietnam. Somehow that sounded safe and boring.

Of course, John looked like a supply clerk. About twenty years old, his hairline already was receding well above his wire-rimmed glasses. John looked like he came from Kansas, even though he claims he grew up in San Mateo, California. I figured upon entering the service we all stood up in one line, and based upon your physical appearance the Army assigned you to various duties. Even that required some organizational skills, which would rule out the Army.

I finally woke up from never-never land and picked up our conversation where we left off. Jess was flying in the Huey helicopters that invaded our living room on the nightly news. We were all curious about where we would end up being stationed. Talk of "down south" or "up north" filtered through the plane. It was all idle conversation as we had no idea of which was better, if there was such a thing.

Towards the end of our second leg of the trip nearly everyone was awake and either reading, talking, or engaged in one of the card games going on throughout the plane. Great fortunes were being lost and won here, but then no one had intended on saving up.

Daylight streamed into the plane as we made our approach into Japan. We all peered out the windows, glued by the countryside, the mountain peaks, and the cities and towns that endlessly appeared as we dropped lower and lower. It was as if we were trying to get a glimpse of how the world looked as we entered "Asia".

While the plane refueled on the airbase, we got a chance to stretch our legs again. The souvenir shop was overrun, and the snack bar ran out of malts. Somehow our brief visit to Japan was a disappointment. The view on the ground was of runways and planes. We could have been anywhere, but then the ticket did not include four days and nights in beautiful Japan.

As our plane took off again, realization crept through the plane that our orders to Vietnam would become reality . . . real soon. Everyone was awake, talking and waiting for the yell that would come announcing our approach to land. The jostling and joking had begun in earnest.

Picking on my basketball playing height of five foot, seven inches, one of the grunts yelled, "Hey Curry, the only reason they let you fly is because you're too short to carry a rifle."

Always respectful of the level of IQ of someone who picks on my height, I yelled back, "Nah, that's cause I can spell words longer than rifle."

The card games stopped when we heard the large jet engines reduce power and begin a mild descent. I thought for sure we would maintain as high an altitude as possible and somehow drop into a tight spiral right above the airbase. After all, we could face anti-aircraft fire at any moment? But the plane kept dropping and then someone spotted the coast. Credit going to the pilots who kept the plane from rolling over as everyone ran to the right side for a look. We all settled down in our seats after we got over the coast and headed inland.

I found myself staring at the lush green of the countryside and the rolling hills and mountains, surely nothing like this back in the Midwest.

I tried to imagine large armies of Vietcong hiding beneath that foliage that seemed to never end. Then suddenly, we made our approach and touched ground.

The plane taxied to a stop and we waited for the staircase to be rolled up. The stewardesses stood at the door and said good-bye as we each stepped out the door.

The first step onto the staircase is burned into my memory, it seemed as if I stood there an hour and stared. I stared at everything around me. The lush green was gone. Red clay and dirt went on endlessly, only broken by the concrete runway. Then the smell hit me, a closeness that at first took your breath away. It smelled as if everything was rotting in this humidity. The air had a heavy closeness that seemed to move with you. A buddy I ran into later at Phu Bai told me the grunts never used colognes or heavy soaps or deodorants. Smells stayed with you, and the sweetness of the Americans gave them away to the Vietnamese.

We stepped down the stairway and were directed to a wooden building that was the closest thing to an air terminal in the old west I could imagine. And then, there they were. The Vietnamese people we had been sent to help, black pajamas and all. They seemed smaller than I imagined, even for a short guy such as myself. I found myself staring at an older Vietnamese woman frantically chewing on something I first thought was tobacco. I noticed it stained black what few teeth she had left. Someone mumbled to me it was betel nuts. I walked past her to the building to await instructions for moving on to where ever it was we were going. The GI's in this old hot, and dusty terminal had the same blank stare I had seen in the old woman.

My mind was like a video camera taking in the bizarre that would soon become normal; the unkempt hair, beads, mustaches, fatigues, and boots that looked like they had been wearing them for a month. The red clay dust seemed to weave itself into everything imaginable; their boots, fatigues, their skin, and I would later realize, their soul.

Everyone was busy sorting this all out in his or her minds. I couldn't remember the last airport that I entered with people milling about with rifles hanging from their shoulders. Everyone seemed to be staring at us, a new target for their taunts. Our shiny new jungle fatigues and boots must have stood us out from everyone else, our stupid grin, and our gaping mouth. It didn't help that we were all sitting neatly in a row waiting for someone to tell us where to go.

"Hey, how short are you FNG's, three hundred sixty five days?" taunted one of the vets.

"Hey, what did he say?"

"FNG, fuckin new guy, they got their own language here."

Every war had its own language. Whatever the words, they all related to the fear, hate, and hopes of the war. Being "short" in Vietnam referred to how many days one had left before shipping home.

I sat in awe of these dusty veteran soldiers sitting across from us. The stories these guys could tell; more importantly, the experience of knowing how to survive, what to fear, what to give a shit about. It would only become more surreal.

The plane we came in on sat on the taxiway refueling for the trip home. A line of these dusty and vacant shells of soldiers appeared for their trip home. Wow, I found myself already hoping for that day when I would be heading the other way. But the cost of the return flight was three hundred and sixty five days of whatever they decided they wanted from us. Anything shorter involved death or worse, if that was possible.

34

As we sat there waiting and waiting, we could watch the comings and goings of this airport. Cargo planes and helicopters of assorted sizes made their way in and out picking up soldiers on their way to different bases and cities in South Vietnam. Places I could never spell correctly, even after a year of saying them.

Finally, the line I was in began to get up and shuffle outside. I guess someone figured out what to do with us. We approached our Army green school bus and noticed wire screening rolled over all the open windows virtually covering the bus.

"Goddamn, what in the hell is that stuff, are we getting on the prison bus?"

John turned around and said, "They say it keeps the gooks from throwing grenades or bombs through the windows."

Shit, now I could pin my fears on something real, but now I began worrying about what else we were in for? The three buses lumbered onto dirt roads following closely bumper to bumper. Dirt roads surrounded by fields and hills of more dirt, dust, and clay. What in the hell happened to all that lush green tropical vegetation we saw on the way from the plane? The buses would come over the top of a hill to look out over more rolling dirt and clay. The heat of the day was broken slightly by the dusty wind coming in through the open windows.

For a while I thought we were being based in the biggest garbage dump in the world I had ever seen. Vietnamese were few and far between on this trip. Several times alongside the road we saw huge corrugated boxes sitting next to each other. One large Pabst beer box had a piece of tin roofing on top of it.

"Yeah, they live in anything they can find," came from the bus driver. I just then realized my mouth had been hanging open, probably since we landed.

"God Curry," I told myself, "don't act like a naive kid."

We arrived at Long Binh to begin in-country processing and assignment to our permanent unit. Long Binh is a large base some twenty-three miles north of Saigon. We were dumped off near an encampment of rows of one story hut like buildings centering on a small open field.

The remainder of the day was spent in lines going in and out of these buildings. Getting to the head of the line meant some clerk opened your folder, copied some information out of it, stamped it, mumbled some obscenities and sent us on to the next line. When they were done abusing us for the day, we got assigned to a "hootch". A hootch was a small wooden building built on legs about three feet off the ground. I would later learn this gave better headroom to the scurrying rats. In Long Binh the hootches were one large room with a row of bunks on each side. They had screened front and backs and a galvanized steel roof. They were built in neat rows surrounding a small field that we would fall out in formation every morning and evening. This made it easier for the Vietcong's aim.

Here we go again, tossed into someplace with twenty guys you'll probably never see again after the next three to four days. I threw my things next to an open bunk and laid on my back staring at the ceiling, wondering how long I would be here and where I was headed. Ever since reporting into Oakland we seemed to enter the twilight zone. No mail, 'cause no one knew exactly where you were, including the Army. And by now I was down to my last fifty cents. We were told no pay until we got to our final unit. God, that enlistment poster with the helicopter screaming over the tree tops saying, "High school graduate, you too can fly," somehow had lost its appeal a long while ago.

Its not something one let out of the bag too easily in the sixties and early seventies. People were becoming quite innovative in avoiding the draft . . . or taking the Greyhound north to Canada. America hatched a huge crop of college graduates during these years. Not getting kicked out of college meant you received a deferment from military service until graduation, and then you began to sweat again. Those with political connections or money could find a rare opening in a Guard or Reserve Unit, which meant they'd be staying safely back home, far from this shit. In the neighborhood I grew up in, nicely described as a "changing neighborhood", college was not in most kids' minds, and certainly not in their parents' pocketbook. So America's armies drew largely upon the poor and the minority. The effects of this war would add new physical and psychological problems to an already large number of underclassed and underprivileged. But there I was, getting ahead of myself again. After all, it wasn't a problem if one never came home.

The days at Long Binh consisted of falling out into formation three times daily to listen to the sergeant. One of the formations consisted of

36

his daily speech for the benefit of the new arrivals. He told them not to worry about standing in close formations since they have never had a mortar or rocket attack this far inside Long Binh. It was during the formations, he read off names of those who would be shipping out the following day. The list of names grew larger. We found out they wanted to get everyone out before TET, the Vietnamese New Year. That's when the Vietcong became a larger threat, as if letting out their anger for another year of Saigon's rule in the south.

The U.S. remembered all too well TET of sixty-eight, when Vietcong and the North Vietnamese launched an offensive in the South, that resulted in month long battles killing and injuring thousands. It was more information we had no idea what to think of or how to gauge. After all, we were still hoping to wake up from a very bad dream every day now for a week.

Our first trip to the mess hall was the beginning of a yearlong love affair I would have, with the john. God, I was beginning to be convinced most of the war casualties came out of the mess halls, you know, friendly fire.

Our little encampment sat on top of a small hill where we could look over to the other's companies in the area. The constant burning piles on the perimeter of each of these camps puzzled me.

I kept asking around what the burning piles were for. John answered me a couple days before we shipped out, "It's shit!"

"Yeah John, but what kind of shit?"

"Nah, I mean the piles are human shit, they burn the stuff cause it's a health hazard. There's no place to dump it."

I reminded him that we'd be safer if they first burned whatever it was they served in the mess hall before it made it all the way to shit.

The days were occupied with boredom and filling sandbags. The annual housecleaning for the Army came before TET. We'd escape whenever possible to grab a soda or more humane food at Alice's Restaurant. A one-room burger pit made from a converted hootch. Converted means they replaced the bunks with some tables and threw in a grill. It's marvelous what little free enterprise does when one has to survive by selling food to people. I was borrowing money from people more stupid then me. Some days I amaze even myself.

Finally, the formation came in which my name was called out. It was rather absurd, like being in a gym waiting for your name to be called so you could get your class schedule. Only this is what some people called the "real world". I could see my mind had already begun to go. I was being assigned to the 212th Aviation Battalion in Da Nang.

Da Nang, I had heard that on the news. Had to be big, either by size or number of battles. That was not exactly comforting. Someone in the formation leaned over.

"That's up north, I'm going to Pleiku, that's up in the central highlands."

"Well, now that's two things you just said that I still don't have a friggin' clue where it is, or what we're in for."

After we got back to the hootch, John pulled out a map of Vietnam and showed us where we were heading. I'm not sure what Standard Station he got it at, but it sure was handy in making you feel you knew where you were.

The four days of boredom in Long Binh gave me a chance to write my first letters back home to June, my fiancé. Writing of the guys I had met on the plane, our first impressions of this country and its people, and our desire to move on to our "permanent" home away from home. It must have been awful reassuring, or confusing. Hell, I'd go for confused.

The order to move out came the next evening. Bags packed, we all sat in the small fall-out field talking for hours, waiting. Then about midnight came the sound of a number of vehicles approaching. Leading and following these three army green "school" buses with their wire-covered windows were several jeeps with an M-60 machine gun mounted in the back. It certainly brought back the reality of where we were. As soon as we were loaded, the small convoy took off. We drove the seven miles or so speeding on small roads bumper to bumper with no headlights. The jeep led us through darkened Vietnamese towns where barely a person or a lighted window was seen. Not a word was spoken on the bus; we were too busy looking for something to come at us . . . out of the rushing darkness.

The darkened airport was a relief to us this second time around. The duffel bags were thrown about as makeshift pillows for a couple hours shut-eye 'til dawn. We awoke with the sounds of helicopters and planes beginning their daily schedule of shuttling troops across the countryside. Watching the commercial jets dumping more troops in their shiny new fatigues made us feel like veterans. After all, we had been in-country four days!

Well, I got my dream of boarding a darkly camouflaged air force transport off a dusty obscure base in the middle of no man's land. That is, after mulling away two days at the Binh Hoa airstrip waiting for the plane to get fixed.

Finally, we entered the large C-130 transport through its lowered tailgate. When this plane wasn't carrying troops; trucks, jeeps, and pallets of supplies were driven through its tailgate. An Air Force sergeant directed us to sit down in rows of seats made out of strapping material, not unlike lawn chair material. We sat facing each other as the large tailgate groaned shut. The last light was snuffed out; the plane had few windows in the cargo area. Unable to see out, we faced each other in the darkness as the four large turbine engines vibrated the plane, lumbering down the runway. The flight to Da Nang was spent in eerie darkness.

It wasn't long into the flight that I figured it out as a well-conceived and vicious plan of the military no doubt, to foil escapes, since you had no idea of where you were or how you got there.

We landed at Da Nang and finally saw life and hordes of traffic bustling around us. Planes and helicopters of all kinds were landing and taking off one right after the other.

Rising directly to the north of this large airport was a group of mountains. It seemed amazing this airbase would be nestled so close beside a group of mountains. I could only imagine the exciting time had by pilots attempting to land in zero visibility, knowing those hills are out there somewhere. Little did I know I'd be there soon?

The commotion was at the beginning of the line as we were being sorted into groups for transportation to our next home.

"Marble Mountain, two-twelve Aviation, fall out over here," was the cry that caught our attention. It always seemed someone in your group was one up on where we were going, or what the hell it was we were going to?

Marble Mountain was a small army base near the coast used for helicopters. To me it was another step on the way to my final destination.

The jeep made its way through the streets of Da Nang on its way to Marble Mountain. The streets were narrow passageways through shack-like buildings. It seemed every Vietnamese was outside, men and women in black pajamas on their way to somewhere important.

Small kids running through the streets were impervious to the jeeps and military trucks weaving around them. Groups of South Vietnamese soldiers hanging around street corners with rifles slung over their shoulders appeared everywhere. Looking out at these people, I wondered where this enemy, the Vietcong was.

Sliding to a stop in the sandy road in front of the 212th Aviation Headquarters hootch, we dropped our bags and went inside. This time the opening and stamping of folders was quick. We were then led over to our "accommodations" to drop off our bags. These buildings were more like the barracks I was used to on army bases back in the states, large two story wooden buildings with outside staircases in neat rows alongside the airstrip.

Led up to the second floor of one of these buildings, I threw my bags on a lower bunk. Then, out with the others to the mess hall, with a silent prayer this one would have "real" food. On the way everyone introduced themselves and the hometowns we each came from. It would be another group of acquaintances, this time with a better chance of seeing each other again, cause we were all in aviation, even the cooks. Lunch was bearable that day; either that or my taste buds had already surrendered for the duration.

That afternoon was spent in a classroom in the hottest damn building I ever had the joy to be in. I was beginning to think that passing out was a real possibility with a potential benefit, if it let time fly by. Twenty of us "new-bees" were getting RVN, or in-country training. Sergeant Terrance Cocker would give us three half days of how not to get your ass blown away.

As with all sergeants, Cocker had a natural ability to make you feel at home with, "OK you assholes, you survived your first four or five days by blind luck, so if you want to last out the other three hundred sixty, you'll give me your full attention."

"You'll be here for four or five days, then we'll arrange for the best transportation out of here to your units. We may rush a little as we want everyone out of here by TET."

Pointing to a map of South Vietnam he continued, "You have been assigned to various aviation units here in I Corps, the northern most military region in Vietnam." He continued for a half hour describing the various units reported to the 212th Aviation Battalion. It was here I learned by default where I was headed. The only unit with Mohawks in I Corps was the 131st Aviation Company in Phu Bai. Phu Bai was a small air base north of Da Nang, just outside of Hue, the ancient capital of Vietnam. It appeared it would be the Mohawks and a number of chopper units with a MASH Unit thrown in. We would be down the road from the 101st Screaming Eagles headquartered at Camp Eagle.

The day's lessons ended as I daydreamed about reacquainting myself with the Mohawk, if I'd ever catch up with my buddies from school, and wondering where and when I would find myself flying. I snapped out of my dream world in time to here Sergeant Cocker end his talk.

"As you noticed you are staying in the two story barracks next to the air strip. These were built early in our involvement here and now our new buildings are limited to one story. They tend to play havoc with your life when you get a rocket or mortar attack."

"So listen up . . . if you get a warning of incoming rockets or mortars, get your ass into the sand bagged bunkers next to these barracks. If the shit's already hitting the fan, it's better you roll on the floor and pull the mattress on top of you. It'll be safer then running out on the stairs with shrapnel flying around you."

Speech finished and it was on to the mess hall for an early supper as the temperature dropped and the wind from the ocean picked up. It would be another chilly, damp evening.

After supper, a small group of us talked the company clerk into getting us a couple six packs of beer, our first taste in weeks. We sat on the barracks steps, nursing our beers while the sun dropped. I was amazed by the pieces of information floating around in this group of new bees. One of the guys confirmed I'd be heading to the 131st Aviation Company in Phu Bai.

"Yeah, that's right outside Hue, some of the war's bloodiest fighting occurred there when the Marines and Army spent weeks retaking the city from the Vietcong in the infamous TET several years ago."

"Well, at least I'm outside of it."

"Shit, they walked through Phu Bai like nothin' happened."

A couple of the guys figured they'd be headed to the Medivac unit in Phu Bai. Seems the Vietcong like to aim at the Red Cross on the choppers carrying away the wounded. The unit tends to go through a lot of pilots.

The rest of the evening was spent feeding on whatever rumors we could find, trying desperately to assimilate what our lives would be like for the next year. Darkness came, a fitting excuse to let time pass quickly by sleeping.

I climbed the stairs to the second floor and threw myself on the bunk. A cool damp breeze was blowing through the barracks. Comforting when we were talking, but when trying to get to sleep, it would send shivers down your spine. The Army must have decided that blankets, pillows, sheets, etc. were unnecessary luxuries in a tropical way station. As I lay chattering on the bunk, my mind worked overtime trying to figure out a way to keep warm. This mental puzzle was solved when I saw Hopkins, who was on the bunk next to me walk across the center of the barracks and grab a mattress off an empty bunk. I quickly grabbed one for myself and spent the next half hour trying to keep the sides pulled down on me. Finally, I gave in to sleep from the sheer exhaustion of trying to stay warm.

The quiet of the night was quickly shattered with the deafening explosion of mortars falling on the airstrip in front of our barracks. The first explosion sucked the wind right out of me. I was instantly awake. In the murky light I could see silhouettes of men jumping from bunks and running to the door. Mortars continued to fall in rapid succession next to us, shrapnel peppering the roof. The roar of the explosions blocked everything from my mind. Running for the staircase I fought back the deafening sounds in order to think. Just as I reached the door, I remembered the sergeant warning us of running out on the staircase into the shrapnel of the exploding shells. Between the shadows and the roar of the explosions I found my way back to my bunk and rolled on the floor clutching my mattress and darkness around me.

42

Then the first blow hit, knocking the wind out of me and dazing me for an instant. It took me a few seconds to realize the blows were being inflicted by the guy in the bunk above me weighing in easily over three hundred pounds; the mattress and I had merely softened his jump. But in his private panic, he continued jumping around on top of me looking for his boots. It didn't take too long to realize I risked death or dismemberment more from this clown, than the mortars. I crawled out from between the bunks and ran for the door. But, as quickly as it had started, the shelling stopped.

I stood outside on the open staircase peering over the immediate camp area. Smoke was rising from the airstrip; several of the buildings next to us were ablaze, men running around tending to the wounded, the fire units arriving to quickly extinguish the fires. We all ran down to join in the effort to help wherever we could. The cries for help quickly faded as the jeeps ferrying the wounded drove off into the distance. Soon the fire trucks left the blackened rubble in the still darkened night. Once again I felt the cool damp breeze, the now eerie quiet. When would it start again, where would it come from?

There was little talk as we all walked slowly back to our bunks. I lay there awake for hours staring at the springs of the bunk above me. This was our first baptism of fire, yet it seemed too short, too sporadic, even though some of us didn't make it. Not that I wanted more, but the enemy and his threat now seemed more confusing. Little did I know the confusion would only continue and intensify?

The morning awoke us with a cool drizzling rain. It was a week to do something useful, like filling sandbags. TET, the Vietnamese New Years was a week away, and with last night's mortar attack, the push was on for more sandbags. Sand was certainly not a supply problem, 'cause it was everywhere. It's as if God long ago knew a century long war would be imminent and disgorged loads of sand throughout the country. I wore it in my socks, up my ass, and ate it in the food. As I filled sand endlessly into the burlap bags, my mind wandered. I remembered the newscasts back home of small flooded towns caught down river with miles of sandbagged walls holding back the river. It must have been the inspiration of immediate destruction that drove such a Herculean task. Because this was the most goddamn boring job, ranking well below peeling piles of potatoes. The walls climbed, oh so slow. I guess being on the second floor barracks, far from the safety of these bunkers, did not help the inspiration.

Our afternoon found us back in the converted barracks turned classroom. The sergeant presented his material very crisp and machine like. Not many questions were asked here. He seemed to upset easily when his machine gun delivery and timing was interrupted by a question. A disturbance like this could prove costly, so the sarge delivered the army's version of Asian military and political history unimpeded.

Pointing to a map of Southeast Asia, he ended with his moral of the story, "Gentlemen, you have been asked by our government to offer assistance to the Vietnamese people in their battle to rid their country of communist insurgency. Three Presidents and Congress have reaffirmed our support of these people by committing Armed Forces to South Vietnam. We expect you to do your job to insure the Vietnamese may one day enjoy their freedoms as do we."

The class ended none too soon. Another tasteless meal and an evening of small talk overlooking the airstrip. The next two days came and went into a vacuum.

Sunday morning arose with the sound of choppers landing on the airstrip next to our barracks. It was time to grab our bags and head for our new homes. A chopper ride over the mountains to Phu Bai seemed a lot safer then a truck convoy through the treacherous Hai Van Pass that was offered to those of us interested in some sightseeing.

The chopper approached Phu Bai directly from the south at two thousand feet. The land north of the hills above Da Nang was flat and low. Rice paddies ran from the coast, well to the west of approaching Phu Bai. The crew chief yelled over the noise of the engine and the rotor blades beating the air above our heads, "Up there to the right of Phu Bai near the coast is Hue, pretty city . . . just get out before it's dark."

The land seemed low and sandy compared to the ocean, more hills appeared to the north and west of this bowel-like terrain. Our final approach brought us in low over the southern perimeter. The airbase of Phu Bai consisted of a single five thousand foot runway, running almost north and south. Directly to the west of the runway, I saw the tall revetment walls protecting the Mohawks. The chopper hovered past rows of various assortments of helicopters. Sand was everywhere. God, I could imagine the building projects this sand would offer to some demented sergeant or commanding officer.

The pilot put the chopper down in front of an old washed out building resembling a control tower with an attached waiting room.

"OK boys, the stagecoach stops here, everyone out."

Hopping out on the concrete runway, we all stared around us trying to take in everything at once. The terminal building in front of us seemed more appropriate in an old Mexican town. Milling about in the small-attached waiting room were about twenty Vietnamese of assorted sizes and ages. They all had boxes or old suitcases filled with their life's belongings. I even thought I heard animals squawking from a couple of them.

"Hey Curry, kinda reminds you of some Greyhound station back home, hey?"

"Well, I guess the army band and welcoming committee got tied up. Looks like we're on our own."

We all said our good-byes and wandered off to our various units located along the airstrip. From the terminal I could look directly south down to the flight line of Mohawks about five hundred feet away. Wow, it had been months since I flew in one of these birds. Their ugliness kind of grew on you.

I grabbed my bags and hiked over to the first Mohawk. The concrete runway had quit, now steel planking called PSP made up the flight line below these birds. Six planes were lined up on the right side in various stages of preparation for flying a mission.

To the left was an open lane for returning aircraft and maneuvering the planes around. Further left was a row of revetments or stalls for the planes. Each revetment was surrounded on three sides by sandbagged walls lined with steel planking used on the flight line. Planes not being readied to go up were packed in these for protection from attack or explosion. I slowly walked past the planes and turned in a walkway just before the flight operations building to begin my hunt for the company clerk's hootch.

As far as the crappily built buildings stretched was sand, sand and concrete sidewalks running between the rows of hootches. I got the feeling the sidewalks kept the sand organized for the Commanding Officer . . . this was not a good sign.

Past three hootches, I could see the company's CO hootch. It didn't have a sign, but the painted white rocks in neat rows in front, outlining the lawn made of sand, gave it away.

Throwing my bags down in front, I gazed out at this flat land of sand and dirty gray shacks. The most exciting color came from the drab olive green of the planes. So this was to be home. "This was Phu Bai."

Opening the door quietly, I could make out this one consisted of a large room with a row of four desks and an office in the rear for the company Commanding Officer. These hootches were a marvel of army engineering. Directly in front of the CO's office were the company clerk's desk and a tall counter. These were obviously placed to delay a direct assault on the CO's office from some deranged soldier, permitting the CO a hasty retreat out the back door. God, I was learning all the time, it was Army tactics and strategy at its best.

The only person on duty the afternoon I arrived at the 131st Aviation Company, was the company clerk, Sergeant Dave Taylor. Taylor was a tall, dark haired company man straight from somewhere in southern Illinois. He was smartly attired in crisp fatigues and recently polished boots.

"Can I help you soldier?" were the first words out of his mouth, not even looking up as he typed on an official looking army form.

"Checking in, I'd prefer a room overlooking the pool," was my reply, somehow knowing my cocky attitude would elicit a similar response.

"All right smart ass, put your orders and files on the counter."

Having carried them outside my duffel bag, I smartly dumped them on the counter, only to begin to wait. Taylor kept typing in his form as if no one was there. I could sense a war of nerves here, but I figured my recent in-country training would be of tremendous benefit to me here. After all, I had spent the last two weeks waiting in lines for schmucks like this to stamp my folder and mumble obscenities. And when I did rush, I got rewarded with filling more sand bags. Nah, I knew when to put time like this on my side.

While he was typing away, halting before each blank space in the form, deep in thought, I looked around the company hootch, god, what a dull place to spend a war. Everything was a dull army green. The green desks straight out of a World War II movie, the tall menacing green typewriters that must have been rushed into service from the archive room of the Stars and Stripes, the official Armed Forces newspaper.

The dim lighting came from several bulbs hanging down the center of the hootch. Numerous plaques and ribbons hung on the wall behind Taylor, but I couldn't make out the writing.

The door behind me squeaked open as another green clad soldier entered. With the bright sunlight streaming in behind him it was impossible to make out who it was, I could only make out a silhouette of a person.

"Curry, you asshole, is that you? I thought you had conned your way over to Germany," bellowed the soldier.

Squinting to make out who this was, I barely made out the nametag on his fatigues.

"Jim . . . damn . . . how in the hell are you? Did any of the others from our class make it here? I thought for sure they used you guys to fill in another company down south."

"Nah, there is a bunch of our group here, let's get you over to my hootch, we got an empty bunk, and it's about time for the club to open up. Now we got an excuse to celebrate."

"Great, let's go," suddenly reminding myself, "but I gotta check in first."

"Dave, can we get my friend here processed? We got some old times to celebrate." Jim's timing was uncanny. As he spoke the company clerk stood up and ripped his form from the typewriter. Sticking it on top of his In /Out basket, he opened my personnel folder and began filing through it.

"Curry . . . good . . . they've been flying everyone pretty hard. Could use a fresh body," muttered Taylor as he began pulling orders from my folders, stacking them in several piles.

"The flight crews sleep back in the fourth row of hootches. Jim will take you back and help you find a bunk," continued Taylor. "Get yourself settled, in the morning we'll get you up to flight operations and checked in. Then you'll get your equipment and weapons assigned."

Taylor spent several more minutes now slipping these stacks of orders into several folders piled on his desk. My personnel records then disappeared with a slam into one of his file cabinets.

Jim grabbed my bags and we headed out of the company hootch and toward the row of hootches that would provide me with my neighborhood for some time. We walked between these rows of nondescript graying hootches sitting several steps off the ground on stilts. We hurriedly tried to bring each other up to date on our lives since we left training in Arizona several months before.

Jim had married Becky, a local Texas gal, when we were in flight school in Fort Walters Texas. She had moved back east to live with Jim's folks after we all got our orders for Nam. That had to provide for some interesting mail, a son runs off to join the Army during a war, and then the next thing he marries a girl from Texas who's now moving back home to mom and dad. Becky was pretty much a free spirit through and through. The sharp language she used regularly to drive her points home equaled her sharp drawl. And now, Jim tells me, Becky is pregnant. Wow, this guy I goofed around with since enlisting, was now married and on his way to being a dad. I think sometimes he seemed as surprised as I was.

As we walked between these dirty gray hootches, music drifted from the doors of damn near every hootch, and blasted from several more. What I didn't realize now was how important this music would become. Long periods of boredom followed by intense moments of sheer terror. To fill that boredom had limited options. Japanese stereos of immense size were available here for pennies on the dollar.

Songs of the sixties and soon the seventies, their messages of life, their protests of death, flowed as a backdrop to our daily lives. Somehow mimicking the debate that had not yet begun in our minds.

And dogs everywhere, the skinniest dogs I had ever seen, seemed to outnumber the GI's walking around.

We turned into a hootch with Jim yelling, announcing my arrival. This hootch was divided into two large rooms with three bunks in each room.

48

Jim threw my bags on an empty bunk as I recognized one of the two guys talking across the room.

"Chavez, how in the hell are you?" I yelled out.

Chavez was a skinny, twenty-year-old kid from Peru, via California. His folks had moved to the U.S., his mom working for the Peruvian Consulate in California. Somehow Chavez had gotten some bad information. He was told, despite being a citizen of Peru, he was about to be drafted. So, in order not to be a grunt, or a foot soldier, ducking his way through the jungles of Southeast Asia, he figured enlisting for a career of his choosing would be safer. Somehow, flying reconnaissance planes alone over the jungles of Laos and Vietnam did not seem much safer to me.

"Hey Curra, haven't seen you in a while, thought you took me up on my offer to visit my family in Peru for ten or twenty years."

"Shit, Chavez, someone told me I'd have to serve in the Peruvian Army chopping down marijuana fields, this seemed more exciting," I replied.

Another reunion, we sat around bullshitting about our recent months on leave before shipping over here. Chavez's wife was now about seven months pregnant. That's all he would talk about, how unfair it was to be taken from his wife and soon-to-be child. Now another skinny twenty-year-old was going to be a dad. It was hard to imagine he could settle down enough to take on a family. And now people were trying to kill him, Jim, hell me. Life was changing pretty fast for all of us.

Chris Southard was the other warm body in the hootch. Jim, Chris and I would share this room and our lives for the next several months. All the Playboy centerfolds gracing our walls were the property of Chris. Tall, well built, with a healthy head of blond hair and mustache, Chris looked as if he must have been plucked off a beach and sent here. Yet I had known him since basic training, straight from the beaches of California. All the hours he wasn't flying or sleeping were spent lounging on the top of a bunker next to our hootch, working on that perfect tan.

The room had walls and a floor of weathered gray plywood. The tin roof above us insured oven temperatures would be maintained during the day inside. Several wooden storage lockers strewn about served as coffee tables. Candles provided "atmosphere" and occasionally a scented room. A small refrigerator kept our beer cold while a few fans attempted to keep us cool, and the largest stereo system I had ever seen stood next to Jim's bed. A huge amplifier, reel-to-reel tape deck, and several speakers the size of some Vietnamese homes I had seen.

"Damn, Jim, where in the hell did you get that setup?"

"My pride, my joy, down at the PX. Shit, you can buy anything there. Cameras, stereos . . . for a tenth of the price you'd pay for this stuff in the states . . . even food," Jim replied as he laid on his bunk.

Chris threw a catalog at me, "Take a look at this, you can order anything our of it, send it here or home. I just sent some china home to my mom as a surprise."

I thumbed through a catalog the size and quality of a JC Penney Christmas catalog. Glossy, full colored pictures of stereos, china, cameras, and jewelry, TV's - whatever one's little heart desired. My heart found the camera of my dreams, a 35mm Ashai Pentex for one hundred dollars. I could see my planned savings of my combat and flight pay being diverted into the commodities market as I paged through this catalog.

The door flew open all afternoon as I met the new guys and reacquainted myself with old friends. Doug, Frank, Mark, Jefferson, and Pops had also made it here from our wild days in Arizona. Somewhere in between all the talking, a case of the cheapest pink champagne showed up. The club had just gotten it in that day. Obviously we lost out on a trade of the good liquor with a bigger club in Da Nang. But nonetheless, it was a rarity in a world of cases and cases of canned beer, beer that was alleged to contain vast quantities of saltpeter and formaldehyde.

The bottles were popped open, and the drinking began, first sipping, later moving on to guzzling. We talked for hours with each other, expressing our fears and problems, letting down our guard, and allowing everyone to walk around the innermost feelings of our minds. After all, this would be members of our immediate family, members of whom I would swear at, confess to, laugh with, and cry over. All those magazines and TV's describing Vietnam were gone now. We were here to play for keeps. To kill and not make that stupid mistake that would get us first.

Somewhere halfway through our case of bubbles I ran into Pops, our adopted older brother. A group of recent teenagers looking for adventure was beginning to question some basic premises of what life was all about. Pops was thirty something, a little overweight, mellowed out, and a bit philosophical. He traveled with a suitcase full of books that he was constantly reading and adding to. I was never sure why he had enlisted at his age, which appeared ancient from our vantage point. I'm not sure he knew the real reason either.

Pops claimed he was searching for his "place." A place to hide from what one could only assume was a wandering spirit. Well he had his place here, only his price was flying eight to twelve hours a day, only then to be left in relative obscurity to his books and thoughts. His serenity was a drawing card to the rest of us. When we weren't sure of ourselves, we went to Pops . . . to talk, to listen. He talked tonight of his new books on Vietnam and Ho Chi Minh.

The night was on a fast roll, picking up speed. As everyone drank, conversations became more involved, and intensely loud, and as an occasional drunk will attest, more philosophical. One began to leave unimportant words, names, and adjectives out of the conversation to speed us to the more important central ideas. And with everyone drinking, we thought we could also decipher this drunken gibberish back into something meaningful.

The champagne gave out halfway through the evening, but rugged military training taught us how to improvise. We moved on to mixing beer and liquor as a champagne chaser. As the drinks flowed the group grew smaller as one by one we slumped into corners, deep in thought, or as a sober person would observe, a drunken stupor.

My mind was racing at great speed through puffs of clouds, racing. . . oh so fast when the tugging on my arm snapped me back into reality.

"Curry, wake up, you're supposed to be on the flight line."

My eyes opened, seeing sheer awesome light, vaguely making out the silhouette of a person. For a moment I thought I might be at those pearly gates. But as I slowly came to, Jim was shaking me, trying to get me somewhat coherent. As I started to pick my head up, an immense wave of pain surged through my head. Damn, I really did it this time.

"Come on man, get up, your ass is wanted on the flight line for orientation," Jim pleaded.

This time I rose up slowly, careful not to make any sudden moves with my head. Sitting up on the edge of my bunk now, I tried to remember where I was, and what had hit me. My first relief came when I noticed all my parts were still attached, even though several were still numb. With my head swimming, I was not wasting any of my obviously limited strength, so I didn't say a word. Jim just stood quietly back, waiting to see how far I could get. The thought of walking outside in that intense sun scared the shit out of me.

I gathered up everything within me, and slowly rose to my feet. I figure it must have been the sudden altitude change on the way up that sent those huge stabbing pains from one side of my head to the other, and back again. Now holding my head in my hands, for fear it would fall off, I slurred, "Wheres we are goin . . . ,"

"Shit Curry, you're still drunk, can you make it?"

"No problem," slurred out as I lied again. The heat was overwhelming, it bounced off the sand, off the hootches, and it was everywhere now sucking the breath out of my lungs. I truly wanted to die, or at least pass out and go back to my dreams. Anything was better then this.

I walked, staggered that is, with Jim to the flight line fighting to regain at least my ability to fake sobriety. Jim took me into another hootch built right next to the flight line. Here we would prepare our equipment before each mission.

A large room, it was filled with storage lockers lining the back wall, and counters lined the full left wall. Here we would pour the developing chemicals into the small tanks that would develop film in the cockpits of our radar planes. This film would show dots of moving trucks and tanks on a map of the terrain below us. We could then plot their position, and coordinate with Air Force or Navy control planes so the gunships could take them out.

I followed Jim around as he described where the various supplies were stored and what preparation procedures to use. I was still fighting to think clearly, but Jim's movements and speech seemed in slow motion. We left the hootch and strolled out to the first Mohawk aircraft sitting on the flight line. Jim proceeded to reacquaint me with the Mohawk's equipment, and the unfamiliar weapons she carried under her wings.

As he talked, I knew I was losing ground fast. The heat and bright sun were taking a toll on what little energy I had left. Jim noticed as the look on my face moved from awkward to obvious sick.

"Damn Curry, don't you know that champagne will keep you drunk and sicker than shit for days. You better go get sick some place. "

I limped back to my hootch, throwing myself onto my bunk, offering God a trade if he removed this pain from my body. As I slept, I drifted in and out of alcohol malaria. Periods of profuse sweating were followed immediately by teeth chattering cold as I laid under three blankets. That afternoon God answered my prayers as the pain and the false malaria subsided. I still talked and moved slowly the rest of the day. For years afterwards, the sight or sound of champagne bubbles popping in a glass would send me reeling out of a room.

Chris strolled into the hootch late that afternoon throwing his flight gear on his bunk. Yanking open the refrigerator door and grabbing a beer, Chris mumbled, "Well, you really did it up last night . . . feeling up to eating anything yet? The mess hall's open."

Lying on the bunk and staring at the ceiling, still afraid to move I slowly answered, "I guess I need to throw something at the growling in my stomach."

Chris spoke as he changed out of his fire resistant Nomex flight suit into the cooler jungle fatigues, "Let's go, but it's your life you're taking in your hands."

We walked to the back of the camp, toward this latest adventure in army cuisine, Asian style.

Chris had just gotten down from his mission flying radar surveillance over the coastal highways of North Vietnam. These missions were flown back-to-back, virtually around the clock. They monitored the amount of traffic moving down North Vietnam's coastal highways, destined to re-supply their troops inside South Vietnam.

Just as we passed the last hootch in our row, we entered a small open area used for basketball, volleyball, and bad outdoor movies at night. On the other side stood the mess hall, made of the same plywood and tin roofing, but much larger and painted green. We entered the mess hall through a screen door when the foul smell of cooked food and vast amounts of cleaning solutions hit me.

"Ah, how could one forget army mess," I muttered to myself as we shuffled inside. Grabbing a large metal food tray Chris told me to watch out for the biscuits, some days two hands were needed to lift just one onto your tray. I carefully picked my food, lifting a sliced beef-like substance with a fork, as if looking for a land mine underneath. A roll, some beef, a spoonful of carrots, and plenty of coffee.

Walking away from the food line, I faced a huge open room with enough rows of tables for at least one hundred GI's. Today the crowd eating here was slim, so we found a table off by ourselves. We talked a lot and ate slowly, picking at ones food became an art form here. The food was nondescript, when everything looks terrible everyday, you lose your objectivity, after all, it's all crap. The taste, well again it all tasted like it looked. If your taste buds picked up something different, out of the norm, it usually was an alert to toss it before it tossed itself. We talked about our dreams, real milk, a coke in a bottle, a biscuit weighing less then ten pounds.

Chris carefully described the types of missions flown; most were on the North Vietnamese coast using our Slar systems, or side looking airborne radar to track truck and tank movement. He also talked about the photo and infrared missions flown in support of area Army and Marine ground units. The radar missions flown down south looked for boat traffic moving Viet Cong or supplies through the numerous waterways. Then there were the nightly Slar missions out west hunting trucks on the infamous Ho Chi Minh Trail. My ears perked up to that one. That was in Laos, taking action, making a difference in this war. I'd want to know more, but I wouldn't find it here.

We left the mess hall long after everyone else had gone, heading back toward the hootch as some began to gather for the evening outdoor movie. We talked for a while, and then exhaustion called out to both of us pleading to get some much-needed sleep.

The next morning found me coherent and pumping down coffee on the flight line before most people rose to face the day. Only a couple crew chiefs preparing the mission planes were moving about at this hour. I jumped up into the cockpit of the first Mohawk in line. The seat was as hard as I remembered. And over a four plus hour mission, your ass was paralyzed from the hardness, and for hours after it would continually remind you of it.

A bright yellow braided ring stuck up between your legs from the front of the seat cushion, another stood out, centered above your head. These were the handles for the ejection seat. With a small explosive charge built in below the seat, it would, upon pulling one of these yellow handles, rocket you out through the Plexiglas canopy above you, hopefully deploying your parachute high above your crippled falling aircraft. This morning it was safety pinned with an attached red flag to prevent a klutz like me from accidentally ejecting himself on the flight line.

The numerous gauges sparkled, as the sun grew high in the sky. I sat back in the right seat of this A-model that had dual controls, grabbing the stick with my right hand, with my left hand grasping the throttles . . . my mind already racing down the runway lifting off into flight.

The Grumman Mohawk was designed for reconnaissance missions in close support of ground troops. Two large turboprop engines that allow an operating ceiling of thirty five thousand feet and a maximum speed of three hundred knots power it. Of course here it would fly at treetops and mountain peaks at whatever speed we could milk out of an unforgiving climate and a constant struggle for parts and repair. It provided room in the cockpit for a crew of two, a pilot and a co-pilot or tactical observer. The cockpit was designed for maximum visibility. It provided large windshields to the front and Plexiglas windows above you. The side hatch bubbled out so one could peer down virtually beneath the aircraft. When one viewed the plane from behind with its unique, distinctive triple tail, its body appeared as a grasshopper poised ready to jump. The plane consisted of four different models designed to fly a variety of reconnaissance missions.

The first model, or the A version, was a dual control Mohawk built for visual and photo recon. It flew low and over country occupied normally by the enemy. If armed we could take on the enemy with the advantage of surprise. However many times we flew without weapons due to the ever-changing rules of war and had to let others decide if they were to be engaged by whatever forces could be assembled. This plane allowed us to approach virtually unheard; the twin turbine engines never gave us away until we were over them and past. Too many times we could peer in on an enemy who never knew we were there. They were loading weapons, stacking boxes, or lying lazily in the grasses. Of course once the sound of two screaming turbines screeching over them at treetop or below level, it did get their undivided attention. Additional passes for more photos or recon info would now involve a firefight of will and shells.

During the day, visual and photo missions were run on suspected enemy staging areas as requested by various area Army ground units, or the Marines headquartered down at Chu Lai, just south of Da Nang.

A pair of Mohawks, the aerial version of the buddy system, usually flew these missions over suspected areas of guerrilla or North Vietnamese regulars. Belly and front mounted cameras would take hundreds of feet of film, while the pilot and co-pilot visually searched for enemy activity. Visual sightings were radioed in immediately. These A-Models were usually the only Mohawks loaded with weapons. These crews doing visual recons could eliminate targets of opportunity. Upon returning to the airbase, the photo film was developed and reviewed by a Military Intelligence Unit assigned to the 131st, located in the flight operation's building.

At night, similar missions would be flown in C-Model Mohawks using infrared cameras. From first dark until dawn, these Mohawks would fly tree top patterns in the night over suspected enemy staging areas. Infrared cameras would pick up any heat sources in the cool jungle, such as cooking fires, generators, or truck engines. When you looked at infrared film, it was similar in appearance to the negative of a black and white photo. The shades of gray followed the different heat returns of the earth. Rivers and water was always cooler, so blacker. Any heat, a campfire, or engine would be hot and show as a burst of light. These positions could be plotted against the curve of a field, hilltop, bend in a road or river. Infrared missions were flown in areas only owned by the enemy, alone and flying just above the treetops at night. Often it was a target in Laos, or somewhere in North Vietnam. It was flown with your heart in your mouth all the time, as it never got easy. While we were looking for Charlie, after the first pass he knew where we were, and some short bursts on our next passes would wreak havoc in ones life and nerves.

After returning to base, the film again was developed and analyzed by a group of Military Intelligence specialists. They would compare any heat spots on the film to recognizable terrain, plot the positions, and relay the results immediately to the ground unit who had requested the mission. In many instances, these photo and infrared missions confirmed suspected enemy positions, and the following days deployment of friendly troops were based on these Mohawks discovery of enemy camping or staging positions. Often the results called for an attack of B-52 for the ultimate destruction, or fighter-bombers to "soften" the area.

By far, the majority of missions were flown in B, and later D-Model Mohawks both equipped with SLAR, the side looking airborne radar. This model had a twelve-foot cigar shaped pod mounted just below the right front side of the aircraft. To deranged SLAR flyers it was known as the "donkey dick." This radar would map terrain up to fifty miles on either, or both sides of the aircraft. In the cockpit, radar film would be developed and displayed to the co-pilot or tactical observer on a TV sized-screen sized display. The film would display a topographic map of the terrain just flown over. Any trucks, tanks, or vehicles moving in this area would show up as "movers", or black dots on the map. A convoy of vehicles through this area would appear on the film as a series of black dots. SLAR missions flown over North Vietnam were used mostly for intelligence gathering given the current bombing halt up north. The results of how much traffic was moving south along the coastal highways would be fed to U.S. Army Command in Saigon to help determine when the next offensive was building, or when the infamous light at the end of the tunnel would appear.

SLAR missions over Laos and the Ho Chi Minh trail were used to call in air strikes on moving traffic. Any traffic in Laos that showed up on film in the cockpit would be plotted, and their positions were radioed to a flying Air Force C-130 transport plane fitted with a command post in the cargo bay. In southern Laos, on the Trail, these command ships went by the call sign "Hillsboro" during the day or " Moonbeam" at night. This flying command post would coordinate all ground and air activity in its sector, and would order available C-130 or C-119 gunships or strike aircraft in on the target.

As I continued flying my daydream, I was startled back into reality.

"Hey, what in the hell are you doing up there?" I looked down to see one of the crew chiefs staring up at me with his hands on his hips.

"Who, me?" I responded, but as soon as I spoke, I realized there was no one else around. I continued, "Just getting reacquainted. I just got into the 131st a couple days ago."

I continued introducing myself to Daze, as I climbed down out of the plane. Daze was the nickname for the crew chief, Don Henderson. Daze was twenty years old with a mustache and long blond hair that was rapidly receding. The beads around his neck, along with his extremely laid-back attitude, contributed to his nickname. Daze turned out to be the perfect person to pump for the low-down on who was important, and who thought they were important. It was Daze's second tour here. He had signed on for a cash bonus and the lure of another year of tax-free income with added combat pay. There was a conflict here in that Daze also hated the war. He talked that morning of his hatred for the killing, and for the political games played in the Army. He also spoke with pride on how he kept his planes running right. When he was off duty, his time was his own; he'd smoke a little pot and listen to his music. We talked for a while, walking around the flight line, as I tried to store all his impressions in my mind for future recall. As we began walking toward the flight hanger, I realized this was a person to play straight with and keep on your good side. Anything else could alter the proper attention on whose plane gets the extra touch.

Just then, a movement next to a parked plane caught my eye. I noticed a short heavyset guy trying to do a chin up on the engine cowling.

"Daze, who in the hell is that," I asked?

"We call him Hump," replied Daze. "Think the Army was hard up for pilots the week we signed that guy up?"

As we walked slowly by, I watched him go through his preflight check of the plane. I had a gut feeling this guy was trouble, waiting for the right opportunity. We walked to the end of the flight line where the maintenance hanger was located. Two Mohawks were sitting inside with their guts half torn out in some resemblance of repair. Under the bright lights they appeared as two large prehistoric birds that had gotten mangled in flight. I only hoped they put them back together, with all the parts back in their correct places.

That afternoon was my chance to hit the local PX after I stopped by payroll to pick up my last two months pay. I grabbed a jeep from the company motor pool and bribed Jim into getting me there before payroll closed early for some unknown holiday. As Jim hopped in, I noticed we didn't have any weapons.

" Jim, if we're going off base to get to the other camp, shouldn't we be carrying weapons?" I asked.

"Nah," Jim answered, "We're not going that far, besides it's a pain to sign them out and back in again."

Hell . . . he's the veteran here, and we sped off toward payroll, money, and the PX.

As we left the company gate, we entered the public road used by the Vietnamese to get to and from the air terminal building. Bouncing along the dirt road, we joked as I watched the Vietnamese walking on the road.

Soon we entered another camp area and wound through the dusty streets pulling up in front of another nondescript army building, with a sign the size of my wallet that said "Payroll." I enjoyed standing and waiting this time, counting the money from the Army's forced payroll savings plan, that of not paying you for two and a half months. I gladly signed for the money, even though it wasn't good old U.S. green backs.

In Vietnam we were paid in military script, it reminded me of confederate money. They claimed it cut down the black market trade, as no Vietnamese was to have any military script. Every once in a while, they would "overnight" change the money or script. We would trade ours in for new bills, any Vietnamese holding the old script would be unable to trade it in, and be left holding the bag. That's how it was supposed to work.

Of course, the local Vietnamese seemed to know of the change weeks before it happened, calling on favors or just plain begging GI's to trade it for them. Unless of course, they could buy cigarettes with it. After all, cigarettes could be used in place of cash, traded for virtually anything, and the Army couldn't recall them.

Straight from payroll my conscience led me directly to the base post office to send the majority of my new found money home to my fiancée' . . . enough to pay off the accumulated borrowing from my leave, with some left over for the bank.

Next stop was the PX. It stood on a slight hill, made of the same galvanized sheeting anything larger than a hootch was made of. It reminded me of a large warehouse, with sand covering the concrete floor everywhere, and crudely built wooden shelves lining the open spaces.

Cameras, stereo pieces, cigarettes, and liquor counters were on either sidewall. The remainder of the open space was sparsely filled with several rows of canned food. I spent time looking at the cameras and stereos I could never have afforded before. Finally, I noticed Jim with arms full of food heading toward a cashier.

"Grab some food Bob, and let's hit the road," Jim yelled as he headed for the counter.

I grabbed a case of soup, and a large number of cans of spaghetti and beans. Most of the food cans had a little tin of Sterno taped to the bottom. This eliminated the problem of how to heat up these fabulous dinners in the privacy of your hootch.

Back into the jeep, we headed east to do some sightseeing at the small villages lining the narrow two-lane road toward the city of Hue. The traffic, mostly U.S. military trucks and jeeps crawled through the small villages of shack-like buildings and storefronts. The Vietnamese milled about the streets, kids darting between traffic, watching us, as we stared at them.

Outside of the village of Phu Bai, we picked up speed as we headed toward Hue. No plan in mind, just driving, bullshitting, and looking at the countryside. The deep rich green of the rice paddies spread out from both sides of the road. Young Vietnamese rode on the back of water buffalos in ditches of water that flowed along the side of the road. Houses and pock-marked buildings broke the green occasionally. Frequently, groups of large bomb craters appeared along the side of the road, along with burned out jeeps and trucks.

As the sun started dimming behind us, I turned to Jim and asked, "Shouldn't we be heading back before the sun drops?"

Jim hit the steering wheel with his fist and muttered, "Shit, day dreaming again. I always loved taking drives back home in the cool evening air back home after a hot day. I keep forgetting that little pleasures here will get you shot, sooner then shit."

Jim spun the jeep around and sped back to Phu Bai. He explained that during the day we, for the most part, controlled the roads. But at night the Vietcong went to work, ambushing anyone stupid enough to be out here, and mining the roads to get the truck convoys that began moving again at dawn.

Arriving at the airstrip after the mess hall had closed, I got my chance to sample my newly purchased canned surprises. The smell of the burning Sterno waffled through the hootch as Jim and I dug into the canned spaghetti. Not bad, of course I was thankful they didn't list the ingredients on the side of the can. I found it hard to believe real food could stand up to months in the hold of a tramp steamer, half way around the world and then more months standing on pallets in the baking heat of a supply depot yard.

Jim and I strolled out to catch the last half of a boring outdoor movie next to the mess hall. We stopped on the way back past Pops' hootch to chew some time and talk. We shared a few beers waiting for the magic hour of eleven p.m., when they turned the hot water heaters on in the showers. Pops was talking about the current book he was devouring, the military history of South East Asia. He was up to Kennedy's involvement. Just then, eleven o'clock came and it was off to the hootch to grab a towel, under shorts, soap, and robe.

Scraping the sidewalk in my cheap plastic thong slippers, I walked in the darkness between the hootches toward the showers. Our conversation got distracted as I tried to make out the noise and racket coming from underneath the hootch next to us.

"What in the hell is that?" I asked, interrupting Jim.

"That's the rats, they start moving around at night searching for food. So don't leave any out at night if you don't want visitors," Chris nonchalantly answered. "They're pretty big when they brush beside you out here while rushing around."

Damn, I picked up speed attempting to get to the safety of the lit showers, explaining to Jim it was getting cool again. I couldn't imagine being wounded in battle by a hungry rat mistaking me for the aromatic mess hall cuisine.

The next morning came quickly, the heat rising faster then the sun. I felt a rush of adrenalin go through me as I realized today I'd find out when I'd fly my first mission. A trip to the mess hall for breakfast ended in bitter disappointment. Cold black toast made enmasse four hours ago complimented the powdered sloppy eggs. I decided on coffee, not bringing myself to canned spaghetti for breakfast.

Pops walked with me to flight operations after breakfast. He had to prep his plane for the ten o'clock mission. Looking on the mission board, I found my name instead listed on an afternoon SLAR mission for tomorrow. Excitement was mixed with fear; my first mission was a radar flight over North Vietnam. Plenty of time today to get my flight gear and get it ready.

The company supply came up with a brand new flight helmet, and survival vest. The vest weighed a ton as I lugged it back to my hootch to check it over. The vest was made of webbed material, with numerous pockets attached on the front where it zipped up. Opening each one was a little like a bizarre treasure hunt. The first pocket had a strobe light, to signal a rescue chopper from the ground if shot down. Another had fishhooks and line, I guess in case the strobe light didn't work. Further down on the vest a first aid kit, with a package of "speed" pills, to keep you awake should you get shot down. I'm not sure of the older pilots, but taking a nap after hitting the branches among charging North Vietnamese, had never entered my mind. And last, but not least, a pocket filled with .38-caliber shells reminded me I'd better sign out a weapon.

Walking into the weapons building, I instantly noticed the incredible cleanliness; a highly buffed and waxed floor, with weapons neatly in their racks, each with a tag hanging to the left of its barrel. Since arriving in country, I had never seen anything so antiseptic. I wasn't sure why I was impressed, but I was. The weapons sergeant then informed me that I wouldn't get an M-16 rifle, but a laminated gun card that I could bring down here in case of attack . . . stand in line, receive my weapon, and turn in my card.

"You've got to be shittin' me," I sputtered out in astonishment. "If we get attacked, they'll blow our asses away while we wait in line for our weapon," I continued.

"Our perimeter defense is capable of holding back a ground attack while weapons are disbursed in an orderly manner," responded the weapons sergeant as if reading from a plaque. "There's much more danger from weapon accidents if we handed these all out."

I couldn't believe this, somehow the stupidity held me speechless. The insanity continued, any Vietcong or pissed-off kitchen help could mount a serious attack by first hitting the weapons building, the ammo shack, and the company headquarters' hootch. After that, they could saunter through the company, blowing us unarmed GI's away at will.

My saving grace, although limited, happened when the weapons sergeant found out during our heated conversation that I flew.

"Oh, you fly? Well, then we sign you out a .38-caliber handgun," the sergeant muttered as he disappeared into the back room. He returned shortly with a .38 revolver and three forms to fill out and sign. He then dug in a bin and poured several handfuls of .38 shells on the counter.

I walked back to the hootch with my laminated gun card, my vest, and a handgun that I had no idea where to stick except in the top of my pants, the shells filling every pocket I had. Army procedure provided that a pilot or flight crew member could be issued a hand gun for protection in a zone of conflict, but it said nothing about issuing a holster to put it in.

As I opened the screen door to my hootch, scaring away some resting cockroaches, Chavez yelled from the next hootch, "Curra, they want you down on the flight line, they want you to go up on a check flight."

It had come faster than I thought. I threw the gun and shells in my footlocker and took off to the flight operations building. I was to make a checkout flight on a Mohawk that they had just replaced part of the tail that had gotten shot off on a recon flight west of Da Nang.

As I made a brief walk around the plane looking for telltale signs of problems, I ran into Gus who I'd be flying with today on the check out flight.

"Well Curry, welcome aboard . . . understand it's your first flight here".

"Yeah, new kid on the block. I'll be glad when the honor gets turned over to someone else," I answered him.

Gus grabbed the plane's maintenance log when we jumped into the cockpit. As I strapped in, Gus read the log that kept a record of all maintenance completed or minor problems still unresolved. It was the pilots' responsibility before flight that he makes sure all the maintenance problems, entered in that book by the pilot or crew chief, had been corrected and signed off.

We ran through our preflight check with the crew chief standing in front, and soon had both engines running, waiting for the airport control tower to give us clearance. Taxiing to our assigned runway, I felt the adrenalin rushing through my system. It had been two months since I had last flown.

"Spud Two-Two, you are clear for take off, runway two-niner," the radio blared.

Looking at Gus, I slammed down the open hatch pushing the handle forward to lock it closed. I flipped the yellow handles above my head and between my legs to arm the ejection seat.

"Roger, tower, Spud Two-Two rolling," Gus answered.

Pushing the throttles forward, the plane rolled down the runway, picking up speed rapidly. Suddenly, the plane leaped forward, freeing itself from the ground below. Gus pulled the landing gear up; the plane lurched as the gear doors slammed shut. We were off, flying hard and fast, past the base perimeter. As we flew over the PX and the village, Gus banked her hard heading out to the ocean.

The advantage of a test flight is you fly mean and hard, and wherever you desire. The goal is to press the plane's performance, to make sure everything is working, as it should be. The only disadvantage might be in finding a part that isn't working correctly while your flying a couple hundred feet off the ground.

Gus took her out, flying the engines wide open, low leveling over the rice paddies and dikes on our way to the ocean.

The world whizzed past both sides of the plane, as if driving a fast car three hundred miles per hour down a country road. The plane was designed that its engines would only be heard after it flew past you. So I watched the Vietnamese we flew past, working in the fields. Then the delayed reaction as I looked down, watching them jump out of their black pajamas a full second after we buzzed past their heads.

The countryside was extremely green and wet. The monsoon season was beginning and the rain would fall for months. The small villages we flew past tended to be small enclaves of peasants who tilled the fields around them.

When we hit the coast, Gus low leveled over the long sandy beaches, buzzing the fishermen bringing their boats in. He finally turned out to sea, putting us into a climbing turn that pinned me back in my seat. Shit, I was getting the full treatment here, and loving every minute of it. He leveled out at several thousand feet and headed south over the ocean toward Da Nang. Flying in a photo recon plane, we had dual controls. Knowing a number of us had some limited flight training in choppers, and even less in Arizona where we begged for any stick time, Gus allowed my indulgence for a while on the trip south.

Taking back the stick, Gus turned and descended to several hundred feet above the ocean skimming the waves. Up ahead was a Navy frigate on patrol. We buzzed past her, rolling our wings as the sailors waved us on. As we neared Da Nang, Gus entered controlled airspace that I was of yet unfamiliar with. The air traffic in and out of Da Nang's air base was immense.

Circling around to the south of Da Nang at several thousand feet, I found myself gazing at the city spread out below. Buildings appeared to be all of one or two stories tall, made of wood. The dirt streets were loaded with traffic, motorbikes, and Vietnamese scurrying about. It was hard to believe a war was going on in this country from up here.

As we came out on the west end of Da Nang, the green hills started, at the same time the bomb craters did. Dirt roads broke the rolling green of the countryside. The first miles seemed barren of any people . . . of any life.

We followed the river west out of Da Nang. The hills rose quickly and the jungle now began to take over. It felt eerie out here. I could relate to the bustling city, but this countryside seemed as if it wanted to reach up, engulfing you forever into the jungles below.

Gus was enjoying every minute of it, for he flew the recon missions down here regularly. We began to climb as the hills and mountains rose before us. The valleys were becoming smaller between the steep crests of the hills. The lush green I had seen when first flying over the coast on my trip here was now only hundreds of feet below us.

As we came up over the crest of another hill, still following the river, we came upon two Vietnamese paddling an enlarged canoe with some sort of boxes stacked between them. They were as shocked as we were to see someone else out in the middle of no man's land.

"Shit, goddamn it . . .VC," Gus muttered pushing the throttles to the wall as we climbed sharply to turn us around and back over the boat we had just startled. As we climbed, turning back I watched the panic as these Vietnamese paddled frantically, trying to get to shore. Gus was in total control here, reacting as he had done it dozens, if not hundreds, of times before.

"Damn, this is no man's land, anyone out here is assumed Vietcong," he explained, straining to keep the turn as tight as he could.

Somehow I knew the wooden crates stacked between these two were not Christmas presents meant for their families.

As we leveled out from our turn, Gus put us into a dive, straining to catch these two who, now more than ever, were paddling for their lives. We raced downward, against the clock, and the approaching shoreline. As we lined up directly behind them, I saw Gus flip some toggles on the stick. It was all his show, for which I had a grandstand seat. I knew how this was going to play out, as if I had been here before, yet I hadn't.

The drone from our racing engines was deafening as we fell, gaining on these frantic two. They had to feel the heat on their necks, as we came down on them, like an hawk on its prey. Out of the corner of my eye, I saw Gus press the before hidden button. The plane bucked as first two, then two more rockets streaked out from under our wings. I followed the thin trails of white smoke, streaking toward their target as we raced on behind them.

The first two rockets hit directly below the water line of the boat. The wooden boat and its cargo flew up in the air, falling back into the river into many splashes. Seconds later, the following two rockets found their home in the capsized bottom of the boat. The splinters of wood and fabric flew high in the air, riding the plume of water upward.

We flew over the churning water of flying debris. Another climbing tight turn, and we came around to view our work. The wood splinters covered the river. The river soon smoothed over, and quickly swept away what had happened that afternoon. As we made several passes over the river, the water returned to its gently running course. There was no longer any boat . . . or crates . . . or Vietnamese. I now knew this is how the VC nicknamed the Mohawk "whispering death".

Gus took her up, and headed north, back to Phu Bai. We chatted on the way back talking shop. Putting the job we were paid for, and what had happened that afternoon on the river, out of our minds.

We touched down at Phu Bai as the sun was beginning to fall. Popping open the hatch, the hot sandy wind blew into the cockpit. I no longer felt like the virgin, the new kid on the block. I hadn't expected it to end this fast. The novelty was over. The work I was sent to do had just begun.

We taxied into the revetments, Daze out in front directing us to our parking space. As we came to a stop, Gus killed first one engine, then the other. The whine of the props slowed till there was the deafening quiet of being back on the ground. My ears ringing, still trying to adjust when Daze walked under my hatch remarking, "A little target practice this afternoon boys?" noticing the empty tubes where the rockets had been.

It was time to grab some beer, a little food, and take in a boring outdoor movie. The time for a cold shower rolled around fast, and when it was time to turn in, I did . . . exhausted.

For tomorrow was another day at the office in the sky, always coming faster than we'd like.

Five-thirty in the morning came early, not that I had to get up then, but I couldn't sleep anymore. Over a long period of time, this was bound to have an unhealthy effect on my body . . . a body that struggled never to rise before the sun did.

My first assigned mission was due to take off at ten o'clock this morning; and with three hours to burn before reporting to the flight line, I needed to find something to pass the time. The only action at this time in the morning was the cheap talk, and even cheaper food at the mess hall.

As I wandered down toward the mess hall in the cool dark morning air, I came up behind Pops heading in the same direction.

"Hey Pops, how 'bout some company for breakfast?"

Turning around, with a book under his arm, he seemed at first startled, finally responding, "Curry, what in the hell are you doing up at this hour . . . problems?"

"Nah," I answered, "couldn't sleep, besides my stomach is growling so bad, it suggested we play Russian roulette with breakfast."

Pops and I strolled in the only cool air brought to this country at five thirty in the a.m. The quiet was broken as I opened the mess hall screen door.

The harsh bright lighting and the pungent odors of cleaning fluids accented the clanging of cooking utensils and the numerous conversations from those already eating. Ah yes, what a life.

Grabbing a tray, we walked through the food line, staring at this morning's entree selection. Cold, blackened toast, half cooked fatty bacon, and soupy powdered eggs that had that "wholesome" orange tint to them. God, the list of shit getting tossed at us was endless. I was beginning to believe that the only way to deal with this place called Vietnam was to become mindless, because questioning it was too painful.

A glint of hope caught my eye just before I was about to make a fatal selection. Cereal, little boxes of cereal, I'd have to put up with powered milk . . . but cereal, the Army certainly couldn't screw that up. They were boxed and sealed someplace around Battle Creek, Michigan. How wholesome can you get? I could almost feel the goodness ooze from these little boxes of joy.

I grabbed a box of Raisin Bran as I watched in amazement as Pops heaped his tray with the bacon, eggs, and toast I had just passed up. I wasn't sure if I was to be impressed with his stomach lining, or look up the hootch number of the company chaplain.

We grabbed an empty table and sat down for a relaxing meal. Pops talked in-between his gulps about his recent readings. He began breakfast talking about France's attempts at colonizing Vietnam in 1876.

Pops' mind was like a steel trap on history. While we were in school in Arizona, he was hot on Indian history, now he changed his geography. I was letting my bran flakes get soggy . . . when they're really good . . . while listening to Pops. I hadn't understood that Vietnam had been under foreign influence for that long. I only remember the "communist" invasion the President talked about in his speeches. That's why we were here, if Nam fell, the rest of the dominos would fall, and all of Asia would be communist.

Pops was up to the 1930 Japanese expansion that eventually sent the French running out of Vietnam, when I put my first spoonful in . . . intent on what he was talking about.

"Jesus shit," I yelled, spitting out cold milk, cereal, and raisins. I continued swearing while grabbing my mouth to begin the search for my teeth I'm sure were shattered.

Pops dropped his fork; with a shocked look on his face, sputtered, "Bob, what in the hell is wrong?"

"Damn," I continued feeling my teeth, making sure they were all there. "Jesus Pops, it felt like I crunched down on a mouth full of steel B.B.'s. I thought I had broken every tooth in my mouth."

Somehow the raisins had hardened to the intensity of cold steel. As I read the cereal box, scanning the ingredients list for steel ingots, I noticed the packaging date.

"Look at this Pops, this cereal is twelve years old!"

I was shocked, and then I wasn't. The Army had gotten me again. Well, the coffee was rotten, but at least it didn't break your teeth; so I drank this warmed motor oil as Pops rolled on. He had his book open as if he were directing his own Asian history course. When I thought he was convincing me on the current folly of the US following France into this war of liberation, he sprung a whole new set of players into the discussion. Now he talked about Laos, Vietnam's neighbor to the west. All I knew of Laos was it was the location of the infamous Ho Chi Minh Trail that North Vietnam had built to run supplies and troops down along the Laotian side of the border with Vietnam where US troops were restricted from going.

I never quite understood these strange rules of war that allowed the opponent a virtual time out while it ferried troops south to kill Americans and South Vietnamese further down south. But then again, who made up rules for war? It was those with the massive weapons and assets, who felt pompous enough to dictate. Of course anyone who played schoolyard games like king of the hill knew they'd be fools to play by the bullies' rules, or anyone called Ho Chi Minh. Their war here was being fought wherever it could, "illegally" in Lao's, in the world press, on the college campuses, etc. And somehow that could not be understood by the best and brightest of the Washington politicians and their bean counters that seemed a gaff that one would dare conduct warfare in such an improper manner. Apparently the only person who learned from the guerilla tactics used by the American soldiers during the Revolutionary war was Ho Chi Minh. You couldn't fault him completely for actually cracking open his history book. But at eighteen years old I realized I wasn't often asked my opinion very often on matters of geopolitical strategy.

But what Pops was describing was the centuries of war that permeated Southeast Asia, where Cambodians, Lao, Thai, Vietnamese and Chinese had each fought for control and expansion amongst themselves. While North Vietnam was waging a worldwide PR campaign of its war for independence, at the same time it was hijacking Laos to serve its purpose in carrying the war south. And it didn't end there; in Northern Laos far from the Vietnam borders it was waging a war to oust a hill people known as the Hmong for a number of reasons. First, the Hmong were not Vietnamese, worse yet; the Hmong had fought ferociously for their centuries old ideal to live free in the mountains, after all, Hmong translates to "free peoples".

Second, the Hmong had for the sake of survival aligned themselves decades earlier to fight alongside the French in their fight against the communists. Memories die hard here, and brutal revenge is a tremendous way of carrying a message of expected behavior.

Third, given the Hmong were seen as racially inferior to the Vietnamese, the Vietnamese could rid themselves of a tough internal enemy that would cause problems down the road. There was a fear by some that the real target was Thailand across the Mekong where a communist South East Asia could be a formable foe not only to the Western powers, but also to their Asian neighbors; China, Japan, the whole the Pacific Rim. It wasn't getting any simpler in trying to understand what in the hell all the shooting was about.

We were interrupted deep into the Japanese rule of Vietnam in the 1940's by some of our buddies throwing down their trays next to us.

"Hey boys," muttered Chavez as he and Chris threw their trays down and pulled up chairs. "Did you hear the great news?"

Pops and I both stared at each other and shook our heads no.

"My wife . . . she had a big, baby boy . . . hey, great hey?" as he beamed.

"Congratulations Chavez, that's great", I reached across to shake his hand. This guy was in his glory now that he was finally a dad.

"Does that mean you'll now bore the hell out of us with I wonder if mom and the baby will be OK?" I asked.

"Yea, I just got to figure out how to get out of here, and get home," he answered.

"That's a good one," mumbled Pops between chewing. "Figure that out and then fill us all in, OK?"

Up until then I hadn't noticed Chris had been sitting there, not saying a word. Well, it was time to head down to the flight line and get my plane prepped.

While I loaded the film into the radar display and ran a systems check, the storm clouds moved in. Soon low hanging black and gray clouds quickly replaced the sun. You could almost reach up and touch one. The rain was incessant, finding every dry spot on your body. It was in one sense a relief from the hot, humid air that sucked the breathe out of you. These monsoons that lasted months were so intense. They would replace day with a continual night, a damp darkness so close and personal it would darken your very soul.

Downing my last pot of coffee, I ran out to the plane trying unsuccessfully to dodge the downpour. As I strapped into my seat, I introduced myself to Lt. Larry Koontz, who was in his late twenties and slightly balding. He spoke in a low monotone voice as he began to check out his instruments. He was almost shy. That's what I thought until he threw something up on the dash. It took me a minute to figure out what my eyes had been staring at.

"Damn, is that a rubber duck?" I stuttered.

Koontz grabbed the duck, petting its head. "Yep, this is rubber ducky, it goes with me everywhere." Putting the duck in front of his face, he asked his rubber friend. "Right ducky?"

"Class, Koontz, pure class," I said, staring at this new flying buddy. It was insanity, but then I knew instantly I was going to get along fine with this guy. Anyone this bizarre didn't stand a chance playing politics like some stuffed-shirt captain praying to be major.

We finished our preflight check with Daze shivering in a poncho in front of us, directing us with flashlights. It was hard to believe it was ten o'clock in the morning.

"Tower, Spud Two-Two, clear to taxi, use runway two-niner," the radio crackled.

As we taxied toward the runway, we watched landing lights appear out of the clouds a hundred feet over the runway, as one cargo plane after another touched down.

"Looks like we're up to something big," Koontz pondered, "haven't seen this much traffic in a long time."

There was soon a break in the landing traffic and we got clearance for takeoff. We rolled down the runway accelerating as the engines strained for lift; an incessant drone filled our ears and head as the rain beat against the windows, the wipers groaned under the strain.

Soon we were airborne, instantly being sucked up into the clouds, rain, and fog. The land disappeared below us, as we were slipped up into the huge white marshmallow clouds that embraced us. Then drops of water on the windshield soon created rivers hurrying to leave. The landing gear shuddered in place and we headed up, and east for the coast. As we climbed, the dark clouds turned into a whiteness that almost blinded us. We felt all alone up here in this closeness, alone except for the radio chatter of planes heading in and out of scattered battles unknown to us.

Our instruments told us when we had reached the coast; we headed north, toward North Vietnam. The sounds were massive, the wind screaming past us, the drone of the engines driving us forward and up, and the radio chatter. And then suddenly it all became background noise, never losing its intensity, but rather my mind learned to filter it out in an attempt to allow me to think, to do my job.

Turning on the radar system, I heard a surge of power in the headsets as the radar unit put its load on the plane's resources. As I pushed the various switches setting the mapping format we were looking for, we continued our climb upward through the never-ending clouds.

Finally, we broke through the clouds after passing five thousand feet. God, it was beautiful up here. The sky above us was a crystal blue, the sun sending glimmering rays against the sea of clouds below us. We could have been anywhere up here . . . except for the radar displaying the land below us, as if there wasn't a cloud in the sky.

Koontz leveled us at ten thousand feet as the radar displayed the coast and inland areas of the demilitarized zone separating North and South Vietnam. As we passed in between Tiger Island and the coast, I knew we were now in North Vietnam. Not that I cared to get shot anywhere, but I had an eerie feeling there would be no welcoming committee down there.

"What exactly are we doing up here?" I asked Koontz, "We can't call in fire on anything with the bombing halt on."

"Well, you heard of the grunts talking about walking point?" Koontz rambled. "Well, walking point is to go alone up front to look for the enemy without the noise of the patrol tipping the bad guys off. Well, we do that up here in the air. Alone and quiet we can see what they're up to, hopefully before we spook them and they try to shoot the crap out of us. Only there is no patrol to back us up if we get in trouble, and the welcoming committee down there is not real friendly. But hey, look for the good news, there's no boss looking over our shoulder up here."

"OK, I feel much better, alone over North Vietnam with no weapons or friendlies. You're telling me we are sitting ducks taking pictures just waiting for these fools to make an example out of us? Thanks Koontz, that's makes this all worthwhile when you put it that way"

We flew north along the coast, mapping and storing the traffic moving down North Vietnam's coastal highways, presumably loaded with war goods to supply their armies hidden in the South. The radar system was state of the art for the battlefield of the nineteen sixties and seventies. A large cigar shaped fiberglass boom was attached to the right side of the aircraft extending slightly past its nose; we fondly referred to it as a donkey dick. From this long pod would be emitted a stream of radar signals downward and out to the side that would then bounce off the ground, hills, rivers, trucks, etc., and return to the pod. This data was sent to computers stored in the Mohawk fuselage behind its massive engines where these signals were compared and analyzed. Any item that had a metal surface over a minimum size, like that of a truck or tank that was moving would be detected. This system used line of sight, so for instance, a truck moving on the other side of a hill depending on the angle might not be detected. This data would then be sent to the cockpit of the Mohawk providing real time intelligence on where motorized traffic was moving.

Where in the A model Mohawk, the right or copilot seat had dual controls for flying the aircraft; in the Slar and Infrared Models, the dual flying controls would be replaced by the massive electronic systems controls and systems. In this Slar or radar model a large screen is positioned in front of the right-seater. Computer displays were yet too large and bulky to be used on small battlefield aircraft during Vietnam. So we carried small tanks of developing fluids along with custom designed photo film we tried not to get exposed to the bright sunlight. Long, thin rollers that spread the developing fluid over the wide film were our most treasured possession. The slightest bang would warp them, even a slight warp would mean only a portion of the film would be developed and that would immediately require that the mission be aborted and replaced by another Mohawk. The screen was just that, a piece of slightly tinted glass a little larger then an eight and a half piece of paper that would cover a wide piece of photographic film that rolled up from its film canister underneath. The roller would apply a thin film of developing fluid to the constantly moving film as it inched up the large screen where it would be displayed in front of you to view.

What would appear before you was a large photographic display of a topographic map of some fifty miles wide of terrain moving up the screen as you flew on. You could see the rivers wind along, the tops of mountains reach their peak, and more importantly, the black dots, or "movers" that would designate one or more trucks or tanks moving underneath the jungle canopy below you. While they drove seemly hidden from view, I watched miles away already knowing their exact position. These movers were instantly plotted onto a map in the Mohawk cockpit on the flights over the Ho Chi Minh Trail in Laos. There we were flying with the 7th Air Force where fighter/bombers or gunships were assigned to our mission. When the "movers" were detected and plotted, we handed them off to the assigned fighters or gunships that proceeded to take them out.

Here over North Vietnam today we are flying under the latest White House bombing halt. So we watched and plotted the trucks heading south loaded with guns, munitions, soldiers and their supplies that would be used against our troops in the south. The next time they'd be heard or seen was after they rained death and destruction on the GI's or the South Vietnamese. Only then would the rules allow someone to shoot back, if they could . . . if they weren't already dead. Our film would be analyzed and plugged into some computer in Saigon or back in Washington. There the bean counters could predict and advise the politicians when the light at the end of the tunnel would appear. Our troops in Vietnam would watch that light appear from the wrong end of a rocket or mortar tube.

This was the never-ending confusion here. War is the absence of politics, where man decides they can no longer discuss solutions, that the last person standing will enact his policies with no compromise necessary. If your goal is to limit your casualties, then a swift road to victory is the only way to insure it. Here the American version of war meant people died for a political statement, or a negotiation tool. A bombing pause or an attack was used to send a message, and people paid for that with their lives. Back in Washington far away from the shit, war was an extension of negotiation. To the Vietnamese, negotiation was an extension of a war they meant to win.

The hard seat seemed to get harder as each hour ticked by, soon my ass was numb. Between watching our heading, the radar, and listening for warnings against enemy planes or SAM missiles, we talked about everything . . . from where we came from, to our thoughts about everyone back at Phu Bai.

At the North Vietnamese port of Dong Hoa, we took a short jog to the northeast to follow the contour of the coast. We conversed with "Pamper", the air traffic controllers now located on the Navy task force to the east of us. Most of the traffic up here comes from this Naval Carrier force launching missions against the North, or waiting to launch as was today.

My first impression of Koontz, that is after rubber ducky, was pretty close. He loved to fly, hated the officer politics, and otherwise wanted to be left alone. He was bucking to fly the Laos missions, get some payback he said. Always the curious one, I pressed him for more background on what would possess an individual to ask for missions that took heavy fire over the infamous Ho Chi Minh Trail.

Our company had four planes, three flight crews, an intelligence chief, and several crew chiefs on the units classified assignment based out of the Royal Thai Air Force base in Udorn, Thailand. They were still assigned to Phu Bai. Their mail came and left here, but that was part of the ruse. These crews flew nightly missions directly for the CIA under direction of the U.S. Embassy located over the river in Vientiane Laos. Laos is a slender country located between Vietnam and Thailand. North Vietnam had built an integrated system of highways in Laos that funneled war goods for North Vietnam into Laos, re-entering South Vietnam through numerous staging points along their long jagged borders. The U.S., Russia and North Vietnam had agreed to the Geneva Convention by not committing their troops into Laos. Always the chameleon, the North Vietnamese simply denied their massive number of troops in place in Laos. The US would choose an entirely different strategy I would later learn, the flights into Northern Laos supported the Hmong hill people who were forced out of their mountaintop villages. The fear was a communist move toward the Thailand border. No one knew where this would end, Vietnam, Laos, Thailand. What had we gotten ourselves into?

So, we fought the war from the air. Our planes flew with ground sensing radar that would detect trucks moving along these jungle roadways. Plotting their position and strength, the Mohawks would radio the information to an in-flight Air Force C-130 flying command post. The southern command was flown by the C-130, call sign Hillsboro during the day and Moonbeam at night. In the Northern Theater of War in Laos, Cricket controlled all the daytime air traffic, and Alleycat took the night missions. Every plane in or out of the air space checked in with these flying command posts. They would take calls for assistance from the ground, all targets of opportunity. From its list of available strike aircraft it directed the best combination of air strikes. For a Mohawk finding "movers", gunships or fighter/bombers would be called in on the targets to finish the hunt. The second part of the Laotian team was flying infrared missions over the treetops to detect heat sources that could only come from NVA units under the foliage.

I found myself fascinated with the Laos missions. Only one of our planes flew the nightly Ho Chi Minh Trail operation the Air Force named Steel Tiger. Two Mohawks flew north to the Plain of Jars, or the operation called Barrel Roll. These planes flew from the Royal Thai Air Force Base in Udorn across the Mekong from Vientiane. The lone trail hunter, Mission Twenty, flew from Phu Bai flew every night changing its takeoff time between ten p.m. and three a.m. to keep the NVA guessing. Its job was to kill trucks heading down the trail.

Somehow, I knew this was where the action was. You found the prey winding under darkness and the jungle canopy to deliver its load of war goods to South Vietnam. Once found, you called for the Air Force fighters or gunships that would deliver the final blow. Watching the explosions from your high vantage point, keeping score and moving on to find more. It was what we were sent here to do, stop the flow of men, arms, and destruction from raining death and destruction on our brothers in the south. I truly believed that stopping the flow of men and materials meant fewer attacks in the south, one less base being overrun, some more brothers that would go home in one piece. I couldn't do anything about the larger decision of if we should be here. Someone out there had a huge hard-on for killing Americans every day, and survival was a daily occupation.

Of course, the anti-aircraft fire here was the heaviest of the war, in fact there were more anti-aircraft guns in Laos then in any theater of war in the world's history including today. These highways were the vital link to keep Ho's war in the south alive, and they protected it well. The AAA (anti-aircraft artillery) consisted of aim and shoot 37mm shells, to the more sophisticated and deadly radar guided 57mm to 100mm, SAM missiles, and MIG jet aircraft. But as every eighteen year old who grew up on John Wayne's war movies will attest, one would live to fight or fly another day.

This mission in North Vietnam was flown twenty-four hours a day, every day of the year. A backup Mohawk crew stood by with a plane ready to roll should we have to abort up here. Soon the radio call came in advising our replacement had just entered North Vietnam airspace. So we finished our third and final pass and headed back, passing our replacement Mohawk as we entered the clouds on our way home.

Our first mission up north had been uneventful unless you took into account a couple of sore asses. We had detected several hundred movers or vehicles on our runs. Their positions would be plotted and sent down to U.S. Army Command in Saigon for analysis.

Waiting in the clouds for clearance to land, it became apparent that all the traffic into Phu Bai was some sort of new build up. After landing clearance, we finally broke through the clouds about a hundred feet over the blinking night-lights of the runway. Of course, we were touching down at three in the afternoon. The rain would keep up for weeks without a break.

Dodging the rain again, we unloaded the radar system, turning in the film to the Military Intelligence group located next to flight operations. Their shack was located next to the flight line. A windowless building, it was humming with activity twenty-four hours a day. We'd walk our films inside and hand them over to an intelligence clerk who would roll the Slar film out on a light table. First, they'd search the long lengths of film for the black dots that would signify a "mover" or truck. With calibrated protractors, they would do triangulation measurements of each dot or "mover", and plot the coordinates off the appropriate terrain map. Where the information, went depended on the mission. Our trip to the North would be transmitted to MACV headquarters down south. There, comparisons with the level of traffic detected would be matched against other intelligence to try and determine the NVA's next moves. Photo recon and infrared missions would be analyzed looking for "clues", their results sent back to the unit who requested the sortie or mission. It might be the 101st next door that asked for a recon of an area out west near or over the Laotian border, or the Marines up in Quang Tri interested in some area near the DMZ. Based on our results, they plan their next deployments in a constant effort to destroy an enemy seemingly always on the move.

Done for the day, or until somebody hunted us down for something else, we both ran back to our hootches for some dry clothes.

Along the run back to the hootch, I noticed the numerous dogs that lived in the compound were huddled below the hootches out of the rain. Either that, or the rats were a lot bigger and furrier then I had imagined. As I swung open the screen door seconds from my dry clothes, the smell of incense and soft music hit me. My eyes finally adjusted to the darkness of the hootch, only lit by candles. I noticed Thomas lying on his bunk, with a letter in his hands staring at the tin roof.

"Hey Tom, another romantic letter?" I asked, ripping off my wet clothes.

"I wish," he answered slowly. "Problems at home I'm not sure I can do anything about."

I suddenly remembered his quietness at breakfast this morning. "What's going on?" I asked.

Tom began to explain that he and Lynda were not getting along. In fact, it was getting down right ugly. She was now seven and a half months pregnant, but insists she can go out to bars at night to relax. Tom is afraid for her and the baby, but the more they argue through their letters, the more often she takes off. Tom had tried to write her, but her letter writing has fallen off to once a week. Half a world away, and Tom was afraid he was losing his wife and his unborn baby.

He suddenly jumped up, changing into his flight gear. "Well, I can't do anything here, and I got to fly."

My few words didn't calm his mind; I wasn't sure what to say. Problems like this had never been a part of our worlds before. Hell, a year ago, all us guys were single and taking weekend leaves from flight school into Dallas and later Tucson. Life certainly seemed much easier back then.

Tom headed out to get his plane prepped for a night mission, as I headed down the line of hootches to see where everyone was hanging out.

I found them hanging at Pete, Turk's, and Phil's hootch. Numerous conversations were going on as I opened the screen door and entered.

Music played on, as the only light in the room was that of a number of candles flickering. The shadows around the room as the strong odor of pot hit me as I entered.

The evening lasted until midnight when only a couple die-hard conversationalists were left. Turk was lying on his bunk stroking Samantha.

Samantha was a young mutt dog, ready to have a litter of pups any day. Dogs stayed close to the American compounds, trading affection for their meals. At least the smart dogs did. Meat was an expensive and rare commodity in Vietnam, and dogs dumb enough to stray into town usually ended up in someone's dinner kettle.

Watching Turk pet Samantha gave me a tinge of home . . . to the dog I left behind, Sarge. Before the evening was out I traded flying four missions of Turk's for one of Samantha's litter. Sounded like a good deal, a lifetime companion for sixteen hours in the air. Besides, I enjoyed flying above this constant rain and clouds. I was beginning to feel extremely claustrophobic. It felt like we were living in an eternal night, resigned never to see the sun again.

I awoke to rain again pelting the roof. The only good reason to fly the early mission was a chance to get over to the PX that afternoon. I was out of canned spaghetti, and in need of a holster for my revolver instead of using my pocket when I flew.

The tremendous numbers of cargo planes were still landing, appearing out of the fog and rain as I loaded my plane. We hadn't received mail for four days now. It was hard to understand. We had more cargo planes landing than people here, and no mail!

Daze walked over in the drizzle and stood under the open hatch chatting, as I ran the systems checks. He had just gotten the word he'd be heading to Thailand to replace a crew chief going home supporting the Lao missions. He was a new man that morning; he finally had something to look forward to, which was getting out of Phu Bai.

I finished my system warm-up and Daze and I strolled in the morning drizzle to the maintenance hanger for some coffee. He filled me in on the latest scuttlebutt he was privy to. The South Vietnamese Army known as the ARVN's were getting set for an invasion of Laos. They were planning to crush the truck depots, highways, and bridges the

North Vietnamese were using to supply their troops in the south. Congress had denied the U.S. military the ability to use ground troops in Laos, in an effort to not widen the war. So now the Vietnamese were on their own here. Except for the air support that would be provided by the U.S. It soon would be known in the history books as Lamson 719.

Phu Bai was now being used as a forward stockpile point to keep them re-supplied. Now all those cargo planes landing here made sense.

"Yeah, they're setting up the depot on the other side of these revetments," Daze explained. "Ammo, helmets, rifles . . . man, they got everything back there. I want to get my hands on some C-rations."

"Now there's an idea," I answered. "Anything is better than the mess hall slop. If you get a deal on some, count me in for a couple cases."

The hour for my mission tolled. As I strapped in, I introduced myself to Taz. Boy, I'd be glad the day I knew everyone. Ted was a tall, slender, twenty-four year old kid, and a nice guy. We ran through our series of checks with Daze standing in the drizzle in front of the cockpit. Soon we were taxiing for takeoff.

As soon as we lifted off the runway, we immediately disappeared into the clouds. We were alone again, racing through this huge world of cotton-like clouds. Only the instruments told us where we were, and if we were flying right side up or upside down. We broke through the clouds again at a little over five thousand feet and continued climbing until we reached our mission altitude of ten thousand feet.

Taz was a typical, wholesome American kid from upper middle class suburbia. He had joined the Army in college by entering the ROTC program. He reminisced about his early "tough" days wearing his uniform across campus amid the heckling and taunts. I laughed to myself at people's different ideas of their "tough up bringing". He had married his high school sweetheart and found himself in Vietnam four months ago.

Taz had been flying the SLAR flights up here in North Vietnam. He liked the relative solitude high up here, versus the tree skimming gymnastics of the photo or infrared missions.

We were picking up plenty of moving traffic or movers along the coastal highways. Plenty of chatter on the radios went on between the Navy and

Air Force flights now making bombing runs further west over Laos, where the roads from North Vietnam wind through the mountain passes to enter the Ho Chi Minh trail heading south.

"Spud One Six, this is Pamper, you have bandits out of Vinh heading one seven five . . . Fighters unknown."

"Shit," the air controller located on the Navy carrier force in the Gulf of Tonkin was advising us we had North Vietnamese MIGS flying out of Vinh to the north of us at a heading of one hundred seventy five degrees toward us. We had no clue if Pamper was aware of any friendly aircraft that could provide us cover.

We pushed the throttles to the wall and continued heading south and east further out to sea hoping these bandits had something else in mind.

A minute later the radio crackled again, "Spud One Six, bandits heading one six zero . . . three minutes to your position . . . Fighters unknown."

I tried squirming in my seat hoping to look behind us. The MIG twenty-one jet was North Vietnamese's principal fighter plane. This Russian plane was not much of a match for our Air Force or Navy F-4 Phantoms, but with a top speed of over a thousand miles an hour, this MIG was more than three times as fast as us, and carried air-to-air weapons, we were unarmed.

"Pamper, this is Spud One Six, we are breaking off mission, request permission to descend immediately into cloud cover to four thousand feet."

Pamper responded, "Spud One Six, descend immediately to four thousand feet. We show bandits still heading one six five. We have fighters enroute, two minutes to rendezvous. Make heading change to one four five."

Given we were no match for a couple of Migs, we had to evade them as best we could until our fighters arrived, a flight of Navy F-4 Phantoms closing on us to provide cover. The best way to evade was to make it hard for them to find us. While we raced to get below the cloud cover stretching out below us at five thousand feet, Pamper had directed us to head southeast, further out to sea. The Migs never wandered too far from their bases, and normally when their radar detected our fighters, they turned and ran.

We reached the cloud cover when Pamper advised us that the bandits were returning to Vinh. We both let out a cheer for the Navy jocks that scared these guys off. Now I had a feeling of how the grunts must feel, knowing the enemy was out there somewhere, but often not seeing him until the firing began. We returned to Phu Bai and landed as the sun began to break through the clouds. Maybe it would be an OK day after all.

I grabbed a sandwich with Pops at the mess hall. Afterwards we walked the several miles to the PX. I loaded up on canned spaghetti, beans, a set of stereo headphones, and a holster for my thirty-eight handgun, thank God, at least I didn't have to pay for the fuel we used. I realized on our hike back, I had loaded up a little too much. We got back to the hootch late that afternoon. Time to try out my new headphones to a group called Spirit, while drinking a beer and writing a letter home.

My letter writing was interrupted by the screen door slamming open as Jim came in tossing his helmet and revolver on the bunk. I wasn't the only one interrupted; the numerous cockroaches sunning themselves on the wall ran for cover.

"Shit, fucking Migs almost got us this afternoon . . . ", Jim nervously began rambling as he opened the fridge for a beer. He sat on the edge of the bed, sweat was pouring off him as he rattled on. It seems the North Vietnamese wanted to keep us out of the area today for some reason. Most of these coastal missions were fairly routine, except for frequent warnings of SAM missile radar emissions. The Migs kept away from our SLAR or radar planes. Trying to take us out of action would excite the Air Force, Navy and Marine fighter jocks always too eager to down a couple of Migs. The ferociousness of the retaliatory air strikes was something the North Vietnamese didn't take lightly.

Jim and Keller had received a warning from Pamper about Migs being launched from Vinh when they had approached their northern turning point of their first leg. They had detected over one hundred fifty movers on the coastal highways on their first pass up the coast. This was several times the normal traffic count; the North Vietnamese were up to something. Keller made the turn and began descending to the relative safety of the cloud cover.

This time the Navy was ready but everything played out a lot closer. Meanwhile unarmed and clearly a slow moving target Keller had put the

Mohawk east attempting to drop altitude quickly, as well as keep an eye out for the approaching bandits. Pamper had given them a play by play every thirty seconds on the position and altitude of the approaching Migs. Of course, the North Vietnamese ground radar was giving the same information to the fast closing Migs.

Jim watched a Phantom come on fast, first appearing as a dot, growing and growing until it streaked overhead heading toward the coast behind them. Then suddenly it had roared past them, he could make out one, no . . . two more coming on fast. They both had a collective sigh of relief as they listened to the ensuing chase over the radio. A flight of Navy F-4 Phantoms jumped in the mixer just in time chasing the Migs back home, thanks to Pamper. Of course, once on the ground the Migs couldn't be attacked without a directive all the way from the White House. So they were safe to try again another day. This one had ended faster then it began as Keller thanked the F-4s, promising the world and his first born should they ever drop in on Phu Bai.

Jim cut his recollections short when he noticed four letters lying next to his bunk, our first mail in a week. He ripped open the top letter and leaned back on his bunk, quietly reading. I went back to writing home when he suddenly jumped up excited; his wife found a job and was getting along well with his parents. Her pregnancy was going well, so the fear of a cultural clash with his parents seemed to be fading. It didn't help that our mail was always a week or two late. Jim was elated; running out the door to find some of that awful pink champagne that weeks earlier had killed a number of my brain cells.

The evening began and ended as many would, I fired up a sterno can and enjoyed a can of beans and chips for supper. I then strolled over to the clan meeting at Turk's hootch. Each evening the camp found itself passing the time in numerous cliques. The captains soon-to-be majors and above, spent the evening drinking and politicking in the Officer's Club. The sergeants, and other men enlisted over the age of menopause, monopolized the Enlisted Club.

The club was actually a large room, three quarters buried into a hill, or one third located in a hole, depending on your outlook on life. Dark and damp, even the rats considered it inhospitable. One could tell time as surely as your grandpa's railroad watch, at two a.m., the club closing was punctuated by fights, loud arguments, and breaking glass.

Booze was extremely cheap, and although the long-term cost was the proper nourishing for a future corps of alcoholics; it solved the Army's more pressing current problem. What to do with a large group of men at war, herded together for a year or more on a small base with nothing to do. Keeping them drunk while off duty was certainly a cheap solution to the problem.

Turk's hootch was a gathering place for the young, restless air jocks that didn't feel like beating heads with the veteran sergeants, or playing second fiddle in a conversation with an upper class officer. Some drank beer; most smoked pot, and all listened to the music. The music was a backdrop to the numerous conversations that passed around the room in the evening . . . talk of close calls that day, new items at the PX, or what's the first thing you'll drink when you get home. It was a tie between Coke in a bottle, or real milk. The more serious conversations came as the evening wore on. A small but growing number of the group felt the war was going to be negotiated to an end, so why not exist and stay out of danger, for what would another death add to the outcome. Peace signs were painted everywhere, including on the helmets of some of the grunts. The conflict that was raging in the U.S. found its way here, no protests, but subdued restraint on a war some felt we couldn't win.

I wandered back to the hootch in time for my evening shower, definitely a high point in my day. As I walked up the wooden steps, I noticed a shadow standing between the hootches. Struggling to focus, I made out the outline of Tom.

"Tom, what in the hell are you doing there?"

"Hey Bob . . . what's going on?" he sputtered out slowly. He began to stagger forward out of the shadows, moving now, I could see under the influence of something heavy.

"Are you OK?" I asked reaching out to direct him.

"Fucking-A man, I finally feel like gold, after what that goddamn bitch did to me and my kid." He brushed past me and started heading down the sidewalk to where I had no idea.

I yelled behind him, " Tom . . . what's going on . . . man, you got to get some sleep." But he disappeared into the night. Wow, this guy was falling apart before my eyes. I didn't know what, if anything, I could do.

Sleep came easy after a good shower; it passed the time and eased the mind of these kinds of problems.

Sometime during the night, I woke up finding myself sitting in my under shorts in a bunker, as the ground around us shook with explosions. We were under a mortar attack. I could make out Jim, Pops, and some guys from the hootch across from us I hadn't met yet. God, it stunk in here. The bunkers were built from sandbags between each pair of hootches. Most of the time they were used for everyone to relieve their bladder during the evening when the latrine seemed miles away, and for the rats to store the goodies recently appropriated from our hootches. As I thought of that I instantly searched the bunker for the illuminated sets of rat's eyes, thanking God I saw none. It would have been a short debate on staying with them, or taking my chances outside with the mortars. While waiting for the mortars to stop, I tried to remember how I had gotten there. Finally silence . . . we waited another ten minutes or so to make sure this wasn't just a required union break for the NVA mortar group.

As I left the bunker, I saw the trail of sheets, blankets, and assorted goodies that got in the way of my feet on leaving the hootch. I picked up my mess, threw a pile in the corner and stretched out hoping to get back into my dream. As I lay there, something seemed odd in the room. Straining in the darkness, I finally figured it out; Tom was sleeping in his bunk. He had never moved during the mortars. Talk about the luck of a drunk, or whatever he was using.

Seven a.m. came early as I crawled around the room attempting to untangle my clothes from the pile I threw into the corner after the mortars.

Tom was still asleep and groaning when I left for the flight line. Enough time to grab coffee, load up and check two planes out. Turk's dog was about to have her pups any day now and I figured I'd better start making my installment payments.

The rain and clouds were back. Shit, two weeks and the infamous annual company barbecue was on. Figured it would probably rain for that too. We were placing wagers on the entree to be barbecued. Spam formed into little chicken figurines was the odds on favorite.

I flew two missions in North Vietnam that day. No Migs, but still detecting plenty of heavy traffic moving along their highways.

I got back in time that afternoon to catch up with Chavez and head over to the mess hall. For today was payday, all I had to do was show my dog tags and sign my name and I got an envelope full of money. Funny money that is, the military script that was designed to thwart the moneychangers in the black market. Of course the line continued after the pay envelope was handed out. There was the officer-of-the-month begging and threatening for Red Cross donations, and a table to pay for your hootch maid.

The hootch maid was a Vietnamese woman who came in everyday and kept everything in your hootch clean, or as clean as the blowing sand would allow. Our hootch maid Nui, was a Vietnamese woman, about forty years old. She spoke broken English and had a tendency to shuffle off to the area of the hootch where we weren't. She washed our clothes every morning at the same time, meeting the other hootch maids at a building behind the mess hall. The remainder of the day she polished our boots, swept out our hootch, and straightened up after us the best she could, all for five dollars per month for each of us. These positions were the most sought after jobs in the area villages. The money, by Vietnamese standards, was good, and it gave access to wheeling and dealing for American cigarettes, better than our military script.

I saw only one hootch maid that entered into long conversations with GI's, and that was with Pops. I'd walk past his hootch and he'd be sitting on the steps next to his hootch maid, a woman at least in her forties or fifties, with one of his books in hand, deep in conversation. I admired that ability as I wanted very much to understand what was going on in the minds of the Vietnamese, what they really thought of the war . . . about us being there. My conversations with my hootch maid were very limited, perhaps because of the giggling after she called me her pet name, Babyson. I found it amazing in a country where children were being killed every day, and young teenagers were scripted into the Army, that she thought it funny that I was barely old enough to come join the fray in her country.

That evening Samantha had her puppies. It was a real family affair. The beer flowed and the pot was openly smoked as everyone came over to congratulate the mom and Turk. Turk was like a proud dad, smiling and standing over his brood. I got there as soon as I heard the news. My eyes fell on the little reddish pup whose build looked like a German Shepard pup. I named her Sally J, she would soon become my buddy here, a little bit of home in this dusty enclave, a half a world away from the real one.

The deals were cut for the remaining pups in record time. I wondered about the one guy, Ellis. Tall, young, . . . he was part of the perimeter guards watching the wire for attacks. It was a duty no one wanted, but many with a drug problem, real or alleged, ended up here. The Army was struggling with the drug and racial problems that were rampant back home in America's streets. But in Asia, drugs of every variety were easily available here and had woven itself into the fabric of this war. For many it was better to get it out of sight, and the perimeter was one of the many places in this war were this piece of insanity festered. Ellis was obviously in another world, heavy into something much stronger than pot or hash. He often wandered through the hootches talking incoherently to himself, later dragging his puppy behind him. Unfortunately, the perimeter duty meant they would have the only loaded weapons in camp while sitting in bunkers, watching night after night through the barbed wire for any attack or snipers. It also meant they were free to do their drugs openly. It didn't give anyone a good feeling knowing they were the first line of defense should an attack occur. Of course, if one wasn't on drugs, the job of peering into the darkness every night waiting for an attack that may or may not come, could present a good argument for a strong nerve reliever of one kind or another. In another world this would be insanity, only here insanity was reality.

The intensity of the daily photo recon missions was at an all time high. The daily photo recon missions along with the nightly truck hunter Slar mission over Laos were taking an impressive amount of fire. Word was the South Vietnamese were getting ready to roll into Laos, that gave the 131st had the job of finding out where the NVA was positioned. Turk was flying with Lange, a tough little career captain, and a hell of a pilot. Jim was flying in the second plane with Ted that day when there was a break in the weather out west, so the goal was to get in and out quickly before the clouds closed up again.

Both Mohawks lined up on the runway, Ted rolling on takeoff shortly after Lange lifted into the air. Their gear slammed in place as they made a tight turn and headed low and fast for Laos passing a number of chopper flights making their insertions of troops into the hills to the west of Phu Bai. The radio was especially busy today, as everyone was catching up on the break in the weather.

The series of valleys they were to photograph were found without too much problem. Lange had flown the border a lot over his past nine

88

months here. Radioing Ted, they coordinated the runs in and over the area in strips in order to create a mosaic of the area in film for the intelligence group.

The passes as always were right down on the treetops, flying tight over the hilly landscape looking for fast approaching landmarks to compare to their maps in order to maintain the proper course. Several hundred feet behind lead Mohawk, flying the strip to the right was Jim and Ted. Close and continuous contact insured they were properly filming the terrain below.

They entered and exited the grids at different points in the imaginary box. While they had to keep the strips fairly straight to insure they filmed the entire area, they didn't want to give any gun toting NVA on the ground the idea of which strip they'd would be flying next.

Flying low and fast, they were constantly searching for any humans, trucks, or tents in this no-mans land, hoping the mission would be a fast and quiet run.

"Spud One Three, we show one more pass, negative on any sightings."

"That's a roger Jim, negative any sighting, one more pass and it's homeward bound," came the answer from Turk.

The final turn was made, and they started the last pass on the western side of our mission box. This strip was near the Laotian city of Tchepone, known to be the major hub of the Ho Chi Minh Trail network. Ted finished his turn a little wide and fell back.

Suddenly the lead plane was buffeted all around, as if one had hit a set of railroad tracks doing forty in an old Chevy. Puffs of black-gray smoke exploded first in front, then all around the lead plane as they flew directly into and through it.

"Break off, triple A," Turk and Lange both screamed into the mike, hoping that Jim and Ted following behind could avoid it.

As soon as the anti-aircraft exploded, Lange put the plane on its side, banking hard. The engines strained, the props groaned, as she fought to maintain the low altitude . . . as she was flying virtually on her side skimming the treetops. Lange was assuming the NVA was firing heavy in front, in an attempt to lead.

They had flown into a group of 37mm anti-aircraft guns. Flying low, they were dead in their sights. The only good news was they were also flying fast, being over them only briefly. Not a lot of time to aim and shoot.

Within seconds they were out of it, Lange continuing his screaming turn, coming about to find the fate of Jim and Ted in the trailing Mohawk.

Ted had made his last turn wide before starting the final strip, dropping further back from the lead Mohawk. He had pushed his throttles forward, attempting to catch up when he saw the muzzle bursts from the 37mm guns just under the tree line beyond a small creek. As the airbursts exploded around the first plane, Ted maneuvered his plane to set up his aim for wing-mounted rockets.

Turk and Lange had come around full circle in time to catch the explosions from the load of rockets Ted had unleashed on the tree line. God it was beautiful, there were numerous secondary explosions as the tree line lit up, pieces of equipment flying high over the trees.

"Yah -- whooo . . . sure do appreciate you guys setting those sorry assholes up for us," Ted screamed on the radio.

"All right, Johnny Wayne, but the next one you find for yourself, I'm getting too short for this," Lange answered, referring to his "short" time remaining before shipping home. Everyone was surprised by Ted's outburst. This quiet guy did harbor some killer instincts. Of course, someone trying to make a hunting trophy out of you would bring out some unpredictable responses in anyone.

The team of Mohawks made a couple more passes over the area with the cameras still running to give the Military Intelligence or the MI boys enough to figure out what the hell they ran into here. Anti-aircraft guns would not be sitting here by their lonesome, unless they were protecting something important.

Heading back to Phu Bai, the chatter on the radio quieted down as the adrenalin wore down.

They touched down at Phu Bai with Ted, now cocky, touching down seconds behind. Folks on the ground think he was trying to reenact those old World War II films of planes landing within feet of the tail of the plane in front of them. He was probably hoping a newsman would be filming us. As both rolled to a stop, the tower was screaming at Ted for not waiting for landing clearance. Ted played the infamous, but now old, "do not copy tower . . . coming in garbled . . . must have radio trouble," game.

Both warriors taxied into the revetments and shut down their engines. As before, the crews took off their helmets, rubbing their ears as the turbines whined down to a stop.

Lange jumped down and began checking out the plane for damage. After Turk's hearing returned to one ear, he jumped down and strolled over to Jim and Ted's aircraft. He stood up under the cockpit hatch, yelling as the props slowly ground down, "Hey, that was pretty impressive out there guys . . . and I don't impress easily."

"Shit man, you got a flak magnet in your ass, I'd get that checked out. We can't be around to bail you out every time," Jim jabbed back.

The days film was turned into the MI boys, and by invite of Turk, everyone headed over to his hootch for a beer. Lange had already disappeared, probably a big night at the Officer's Club. Turk had lucked out, better yet; he had adjusted the fridge to keep the beer near freezing. The beer was so cold; one could lose their eyesight on the first gulp.

"Well, how does this compare to SLAR flying?" I asked Jim as we all gathered to hear the details no one wanted to experience firsthand.

"We finally get a chance to fire back. But . . . it's a lot faster reaction time. Flying Slar you're up high enough that you could be in their sights a long time. And they got SAM missiles, and radar guided 57mm to get you down with. Nah . . . you can end up dead either way, doesn't really matter which way you go," Jim slowly answered, nursing his beer.

Jim continued, now turning to Turk, "But you know, you and Lange lead so well, maybe next time you can try the crippled bird approach. Yeah, you guys shut down one engine, and appear to lose altitude over the trees . . . almost stalling. They will think it's such an easy kill; they'll open up with everything. See, then we'll be laying back, and once they start firing, we'll blow their butts away."

"Jim, . . . fuck you."

Everyone nursed the cold beers and bullshitted for hours. Jim and Turk were both good eggs now having calmed down from the days excitement. We all argued a little over the ongoing political quarrel, debating if the war would be negotiated to an end. And if any of these missions would even factor into the final resolution, if another death meant anything now? I slipped that I wanted to start flying the nightly Laos mission, attempting to argue that the Laos mission was stopping the flow of war goods to the south, helping the Hmong Pop's talked about. Jim being married, and having his ass almost blown off was more concerned with the anti-aircraft fire they ran into almost nightly. Then I saw Jim sneak out the side door as I fought the stabbing pain in my forehead from drinking the freezing cold beer too quickly.

Soon after a knock came to the door, Turk opened it.

Standing outside was a GI claiming he was from Military Intelligence. "Turk, the operation's desk sent me here to get you. They want you to re-fly your mission. It appears the rocket explosions exposed the film. So we got nothin'."

We all stared at each other. Tom led off, "What the shit . . . you're kidding us right?"

"Nope, they want you down there right away."

Everyone swore as Turk put down his beer and walked out the door, obviously in no condition to fly, much less walk straight. Something was up, it was already late and we knew they'd never let anyone near the flight line like this.

As Turk rounded the corner of the hootch, Jim was there with a beer in hand, laughing and banging his fists on the hootch, "Ha-ha, got you asshole. Now we're even." Turk just about fell over laughing, he'd already had way too many. More chatter and soon it was time to turn in for this thing called sleep. Time to dream about what insanity was in store for all of us tomorrow.

The next morning found me requesting to fly mission twenty when it became available. There wasn't a long line on this list; most of us learned long ago volunteering for anything in the Army was un-American. Politics aside, as long as we were here, the only air action the politicians allowed was the secret shit going on in Laos. And that war seemed to make sense. The southern missions were killing trucks on the

Ho Chi Minh trail, which meant a couple less mortars and rockets hitting our brothers down south. And in northern Laos I keep hearing of the North Vietnamese Army trying to exterminate the mountain people called Hmong. Here was a people actually fighting fiercely for survival. Unlike the South Vietnamese Army who you weren't sure whose side they fighting on a given day. That seemed to make sense in a world gone crazy.

I was born on May 3rd, 1947, the second son of my father and mother in the village of Nonghet, Laos. A Hmong man is given two names during his lifetime. The first is chosen by his parents when he is born, my parents named me Neng. The second is given later in a mans life. My last name or clan name is Lee, so I was known as Neng Lee.

I had been born just a few months before Luis Alvarez dropped his atomic bomb on Hiroshima Japan. Soon after my birth, the Japanese would leave Laos and neighboring Vietnam. My uncle had watched a group of Japanese officers in a nearby camp commit suicide when news of their final defeat arrived. We were not sad to see the Japanese leave; they had treated our people worse then cattle. Many who had worked for years in the mines for the French were forced to labor there under the Japanese for long hours or days with little or no food. Many of the French died at the hands of the Japanese, so we were very happy to hear of their defeat, we knew that this would be the only way they would leave us alone.

We had fought beside the French who remained here during World War II. We hid them in the caves, fed them, saved them from starvation, from the Japanese. We saw how the Japanese treated the French they caught. They treated them like animals. How could people do this to others? They arrested them, cut their ears off, pierced their noises only to pull ropes through the holes, and then pulled them like animals through the streets. This was to show the French were weak and no longer the strong leaders of years past. The French now bowed to the Japanese, and the Japanese would pick the exact day and time of their death.

But with the Japanese now gone, we all thought that perhaps our freedom would truly return, that for once since our families who had fled from China over a century ago might find the peace we so want. That peace was to raise our children among our extended family, our clan of Hmong.

The Hmong, like many other people believe in one "higher power" or one "God." We believe that God knows everything and punishes anyone who does wrong. Therefore, our parents stressed to us, as we stress to our children to be good, that God will protect us from harm when we ask him to, through meditation or prayer. Little did we realize we would truly be tested in the years ahead?

Our people originated in China thousands of years ago where most of our people lived. We also spread throughout the border areas of Burma, Vietnam, and Thailand. The Chinese had attempted for centuries to take away our culture and history. Our forefathers were forbidden to write the Hmong language, if they did, they were to be killed immediately. For centuries, our Hmong women attempted to continue our written language by hiding it in their artistic tapestries

In the mid 1800's another war erupted between the Hmong and the Chinese. A number of Hmong clans determined that the Chinese were too many, too strong. They did not want to yield or surrender the ways of our people, so they decided to move south to the high mountains of Laos. There were few people that lived this high; most of the Lao people lived below the mountains further to the south, where they grew rice next to the powerful Mekong River.

Then, more and more French returned to begin again where they had left off. But this time they brought the hate of the Vietnamese who followed a new leader, a communist named Ho Chi Minh. But our people had seen this Vietnamese person, the one who talks of freedom from the French. My father remembered this Vietnamese person who traveled with his French master before the war with the Japanese. When this Vietnamese person was without his French leader, they looked at the Hmong like the Japanese did. My father could see the look in his eye, how he looked at the Hmong as inferior, weaker then he. So many amongst the Hmong took up our cause alongside the French who promised to protect us from the communist Vietnamese. They also provided education, which the Hmong always treasured. You see, after the King, Hmong respected most the teacher.

My village was located on the border with Vietnam. I remember growing up as a child seeing the French and Hmong soldiers come and go from my village. My friends and I watched the many airplanes in the sky, drop bombs and fire guns. Then the sounds of war came closer and closer, soon there was shooting outside my village, then through it as the French and Hmong fighters fought the Vietnamese.

My parents, now scared for their family, my brother and me, took us and moved whatever they could carry to the of Xiengkhousang, which was some seventy kilometers to the west. They hoped the war would not follow, that we would be once again safe.

Several years passed and the word of the defeat of the French at Dien Bien Phu came to the village. The French had gone to Dien Bien Phu to stop the Vietnamese from entering Laos. Dien Bien Phu stood in the way of this natural gateway into Laos, toward the Plain. A number of older Hmong sent our soldiers to see if any French were still alive, so they could help them find their way back. After all, we had seen how the Vietnamese treated its enemy; they would torture, and then kill them as examples to all who were not Vietnamese.

Our people found a few French hiding in the jungle and led them back, fed them, gave them medicine and cared for them. But we heard the French, as a nation had grown tired; therefore, they would send no more soldiers. And most of the French who were here eventually disappeared, to return to their far away home.

The next years were quiet as I grew and learned, learned in school to help my family by growing stronger and smarter, for my dream was to become a teacher for my people. The country of Laos wanted to live peaceably with its neighbors if it could.

Then the calm was shattered when in 1960 a captain Kong Le, a parachutist in the Lao Army made a Coup d'Etat in our capital of Vientiane. The country was thrown into a war amongst itself. But again, there were other countries that saw an interest, an opportunity where Captain Le and his army had taken over the Plain of Jars. There, many large aircraft from the Soviet Union began landing with guns and supplies. They brought with them the North Vietnamese, the communists. The Hmong leader Vang Pao knew of these communists, he told the King and us that we could not live with the communists. We would have to fight or we would have to leave.

The country was again at war, and the schools were closed. Those above grade five were asked to volunteer for the Army. I quickly signed up for the Army at thirteen years of age; these were my people, this was my call. It was during this time General Vang Pao had met with some Americans here in our country. They promised him guns, and food, and help if he would fight with them. The French we knew said these Americans would help us fight, to save our freedom and our home.

96

So we fought. My Uncle showed me quickly how to use a carbine rifle and a grenade when the enemy attacked. General Vang Pao sent others and myself forward to the front lines; I was assigned to Company one-eleven of the twenty-first battalion. I remember my first battle clearly. I followed the older Hmong soldiers with my gun in the middle of the night walking through the forests; it was so hard as there was no light. We fought the communists in the dark. I remember the shooting, the noise, and the confusion of that night. I remember the many enemy soldiers dieing in front of me, close to me. It was my first battle and we had lost two of our own. I was thirteen, but that night I was turned into an older, more mature man. I had seen death violently, loudly. I saw what I wished I hadn't. But I could fear nothing now. I was Hmong, this was our home.

We fought for two years, until the leaders from both sides and the world community of nations met and agreed to the neutrality of Laos in Geneva. Once again, Laos was a neutral nation governed by Prince Souvanna Phouma. Again, there was hope we could enjoy peace, and I went back to school again.

But while this peace began, we saw that the Vietnamese Communists did not leave our country. Here in northern Laos, they moved east to their border area of North Vietnam. A number of Lao joined them, and organized the Pathet Lao, or the communist Lao. We heard the Vietnamese were building roads in the southern area of Laos underneath the thick jungle. It looked like they were going to war with the Americans in Vietnam. And to do this, they need to use the hidden roads in southern Laos to get the materials of war to South Vietnam. The clock was ticking, and the mood was anything but at ease.

Then the communist began attacking the Hmong again. They wanted to control their roads to the east and south. But they wanted pay back from the Hmong for their alliance with the French a decade before; these communists had long remembered the past. Several leaders felt they eventually wanted to control all our Laos, but we Hmong, we mountain people were in their way. We could see that the same look in their eyes was the same look in the eyes of the Japanese before them. They looked at the Hmong as less then they, as inferior to the mighty Vietnamese. Maybe that made the killing easier? And then we were at war again.

Choa Say Kham, the Governor of Xiengkhouang estimated the population of the Hmong in Laos to be four hundred thousand, very small when compared with any neighbor along side us. There would not be enough soldiers if the Hmong selected only the adults over eighteen years of age to serve in the army. So the decision was made reluctantly to take younger men into the military also. We would not foresee the devastation of an entire generation of our men and the considerable number of widows that would face life on their own.

The war increased in its violence, in the breath of its destruction. Many Hmong lost their lives at Pha Thi, Hong Nol, and Nakhang. After the triumph of the Vietnamese, they now wanted to attack the Hmong at Bouam Long, an area not far from Pha Thi and Nakhang.
Aside from Long Chieng, our headquarters, Bouam Long was most important to the Hmong. The battle lasted for days, the communist lost thousands of their best soldiers. Our men were strong and clever. We knew the mountains, the land away from the road, and we were used to climbing in the high altitudes. We could walk like the wind and carry the attack on the enemy, then disappear into the jungle of the hills. We knew guerilla warfare better then the Vietnamese; they had to react as they did with the large Armies they fought elsewhere. When they did, we killed them. Then we destroyed enough of them at Bouam Long, we withdrew to fight again.

We battled over the Plain of Jars, our homeland in each of the years. By now some American Special Forces and those from SKY, the CIA fought with us and showed us how to use the planes the American's flew. We would learn to use this fire from the sky to drive the communists into the open and then destroy them from the large guns above us.

Then came an opportunity for me, I was able to go south to the University of Vientiane to learn math and to become a teacher. I graduated with a degree in teaching math and moved north hoping to be soon married.

Each year we celebrate the Hmong New Years where the head of the household must give thanks to the spirits of our ancestors and prepare a special meal for them. This meal usually consists of a bowl of rice and a cup of alcohol. This celebration lasts many days. During the New Years, men and women gather to ball toss and sing traditional love songs in order to impress and pursue each other. In Hmong culture, there are many different clans. Within each clan, one cannot marry another. My heart belonged to a beautiful girl from another clan. In these ceremonies, if a couple is ardent, it is not rare that they will decide they are ready to marry. If it is decided they are fit for each other, the bride-to-be will accompany the groom-to-be to his parent's house. Three days later, the boy's family will look for two "Mej Koob" (may kong) or wedding mediators to represent his family alongside two "Mej Koob" from the bride's family. The parents of both sides meet to discuss how to organize the weddings of the newly weds.

In general the elder men and women will chose a date in the first appropriate month of the year. The month chosen must be an even numbered month, and the date must be before a full moon occurs. It is believed that odd number months and days after a full moon occurs is not a good time to marry, it will bring bad luck for the newly weds.

After the birth of my firstborn, I received my second name from my father and mother-in-law and am now called Chong Neng Lee. This name signifies I am in charge of my family and now connected to two families with many responsibilities. My responsibilities would extend to the community that included monetary contributions to weddings and funerals as well as participation in community events, the funeral process, and governance.

It was a few short months after my marriage when I was recruited back into the Army. This time I was trained in Military Region Five where I was again sent to the front line.

I learned to fight and kill the enemy where he stayed and slept. Then, I learned how to operate aircrafts where I not only showed the Americans where the enemy was, but also showered the enemies with bombs and fire. My cousin was the famous Hmong Pilot Lee Lue. I flew with him the day before he was shot down and he was killed. Lee Lue was a teacher like me, but when he saw the plight of our people he decided to fight. He soon became a revered pilot that was honored by the Americans and the whole of the Hmong nation. He flew from sunrise to sunset, only returning to rearm or refuel his plane. When he landed at the end of each day, several Hmong had to assist in lifting his tired body from the cockpit and help him to his house. His death brought a great sadness to the Hmong people.

And then a number of our Hmong took to the skies and destroyed the enemy from where they couldn't go. By the late sixties, the fight had taken many of our good men and women. In some villages, the families lived alongside their soldier husbands, brothers and sons. When the communists fought, they didn't care who died. If they would overrun a base or village, they would parade out the Hmong men, cut their penis off and stuff them in their mouth, to show the others and the women they

99

no longer had men. Then they would rape our women and shove bamboo up their vagina so they could no longer bare children. This was not war; this was extermination, and we were fighting for our lives, for our people.

Funerals became a regular almost daily occurrence for our people. When a person dies, the Hmong people say he or she has reached one hundred and twenty years old. In our villages we would open fires three times in the air to announce there is a death. As there was no proper way to preserve the bodies, the funeral would be held within a day after death. Thirteen days after the death, the spirit would be called home for the last time. This is called "Tso Plig" (chaw plee) which means the releasing of the spirit of the dead. For the Hmong, the spirit may stay in his or her home until the Tso Plig ceremony occurs. If the spirit is not released, it will remain in the home, where the home is called "muaj dab" (mua da) or haunted.

So the war went on, the Americans would fight from the sky. The Air America people would fly us from base to base, bring us our food and supplies and fly our wounded back to the hospital and our dead back home. Every year there were more and more communists that would attack us in the dry season, when they could move up the winding and dangerous roads. There was no time to grow crops or even take a breath. We raised our families under the clouds of fire, and the fear of death.

But we were Hmong strong in our love for family. Our fathers had stood the test of time for centuries against other great enemies who would plot our defeat and pray for our death. And we would pray to god for help as he is always with us if we ask him. We also had our Shaman or Sheyee, a spiritual doctor. This is a very special person in our culture. He or she does not decide to take on this role. Rather he is chosen for it. The person will know he has been chosen when he becomes very ill and depressed. He will remain so until he accepts this new responsibility. This great sadness and illness is caused by an ancestor who has called him to his duties. The Shaman has abilities to heal the wounds of the body and of the mind. New Shaman must learn from experienced Shaman who will pass their knowledge down to them, teaching them how to communicate to the spiritual world.

You see, the Hmong have a great respect for the dead and their spirits. We believe a person has many spirits within him or herself and that every part of our body; hands, feet, eyes, etc., all has a spirit. We believe

100

that there is a major spirit in each person that he or she cannot live without, for the body would die if it permanently left. When a person is sick or injured, we believe that the spirit has left the persons body. Therefore, we must call the spirit back in order to heal the person. Many times, the departure of the spirit is due to fear or distress the body is under. For example, after a battle of horrendous death and destruction, the person may have been shaken beyond comprehension. When the Shaman has determined the distress, he performs the hu plig ceremony where the Shaman calls the spirit back.

Xwm kab(sue ka) is a special paper that hangs on the main room wall of every traditional Hmong household. In the center of the paper, feathers of a rooster are arranged in a specific way. The feathers on top represent the eyes, and those on the bottom the mouth. We believe that the xwm kab represents a home for the main spirit of our ancestors. We welcome the spirits of our ancestors, because they protect our families and keep evil spirits out of our home. At the end of the year, we sacrifice a rooster to the xwm kab to thank and honor our ancestors for protecting us.

Within death, there comes life. There is nothing as exciting as a new baby, a new Hmong life in the midst of all of this misery. When a baby is born, it is believed the baby's spirit has yet to attach itself to the body of the baby. Therefore the head of the household organizes the hu plig ceremony to call the spirit to join the body. The baby's parents or grandparents will be the ones to name the baby.

In 1969 General Vang Pao's About Face campaign had taken the Plain of Jars away from the enemy. I moved to Muong Soui, Lima Site 108. There I fought and few to find the enemy. With an increase in American air power, we had enough planes waiting for a place to drop bombs to kill the enemy. But every year, the Vietnamese sent more troops. They seemed like young boys who were not so sure of this mountainous country we called home. We knew the forests and the mountains. The Vietnamese stuck to the roads. They stayed in large camps to protect themselves from the land and people they didn't understand. One of our American advisors told us this was the opposite of the war not far away in South Vietnam.

Because here we could attack from the forests and the mountains and then disappear like the wind, we were the Hmong of the Mountains.

I had a chance to sleep late the next day, but unfortunately the heat drove me out of the bunk before ten. I wandered down to the mailroom with Tom hoping to get some mail, or a care package. I had written to my fiancée' asking for cookies, brownies . . . any human food. And potato chips, I had a craving for them. No mail again, so Tom and I headed over to the mess hall and grabbed a sandwich of some type of processed meat that didn't have a name, or much taste either.

I tried to pump him over lunch as to what was going on. I had known this man closely for the last year, but he was drifting away. He told me Lynda had moved out of their home. She was still living with some "freaks" near the university. He figured she was just waiting to have their baby any day now, and then she'd leave him. He got a letter from her once a week or less. They were always very short now, and seemed to center on some more items she would like Tom to buy from our catalog and ship home. The last one even asked him to ship it back to her digs she was sharing with several nameless friends.

We finished lunch as the crowd began to hit the mess hall. It was hotter then hell now, over hundred and ten degrees with insufferable humidity. I had to go down to the flight line and see what time I flew tonight as Tom headed off toward some newfound friends on the edge of camp.

I wandered into the intelligence room next to the flight operations where all the film was analyzed. The room was filled with large flat drafting tables. Many had lights under the surface so the film could be lit from below. Maps hung from the wall pinned on flat sheets of cardboard so they could be pulled down to use in planning or debriefing a mission. Tyrone Sumner was bent over one of the tables with a magnifying glass trying to make out some shadows on film from one of the recent photo missions.

"Hey Tyrone, anything interesting?" I asked walking over to his table.

Not even looking up, Tyrone responded, "You trying to get out of the heat too Curry?"

"Tyrone, buddy, I came in here to see you."

"Yeah, bullshit you did . . . didn't have anything to do with the air conditioning?" still looking down at his film, circling things with his red marker.

Tyrone was twenty-four years old, black and college educated, with the draft catching him right after graduation. For a draftee, Tyrone was continually involved in his work. He was always back here hunched over some film, or helping some of the new guys with theirs. Of course, it could have been the air conditioning.

This afternoon Tyrone was trying to catch up on the crush of missions flown for the Army and Marines. And now a flood of requests was coming in from U.S. Army Command in Saigon, presumably for the rumored South Vietnamese push into Laos. C-130 transports were landing every ten minutes up here now on this remote airstrip disgorging huge amounts of supplies that are being hastily stacked behind our revetments. It was apparent to everyone something was coming down soon. With the monsoons coming to an end soon, the good weather brings on advances from the NVA.

Tyrone went back to studying his film. I figured it was time to see if my plane had been assigned yet. The mission board had just gotten in assignments from maintenance; I'd be flying Spud thirteen, how lucky. With nothing much to do, I wandered out to the flight line to nose around and check Spud thirteen's logbook.

Daze was around as always, running around getting planes out on their missions.

"Hey Bob, two more weeks and this place is history," he yelled before giving an outgoing plane its final checkout of its controls. As the plane taxied out for takeoff, Daze wandered over. He had gotten his official orders, and heard the crew chief he is replacing was already packing his bags. Daze filled me in on the rumors about Udorn. The food was great, the women were beautiful, the food was great, the bars stayed open all night, and the food was great.

"Oh, shit . . . speaking of food, I got these C-rations for you, three cases".

"Hey terrific, let's go get 'em if you got them handy. I'm running out of the canned spaghetti from the PX."

As we wandered down the flight line, one of the Mohawks parked in a revetment we were approaching, fired up first one, then the second engine. I could make out Hump in the cockpit as he ran the engines up, testing them for what reason I wasn't sure. As we passed him he was racing the engines, standing on the brakes while the props were kicking up all kinds of dirt and sand.

As we got past the revetment, all hell broke loose. The plane had suddenly broken loose and spun wildly in the revetment. The sounds of a spinning Mohawk sent Daze and me scurrying for cover. And as quickly as it began the plane came to a halt; the engines began winding down until there was absolute quiet.

Daze and I peered around the revetment wall to figure out what in the hell happened. The Mohawk was now facing the back of the revetment as a rustling noise came from the front of the plane, we watched a pair of feet dangle from the cockpit. Suddenly a plump body fell to the ground in a heap. Daze and I both realized Hump had fallen out of the plane, obviously disorientated from his short flight in the revetment. He had been running the engines to check out the gauges, when he unfeathered one of the props. This would cause one of the engine's props to twist into a thrust position on one side of the plane. With only one engine providing thrust, the plane would spin like a top, especially at the RPM's Humper was running at.

Daze became unglued running toward Hump he began yelling, "Judas Priest, what in the hell have you done to another one of my planes?"

I watched Hump stand up, brushing himself off, still stunned. His face turned beet red as Daze read him the riot act. Hump stood there dumbfounded, never saying a word.

I couldn't take it anymore; my morbid sense of humor sent me into laughing hysterics. The incompetence of Hump had reached a new height today, but I had to give it to him, this was original. And God knows the Army would probably find a way to give him a medal "for bravery in the face of a revetment wall".

As I held my sides in, Daze passed me mumbling how this man was going to kill him yet before he escaped from Phu Bai to anywhere. I ran after him and suggested perhaps Hump would be the pilot who flew him over to Udorn. Daze stopped in his tracks, before he could mumble a response, I said my good-byes and walked away. I could see the fire in his eyes.

Compared to the afternoon, my evening mission with Keller was quiet and uneventful. Traffic was picking up heading south toward the DMZ and the Mu Gia Pass. The Mu Gia Pass in North Vietnam was the major funnel where supplies entered the Ho Chi Minh Trail into Laos. With the frequent bombing halts, the North Vietnamese could warehouse their war materials and quickly transport them to the Lao border without fear of the Americans planes that could easily destroy them as they drove through the open lowland rice paddies of the North as the White House had ordered a bombing halt in the North. I watched them every day and night up here, driving as safely as traffic on the highways around any American city, except the trucks racing like ants below me were filled with death and destruction on its way to a target in the south.

Finally when the supplies and troops reached Laos and disappeared into the forested slopes of the Annam Mountain range would they fear anything. It was first here that the voluminous rules of war written a million miles away, were our planes allowed to hunt them. Only now they were safely under the triple canopy jungle of the lush forests and jungles of Laos.

The Ho Chi Minh Trail was North Vietnam's bloodline to feed and supply its troops in the south. Replacements were critical to replace the thousands being killed or wounded in the ongoing battles. With the border between North and South Vietnam a virtual no mans land; deforested, sprayed with herbicides, mined, and watched like a hawk, any infiltration here was pure suicide.

But Laos, which ran down the western side of both Vietnams with its dense jungles, valleys, and mountains, was the perfect hiding place to race troops and supplies south. After all, the Geneva agreement signed by both sides prohibited foreign troops from entering Laos. For the North Vietnamese, agreements were all part of warfare, deceive and destroy. They couldn't fight the US playing by western rules, but it could use the rules of the west against them.

So the Secret War in Laos was on, the North Vietnam simply denied they had troops in Laos. The US would fight the war in Laos from above with air power, and on the ground with indigent troops, sensing technologies, "sheep-dipped" or clandestine forward air controllers, and Special Forces. The war in southern Laos was directed at stopping the movement of troops and supplies from entering the war in South Vietnam. The Ho Chi Minh trail originally hugged the eastern side of Laos, but as the war progressed, the focus of the NVA changed to taking over the entire breath of the country in south, pushing the Lao troops back to its Mekong border with Thailand, effectively evicting them from their own country.

In the North of Laos far from South Vietnam, the NVA had a more sinister purpose, that of evicting, of exterminating the Hmong from their mountaintop homes. This war had no purpose in their war of "liberating" the whole of Vietnam. This was purely a war of aggression and destruction, a war to take Laos. A war many in Thailand feared would soon embroil them in their own war of survival.

As the war waged, the network of roads known as the Ho Chi Minh Trail were constantly improved and expanded in order to offer more routes for the NVA to hide from the constant harassment of US air power. The trail had started with jungles hacked back to allow the eighteen foot width dirt path necessary to get a truck through. The annual wet season would turn the roads into a quagmire that virtually halted the flow of war supplies south for months. Later, heavy earth moving equipment would be employed to widen and smooth the roads. Paving and gravel were added to allow faster passage and counter the quagmire the rainy season brought slowing supplies to a crawl. Troops were continually added to both improve and protect the roads. By 1970 over fifty thousand North Vietnamese called Laos home, in a Laos that was to have no foreign armies.

The journey down the trail was complex and dangerous. Almost all traffic moved in darkness, beginning shortly after sunset in short journeys that constantly transferred men and material from one driver to another. As the dark and winding roads were dangerous by themselves, drivers became experts, driving their own familiar winding route night after night. Several hours before sunrise the focus switched to hiding and concealing the materials, men, and trucks that had moved all evening. Daylight brought more US airpower searching for truck parks, bridges, and roads that could be bombed to stop the evening rush hour traffic. When bridges could no longer be found, a surprised US watched trucks seemingly float across streaming rivers, then realizing the NVA had begun to build the bridges underneath the water line, hidden from the eyes in the sky above. It was a constant cat and mouse game of tactics, each side responding to a cleaver idea or technology employed by the other.

I returned to the misery called Phu Bai and hit the bunk hard. By the time I awoke, the rains had returned. For the next two weeks it felt as if we were living in eternal darkness. The photo and infrared missions virtually ceased, as did most of the helicopter activity. The grunts and the enemy got their much-needed rest, as the rain and mud prevented much movement, other then sporadic small guerilla attacks.

The hours I wasn't strapped into a Mohawk flying through the clouds, rain, and darkness flying the skies over North Vietnam, I was over at Turk's place. Sally J was growing daily, playing with the other pups as I waited for the day she could leave mom. The mail came in batches every four or five days. Tom was becoming more distant; the occasional mail only seemed to infuriate him more.

The wet spell finally broke when I awoke one morning to blinding sunlight and intense heat that could be mistaken for hell. Steam rose from the ground and bunkers as Mother Nature began taking back the torrid rain she had dealt us these past weeks. I felt lucky, for today was the day I brought my new pup, Sally J home.

With the good weather came an onslaught of missions. The clear weather was now on, and both sides would try to advance their positions. With the photo and infrared missions claiming their pilots back from flying SLAR, we were all stretched, most flying two long missions a day. The morning mission got me back at the peak heat of the day. I stopped by my hootch to find mail had arrived, including a CARE package from home. Damn, what a day. I scavenged through the package finding homemade cookies, sausages, nuts and chips. Some of it was crushed, but a sweet tooth lunch was what God had granted me, who am I to argue with this guy? I packed the rest away, minus some samples for whoever was in Turk's hootch.

Heading over to pick up Sally J, I ran into Chavez. He was beaming; having just gotten confirmation he'd be heading on R&R to Hawaii to meet his wife and baby. R&R was a weeks rest in the middle of one's tour in Vietnam designed to give you a break from the rigors of war. The choices were largely in the Far East, Japan, Hong Kong, Bangkok, or Australia; Hawaii had just been added to the list. Chavez had his wish, now we'd have to put up with talk of his dream trip home every time we ran into him.

Turk was sitting on the steps of his hootch drinking a cool coke and watching mom and the pups laying in the shade.

"Hey Turk . . . came to pick up Sal J. Oh, and I got a gift for the Grandpa," as I handed him some homemade cookies.

"Wow, this is like gold," soon speaking with a full mouth of chocolate chip cookies. I ended up trading off some more cookies and a sausage for the remaining missions I still had to fly for him in trade for the pooch. The right-seaters traded mission like currency, the pilots were never sure whom they'd be flying with until they were both strapped in and taxing out. Turk sat down as talked about his dream to buy a Honda thousand cc motorcycle and tour the U.S. when he got back. I finally scooped up Sally J and headed back to my hootch, wanting to acquaint Sally J with her new home before I had to fly my late mission back over North Vietnam. Tomorrow would be my first Laos night mission. Cradling the little pup in my arms, I entered my hootch, eyeing Jim lying on his bunk.

"Hey Curry, guess what, I'm a dad," he excitingly spit out.

"Goddamn Jim, congratulations," as I put Sally down on my bunk and reached over to shake his hand. "Boy or Girl?" I asked.

He shook my hand weakly as he answered, "I have a baby girl . . . mom and baby are fine."

As my eyes adjusted to the dim light, I knew something was different, Jim was finally rested, the daily fear wondering if his wife and baby would be ok a million miles away had been overwhelming. I loved this guy like a brother, and looking back over this past year was hard to put into any perspective. Now we were sitting in the middle of a sand box a million miles from home, whatever that was, never knowing where the next threat was coming from, a mission over no mans lands that went to hell, a mortar in the middle of your sleep, or the mess hall food finally claiming a casualty. I had a new respect for a cat, which never slept with both eyes fully close, with one's ears always open to hear for the thump of a mortar tube in the distance. This place was a daily rape of the body and mind, and we learned to survive today however we needed to, it was the only way to get to tomorrow.

"Congratulations dad, let me know if I can pick up one of your missions in place of a baby gift, I don't think black pajamas are the "in" thing back home." Little did I know on some campuses they were?

There was a long delay, finally he answered, "Thanks Bob, just trying to sleep once and not worry. You might want to find out what's up with Tom; he got word today his wife is suing for divorce. He read her letter to me; she quit her job and was off doping up with some hippie fuck. Somewhere in there she found religion, God knows which brand. She blamed him for all this killing shit, like it's his fault."

Jim explained he watched Tom walk off, not listening to any of his words of consolation, and only mumbling acknowledgements. We both knew he was hurting bad, only neither of us realized at the time how much he was losing himself in drugs. I realized much later that the signs were already there; the pot was long behind him. Assorted tablets and bags lay around his locker as he experimented, looking for the one that would solve his problems. He scheduled his self-imposed medication for those off days between missions. Somehow he was still flying with a clean mind, fearing the ever-present flight surgeon looking for the next break down case. For how long, none of us knew?

I threw Jim some cookies as I realized it was time to fly. I looked down noticing Sally J had long fast fallen asleep on my bunk. Bending over I scooped her up in my arms, and kissed her good-bye. She lifted an eye in acknowledgement. Animals seemed a lot easier to understand.

I ran over to flight operations as I buckled my gun belt around me. Looking up at the board, I realized I was about to have my initiation flight with Humper and in Spud thirteen. Damn, a day that started off on a good note was fast turning to shit. I ran up to the plane in time for Hump to appear. Strapping myself in, I watched as he mumbled to himself running through his engine start-ups. The tower gave us takeoff clearance as we rolled, slowly lifting off into the darkness of night.

I tried pleasantries as a way to establish communication with this much talked-about man. Hump tried, in his own limited way, to talk intelligently. God this was harder work then I thought.

We arrived over North Vietnam with a slender slice of moon occasionally sparkling on the water below us. Some towns along the coast were lit, as flares began lighting up the skies over the coast.

"What in the heck is that?" Humper gasped as he appeared startled from the first flare. The radar lock on warning had been heavy during the day, as well as radio warnings of bandits, but none appeared. Every one was very nervous lately.

My morbid sense of humor took control of my body as I answered, "Oh shit, that's probably some NVA choppers following us along the coast."

Humper tensed on my words as he turned in his seat trying to make out a shadow or shape in the darkness. "Damn, damn," he uttered, obviously deep in thought . . . or as deep as Hump could get.

As we continued our runs up and down the coast, the flares continued to light the evening sky with Hump intent on watching for the fateful enemy. The first half of the mission, I thanked myself for the limited conversation that had occurred since my comment. As the mission grew on, it changed to worry as I realized this man was deeply disturbed.

He was looking for an enemy that, at the moment, was not there. In fact, he was beginning to rattle me, as I wasn't sure what he was up to any one moment. I tried every possible conversation to get Hump's mind back into reality. I knew it was to no avail when he radioed the Navy carrier group in the Gulf of Tonkin of enemy plane sightings. They were puzzled, as the only plane showing up on their radar in our sector was our Mohawk. But Hump insisted, at times demanding that the Navy send us fighter cover. I wanted to interrupt the conversation . . . to tell the Navy to forget the request. The only thing flying up here, besides us, were flares . . . to tell the Navy this man was an idiot, but then he was doing that one all by himself.

The night and the insanity wore on, and the mission ended none too soon for me. The stories I had heard about this man took on new meaning tonight. The weather was good for the next week. We were each flying two missions everyday now. The NVA and guerilla activity was increasing dramatically as the weather allowed easy movement of supplies and troops.

Sally J was getting bigger everyday. She slept at the foot of my bed every night. Many nights I would awaken to hear her scampering across the wooden floor, scaring away the patrolling rats hunting for food. Every morning at sunrise, she would leave to stand in line at the mess hall, begging for scraps along with the other dogs. It wasn't long before she was constantly scratching, a sure sign of fleas. An emergency letter went out to my fiancé June for a care package for Sally J.

Weekends are hard to distinguish in war, the schedules, the flying, go on as any other day. But this one was significant, the much talked about company picnic. I lucked out and flew a morning mission with Keller. We touched down just after noon, both of us heading to our hootches to get out of our hot flight suits. On the way we watched a group of "volunteers" set up large barbecue grills made up of grates, over split-open barrels. Everyone else lucky enough to miss the "volunteer" roundup, was sitting out on their hootch steps. The huge stereos bought at bargain basement prices at the PX up the road by the 101st were blaring from behind the screen doors. Beers in hand, everyone was talking, waiting for word of when this hallowed event would begin.

Another hour passed until word filtered around that the barbecue was on. We arrived by the flight line to see numerous grills in full swing. Helicopters and jeeps were arriving, dropping off a number of high-ranking army brass. The area became wall-to-wall people in a short period of time. Jim, Turk, Chavez and I pushed our way to the food grills. We took a couple of swigs of beer, staring at the army brass starting to mingle through the crowds. Protecting our cups we started our journey to the food.

It took only ten minutes to reach the food, I only hoped it was worth the effort. Just then my eyes realized what was on the grill, "Jim . . . take a look at this, my God it's chicken . . . real chicken!" My mind was groping with what was being put on my plate.

Jim was speechless, other than an occasional "damn" sliding out. The cooks stacked the chicken on, and then added corn and baked potatoes. This corn was the first yellow food I had seen since I arrived in-country that was edible and didn't first start out in a powdered form. And baked potatoes, it's still hard to believe that the Army didn't first reduce them to powder so they could add water.

The food and beer flowed endlessly as everyone milled about, talking and eating. The newly arrived army brass were walking around, stopping to ask questions and engaging in pleasantries. We all felt uneasy with their questions, not sure why they were here, or what they were up to. Our answers were guarded; even the beer wasn't enough to get us loosened up.

Turk, with his street sense, pieced it all together for us. He had overheard a group of battalion supply sergeants discussing the horse trading that went on to get the fresh chicken, corn and potatoes. The CO had set up the barbecue to show off to his superiors that the rumors of strife and fatigue were only that, rumors.

The complaints had been numerous; many of them were beyond the CO's control. And many were problems rampant throughout the military in Vietnam. The holding action in units throughout Vietnam had invited boredom, drug abuse and racial strife. With the news talking about Nixon ending the war, no one wanted to be the last guy killed for a war we were exiting. There was a new war within a war going on everywhere now. And to the older officers, the drugs brought a new threat to morale and peace in the units they couldn't understand. Many times a CO would bury his head; those who turned to drugs, or who were merely "suspected" of using drugs, often were shipped out to guarding the camp perimeter or worse. And they stayed there unless shot, killed, or shipped home at the end of their tour. Out of the way, the problems were, "eliminated."

The problems that seemed fixable affected everyone on a daily basis, such as not getting mail for weeks at a time, poor food, not enough spare parts, were similarly ignored. On a larger scale, dieing for ones country was never a plan of any soldier, but he or she knew it was a reality. And if it was a reality, one hoped it would be for some noble purpose. But those who were returning to Vietnam for additional tours told of the hatred in the streets for what was going on over here, and that the targets were anyone in uniform. The confusion was draining, so basic survival won out. Whatever the political motives, today we kept enjoying the food, beer, and talk amongst ourselves. Who knows what would come crashing down tomorrow.

As I walked back to the beer line, a deep black voice rang out from behind me.

"Hey you . . . Curry, I'm talking to you man."

I turned around, not quite sure what to expect. And what I didn't expect to see was the black crew chief, Jess McGee; I had flown over to Nam with.

"Damn, Jess, you taking speech lessons from a black militant?"

"Got your attention white boy," he chuckled.

I found out and a couple of his buddies had been assigned to the 180th Medivac chopper unit located behind us along the flight line. They flew in the Huey helicopters with the large red crosses painted on the sides to evacuate the dead and wounded from a battle. The Vietnamese didn't follow the cookbook rules of war, known as the Geneva Convention. They often used the red crosses for targets, unarmed targets carrying away the wounded who had already seen battle . . . too much of it.

I introduced Jess and his party crashers to our group, and traded gossip all night. The barbecue ended with Jess talking me into flying with him on a "pickup" so he could fly in a Mohawk. Wasn't sure how I'd pull that off, but horse-trading was the name of the game here.

Hitting the bunks felt real good, as we were tired from the hard work of partying, although there were very few stumbling drunks. The sleep we fell into so fast was broken at three a.m. by mortars falling in the compound. After the race to the bunker, four of us sat only in our khaki green jockey shorts, inside the urine soaked bunker, waiting for the shelling to stop.

The mortars stopped, and then came the dead quiet. We waited, as the Vietcong would sometimes wait for everyone to get out in the open, and then mortar again. If they could only aim today, they would have been dangerous.

The days came and went, all blending together, flying, eating, attempts to sleep, and always counting the days down to when this insanity ended. I had become a cat, always keeping one eye slit open, and one good ear listening for the telltale "whoosh" of incoming.

Another hot evening found me half awake laying in the darkness, I heard the whoosh of a mortar tube somewhere out there, then the random explosions over the base as I ran my ass into the nearest bunker. I was staring at several half open eyes I couldn't make out yet when a violent explosion filled my ears and head, it sucked the breath out of me, sat on my chest and then everything became black. My heart was racing as I knew I was in trouble, I just couldn't slow my brain down enough to think. Now I knew I had an incredible weight on my chest, I was struggling to breathe, and when I could I was eating sand, not breathing in air. And then it all went quiet.

Somewhere in my thoughts I could make out muffled noises, yells and screams. I thought I could hear men running past, outside our bunker. Not sure what was going on, I realized that the bunker had collapsed onto itself, and we were somewhere under tons of sand.

Unknown to us, outside men were running everywhere, trying to pull the hundreds of sand bags off of what used to be a bunker, while trying to anticipate when the next round of mortars or rockets would be incoming.

By now several dozen men had formed a chain gang allowing only a couple to stand on top the pile to throw down the bags. There was already enough weight on those of us inside.

"What in the hell happened, mortar hit?" Jim asked throwing the bags.

Someone yelled back, "The mortar fell a hundred feet behind it . . . this damn rotting bunker just collapsed."

They kept throwing the sandbags frantically, unsure who was inside or what condition they were in. Then . . . they heard a voice yelling from beneath them. They dug where the voice was coming from. Suddenly they saw someone appear in the darkened opening beneath them, it was Chavez. In one move, someone reached down and plucked the skinny Chavez from the dark hole.

Instantly I felt a tug on my arm; I could make out light and finally air, precious air. Luckily I had been near the entrance, I coughed my guts out, sucking in as much air as I could, spitting out a rice patty full of sand. While I was standing there, making sense of what happened, trying to pull it together, I heard Chavez yelling, "Hey, you got to help Pops, his arm is hurt bad, he's still in there," Now Chavez coughed out, wheezing, trying to breath the fresh air.

Everyone tore at the opening, pulling away the remaining bags. They saw Pops laying there, groaning in pain. A group grabbed at him, straining to pull his huge bulk from the hole.

I heard someone say, "He's barely breathing . . . he must be in shock."

Those around yelled for help. Someone suggested they put him in a jeep sitting down the road and get him to the MASH unit at the end of the runway. Before anyone answered, a group of guys had Pops picked up and slumped into the right seat, Lange soon had the jeep spinning between the hootches in search of the road to get Pops to help. Chavez and I shook off the sand and the terror and made our way back away from the commotion trying to take everything in. The pile of sand bags, the blackened clump of wood was all that remained from the hootch that took the hit.

By the time Pops was speeding on his way to the hospital, the bunker had been totally dismantled and no one else was found.

Everyone stood around for a while as if expecting something else to happen. Word came back from the MASH unit that Pops was OK, except for an arm shattered in two places and a mild case of shock. The officer on duty that night walked up with a pipe sticking in his mouth pointing and talking with various GI's standing around trying to figure out what had happened. Somewhere through the conversation he noticed his jeep was missing and launched into a tirade. When he was told Lange took Pops to the MASH unit, he seemed to calm down. He glanced over at Jim and I, first nodding recognition, then giving us the once over. I suddenly felt naked, and looking down I realized I was standing there with nothing on but my jockey shorts. It became apparent it was time to catch what sleep I could before the heat of the morning drove me out of my bed.

I awoke to the sound of Vietnamese girls chattering between themselves outside the screen door. This place was always a surprise; I wondered what in the hell was going on now. I got dressed in fatigues, as I wasn't flying until midnight, which would be my first mission over the Ho Chi Minh Trail in Laos. It was too late and hot for coffee, so I grabbed a Coke and went outside to see what all the commotion was about.

There were about twenty young Vietnamese girls chattering in a group around the remains of the collapsed bunker that everyone was plucked from the night before. The weapons sergeant, with a Vietnamese interpreter, was trying to organize a construction team of cheap labor to rebuild the bunker. New bags were in a pile waiting to get filled and stacked.

"Hey Curry, better watch out, they'll have you filling bags too," came from behind me. Turning around, I saw Chris on the top of our bunker sunning himself as usual.

"I wouldn't talk too loud up there, you could cause this bunker to collapse," I slung back.

115

I gingerly stepped up on the bunker to watch the excitement with Chris. The weapons sergeant was about to lose his mind with these women. He had already lost his cool with the interpreter, resorting to the Army's backup contingency plan . . . yelling and screaming multiple obscenities. Finally progress, as half of the group began shoveling sand into bags while the others started stacking the bags around a shell of galvanized steel.

Tom filled me in on the proper ways of beach life and safety in tanning as the bunker slowly went up. Several Cokes and sometime later, I was watching these girls work when something shiny glimmered from the sand pile. I watched closely out of curiosity, when I finally realized one of these Vietnamese had a pile of rifle shells she was sticking inside the sandbags. The idea was that a close mortar, or shrapnel hit, would cause the bullet to fire into the bunker. It was a million to one long shot, but given my luck it would probably graze me in the ass.

"Sarge, hey Sarge, you got a problem here!" I yelled, jumping down from the bunker on my way to the scene of the crime. I explained to the Sarge what was going on. He screamed for the interpreter, and both went over to the girl I had pointed out. Sensing I was on to her, she had tried to hide her stack of shells deep under the sand. The interpreter questioned her, but she replied crying that she was doing nothing wrong. Son-of-a-bitch, this was enough; I grabbed a shovel and dug around where she was filling the bags. Bingo, I hit into a pile of shells just under the sand. Now the Sarge responded by yelling more at the interpreter. The Vietnamese were then all checked, over protest from the interpreter. Four more were found to be burying live shells in the bags they were filling. They were immediately thrown off base without any pay.

Pops came home that afternoon with his right arm in a sling and his chest taped up. I spent the afternoon at Pops' hootch arguing about our role in Vietnam. I took a number of current events and political courses in high school and felt quite informed, but Pops was setting me up that afternoon. After I spilled my guts about the need to protect the freedom of the South Vietnamese from communism, Pops pulled out his tattered history books. I didn't know that the U.S. supported Ho Chi Minh and his guerrillas during World War Two to fight the Japanese, or that Ho Chi Minh had on numerous occasions, written to President Roosevelt asking for U.S. support in remaining a free country after the war. I never knew that the U.S. supported France in returning to its role of ruling

South Vietnam after World War Two in exchange for France's support of U.S. plans in Europe. But were the Chinese and Russians duping Ho, using him as a pawn for a larger empire? You know, the communist threat? I remembered the air raid sirens of the early sixties when Kennedy stood the US on the brink of war over nuclear weapons in Cuba. It was Korea before that, now it was Vietnam, wasn't it?

Then Pops went back to his stories of the Hmong asking me what I knew of them.
"Yah, they're the mountain people in Laos fighting to stay on their mountains?" I answered unsure where we were headed.

Pops then exploded about the war in northern Laos, far away from the Ho Chi Minh trail the NVA used as a convenient highway to get their war materials into South Vietnam. High in northern Laos, near the Chinese border the NVA was trying to exterminate the Hmong from their mountaintop homes and villages. The Hmong, persecuted for centuries by the Chinese had moved in the early eighteen hundreds to the relative sanctuary of the remote mountaintops of Laos. Later they would find themselves in a battle between the French and the Vietnamese. The Vietnamese had always treated the Hmong cruelly, seeing them as simple mountain people who were always in their way. They also viewed how the French controlled the Vietnamese, especially in their presence. So the Hmong began to see the French as protectors and allies; they admired their power and technology, but especially their education and schools. The war quickly found the Hmong fighting fiercely with the French against both the Japanese and later the Vietnamese. Now with the French gone, the Vietnamese were out for revenge on these simple people who had no plans of expansion. Who only wanted to live their life free in the high mountains in northern Laos. Unfortunately, the Hmong had been a loyal and fearsome ally of the French, and the Vietnamese would not forget.

I ended the history lesson early, claiming it was an overload for my young, growing mind. But it started the questions that would haunt me the rest of my tour . . . what in the hell were we really doing here, why did it sound so different there? I was beginning to feel the insanity build.

Pops told me he had several months to go before he was discharged, and these injuries would keep him from flying any more missions. He was content to stay in Vietnam in relative obscurity, to be left to his books. Pops and I heated up some of his PX spaghetti for supper, and headed over to watch the occasional outdoor movie between the hootches. It

117

consisted of a family sized movie screen set up nightly on the volleyball area. Well, a volleyball court could have been anywhere in Vietnam, put a net down and you got a sand court. The projector was duck taped together and we got the left over films that the big bases in Da Nang tossed aside, but hey, beggars can't be choosy. I left the black and white John Wayne western early and got dressed for my nightly mission.

I would fly the mission with Koontz, his first Laos mission also. That made a lot of sense, we could both get lost and killed together, but then again, this was the Army.

We took off at midnight. It took us twenty minutes to get to our starting point in Laos. We would fly seven separate legs that would form a number of boxes crisscrossing the Ho Chi Minh trail. The "trail" was actually a large network of roads that weaved under the jungle canopy. Bridges, truck parks, anti-aircraft emplacements, the commitment, all were impressive . . . a sign of how important these roads were to Ho Chi Minh's war in the south.

We flew southwest out of Phu Bai to enter Laos on its southern border with Cambodia. This is where the trails would be entering Vietnam and branching into the sanctuaries of Cambodia. We would soon be in never-never land Laos, the land of a million elephants, of roaming tigers and bears. This was a different war; here the US would attack the North Vietnamese who are the large uniformed and well trained Army holding strategic location, roads, shops, storage facilities, barracks, etc. Their job was to protect the all-important lifeline that supplied their troops in the south of Vietnam. And we would do it at night, when they felt protected by the black of night. We were about to turn someone's journey in darkness a living hell.

Our first leg didn't turn up any activity, which was good, as we were getting acquainted with our flight paths and the airborne Air Force command ship called Moonbeam that we would coordinate our activities with. We could see the red tracers of anti-aircraft fire to the north of us where we'd be heading. The radio was alive with flights of aircraft getting their target assignments. We all flew out here with our "Christmas tree" or navigation lights on. The air out here was like a freeway on a Friday at rush hour. Half our job was keeping track of all the other planes flying in our sector to avoid collision.

All traffic into the theaters in Laos were controlled by a flying Airborne Command and Control Center or ABtripleC, whose job was to keep track of every type of air traffic flying in its sectors. An electronics van of communications equipment was loaded into the back of a C-130 and manned by various teams of communications and intelligence officers and enlisted men who took requests from forward controllers, special ops teams on the ground, Hmong, Lao, or Thai troops in need of air strikes. Then the mission was matched up with the appropriate air strike craft available. In southern Laos, the night command was known as Moonbeam, the day command ship went by the call sign of Hillsboro. In northern Laos, the nighttime command ship was known as Alleycat, its daytime counterpart went by call sign Cricket. It was a Herculean task of juggling a constantly changing inventory of missions and requests for immediate firepower anywhere in this country. And when the call went out of a pilot down, every resource was allocated to the task of quickly getting the pilot and crew out safely. It was well known if taken prisoner here by the communist Pathet Lao, the chances of survival were nil.

Soon after our first turn heading north, I started picking up movers on our radar. With the map mounted on a board on my lap, I plotted the truck's positions and called in the coordinates to Moonbeam.

"Roger, Spud, we copy coordinates, will assign short," the radio responded.

The air war over the trail consisted of the largest array of aircraft from multiple generations the world had ever seen gathered for a fight. The goal was to blast the elusive NVA trucks and tanks rumbling under jungle canopy along winding roads attempting to deliver their war goods to their troops in the south. Of course it might have been easy to blow them away in the marshalling yards of North Vietnam, or buzzing through the flat rice lands of the North on their way to the jungles of Laos. But Washington decided that wasn't a way to fight the war. So the war would have to be fought from the air, with limited operatives, Special Forces, and our Hmong allies on the ground in Laos.

Prior to Vietnam, the focus of the Air Force called for more of the same, fast fighter jets ready to take on the Migs of the Russian bear. But here in Vietnam, speed was not the most important asset, unless you were trying to outrun an anti-aircraft artillery shell aimed up your ass. Putting massive firepower directly on a target often made the critical difference between success and failure. Time over target meant you could destroy more of the enemy, or spend more time defending your troops under attack. So those in command in this theater were willing to reach in a bag of tricks to pull together the right strike force for a most unusual war. And sometimes that meant pulling planes out of mothballs made for an earlier war, or refitting planes once designed for other purposes. It was a work in progress, but some of the greatest military minds put on one hell of a fight in Laos with limited assets.

The war over Laos was being fought from two sides, from Vietnam in the east and from the west in bases in Thailand. But most of the Air Force assets and special ops teams for the Lao operations were assembled on various Royal Thai Air Force bases in Thailand. America's war in Asia began in Laos well before Vietnam would invade our living rooms through the nightly television news. In 1954 the Geneva Accords guaranteed Laos' neutrality. But, the late fifties shattered this peace as the communist Pathet Lao and the North Vietnamese began attacking Lao Army troops resulting in a struggle that would last till the end of the Vietnam era. While the North Vietnamese patently ignored the Geneva Accord by camping upwards of fifty thousand troops in Laos, the US policy of not letting Laos topple into the communist camp involved a program of CIA operations, Army, and Air Force Special ops. Then an Air Force Major later rising to Brigadier General, Heinie Aderholt was given the job of setting up Air Force special operations in Thailand in the early days of this conflict. The job began as supporting CIA operations in Laos who was using various contract air carriers such as Air America, Continental and Bird Air to fly food, ammo, medical supplies to the Lao military and Hmong troops spread thinly throughout Laos. Cargo planes of various eras were used in this "private" operation. A number of World War Two and Korean era prop aircraft were being turned over to the Thai, Lao, and Hmong troops to use as their Air Force. Heinie introduced the Helio Courier as the first of the STOL, or short takeoff and landing aircraft to land on the short rough landing strips hacked on a hillside or out of a jungle to support remote ground teams.

More importantly, as commander of the 56th SOW group, he argued for an Air Force that could be used for close air support and interdiction of the enemy moving down the Ho Chi Minh Trail or in the mountainous jungle terrain of northern Laos. He argued that propeller-driven aircraft were well matched to the war in Laos. With their slower speeds they had the inherent ability to observe the battlefield correctly, stay over the battlefield longer, and deliver fire with more precision. The Spooky, AC-119 and AC-130 gunships along with the A-1's and T-28's, OV-10's, and OV-1's were demonstrating this every day by destroying more equipment and enemy in Laos then all the jet power combined. Heine did this at great personal risk to his career while the Air Force brass back home were still blindly committed to a high speed, all jet force.

Another ingenious warrior, Bill Lair put together the plan to fight a low intensity war allying with the Hmong forces on the ground that were already fighting the communists. He would order the placement and construction of hundreds of landing strips or Lima Sites throughout Laos to support this new type of warfare. For here in Laos, America and her allies would become the guerilla force attacking the bases and logistics of an in place formable army known as the NVA. They would learn to fight a new type of warfare at troop levels approaching that of ridiculously low when compared to the fight in Vietnam.

Aircraft became instrumental to Lao and Hmong forces on the ground that were vastly outnumbered and outgunned by a well trained and equipment NVA Army, complete with tanks and artillery. Controlling air strikes in Laos was handled on the ground and in the air by a combination of American, Lao and Hmong volunteers.

The first groups of these were Air Force enlisted men known as the Butterflies, later the Ravens would enter. Names like Larry Sanborn, Jim Stafford, and Charlie Jones began to enter my vocabulary. Scattered throughout Laos, they flew in the slow moving O-1's over the treetops to find and locate the enemy, then directing the attack aircraft of every shape, speed and ordinance in on to destroy, often within yards of friendly forces. They lived with the Hmong in the thick of it all, having been sheep dipped, the protocol of being "unassigned" by the Air Force, and acting as civilian contractors so they would not violate the Geneva Accord of having US troops on the ground of Laos. They also took the most causalities of any Air Force unit in these wars of Southeast Asia. All in a war that didn't exist, according to a speech to the country by President Nixon in 1969.

As the war grew, so did the aircraft and the missions. Besides the aging bombers, fighters, and cargo planes, an assortment of helicopters added flexibility to this growing odd assortment of aircraft. The list of aircraft in this strange war was long and varied, it included T-6's, T-28's, O-1's, A-1's, C-47's, O-2, the Huey, OV-10's, B-26's, CH-53's, C-130's, C-123's, the Porter and Helio, the OV-1, etc. Now add the conventional inventory of the Air Force and Navy; the F-4's, 100's, 105's, F-111's, B-52's, Corsairs, A-6 Intruders, B-66's, etc. And that was just the air war; now consider the special ops on the ground, the Hmong troops,

Royal Lao and Neutralist Forces, Green Berets, the electronic sensors program, etc. Laos, it was a handful one might say.

Fighter aircraft were put in action early dropping bombs on targets, strafing convoys, or taking out radar or Sam missile sights. They also provided necessary fighter escorts with other aircraft to protect against the North Vietnamese Migs who became more venturesome as the war progressed. We didn't know of Kissinger's secret negotiations with North Vietnam, but we felt this new aggressiveness on behalf of the enemy. The jet fighters had to chose between their bomb load and fuel as their appetite for speed consumed gas like it was going out of style. It was easier flying fast and hitting targets during the day, but most of the traffic moved under the safety umbrella of darkness. Our sensoring equipment had the ability to see through the darkness and find the enemy. Once located, we'd radio Moonbeam with the target list. Moonbeam would chose from a list of strike aircraft in the target area to take out or kill the enemy. Fighters at night were limited to their time on station, as fuel was the limiting factor in how long they could stay up there orbiting. Many times putting a fighter on coordinates in the night sky of a jungle also required putting in a flare ship first, to light the night sky to aid in the sighting and bombing.

Several groups of the Air Force had been working on a better platform for close air support, for massive firepower that could be closely directed on a target for an extended period of time. And to find a way to bring the war to the enemy during his curtain of darkness, when the trucks fired up and ran supplies south until dawn and the fighters returned. We were about to work with one of the best.

"Spud, we have Stinger one-three enroute to your targets" crackled the radio.

Moonbeam had looked through its airborne inventory of strike aircraft available and picked out Stinger one-three, an AC-119 gunship designed to put massive firepower onto the targets we had detected. On a separate radio frequency they had given Stinger the target coordinates we had just called. We could map out to fifty miles on either side of our plane, we could find the needle in the haystack anytime of the day or night. But night was when they moved, when they least expected us. Once we had the coordinates of these "movers", we could give the Stinger the area for them to pinpoint the trucks, to scc thcm moving under the illusion of safety in the darkness of the remote jungle, and to take them out. We were the hunter and Stinger would be the killer tonight. Shortly afterward we saw a set of navigation lights appear in the air over our sightings. The lights soon disappeared as the Stinger went "Christmas Trees out" and began to move slowly in a circle over the area. Suddenly, streams of red fire poured from the sky. It was an awesome night spectacle in the skies before us.

Stinger was an Air Force C-119 designed originally for cargo hauling, but now living a new life as a floating gun platform. It was an updated version of the AC-47 or "Spooky" of movie fame thrown into duty to prove the concept. The AC-47 was limited in availability and the load of guns and equipment it could carry. So the Air Force had started reengineering the cargo plane workhorse, the C-130. Known as Spectre, the C-130 gunship originally carried night vision equipment, four veracious 20mm gatling guns and four 7.62mm mini-guns. Later Spectre models added 40MM bofors and in 1971 began carrying a 105MM artillery piece. The Spectres were flying the skies over Laos from the special air warfare base in Ubon in east central Thailand, directly west of the Ho Chi Minh Trails. But the numbers of C-130's for gunfighter duty were limited; the priority was being given to its cargo and troop hauling duty. So the hunt for more plane resources continued, and the C-119 was selected as the third gunfighter platform. Retrofitted in the US with new engines, night vision systems and a combination of 7.62mm miniguns and 20mm gatling guns lining one side of the plane, they were sent to fight their new mission over the jungles of Vietnam and Laos. C-119 missions flown in support of US troops in Vietnam went by the call sign of Shadow; those killing trucks on the trail went by the call sign Stinger. And tonight on our first hunter killer mission over Laos, the combination of Spud and Stinger would help end someone's quiet drive through the jungle attempting to bring loads of troops and weapons to continue the war in the south.

The radio crackled as Stinger confirmed our sighting. Unlike the fighter and flare ships, the night vision equipment on the Stinger allowed its operators to see the trucks we had located. Once they confirmed the sightings they would circle slowly putting the targeting information into the guns. In an instant, the Stringer cannons interrupted the safety of the darkness, each gun firing two thousand shells per minute onto the trucks and tanks below they had been silently watching. From our vantage point, hanging in the air over the Laotian jungle, we saw rivers of red fire arch from a hole in the sky toward the ground. Within seconds, the bullets found their targets as explosions from the trucks' fuel and weapons they were carrying erupted into flames. It was a weird reversal of a fire works display, this time the red trail of the rockets began in the sky and exploded on the ground into a multiple of colors and shapes. Now the Stinger with its slower airspeed and its night vision systems could easily circle in the sky continuing to aim its rivers on death on anything below that was still moving, trying to escape the rain of death that came from above without warning. The rivers of red tracers were deadlier then even we could see, as a red tracer round was inserted only every fifth round. But to us, the tracers appeared as solid streams of fire heading toward the ground.

We were riveted to the cockpit glass, watching as if we were kids for the first time. Suddenly the ground below this red rain erupted into a number of new explosions, white and red. The streams of fire continued as the Stinger continued its dance of death high over an enemy whose night was ripped away by the explosions and death now all around them. Soon we could make out numerous burning hulks of trucks bathed in the light of their own flames.

"Moonbeam, we have confirmed twelve truck kills with eight large secondary explosions, numerous smaller ones," radioed the Stinger.

"Good hunting guys" came the call from Moonbeam to Stinger and Spud; the Hunter Killer team had done its job.

Our plane was filled with screams as Koontz and I went crazy over our kills. We yelled and slapped each other on our first success. The feeling was electric. We were stopping, in some small way, the war from reaching the south. We were busy the rest of the mission, between watching out for other flights and calling in truck finds. Finally we were kicking ass and taking names, like it was a high school football game. How would we ever explain this to anyone back home? How would we explain the incredible high from the adrenalin rush over killing dozens or more that night, or the next night, or the next? It was the macabre of the bizarre and everything in our life here was another piece of it. We were learning to enjoy the hunt, the kill; like a lion tasting blood, could we ever go back?

By the time we landed back at Phu Bai shortly after 4 a.m. we were excited over our successes, but couldn't find anybody up at that hour to dump our excitement on. The adrenalin pulsing through my body wouldn't let me go to sleep, even though there was nothing to do. I took a long shower and lay on my bunk for the next hour staring at the ceiling, reliving the flight, reliving the thrill of the burning fires.

The heat drove me out of bed at ten. God, I was going to have to devise a better way of getting sleep before I turned into a zombie. Grabbing a Coke to get some caffeine in my system, I peered out the door to see at least ten guys filling sand bags, rebuilding the bunker next to our hootch. I could make out Chris, Jim, and Chavez in the group working. Shit, another "volunteer" chain gang. I hid inside till lunch when the group was released to eat. There was another advantage of flying nights, we slept days and tried to became invisible to the numerous make work projects routine to any military base.

At lunch I caught up with Chavez at the mess hall. He explained that they let all the Vietnamese go after the attempt to sabotage the bunkers yesterday. And the CO had ordered all the bunkers be ripped down and rebuilt, as they were unsafe. So anyone moving around in the morning was conscripted for the work gangs. I began to appreciate my Laos missions for now another reason . . . keeping me from my aversion to massive building projects involving sand.

Jess had a day off from Huey duty and offered to take me to the PX that afternoon. He had a jeep checked out of his motor pool, and had to make just one stop along the way.

"Hey, I'll give up a long walk on the dusty road," I answered, "let's get the hell out of here before someone volunteers me to rebuild those bunkers."

It was our first break in two weeks. The monsoon rains had given up, at least for a day. The sun and heat were working overtime trying to soak up the water and humidity from the last week's constant rain. And the recent outbreak of flu had ended, meaning several of us got our first break in weeks from flying every day.

Hopping into the jeep, we buzzed past the company gate, dumping pounds of dust from our spinning tires on top of Daze, standing at gate duty that afternoon. Bouncing down the dirt road we laughed about the load of dust Daze had just eaten, and how close it probably was to today's mess hall lunch.

Jess grabbed a jeep as often as he could. He had never discussed his errands, and none of us ever gave his little jaunts a second thought. As we bounced along the road, the conversation turned serious. Jess got real sullen, his voice cracking a little, as he explained he and his wife were unable to have a baby. Hell, I didn't even know he was married, as he never wore a ring. He had grown up in the neighborhood with his wife and knew she was unable to have a child due to a childhood accident. Somehow we were too young for that, but I had heard some of my buddies back home were married with kids already on the way. We got to be true friends on that ride, as we both struggled with growing up faster then we ever imagined.

We got to old Highway One, and headed right toward the village of Phu Bai. Traffic was slow going on this crowded two-lane road. It appeared as everyone was taking advantage of the sun. There looked to be as many joy riders as military trucks. We slowly pushed through town, talking while staring at the hustle and bustle of the crowds of Vietnamese on their way to somewhere. Their little blue-green motorcycle buses wound their way in and out of the line of larger military vehicles.

Once through the small town, we were able to pick up speed before Jess pulled us off on a dirt road towards a set of whitewashed buildings set about a quarter mile up the dirt road on a small hill.

"Where in the hell are we going," I asked, never having been off the main roads in the forbidden country.

"My errand, remember? I always visit this orphanage to drop off extra food or clothes my wife sends for the nuns."

As we drove through an old crumbling stone gate, I could see our airfield in the distance behind us. Children of all ages and sizes came running toward us to see who the visitors were.

A small Vietnamese nun approached us from one of the buildings smiling. "Jess, I so glad to see you . . . the rain, you fly much? We worry for you . . . no see you for while," she haltingly asked.

As Jess pulled a couple boxes from the back of the jeep, he answered the nun. "Sister, I'm sorry I couldn't get here for a while. We were flying too much, and no mail or packages from Jan for the last week. We finally got some packages yesterday."

The nun smiling reached up to pat Jess on the shoulder as he carried the boxes up to the first building. As I followed these two, the nun turned, smiling at me, and asked Jess, "Who is your friend?"

"This is Bob," Jess answered, "he's a flying buddy of mine."

"Welcome Bob, to our home," she continued, "a friend of our Jess is always welcome here."

She grabbed my hand, and asked Jess to take the boxes on ahead as she showed me around. The children were running around us as we walked toward one of these whitewashed buildings.

"The children, they came in on their own or are dropped off by the villagers or the Army," she began to explain. "Their family is killed, or they get lost from them in the war. And to these children, we are now their family. We give them love, and they know, we care for them."

My god, there had to be over a hundred kids here. In the background I heard babies crying as I noticed several nuns in the building we were approaching, cradling them in their arms.

I found myself staring at two small children, arms around each other, staring at me, not saying a word. They somehow looked different, but I wasn't sure why.

"That's Thuy and his sister Tin Hoa," the sister answered noticing my stare. "There father is American, their mother is Vietnamese. We don't know where the father was; perhaps he was back in the U.S. The mother, she left them at our gate one night."

"My god, why?" I asked. "Couldn't she care for them?"

"No, these children of mixed races are not welcome in Vietnamese society. Their mother in order to survive will many times abandon these children. Or her family, her village will abandon her and her war babies. She not accepted anywhere, with no where to go, no one to care for them after the GI father go home, it only certain death for them all."

The cruelty of this prejudice, a continent and a culture away from us, sent a shiver down my spine, in the hundred ten degree heat.

"Bob, these are the lucky ones. There are hundreds of these kids living on the streets of Da Nang and Saigon to fend for themselves. These two are lucky. We will love them and care for them. But when they grow older . . . I not so sure."

It wasn't until later that evening when I wondered, how many GI's went home, knowing the children they fathered would be left to fend for themselves . . . or die alone in the streets. And which culture should bear the responsibility.

The buildings that housed the children looked adobe like, with their whitewashed walls, tin roof, and broken shutters covering few of the window openings. The inside was one large room with mats lining the walls. The few belongings of the children lay on the dirt floor next to them.

I suddenly noticed some of the children were sleeping on their mats in the afternoon heat. Just then, Jess came around from behind the building, with a little girl following beside him. "Bob, meet Kim."

I looked down on the sweetest four-year-old girl I had seen in a long time. She just stood there with a smile barely cracking out, I then realized she was part Vietnamese and part Black. She was a little scared by this new American in an unfriendly green uniform. For most of these children, uniforms had brought the death and destruction of their families. It didn't matter who wore them.

I knelt down in front of her, took her tiny hand, and said, "Hi Kim, my name is Bob. Can you say Bob?"

She looked up at Jess, unsure of what to do. He smiled and nodded his head. Her face broke open a wide smile as she quietly said "Bob."

"So this is your errand into town," I said looking at Jess, "you can't stop rescuing people."

"I met Kim here months ago when I was dropping off some extra food with the mess sergeant. She just walked up to me, all alone, and stared up at me with those eyes. Kinda got to me."

"Yeah, I can see how," I answered, "She sure is a cutie." I noticed her tiny hand was holding onto Jess 's.

"I'll meet you back at the jeep Bob, Kim wants to show me something," Jess shouted as he had turned walking away.

"Fine, take your time." I answered. He was obviously head over heals in love with that little girl. I slowly walked back to the jeep with Sister Thoua. She and her group of nuns had been in this spot for over fifteen years. She had seen the French leave, and the Americans come. She tried not to understand the politics, so instead spent all her waking time caring for the children. They had seen hundreds of kids come and go. They leave when they are old enough to care for themselves . . . or when a young one dies from a wound or illness.

The orphanage survived primarily from the area army units who dropped off extra food rations; or with GI's like Jess, who fell in love with these little urchins, and wrote home begging for clothes from their family and friends. I had seen several loads of canned foods leave the mess hall for the orphanage before. One day I cried over cans of yellow corn leave, yellow corn we hadn't seen since the states. Oh well, at least it was for a good cause.

The cruelty of this war often brought out hatred for the Vietnamese. The name calling, the "gooks" or "dinks" made them less than human, certainly less than equal. This enemy that killed and maimed our friends, also killed their own people. These children were the innocent ones. In their tiny eyes, you saw the pain and suffering. You found yourself imagining someday your own children in their place. Their questioning looks of why . . . why was this happening to them. I began to feel uncomfortable, because there were no words. I wasn't sure I understood it myself. The politicians seemed to know all the answers two months and a million miles ago. But I wasn't so sure today.

Jess finally came jogging down the hill yelling excuses why he took so long. Panting, out of breath, he stammered, "Sorry I took so long, let's head on down to the PX."

We said our good-byes, hopped in the jeep, and headed back down the bumpy road toward the highway. I'd make sure I'd write the church and school back home for old kids clothes, they were wearing rags here.

Traffic was still heavy but moving at a good clip. Finally a break came, and we turned in behind a jeep of MPs heading back toward Phu Bai.

Jess told me he had sent a picture of Kim home to his wife shortly after his first visit here to the orphanage. And in their letters they discussed the possibility of adopting her. Now with the recent excited letter from his wife, he was certain they would try to adopt Kim. He was waiting to hear from his wife about it. The procedure would take months, but just maybe they'd have a little girl of their own.

As we approached Phu Bai, traffic slowed to a snail's pace again. Nothing new here, there wasn't any other roadway through the area as this thin piece of Highway One snaked from one end of the country to another winding through cities and rice paddies. The temperature was now a torturous one hundred twenty degrees with humidity that you felt dripping down the back of your neck. As we talked about the cold beers waiting for us after the PX, I suddenly noticed the hustling Vietnamese that lined the village streets on our way to the orphanage had totally disappeared in the middle of the afternoon.

Just as I was trying to make sense out of this, a huge explosion shook the ground, a jeep up ahead of us literally leaped into the air, falling to the ground seconds later charred from the explosion. Before our jeep screeched to a stop, gunfire erupted from all around us . . . more explosions occurred to the front and rear line of traffic. I turned around to see a truck not far behind us hit by gunfire veer off the highway, smashing into the hootch next to the highway.

Everything happened so fast, yet at the same time, appeared as if we were all moving in slow motion, Jess and I could only react. Jumping out of the jeep, we both crawled underneath hugging the pavement. The loud popping sounds of gunfire were getting heavier. The occasional plinking of shells against our jeep overhead made us dig deeper into the pavement.

As we watched from under the jeep, we could see bare feet and black pajamas moving between the shacks in the distance, and then we heard shooting ahead of us along the stalled line of trucks. Further ahead of us, some GI's were returning the fire. More sporadic explosions occurred as grenades were tossed at the stalled vehicles.

Once the heartbeat slowed, I could only feel total helplessness as I then realized we had not carried any weapons with us. Complacency had slipped into our lives as we had often made off-base trips to the PX without a hitch. Looking frantically around us for a weapon, the gunfire seemed to increase. Bursts of it pinged against the jeep and the street beyond us. The fear turned my stomach to shaking as I felt we were going to die, it was now only a matter of the Vietcong walking over here and finishing us off. At times I thought I wanted them to hurry, before my heart burst out of my chest.

130

There was no movement from the jeep ahead of us with an open area of a couple hundred feet. Looking behind us was a truck burning, part of it was smashed into the wall of what used to be someone's home. Looking at the MP jeep in front of us, I figured if anyone had weapons, this jeep must. Besides we had no other options, we couldn't risk just waiting for the inevitable.

I looked over at Jess who was thinking the same thing I was. He shook his head and waved me on. "Fuck you," I screamed, "we both go." Soon we both were crawling on all fours to the jeep ahead of us, going as fast as we could manage while hugging the ground. I didn't look up, just tensed my mind and crawled, waiting for a shell to find me.

As I got next to the jeep, I stopped, now on my knees, trying to catch my breath. I listened for some telltale sign of movement of the enemy across the highway. But my heart was beating too loud; I couldn't hear anything.

Several more explosions occurred further down the line. More grenades or gas tanks catching fire, I wasn't sure. Our return fire at the head of the line seemed more intense, still . . . no one was moving. They still had the line pinned down.

Kneeling next to the MP's jeep, I looked over at Jess, finding him staring at me again. Suddenly he was up, crawling into the jeep over my head. Shit, I was afraid of this, it was time to stick my head up.

Suddenly, I pulled myself up to the side of the jeep. Time stood still for a moment till a scream from the other side of the jeep finally made it through the numb passages of my mind.

"Curry, the gun . . . get the goddamn gun!"

As w both crotched there; Jess grabbed the only rifle lying in the back of the jeep. Sliding down next to the jeep, we both tried to figure out our next move as we crawled behind the jeep.

"Shit Curry, what the fuck were you doing, trying to get us killed," Jess screamed.

I didn't answer, I didn't know if it really mattered now.

The firing was continuing around us, extremely fierce at the front of the column. We had to see what was happening . . . to use this damn rifle to stop the shooting . . . to stop the damn noise. He pushed the rifle safety off setting the butt into his shoulder as he now kneeled next to the jeep.

Both our eyes were furiously searching the row of hootches across the road for movement. Jess seemed ready to blow anything away that moved, or at least scare the shit out of anyone with plenty of near misses . . . but nothing moved now. It had ended as fast as it had begun. The VC had made their move causing quick death and destruction, and then quietly left before the American's firepower could be directed back at them.

The air soon filled with the noise of helicopters. Gunships were firing into the fields behind the buildings lining the road. Dust filled the air as Medivac choppers landed on the roadway up ahead of the line directed by frantically waving GI's looking to get their wounded buddies out of here.

We stood there staring at the road filled with burning and smoking vehicles spilled over both sides of it. Walking through the debris scattered across this little piece of Highway One we came across the road brightened in spots with the red blood of some GI or villager who weren't as lucky as us. Several villagers who got caught in the crossfire were being dragged away by families screaming in the horror. We stood there speechless as the arriving medics carried away the dead and wounded. Within hours the wrecks of the battle would have been dragged away, and traffic on Highway One would continue as if nothing had happened.

Except for those who spent a lifetime there one afternoon.

The next days came and went in a vacuum, flying and staying alive was the game plan, which was until Chavez Day came. This was the afternoon that Daze was packing up and flying off to Thailand . . . for good he claims, and Chavez was heading to Hawaii to meet his wife and baby on R&R. Everyone said their good-byes at our hootch that afternoon. In the back of my mind I was hoping it would only be a short time before I caught up with Daze. I wasn't so sure about an R&R to Hawaii. Chavez and I talked about it that afternoon. I asked him, why go back to a U.S. way of life for a week, meet his kid and wife, and then leave them to come back here for another six to eight months? Chavez argued vehemently with me, he saw it as no problem. I didn't want to ruin his leave so I dropped the subject. Who knows, maybe he knew something I didn't.

Chavez left mid afternoon on a C-130 transport from the air terminal, so a group of us saw him off. The Vietnamese were in the terminal with their live poultry heading south. I'm not sure who was more bizarre, the Vietnamese getting on a DC-9 with their chickens and pigs, or a bunch of soldiers waving to a camouflaged C-130 taking off.

Dazes' exit was quite low-key. He was flying with Pappy, one of the 131st's more respected and experienced pilots over to Thailand. Pappy was taking over command of that unit. Originally Daze had planned on leaving late afternoon, arriving in plenty of time to party in Udorn, Thailand. But Pappy was waiting for some parts to show up so he could ferry them over. He said his good-byes and left with his bags for the flight line later that afternoon.

My next mission ran into trouble on the west leg of Laos. It figures, we'd been having pretty good success with fishing for trucks that night. Moonbeam had assigned us a Spectre gunship, so the dead truck count was well over thirty. We'd taken some triple-A west of Tchepone, but the NVA's aim was off so there would be no soiled seats this evening, or so I'd thought.

"Do you hear that?" crackled the headset.

I looked over at Jim puzzled, "hear what?"

"Think we got a problem with number two," pointing over to the engine on my side.

"Awe shit," I thought as I peered out my hatch making out the silhouette of the props spinning, as if I could make out any problem in this dark night air? I did take note that the props were still spinning, that was good I thought.

Shereck continued to egg me on to the point where I did hear trouble. I was now convinced we were about to lose number two. And then what in the hell would we do?

"Moonbeam, Spud two-two is declaring an emergency, we'll be RTB to Ubon to check this out," Jim alerted the flying command ship.

"Roger Spud, RTB, will advise Ubon, fly safe," a curt Moonbeam replied.

Ubon was the closest Thai Royal Air Force base to us. Seven huge Thai bases housed the enormous inventory of American planes continually bombing Laos or North Vietnam. Within fifteen minutes we were on the ground taxing past rows and rows of an incredible number of aircraft finally coming to a halt in guest parking. Shereck pulled back the throttles killing the turbines as I pulled off my sweated helmet to the high-pitched whine of the props as they slowly wound down. Warm wet air was rushing though the open hatches as I wondered what we'd do now. We were on an Air Force base on the other side of a war far away from any parts or crew chiefs that knew what in the hell a Mohawk was.

"Supper?" was all Shereck said as he stood on the ground underneath my hatch giving a quick look at number two engine.

"What the hell . . .?" I answered throwing myself down from the cockpit. Just then a jeep pulled up with an Air Force sergeant welcoming us to Ubon and asking what they could help us with.

"Officer mess would be appreciated," Jim responded as he pointed to me to hop in the back. And with that we were off, winding through nicely paved roads past row after row of aircraft and buildings, this place was enormous.

We entered a building full of Air Force officers in neatly pressed blues sitting at tables with real plates, glasses, and tablecloths. Then the most beautiful Thai woman I'd ever seen came up to our table, poured coffee and asked if we knew what we'd like. This was going much too fast for me, I was now convinced we had crashed and I was in heaven, no better yet, Disneyland.

"We'll both take steak and eggs, thank you very much," Jim ordered, as I watched this beautiful woman walk off to place our order. My eyes then caught the stares of every prim and proper Air Force officer sitting in this room. We had to be a sight for sore eyes, both Jim and I were sitting in our red clay stained Vietnam nomex gear, three weeks past a haircut, and a couple days shy of a shave.

Jim stood up and waved his hat to the now suspicious crowd offering up, "Evening gentlemen, we're here to inform you that we got your flank covered to the east and tonight everything is alpha-oscar-kilo-mike-foxtrot"

The place broke into laughter as I realized Jim had told them that everything in Vietnam was a-o-k motherfuckers! A now seated and beaming Jim then explained there might not be a problem with engine two that an hour cooling off in the beautiful air of Thailand wouldn't fix. That everyone on mission twenty was indoctrinated with the Ubon detour and tonight was my turn. We sat back and had the greatest meal of my then young life, enjoying the food, watching the beautiful Thai ladies, joking with the Spectre and Stinger gunship jocks, and just bull shitting with Jim. On that evening, life didn't get any better. Later we took off into the still night sky as we checked back in with a surprised Moonbeam as we flew across Laos to re-enter Vietnam and our life of shit and despair. Oh well, at least we knew how to dress properly for shit and despair. The flight back was uneventful, a perfect evening in this sea of shit.

Arising at noon from my much-deserved sleep, food again became a priority. I ate some of my C-rations I had bought off a group of Marines moving through Phu Bai as the mess hall was again serving a dish resembling beef jerky strips in foul smelling dark gravy. After supper I wrote some letters home, put on my flight suit and headed to the flight line to prep my plane.

Arriving there I met Jim and Hump as they were strapping in. Jim didn't say much sitting there next to Hump, but I knew his prayers had been said, and now it was up to the gods. After they sped off into the evening sky, I checked out my plane's systems and spent the next hours waiting in ops as mission backup, ready to fly in case one of the birds out flying developed problems. Tonight that wasn't necessary, every once in a while things go right in the Army, that's just to keep you wondering.

Getting back to my hootch, my luck took a turn for the better. I had three letters and a care package from home lying on my bunk. I ripped open the box in record time as the letters could wait. I found some of my fiancées' infamous chocolate chip cookies, small tins of ham, and a flea collar and rawhide treats for Sally J.

Sally was on the bunk sniffing the whole time, knowing she was on to something important. She snatched a rawhide treat from my hand, disappearing under the bunk for the rest of the afternoon. Chris walked in, grabbed a stack of cookies and popped open a beer. He was in an exceptional mood. The anti-aircraft must have snapped him back into reality, or at least made him realize he had to take care of himself here; that he couldn't change what was going on back home. I left him to guard the care package while I hit the cold showers to remove the mud and musk from my evening in the rain. I realized too late that was like leaving the lion to guard the kill while I stepped out for a minute. My return found a roomful of "buddies", some I'd never seen before, drinking beer and eating my cookies. Chris merely shrugged his shoulders and chewed on another precious cookie.

The cookies gave out and the party magically ended. As everyone left, Chris sleepily tried to explain, "I was threatened with my life by this gang of starved GI's. I knew you'd understand."

"Sure I'll let you make it up in trade when you get your box of cinnamon bread from that little bakery back home."

Heading out toward the company gate, my eyes fell on the mail jeep sitting outside the Officer's Club, with Jim sitting in the drivers seat.

"Jim, where in the hell are you going?" I yelled across the road.

"Not so loud," as he waved me over. "Turner's drunker than a skunk, and I thought he'd never miss the jeep while I ran to the PX."

"Move over buddy, I'll ride shotgun," I announced while jumping in.

We both shut up while our heads swiveling to see if anyone was watching. Jim turned the starter switch; magically she kicked over on the first try. I quickly looked to see two M-16's sitting in the back. But unfortunately in Jim's haste to make a quiet and quick getaway, he spun the tires kicking up a street full of dust. Hearing the door on the mailroom kick open, Jim gave her more gas. We sped past the gate spewing dirt over anything and anyone in our path.

We made it to the PX as they were loading up the shelves with cans of food. We loaded the carts with anything that wasn't stewed, pruned, or contained animal tongues or hooves. Thank God we had the jeep.

"Do you mind if we make a detour?" I asked Jim.

His eyes widened, "Nah, you know some local woman in need of companionship?"

136

Not wanting to burst his bubble I answered, "Yeah, you could say that, move over I'll drive." I figured the brisk drive would cool him down. We headed up Highway One and rolled through Phu Bai. I found my mind wandering back to the day of the ambush. The tire and scorch marks were still on the road. I found I had been gripping the M-16 sitting between us. There wasn't much traffic so I punched the accelerator. I wanted to get the hell out of here.

It wasn't far before I saw the dirt road heading up to the orphanage. Turning off the highway and bouncing up between the ruts, I turned to see that puzzled look on Jim's face, the same one I must of had the first time I came here with Jess. I knew by that look, his passion was now replaced with fear. Good, it would make explaining easier.

By the time we had bounced through the broken gates, the children were running out of their ramshackle buildings toward our jeep.

"Time to meet your girls," as I tapped Jim on the shoulder, we came to a stop. "Oh yea, and close your mouth, you're making a spectacle of yourself.

"Sister Thoua shuffled up to us as I began unloading the boxes of canned goods out of the jeep.

"Oh Bob," she struggled, "it is nice to see you again," staring at Jim, "and you bring a friend?"

"Oh yes . . . sorry Sister, this is Jim. Jim's been a long time close friend of mine."

Tugging on Jim's arm, Sister Thoua ordered, "Jim, get up."

Jim startled, jumped up and stood there, as if waiting for the Sister's next order.

"Where can I put this Sister?" I asked while picking up several boxes of the food.

"Oh Bob . . . thank you, please put in first door," the Sister answered, "I take care of Jim."

I carried the boxes up a small hill with a group of curious youngsters following me. I watched as Sister Thoua walked off holding Jim's arm as she led him on his introductory tour. I had to hand it to her, she was the best damn unassuming salesperson this orphanage could have.

I stacked the boxes at the door to the makeshift cooking area. I sat down in the shade next to the building to wait for Jim to come back. As I sat on my butt, a group of quiet kids stood in front of me, just staring.

"Hi," I said, breaking the silence.

A bunch of giggles emerged, then turned and talked to each other in excited Vietnamese. This was going to be interesting as we began a game of pointing to ourselves, and then to items around us while saying the appropriate words in our languages.

After a while, a new member joined the game. I looked up and noticed Kim, Jess's hopeful future daughter.

"Hi Kim . . . Bob . . . remember?"

She smiled, opening her mouth, " . . . Bob?"

All the kids excitedly bubbled more Vietnamese. Suddenly I was a trusted old friend. We continued to play our game. It's amazing the amount of Vietnamese profanity I learned from these urchins. Sometime later Jim and Sister Thoua showed up.

"Thank you boys for all your help, thank you," as she held our hands pressing them, struggling to say the right words in English that would repay us.

"Sister, thank you, we all do what we can. These kids repay us every time we come," I replied.

Jim noticed the sun was beginning to drop, grabbing my shoulder and pointing to it. I knew I didn't want to be out here after dark. We both hopped in the jeep, this time Jim was driving. As we sped off, we yelled good-bye to these kids innocent of everything that was going on around them.

The next day came too quickly as I awoke to Sally J's warm tongue licking my face. Grabbing her, we wrestled for a bit, then I put her down

138

and opened the refrigerator. Pulling out a Coke for myself, I grabbed a near frozen rawhide for Sally. I kept the rawhides hidden in there . . . hopefully the rats hadn't figured out how to open the door yet. Sally J took the rawhide strip and instantly dropped it. She wasn't sure what this frozen treat was. Lying there sniffing at it, she knew it was a treat she wanted, just wasn't sure what the problem was. As I reached for the rawhide, she gave me that fierce puppy growl. I petted her head as she continued growling, letting me know whose property the rawhide now was. We had gotten the word that rabies had broken out on the base with several of the dogs. So I had a day to turn Sally into the Vet for a week's quarantine. Any dogs out after tomorrow were to be shot by the MP's.

Strapping on my revolver, I said good-bye to Sally, now involved heavily into shredding the rawhide to pieces. She certainly had lots of practice, given the tenderness of army food scraps; this rawhide was a piece of cake. I headed over to the mess hall to grab some breakfast with Turk and Pops.

Sliding my tray down next to Pops, I asked, "Hey Pops, how's the arm doing?"

"Great, good enough to turn the pages of my books, but bad enough to keep me from flying any more missions."

Turk slurping his cereal jumped in, "Yeah, even with his cast, give him a Playboy magazine and an empty stall in the latrine with a door and he'll never miss a stroke."

I choked on the eggs as Pops' face turned beet red.

Having to fly the eleven a.m. mission, I showed up at operations, coffee in hand, to check on any delays. Looking up at the assignment board, I noticed whom I was flying with. Shit, it was Hump. It wasn't only that I considered him totally dangerous, he was a complete and total bore. And four hours in the air talking to someone with the personality and intelligence of a brick, was not high on my list of ways to pass the time.

I got my plane readied, checking out the radar systems twice, I didn't want a problem today. If we had to abort this mission, we'd have to fly an evening makeup mission. The last night mission I flew with him was an experience I didn't want to repeat. While I waited for the Hump to show up, I drank more coffee talking with the crew chiefs on the flight line. The whole discussion focused on how short everyone was. After even a day in Phu Bai, there was the constant math of how many days left till one could leave the insanity. Finally Hump appeared, mumbling pleasantries to us as he did his walk around the plane.

As Hump continued his outside check of the plane, I hopped inside. Strapping in, Hump finally climbed up in, mumbling as he went through his cockpit checkout. The crew chief standing in front of the nose gave us the signal to start engine number one. The turbine whined as the props slowly began to turn and then rapidly picked up speed to where they now appeared as a blur. Engine two started and we taxied off the revetment ramp waiting at the taxiway edge for clearance from the tower.

"Spud one-two, clear for taxiway one, use runway two-niner," crackled the radio as the tower cleared us for a routine takeoff.

We taxied down the runway with our hatches open to get some air in the cockpit as the temperature was approaching a hundred twelve degrees. The wind kicked back from behind us, blowing hot whiffs of exhaust with the smell of burned kerosene in through the windows as we watched the gauges for any signs of problems. At the end of the taxiway we stopped and called the tower for clearance.

"Roger, Spud one-two, you are clear for takeoff on two-niner," crackled the radio again, as we both grabbed our hatch windows, slamming them shut, and pushing the yellow locking handle forward. We then flipped our yellow safety handles to arm our ejection seats.

As Hump pushed the engine throttles, the plane lurched forward and began its roll down the runway. I had my hand positioned on the red emergency wing handle. Pulling this handle in the event we lost an engine on takeoff would send our attached two thousand pound wing fuel tanks, and any armaments, falling to the runway below. This would hopefully get enough weight off the wings to keep us airborne.

The plane bounced along the runway, picking up speed rapidly, as we approached fifty knots. There was a sudden large pop . . . then dirt and air rushed into the cockpit. Shit, Hump's hatch had popped open.

Hump immediately reversed the props and stood on the brakes to abort the takeoff. We came to a stop two-thirds down the runway and pulled off on a taxiway.

———

As Hump checked for any damage to the hatch, I called the control tower to let them know that the aborted takeoff was not an emergency. Thank God it happened here. If the hatch had popped once airborne, the wind pressure would have ripped it off and sent it into the engine or the rear control surfaces. That could have caused us to lose the engine, definitely impairing one's ability to control the aircraft.

Everything appeared OK, so we called the tower, obtaining clearance to taxi down for takeoff again on two-niner.

We sat at the end of the taxiway and waited for two Air Force C-130 cargo planes on final approach to land and taxi off. All this time Humper talked of how stupid these hatch latches were designed. I really didn't give it a second thought, as these hatches appear latched when one's in a hurry and occasionally pop open. Even my disregard for Humper's intelligence didn't enter my mind.

"Spud one-two, clear for immediate departure on two-niner," radioed the tower.

Humper pulled us on the runway as we again closed the hatches, locked the handles and armed our ejection seats.

"Roger, tower, Spud one-two rolling," responded Hump as we began our acceleration down the five thousand foot runway. Hand again on the emergency wing handle; I watched the engine gauges for any indication of trouble. As we hit sixty knots, Hump's hatch exploded open again. He delayed aborting for a second . . . a second that lasted a lifetime. We had hit seventy knots before he reversed the props, pushing the brakes as far as they would go. Shit, we had passed the last taxiway before the plane shuddered to a stop.

"Damn, goddamn hatches," screamed Hump as he pulled off the runway, beating the instrument panel with his fists in a fit of anger.

"Davies, are you sure you checked that latch," I asked pointedly as his pounding and screaming was getting out of hand.

"Yes, dammit, don't you think I'd make sure the second time Curry?" yelled Humper.

Oh well, stupid me, I called the tower and explained our problem as Hump mumbled and argued with himself. He finally settled down and taxied back to the start of the runway.

Sweat beaded on Hump's face, as he said nothing, staring ahead, waiting for another takeoff clearance from the tower. I noticed he hadn't disarmed his ejection seat as we sat there awaiting clearance.

"Your seat is still armed," I said into the intercom.

"I know, who in the hell do you think is in charge of this plane?" he yelled, staring outside. Shit, I had been developing a bad attitude toward prima donna captains, and now this one was trying to kill us.

"Spud one-two, cleared AGAIN for takeoff," boomed through the radio.

Hump pushed the throttle forward, turned us on the runway and began to quickly accelerate down the runway. Shit, I grabbed my hatch, slamming it shut and arming my seat. Humper grabbed his hatch, momentarily letting the controls go as we continued our roll down the runway.

With the look of a crazed wild man, Hump was bent on getting us in the air. That smart remark from the tower set him off again. As I grabbed the emergency wing release handle, I noticed the engine temperature gauges were running close to red line. Suddenly, there was an explosion of noise, air, and sand rushing into the cockpit as Hump's hatch swung open wildly in the passing air.

As Hump threw the props in reverse and hit the brakes, I tried to think of how I could kill this man. It was as if his mind, what he had left of it, was off in another world. A hatch could fly open once, not twice, but now three times! The engines were beginning to overheat, and the stress on these over-flown planes in this heat could cause another more serious problem. I had had it, captain or not, this guy was finished in my book.

Hump arguing with himself, banging the instruments swung the plane off the runway, and proceeded down the taxiway. I keyed the mike and called the tower advising them we were OK, another hatch problem.

"Spud one-two, tower advises you have mechanical attention before attempting another takeoff," crackled the radio. Thank God, the captain couldn't argue with this one. Looking over at Hump, I wasn't sure he had heard any of this conversation. He was still mumbling to himself, occasionally hitting the instrument panel with his fists. As I was about to say something to him, a red glare in the bubbled open hatch window caught my eye. Sticking my head out the hatch, my heart stopped for an instant. Flames were licking up the right landing gear. Hump's heavy foot on the brakes overheated and locked a brake that started the tire on fire.

Keying the mike, I yelled, "Hump, stop the plane, we got a wheel on fire!"

Hump looked over at me, still mumbling to himself, staring as if I hadn't said anything. As he gazed, he increased the throttles, picking up speed down the taxiway.

"Tower, Spud One Two has an emergency . . . fire in the landing gear," I rattled off trying to make sense out of everything happening so fast.

"Hump!" I screamed. "Stop the goddamn plane . . . if you take it in the revetments . . . you'll blow every other damn plane up with us."

I wasn't sure if the flames would put themselves out, or if it would set fire to the hydraulic fluid in the landing gear, moving up to the wings and fuel tanks? This bit of science wasn't covered in school, but I was sure I didn't want to find out.

Hump continued to give the plane more power, racing to get back to the flight line.

I looked out the hatch; the racing props were now fanning the fire, working its way up the gear.

"Spud One Two, tower advises you to shut down immediately, emergency vehicles en route," the radio blared.

Hump only continued to get back to the flight line, oblivious to anything that was going on around him, including the tower's instructions. As I looked out the cockpit, I saw standing between us and the flight line, an Air Force C-130 cargo plane with one engine running, waiting for taxi instructions and a parked Navy A6 fighter that was forced to land at Phu Bai when it ran low on fuel yesterday.

"Goddamn it," I screamed, "stop this fucking plane." Suddenly the engines died and the plane came to a quick halt. I released the straps holding me in my seat and turned to unlatch the small fire extinguisher behind me.

As Hump was now screaming over the radio at someone or everyone, I was debating if and how to jump out of the plane. Then I noticed a number of figures running out to us from off the flight line. The airport fire trucks with sirens wailing pulled up and a number of Vietnamese firefighters appeared, turning several larger extinguishers on the flames lapping up the strut.

The fire was out quickly and I found myself staring at these four-foot plus Vietnamese who fought this fire in their oversized American fire fighting gear. It seemed bizarre, as if they had their dad's clothes on, playing "fireman".

As Hump argued out of range with a group of officers gathered, Daze walked up to his plane in disbelief. Staring at the charred strut, he could only shake his head and mutter to himself. Soon, a maintenance truck with a couple of crew chiefs pulled up with a new tire to put on the plane so they could tow it back.

I pulled myself back up to the hatch window to grab my maps and gear. A small group of spectators milled around the plane as I turned and headed back to the flight line with Jim and Chavez. As they had just happened upon the excitement, both could only shake their heads in disbelief when hearing how it started.

"Hey Curry . . . Chavez . . . hold up there," came a voice from some distance behind us.

As I turned, I saw the Operations Officer running up. Red ran the flight operations with a tight fist. He was probably the first one out here after listening to the radio talk between the tower and us. Red was about forty years old, fiery red hair, and word was an ex-Methodist pastor. He was a fierce character most folks chose not to argue with. I always cringed when he wanted something, as he was very uncompromising. Chavez and I slowed down, wondering what in the hell was on his mind now.

Catching up with us, a much-winded Red said, "Curry, we got the standby plane up to cover for you and Davies' spot, but I got to reschedule you two for a mission later today." I couldn't believe what I was hearing. Staring at Red in disbelief and anger, the words rolled out of my mouth, "What . . . you're saying I have to fly with that ASS again?"

"Curry, you're talking about an Army captain here, and yes, I need to reassign you for later today. We don't have the luxury of extra crews," boomed Red, the color of his face now approaching the color of his hair.

"Captain," my voice tensing and getting louder. "That asshole is not fit to fly, you and I both know that. And today he almost killed us. I'm not giving him another chance." I lowered my voice, noticing I was beginning to attract attention. "I will never fly with that man again. You do what you have to, but I won't go up with him."

There was a moment of silence as Red, Chavez, Jim, and even I were shocked by my outburst. I had attacked the sacred institution of captains. The silence was quickly broken by Red, now outraged, flinging his arms about wildly as he spoke, "Curry, you are talking about a United States captain here . . . ", he began, "do I have to remind you . . . " then there was silence as he searched for the right words.

I didn't care anymore as I cut him off, "Captain . . . I do not fly with that man . . . period. My odds of surviving are better with the enemy."

I walked away from him as he fumed. He quickly turned to see if anyone else was watching, and where Hump had gone. Jim and I walked back to the hootch. I threw open the fridge, grabbed two beers and threw one to Jim. I flipped the stereo on to listen to some more Spirit. We listened to music all afternoon, nursing our beer, talking about home, and of course, Jim's wife and baby.

I never flew that day.

And I never flew with Hump again.

The invasion of Laos was now sapping up every resource in country. And it seems we really pissed off the natives as we were getting rocketed every night. I was wondering if it was just easier to sleep in the bunker, but ever since the collapse I only wanted to be under tons of sand again only if my life seriously depended on it. The rumor mill was rampant; sappers attempting to get inside the wire were testing the perimeter almost every night. We could see the flares going off by the wire from dusk till dawn; hear the bursts from the M-60's firing off.

Several firebases off west in the hills were fighting off NVA charges to dislodge them. With the troop strength declining it was easy to see that the bad guys were becoming increasingly bold.

The Mohawks were flying overtime on an always-stretched parts situation. If not shot up, the heat and humidity were taking its toll. Some planes became cannibalized for parts in order to keep the others flying.

The constant rain had quit today as I readied the Mohawk for another flight into North Vietnam. Film loaded, fluid levels checked as I threw a towel over the Slar screen in the cockpit to protect the film was being exposed in the hash mid day sun. Franks finally came out of flight ops, did his pre-check and we were soon airborne flying over Quang Tri. Just below the DMZ I fired up the Slar systems to get them on line before we passed into North Vietnam. The imagery began rolling and we were in business mapping all the truck traffic moving down from the north. Several minutes into the flight a large power surge went through the plane and our headphones as the Slar system briefly stopped and then restarted. Beside the electronics, all the gauges went to zero before fluttering back to their operating position.

The missions up here were critical, Saigon wanted a twenty-four hour monitoring of all the traffic moving down the highways of North Vietnam heading to the south and west. As we continued north, the power surges continued momentarily bringing everything to a halt, but quickly restarting. Something was shutting down the electrical supply but quickly bringing it back online. We radioed Phu Bai to advise but were told to maintain the mission, they only wanted to send a replacement aircraft if absolutely necessary. So for the next four hours we flew the skies of North Vietnam with the large power surges increasing, clearly amplified through our headsets. It was a war of nerves and we weren't sure if the power supply finally died what impact it would have on keeping us flying. With the luck of someone above we finally landed back in Phu Bai right before sunset. Franks wrote up the power problem in the logbook as I removed the film and delivered it to the intel boys. We both thought the plane should be grounded. But recommendations of nineteen year olds didn't rate high here.

From there it was over to see how Sally was doing, as she seemed sick ever since I got here back from the rabies quarantine at the vets. By the time I got to the hootch, I found Jim had taken Sally back into the vets as a number of the dogs had gotten distemper while in quarantine. The bad news continued, now they were keeping her for the second time in two weeks. I was able to grab some mystery bologna and several ten-pound rolls from the mess hall before they closed and wandered over by the outdoor movie. A black and white western lulled me for the next hour before I had to head over to the Slar shack. Tonight I was sitting backup for the nightly missions up over North Vietnam. I prepped a plane so we could quickly get airborne if one of the planes in-flight developed problems and had to return. I was hoping I'd be able to doze off in the reclining desk chair for a good part of the evening. That would limit my exposure to injury to a bad back, or a possible collision with the wall should the chair wheels kick out from underneath me.

Somewhere in the darkness of the early morning I was awoken with a commotion as one of the guys in flight ops called saying there was a problem with flight twenty. I walked into flight ops attempting to wake up to some level of coherency when I quickly realized they were in real trouble. Shereck and Tim were flying the plane Franks and I had asked to redline on our return earlier that evening. But in the strain for flyable aircraft they went up in the plane that had scared the shit out of us for four hours this afternoon. Now they were returning from their mission hunting trucks over the Ho Chi Minh Trail when the power surges began rapidly increasing, the power going out for longer periods of time before coming back on.

Then the word came they lost both engines just west of Phu Bai. They were attempting to coast and restart the engines. Shit, both engines at the same time, that was impossible but it was happening. Not a mechanic by any means I thought of bad fuel, no fuel, no pumps; whatever, it didn't matter, as things were getting desperate.

Soon the word came they both ejected near or over the runway. People still awake were now flooding the ops desk as runners were waking up anyone they could in a panic to do something, anything. The order of the night was confusion, massive confusion. Several groups of us ran to grab any vehicles that would drive and headed out to search for what we weren't sure, chutes in the sky, guys walking in the distance?

Word came that they found Tim, he was down although injured, his arm and shoulder appeared broken or mangled. They were rushing him to the MASH unit to get medical attention. More confusion followed by quiet, then word had come the Mohawk had crashed not far from the base near a village. Then more of nothing, without radios we had no word on where Shereck was.

Finally we got word or a rumor that he had come down into a fence on the base next to our communications hootch. We raced out to find a number of people huddling around something we couldn't make out. As we ran closer we saw a large bundle, it took several seconds to realize this was Shereck, and several more to realize his parachute had never deployed. He had ejected out of his stricken Mohawk, fell thousands of feet and the fucking chute never opened. And now he lay silent as his buddies removed him from the fence. A number of us followed swiftly to the MASH unit hoping against all odds they knew of a miracle that could revive him from the fall of thousands of feet, that all the kings horses and all the kings men could put him together, to bring him back to life once again.

And this was the same plane we had all the power surge problems on the previous mission over North Vietnam hours earlier. They didn't want to bring us back then, even though we were hanging our asses directly over North Vietnam? Then didn't we bitch enough to keep it grounded, to make them switch planes and this never would have happened? I wasn't sure what I was feeling, fear from almost biting it up north, or guilt for not bitching enough? But who would have listened, there were too many questions, none of this made sense. One thing for sure, we were killing ourselves faster then the enemy.

Somehow we wanted to know that death didn't take a guy as spirited and full of live as Jim. We all lost him that dark morning, and in that we all lost a piece of ourselves. We became a little more hardened everyday, because it was too fucking hard to care that much, especially when those back home saw guys like Jim, like us, as the villains.

Fire Over the Trail
Chapter Seven

Having my fill of coffee, waiting for Lange, I glanced up at the clock. Ten minutes to midnight and takeoff, where in the hell was he? I finally realized I'd have to make the trip to his hootch in an attempt to find him. The night air was exceptionally cool as I ran down the sidewalks and dirt road to Lange's hootch. I banged on the door, waited . . . nothing. I couldn't understand where in the hell he could be. Lange was a terrific pilot, a God given talent to play tricks on anyone, but a true blue soldier died-in-the-wool. It was hard to imagine him missing a mission unless he was dead . . . and even that could be open to debate.

With no other options popping in my mind, I proceeded to beat the living daylights out of his door. In the midst of my fit I thought I heard something from inside, so I stopped. Yeah, there it was again, growing to a faint voice that slowly approached the door. It took a couple more minutes and the door finally cracked open. Hunched over, one eye open and standing in his jockey shorts, Lange stuttered, "Curry, wha . . . what in the hell do you want?"

"Mission, we got to fly the Laos mission. I've been waiting for you. We already missed our takeoff time," I replied.

The adrenalin shot through Lange's body so quickly that his head jerked to attention, both eyes now fully open. Loudly the words came out, "Shit, I forgot I had to fly tonight . . . you hurry, I'll be right there."

His arms and legs were now moving frantically as one side of his body raced for his flight suit and the other side slammed the door shut in my face.

I stood there for a moment in the darkness as I heard him bouncing around inside, knocking things over.

Me . . . hurry . . . for what, I'm ready to go, I said to myself as I slowly walked back to the flight line. By the time I sauntered up to the plane I could hear Lange's feet banging against the steel grated flooring on the flight line. The son-of-a-bitch literally leaped into the cockpit. As I climbed up into my seat, he glared over at me, as if I was holding him up. I felt restrained, as I was the only one who flew this mission every night. I knew the countryside, he didn't.

The cockpit hummed as we fired up the engines in record time and taxied out for takeoff. We streaked across the darkened countryside as we headed west for Laos. Lange settled down enough to take the chip off his shoulder he had placed there earlier. We had time to chat before the time came to fire up the SLAR system and begin hunting.

Flying in the darkness, we had to rely solely upon our compass and instrument readings. Until I threw the radar on, it was impossible to make out anything below us in the never-ending black jungles.

With the instruments warning us of our point into Laos, I fired up the SLAR radar systems that would soon display a fifty-mile width of the jungle below us.

 Lange made our final turns, positioning us on our first leg. I laid out the maps and called up Moonbeam, our Air Force flying command ship we checked in and out with. Moonbeam acknowledged us as our first SLAR mapping appeared on the screen in front of me.

As we made our way west, the mapping displayed terrain that I had not seen before. Not sure to panic, I continued our small talk waiting for a river or landmark to appear on the film so I could plot our position.

We flew for another ten minutes with the SLAR film showing nothing but unfamiliar jungle canopy below us. I had a sinking feeling we were way off course.

"Lange, do you have any idea where we are?" I asked.

First giving me a puzzled glance, he looked at his instruments and slowly read off our position and heading. Plotting them carefully on the map it showed us fifteen minutes into our first leg, a little north but not seriously off.

"Well, what you give me says we are here," as I pointed to our supposed position on the map to Lange, "but I have never seen this terrain before."

Lange shrugged his shoulder not sure what to suggest.

"Why don't you turn ninety degrees and head north? Maybe I can pick up a river or landmark to plot our position from," I suggested.

The radar film in front of me rolled up slowly from the bottom of a backlit screen about the size of an eight by eleven sheet of paper. A tray of developing fluid inside the display painted the terrain we were flying over like a topographic map. You could see the river bends, mountains growing to their peaks and, after experience; you could sense where the roadways were running. I was hoping to catch a piece of river on my film tonight. Each river had its own unique bends and twists, a reference point easily found on a map.

Lange banked the plane heading north, occasionally banging the compass with his fist hoping the needle would move to the correct position . . . whatever that was.

Another ten minutes north and I was convinced we were lost. And lost somewhere in no man's land over Laos was not very comforting.

"Lange, I'm getting nothing familiar here, I still have no idea where in the hell we are. But I know we are not where the instruments show us.'"

He stared at me as if I were crazy. Suddenly he stiffened and began firing questions. The words bouncing through the cockpit reached me faster then the same words booming through the intercom. "Shit, is this Spud thirteen . . . did you check the log book?"

I said to myself, "Yes its Spud thirteen, and shit no, I didn't look at the maintenance log."

Before I finished, Lange had reached over the throttles grabbing the logbook from beside my left leg. Opening the book he read aloud the last entry, ending it with, "Shit, this plane was red lined. None of the instruments are giving correct readings!"

It now made sense. We were flying in a plane that had been red lined, meaning it was not allowed to fly because of serious mechanical or instrument problems. Somehow no one had informed flight operations before they assigned the plane for our mission. But the responsibility was Lange's and mine. Before taking off, the final check was the pilots. He was to read the logbook and make sure there were no entries of unresolved repair problems. In our rush, we both assumed each other had done it, and now we were in trouble.

Now we were flying somewhere over no man's land, somewhere west over Laos or Cambodia. It was useless to continue, even if we picked up something on the imagery to plot our position from, the gauges were probably not reading the engine and fuel properly.

Lange radioed the Air Force sector control C-130 that we had mechanical difficulties and was returning to base.

"Roger, Spud One Three, are you in need of assistance?"

"Negative Moonbeam, not at this time, thank-you."

With that, Lange turned the plane on its side to head us back east, or as close to east as he could remember. After a while we could make out the twinkling lights of the coastal cities of South Vietnam below a haze of clouds moving in from the ocean. I could make out Da Nang, and further to the north the cities of Hue and Quang Tri. It was easy to see what a target the cities made for the NVA with rockets or mortars in the hills. That evening it was hard to imagine a war was on. The radios over Laos had gone quiet. The trucks on the trails were not moving; the anti-aircraft fire was non-existent. This was the evening of the South Vietnamese invasion into Laos . . . maybe it would work after all.

I changed the radio frequency and raised the air traffic controller positioned off the coast on a Navy ship, requesting clearance back into channel six niner, Phu Bai.

"Acknowledge, Spud One Three, turn zero two seven degrees. You are currently six-five miles southwest of Phu Bai. Weather at Phu Bai is seventy five degrees . . . visibility falling . . . currently one mile."

We acknowledged the instructions and began our turn. I shut down the SLAR system to save on the life of the rollers that spread the developing chemicals across the film. The slightest bend and they were no good, and they were extremely hard to come by. There were not many Mohawks around and we were a pain in the ass to every supply sergeant in the Army. Needless to say, we were not heaped in spare parts; having had to cannibalize the worst planes to keep the others running.

As we flew north, the haze we had seen creeping in from the ocean quickly grew to massive cloud cover, stretching across the countryside several thousand feet below us.

"Spud One Three, turn zero-zero-nine degrees . . . descend to seven thousand feet. You are on a thirty mile final approach to channel sixty nine," crackled the radio. The Navy air controller was giving us our final instructions before turning us over to the controllers at Phu Bai.

Lange was busy writing into the logbook. As we were flying on automatic pilot, I turned the dial on the heading compass to zero-zero-nine degrees. The plane banked and turned us to the corrected heading. We were to drop into the clouds and land under instruments, while I waited for Lange to finish up his notes.

"Spud One Three, descend to seven thousand feet and bring your heading to zero-zero- nine . . . acknowledge," blared the radio.

Lange now looked up, and then stared at the compass. It read zero-zero-nine degrees.

"Son-of-a-bitch." He keyed the mike, "Navy, we are having instrument problems. Request number of degrees left or right of current course as our compass is not giving us correct heading."

"Roger, Spud, turn two-two degrees starboard to zero-zero-nine. Descend to seven thousand feet; I will be turning you over to channel six-niner shortly.

"Acknowledge . . . Navy . . . turning now."

We both read off the degrees point by point till we had counted twenty-two. This was going to get real interesting landing solely with instruments that were giving us incorrect readings. I expected Lange to cut back throttles and nose us down, to begin our descent to seven thousand feet. Instead he picked up the logbook and quickly finished off his entries.

Finally slipping the book back into its slot, he nosed us over and cut back on the throttles as we rapidly began our descent. The cloud cover stretched as far as we could see; turning into a huge billowy cotton blanket we were about to poke a hole into as we headed toward the ground.

Just before we were about to nudge below the clouds, Lange gasped. I had been busy rolling up the radar film when I looked ahead to see us swiftly approaching the clouds with a . . . a . . . dark treetop barely sticking up through the clouds.

"Fuck . . ."

I heard the roar of the engines, the props straining as Lange pushed the throttles to the wall. He pulled back on the stick with both hands as I prayed. We momentarily sank below the cloud cover . . . the inertia of our descent still propelling us downward. My heart sank as I realized the asshole controller hadn't realized a seven thousand foot mountain was hiding beneath the clouds in our path. Seconds seemed eternities as the plane groaned, straining to get lift, to climb. We broke out of the clouds when suddenly the plane shuttered as something big struck our belly, then rubbing itself along the fuselage, as we broke free, climbing back above the cloud cover.

Floating higher above the clouds, we vainly looked for any damage. Wings, props, engines . . . all seemed to be fine. The gauges never moved a tab. We must have brushed the top of some trees on the mountaintop. For whatever reason, Lange decided to write his last lines in the logbook . . . it was a stroke of luck. If we would have descended when the controller instructed us to, we would have went into the clouds miles in front of the lonely black stick of a tree top which Lange saw, and ended up plastered on the side of a mountain.

Lange radioed the controller screaming a string of obscenities that must have floated out over all of Southeast Asia that evening, bringing a gasp to even the most ruthless tyrant. The controller's response was deafening silence. For a moment I thought we must have lost our radio. Lange sat there, expended from his verbal assault.

The crackle on the radio was finally broken, "Spud One Three . . . we apologize for any possible misunderstanding . . ."

Lange cut him off, "Misunderstanding . . . you asshole . . . you about killed us."

"Negative, Spud One Three, we show you twenty clicks east of any mountain range with that height."

Lange was incessant now; the controller was trying to worm out of his error. "Do you want me to walk outside right now and pull the tree needles from the goddamn wings to show you? Where in the hell do you buy your goddamn maps from . . . the fucking North Vietnamese?"

It took another ten minutes before everyone got calmed down enough to attempt to get us back on the ground in one piece. I kept kicking myself for not having looked at the logbook before we took off.

"Spud One Three, we are going to give you corrected headings into Phu Bai . . . stand by."

"Negative Navy, we are not going into Phu Bai. With this weather and the condition of our instruments, we are going into Da Nang. I feel a lot safer with their equipment. Request vector to Da Nang."

"Roger, Spud One Three . . . I'm not sure we have you on radar, please squawk emergency."

"Shit, this is getting ridiculous," I muttered to Lange as I reached up to switch on our transponder to emergency squawk. The Navy's radar shows blips on their screens of all aircraft in their control sector. With the confusion over our position everyone was getting gun shy. Squawking meant we would transmit an amplified signal that would "squawk" or flash on their screen four to five times larger than any other blip or plane showing, giving them the plane ID, altitude, and heading.

"Spud One Three, we think we have you. Head one two zero, or one hundred and thirteen degrees starboard from your current heading."

"This is fucking great," uttered Lange as we banked, counting the degrees till we were heading east, southeast. They were taking us out to sea, around the mountains to the north of Da Nang. The bad weather was growing worse. We had been flying in the storm clouds for sometime now, our asses slamming from the increasing turbulence against the hardened ejection seat. Fuel was beginning to be a concern. If the gauges were working, we'd have enough for one approach into Da Nang.

"Spud One Three, turn heading to two six five degrees and begin descent to three thousand feet."

Bouncing through the turbulence, we made our turn and dropped to three thousand feet. We were now on final approach into Da Nang, having been turned over to IFR control. As we shuddered downward through the rain and buffeting winds, the wing lights cast a glow that flickered against the ceaseless clouds that rushed past the cockpit.

The Da Nang controller read off second by second instructions and course corrections as we sped ahead, intent on meeting a runway somewhere out there, unseen in front of us. "Spud One Three . . . dropping below glide path . . . turn three degrees right."

"On glide slope, turn zero two degrees right."

The radio was never ending with pieces of minute course corrections. I had a shiver run through me for an instant. I feared the mountain that sat next to the Da Nang airfield would suddenly appear for a brief second through the clouds. Then it would all be over as we smashed over the hillside at two hundred knots an hour. God, somehow it all seemed useless . . . but then why should it be different for me. Everyone here felt they were to live on, kept alive for a higher purpose; but they died everyday . . . boys and men with loved-ones back home. It was tough becoming a realist at nineteen.

"Spud, you're over the lights," came over the radio, snapping me out of my trance. We both sat up, straining against the harnesses holding us firm to our ejection seats, to see the bank of bright lights that announced the start of the runway we so needed to meet. Skimming a couple hundred feet off the ground, we could still see nothing . . . nothing but more clouds and fog. For a moment I felt as I did earlier. This controller had someone else on his radar, that we were skimming a hundred feet off the ground miles away.

Then I thought I saw something . . . a warm glow out of the clouds. No, it was yellow . . . yes, there they were, two rows of the brightest goddamn lights breaking through the clouds. We both screamed out as we streaked past the lights dropping onto the darkened runway draped in fog . . . pelted in rain.

We floated down onto the runway at a hundred knots, first one wheel touching with a jolt, bouncing up for a moment, then both sitting down. We rolled down through the fog, never seeing more then forty or fifty feet in front of us as the fog kept the rest of the world hidden.

"Spud One-three, welcome to Da Nang. Use the first taxiway, then proceed to guest parking."

"We got it," Lange screamed out, as we both unclenched our fists and sat back in our seats. We turned off on the taxiway, heading into the darkness to find our spot to shut down, and get out to kiss the ground.

Suddenly the ground shuddered as several explosions blew up on the taxiways and revetments off in the distance to our right.

"Shit . . . mortars!" I screamed, as Lange pushed the throttles forward attempting to race the incoming rockets or mortars to the parking area. The explosions continued around the base as they often did, seeking to find a target not so much by dead aim as blind luck. Lange was taxing so fast the bumps on the runway sometimes lifted the plane briefly in the air as our speed increased. Suddenly out of the fog came the parking area, at a ninety-degree angle to us. Lange slapped back the throttles, steering and hitting the brakes, somehow hitting the right brake harder, attempting to make the turn or we'd run off the taxiway and eat the fast approaching ditch.

Miraculously he made the turn without flipping the plane. We careened into the parking area as Lange shut the engines down. As the turbines wound down, their high-pitched squeal blocked our ability to hear anything. After several hours in the air our hearing took several minutes to return to normal. With the rushing air, radio traffic, and the whine of the turbines, one was reduced to yelling for a bit once it all stopped in order to hear or be heard. We quickly dismounted the plane pulling off our helmets and rubbed our ears in an attempt to hear again. As the props came to a stop, we realized the shelling was off in the distance now as the Vietcong continued to walk their mortars around the airfield hoping to get many of the parked aircraft that normally would have been flying missions in better weather. They had a lot of expensive targets tonight to choose from. As we couldn't see where the mortars were coming from, the good news was they couldn't see what they were shooting at. They could only fire into the rain and fog, hoping to hit their targets hidden by the weather.

We laid on the side of a small earthen mound to wait out the action, and then finally the quiet came. It had come earlier, but my hearing was still screwed up. Unsure at first, I scanned the portion of the field not hidden by the fog, the corner of my eye caught Lange twenty feet to my left doing the same thing.

Trucks and sirens began to appear from out of the fog, appearing briefly into our vision, then quickly disappearing into the close fog and rain to another part of this base we couldn't make out. We had a bizarre seat here for an unfolding show of fire crews and ambulances racing along the taxiways. Smoke now mixing with the fog and rain hid the field from us in pieces, floating off to our right. We could catch pieces of voices, yelling out commands in the distance. Shadows danced in the distance from flames and the headlights of the ever-racing trucks. I strained to find our Mohawk . . . somewhere I think to our right. Slowly a large cloud of steam and smoke drifted away revealing our plane still standing there in one piece.

Lange and I walked over to see what damage, if any, we would find. Several ambulances cruised the flight line looking for human wreckage. Lange started swearing as we walked up to the right wheel strut. The tire was pretty low, from what we weren't sure, a piece of shrapnel or old age, one's never sure here. We looked over the rest of the plane for any other signs of damage. We were lucky; apparently she hadn't suffered any other damage from the evening events. Lange approached me from the tail with something indistinguishable in his hands. As he got closer, I made out a tree branch in his hands.

Lange yelled, "Look what got caught in our tail. Fucking Navy SOB, I'm going to take this to him personally and show him where this goddamn invisible mountain is. Then I'm going to show him how this would feel, shoved up his tail at three hundred knots."

"Now Captain, let's show some restraint . . . we were only doing two hundred twenty knots."

The night's tension finally broke with laughter. We had two attempts on our lives by our forces, and one by the enemy, something was out of balance here.

Lange threw his helmet up in the cockpit, turning to me, "It's five a.m., let's go find some chow. I hear these Air Force bases do pretty good."

"Yeah, after almost eating that hill, I've had a craving for something less substantial. If it's any good, we might consider lunch. After all it will take Phu Bai a half a day to fly us in a tire."

We headed out for the row of buildings off the flight line in search of a mess hall. It wasn't hard to find at five thirty in the morning. We just wandered in the rain till we caught a live body . . . at this hour they were all heading to the mess hall.

Appearing from the darkness behind the screen door, into the harsh light of the mess hall, we were a sight for sore eyes. All the conversations and clanging of dishes came to a halt. This man's Air Force impressed me yet again as the prim and properly uniformed Air Force officers stared at two rain soaked and muddied army flyers.

Lange broke the silence with, "Sorry about the mud boys, but we ran into your local VC redoing some of your landscaping with a few mortars." The silence was broken with a few chuckles as everyone returned to their conversations and breakfast. Lange was right; this was the best food I had in a long time. Finishing breakfast, we returned to the flight to beg some Air Force mechanics into pumping up our low tire and sparing us some precious fuel. While awaiting these necessary items, Lange and I were able to catch up on a little sleep alongside the plane before the mid morning sun made that unbearable. We debated over flying again with the gauges inoperable, but with clear skies and full fuel tanks felt the risk was manageable.

By noon we were airborne again. The sun was bright, with not a bit of the previous night's fog or rain. The previous evening's excitement now felt like a distant nightmare. Before long the rice paddies and endless sand brought us back to Phu Bai. We touched down amid a flight of A-Models heading out on their afternoon photo recon missions.

More flights over Laos every night blended together in a macabre routine where the goal became surviving another day, as tomorrow would take care of itself. If you thought too much of where you were, or why; there was never an answer that made sense.

The firefights over and in Laos continued to take its tool. Returning one evening from over the trail, one of the crew chiefs approaching my open hatch after directing us to our shut down spot and said, "Looks like you guys weren't the only ones with excitement," shouting over the engines winding down.

"What in the hell happened?" I asked.

"Hower and Ralph were flying lead on a photo mission out west in Laos. They apparently flew right over the top of a 37mm anti-aircraft gun when it opened fire. I'm still not sure how in the hell they ever flew the plane back. That stabilizers just hung on by the control cable."

Somehow the crew had pulled it together and flew the crippled mess back into Da Nang. Quite a feat, as the Mohawk has a large distinctive tail, one consisting of three stabilizers that gave it excellent maneuverability, given it wasn't dragging and hanging off the plane. Jim said we had the best looking "ass" in Vietnam.

That bird would most likely become a good candidate for the scrap heap. Because of our shortage of parts, and the Army's inability to get us any, the crew chiefs would probably cannibalize her for parts.

Lamson 719, the South Vietnamese invasion of Laos was now well underway. The US was losing helicopters by the hour ferrying in and out the South Vietnamese troops and supplies. And with round the clock Mohawk flights, the NVA was taking its toll on our aircraft. The NVA could not afford to lose Laos, and it was putting up a tremendous fight.

Our nightly Slar missions took us dead over Tchepone several times, in different legs of our missions. Our path there would roughly follow the path the South Vietnamese would be taking. It was going to be interesting to see what happened tonight.

I headed back to the hootch for a catnap, as the evening would be another long one. I awoke after the chow line had ended, and headed over to see if they were showing some bad movies outdoors by the volleyball courts. That would be the sand lot without nets or balls.

The nightly outdoor movie had just broken up when several explosions went off near the flight line. Several voices screaming "mortars" rang out in the momentary silence that followed. Everyone ran for the nearest bunker they could find. Turk and the boys were already inside as I ran through the entrance. The mortars continued sporadically, several seemingly close.

"Did you guys get the word on Chavez? Turk asked during one of the many lulls.

Jim piped up, "Yeah, not bad hey, I though he was up to something."

"What in the hell are you talking about?"

"Chavez grabbed his wife and kid after he got home on leave and went to Canada, he's gone man."

Several cheers went up for our buddy who never should have been here. Not that we were excited about being here, but Chavez was a citizen of

Peru. Many a night after this we would give a toast to his success and a hope that his family is ok.

Outside we could hear voices now, and some scurrying in the direction of my hootch. Deciding that the VC has used up their Phu Bai allocation of mortars we ventured into the night. Coming out of the entranceway we could see flames leaping in the sky by my hootch. The race was on to see if my fears were true. Shortly we joined the crowd to see the hootch across from Jim and mine now half engulfed in flames.

"Mortar hit it, the Vietnamese fire fighters are on their way," came an explanation out of the crowd.

The flames were racing through the hootch; several of the guys living there had quit running in to save anything else. It didn't appear anyone had gotten injured. Screeching up to the hootch were two trucks of Vietnamese firemen now racing out, getting hoses hooked to a water tanker and aiming them on the hootch. But the flames were licking the sky, fed by the dry plywood construction. These Vietnamese, only around four feet something, were drowning in fire gear designed for much taller Americans. The fire was now taking on a festive air as soldiers stood around, drinking their beers and watching the proceedings. As the fire now aimed to engulf the remaining quarter of the hootch, shells from someone's gun left inside started cooking off. The Vietnamese firemen starting ducking, some were running behind the truck. Quiet would soon come and they'd venture out to pick up their hoses and attempt again to put out the fire. Then another single shell would go off and they were scurrying for cover. The cycle continued as the soldier spectators rolled in laughter. It was scene out of a Three Stooge's movie; the oversized fire gear gave them the appearance of a bunch of kids tripping over themselves as the hootch turned to ashes.

What had become a social event now died as the fire turned to glowing ashes. The firemen continued to pour water on the smoldering mess as the crowd broke up and went their ways. It was time for me to get my flight suit on and get down to the Ops building for my hunting mission over the Trail.

The nightly Mission Twenty over the Ho Chi Minh Trail took on a festive air, as the skies were full of navigation lights of a wide variety of aircraft working targets on the ground in a war that didn't exist. We finally had enough gunships for every target we detected. A good portion of our time was staying clear of the other aircraft all with different speeds and changing altitude. Then when anti-aircraft fire itched its way into the black sky from beneath us, we turned off our navigation lights to avoid giving the NVA a target, then praying to god we didn't run into another darkened aviator. There was room for few mistakes out here over no man's land.

My next day was to be a relaxing one, time to go down to the PX and hunt for any type of canned food available. I had traded Ralph the chance of a lifetime, hunting trucks over Laos while I relished a quieter evening over North Vietnam. Jim and I grabbed a jeep and decided to hit the PX on the base of the 101st Screaming Eagles. It seemed to take forever; we'd no sooner come over the top of one dusty hill than the dirt road stretched out in front of us to the next. We passed small clumps of buildings, almost like lonely outposts in the old west.

"There's the hootch Moose has targeted to steal some air conditioners from," Jim mentioned as we sped by.

"Nah Jim, not steal, it's midnight requisition," I corrected him.

Finally we reached the large metal building that housed the PX. Most of the 101st must had been put in the boonies, as we filled the jeep with canned potato chips, spaghetti, beans, and yes, Spam. It felt like Christmas, but what made the day was my purchase of an Asaihi Pentex 35mm camera I had been hunting for. Now I could get some good photos to send back home.

Jim and I quickly buzzed back to base; I spent the late afternoon heating some of my new purchased spaghetti. The smell of burning Sterno waffled though the hootch as I played with my new camera. Before long, the sun settled and I sauntered down to Turks hootch to catch up on the days happening. A group of a dozen or so were drinking beer or smoking pot, as they had finished for the day. The SLAR flights over North Vietnam had been quiet today; the recon flights out west near the Laotian border had uncovered an NVA division moving toward Khe Sanh. I wasn't taking off till late, so I had time to catch the outdoor movie by the mess hall; tonight's feature was a cheap horror flick. I guess we needed something scary to keep our minds sane.

Standing in the Flight Ops building waiting for Captain Fletcher, I was listening to the small radio traffic with one of our Infrared birds heading back. Lt. Arzua was a UCLA graduate whose parents had emigrated from Japan in the nineteen thirties. He was always taking shit for his strong Asian looks, and tonight was no different.

Baker holding his nose spoke into the mike, "Spud one three what's the weather up there."

A moment passed and a puzzled Arzua came back, "hot and humid, does it ever change."

Baker, again trying to disguise his voice, "Well, we heard there's a little 'Nip' in the air tonight."

As Baker and several others just about fell over laughing at the cheap shot, Arzua immediately came back, "Baker, I'm going to kick your ass when I get back..."

Just then Fletcher came in, "Curry, ready for our flight."

"Ready as ever," as I grabbed my maps and books and headed for the flight line with Fletcher. I had already pre-checked the systems so we were ready to hop in, fire up the engines, and head north. I had never flown with Fletcher before. He was a large man, somewhere in his forties, kind of John Wayne'ish' looking. We chatted very easily as we floated north heading across the border. Our mission would take us just off the coast of North Vietnam from the DMZ up to Dong Hoa. We would monitor the amount of traffic along North Vietnam's highways heading toward South Vietnam. Gunships or fighters would not be called in here after we detected traffic. There was another halt put on bombing in the North, another Washington hope that it would prod the NVA at the peace table. Our movers would be counted, their positions noted and fed to the computers at MACV, the US military headquarters in the south. Then it was massaged with volumes of other information. It was rumored to be useful in plotting the arrival of the much anticipated "light at the end of the tunnel."

Just south of the DMZ I fired up the radar systems and we started mapping. The night was clear as a bell with a partial moon. The lights of the coastal cities twinkled as we now passed into the north. The cool fresh breeze felt good up here.

"Bob, I'm going to keep her at eight thousand feet tonight," Fletcher informed me over the intercom.

"Fine with me," I replied while studying the film coming up. Every mission up here was flown at ten thousand feet, that way the guys in Military intelligence who read our film didn't have to change the scale when they plotted the detected traffic. Three complete round trips between the DMZ and Dong Hoa would give us six complete sets of film for the boys down south. We now settled in for our flight, which would last about four hours on station. The hard seat necessary for use as an injection seat started to numb my ass already.

"Spud two-two, this is Pamper, we have an unidentified aircraft ten miles west of your position. It appears to be following off your seven o'clock position," crackled the radio.

Both looking at each other, I broke the silence, "probably some NVA chopper heading north. I hear they got some large Russian choppers that can keep up with us."

Fletcher nodded and keyed the mike, "Roger Pamper, we copy. Appreciate if you keep an eye on it for us."

We both peered left through Fletchers hatch, trying to see something in the darkness. Whatever it was, it was not flying with navigation lights. After several minutes of peering into the night I grabbed my Thermos and poured both of us a cup of strong black coffee. The aroma filling the cockpit was heavenly; the little jolt of caffeine was perfect for the cool evening air up here. We continued our flight north casually chatting in the warm red glow of our instruments. At Dong Hoi we made our course direction northeast to follow the eastward protrusion of the coast. In the clear night air we could make out lights from about eight to ten Vietnamese ships or fishing junks below off Dong Hoi.

We completed our trip north and returned to the same correction point at Dong Hoi. Now below the bay had lights of some twenty to thirty ships. I remarked to Fletcher about it, but we passed it off without another thought.

"Spud two-two this is Pamper, we still have traffic following you, still ten miles west of your position."

"Roger Pamper, we are turning off our Christmas lights, keep us appraised, thanks," responded Fletcher as he flipped the toggle that killed our navigation lights. The sky around us was now dark except for a partial moon that shed its reflection over the ocean below.

164

Things were beginning to get strange, for some reason we were being followed; yet the aircraft had made no attempt to attack us. The increasing numbers of ships in the bay of Dong Hoi was forgotten, as we were now puzzled by our intruder and what he was up to. The North Vietnamese had rarely interfered with our units flying round the clock flights up here. With the bombing halt, any attack on reconnaissance planes would bring an immense armed response by Navy, Air Force, and Marine fighters who were itching for a lick up north.

On our second trip down the coast, Pamper called and informed us that our intruder had now departed. They showed us as the only aircraft up here in the sky. We both let go with a collective sigh of relief; it appeared as if, we were getting concerned over nothing. At least it made the time go faster. As we approached our turn at Dong Hoi, I decided to count the ships below that had mysteriously grown with each pass.

"Jesus Christ Fletcher, there's got to be fifty...or eighty boats down here, take a look."

Both of us peered below at the sea of lights bobbing in the bay off Dong Hoi. Neither of us had seen anything like it before. This was certainly becoming a strange flight. We had another trip down the coast, then it would be back up to Dong Hoa and down again before we could head home. My butt and legs were numb as I struggled to move about in the constraints of my straps, hoping to return some flow of blood below.

I was wishing I had saved some of that coffee when the world above us exploded in light and shock waves. It happened so fast; our brains were still trying to decipher the events when my eyes fixed on a shaky white object streaking from the ground in front of us, then it seemed to turn and head toward us, seeming to stop for an instant above our heads. At the same time Fletcher had caught another white streaking object appear from my side of the plane along the coast and turn over our heads. Then the world above us exploded again and then again. The sky lit up for several seconds like daylight, two fireballs seemed to rain fire on us from above as we shook in the night sky.

"Jesus shit, SAMS," Fletcher screamed into the intercom.

The fear pulsed though my body with those words, SAM's were the size of telephone poles that streaked through the air faster then we could run. The only hope if there was more SAM's was to out maneuver them, to turn quickly within the radius of their ability to turn, thereby breaking their targeting. And in the night sky you needed to do it without seeing where they were coming from, or if.

Fletcher by now had pushed the throttles to the wall and put the Mohawk in a tight descending left turn out to sea, the altimeter was spinning, we dropped altitude as if we had lost both engines.

"Pamper, Pamper, this is Spud two-two, we've had three SAMS launched at us, we are heading one zero-zero degrees from last position," I yelled into the radio.

As we headed balls out to sea we both prayed that we were out of range, where another SAM wasn't streaking up our ass at this minute.

"Spud two-two, this is Pamper, we copy. Are you in trouble, do you need assistance?"

We both scanned the instruments. Oil pressure, temperature, fuel; no, everything looked OK.

"Pamper, Spud two-two, we appear to be OK. Please advise Phu Bai we are RTB out of here," Fletcher advised our Navy buddy.

"Spud two-two, roger your RTB, will advise Phu Bai. We will report attack to CINPAC. We will reciprocate Dong Hoi for their attempt. Have a better evening guys."

With that the radio went quiet. Fletcher had stopped our decent and turned us back to the south. We were well out of range of the coast at this point. I was thinking that the quiet mission I traded Ralph for, almost bought me the farm.

By the time we had returned to the relative safety of Phu Bai, the Flight Op's officer and several others were waiting for us. Fletcher and I replayed everything that had happened that evening. What we didn't know until the next day was the North Vietnamese had decided to get a Mohawk that night. The intruder Pamper had detected following us was most likely a large North Vietnamese helicopter that was plotting our position and flight path; they already knew we flew all our missions at ten thousand feet. The large numbers of boats in the Harbor of Dong Hoi were there to pick up Fletcher or I if we survived the attack. Three SAM's were launched at our turning point over the harbor at Dong Hoi.

The good new was the SAM's were not radar directed, as they would have known we were at eight thousand feet, and not the ten thousand feet the SAM's blew up at. But I owed my thanks to Fletcher, who unlike everyone else who followed the daily routine, and always flew at ten thousand feet decided to be different. And because of his indifference to the routine, we were both back at Phu Bai, shaken, but safe.

The rain had stopped for a week now, but the flu or influenza still was rampant throughout the company. We had been flying double or triple missions for three weeks now. Even the amounts of drinking and smoking after the missions were affected. Walking from hootch to hootch, one could always find someone sleeping, even in the heat of day.

The trip to the mail shed found good news and bad news, a care package from June, several letters, and the daily listing showing I was volunteered for guard duty tonight. Great, now I had to fly till two am and come back and guard the flight line till six am. Not that anything would happen, but I had always feared that only on my duty would the time come.

Supper came and went as I pigged out on chocolate chip cookies my fiancé had sent in the care package washed down by some coke. Shortly afterward I was on the flight line and off to find trucks over Laos.

Koontz and I returned from our Laos mission about two in the morning feeling like shit, something a couple nights sleep would dent. Tonight we had left the Air Force pounding about twenty trucks near Saravan. Not a bad night as both of us went back to our hootch's to change into fatigues, grab our steel pot, and head over to check out our M-16's and clips of ammo. In the quiet of the morning I started having conversations with myself, scared that I was going to fall asleep in the lonely bunker on the flight line and get my throat slit. Then I remembered my survival vest had a container of speed tablets in it. God forbid one got shot down and was urgently in need of a nap, these tablets would certainly help. I opened up the container, threw a tablet in my top pocket and headed for the headquarters hootch.

There was Koontz, in charge of the last shift of guard duty, having us fall in for instructions. Reluctantly we all stood in line as Koontz went though an abbreviated instruction set on how to hold off an NVA division with an M-16 and two clips of ammo.

In case Vietnamese approach our position, Koontz advised us if they keep approaching or take off running, you are to fire two warning shots ... in the direction of their backs, then yell halt."

With that I was off to replace Jim who had been guarding in a bunker at the end of the flight line. As the sound of his footsteps disappeared behind me, and the immense quiet and darkness of the early morning engulfed me, the fear of falling asleep on guard duty was becoming very real.

As I struggled for a while to remain alert, the fatigued finally over took me. I started closing my eyes for brief periods until a large rat moving around the bunker in search of food startled me. With that I took the speed tablet out of my pocket, briefly rolled it around in my hand for a minute and then took out my canteen and popped them down my throat. I stood there quietly, waiting for this massive explosion of what I didn't know. Perhaps my eyes would pop open or I'd have a desire to dance or at least shake. But nothing; it figured, this was Army issue. This was the same Army that served twenty year old Raisin Bran that months earlier had nearly taken my teeth out.

So I continued to stare down the runway, or behind me down the flight line. I looked for a shadow to move and prayed for the sun to rise. After several more minutes, I pulled out some pen and paper I had brought out to write a letter home to my fiancé. I must have had a lot to say, because the eight-page letter took only a few short minutes to write. It was much later I realized the drug had worked, the letter was devoid of any verbs, or "the's", or names. I decided to rip up the incoherent rambling of a 'now' mad man, and wait out my duty. But the fear of falling asleep now turned to a panic of being found "under the influence".

Dozens of thoughts ran through my mind as time rambled on, until the sun finally rose. It was over, I could go back to my hootch and disappear, and maybe I'd make it yet. My mistake came in taking the short cut past the flight Ops building. There I was invited to a group of air jocks getting their buttes reamed by "Red". The ten of us were at attention as he walked by each of us, quickly turning inches from ones face to continue his lashings. I'm not even sure what it was about, my mind was consumed with the fear he'd see I was on something. My god, I was sure my eyes were bloodshot and dilated, that my pupils were spelling out fear. It was all over, I was had.

And then Red was gone.

"Bob, . . . hey Bob, lets go man before he decides to come back."

With that I shook my head, and saw Jim standing there talking to me. Thank god, the gila monster with the split head, one of the heads yelling at me had left.

"Yah . . . oh, sorry Jim. I was thinking of something else. Ah, what are you up to?" I struggled to make conversation as I regained my composure.

"Six two or three, depends on the humidity."

I was to survive the day, in fact hitting the PX and Post Office without hitting the bunk. Sleep would come broken by ever-present Vietcong mortar harassment corps who took joy in screwing up the one bit of peace we thought we had.

The excitement turned to routine; even the increasing amount of enemy fire was expected, no longer a surprise. We were taking out trucks every night now and that's what it was all about, a chess game, only the pieces we were playing with were alive, or dead. The routes we flew were pretty standard; they were designed to get the best shot of the trails from a number of different angles for the radar. But we could change the time of when we flew, and that worked like a charm, catching a fair number of unlucky drivers every night. We'd return home with the glow of trucks burning in the jungle every night now, and that's what our job description called for.

Of course one had to remember to whom we were working for, the US Army was always dreaming up something to keep life interesting. This afternoon I wandered out on the flight line to see what planes were set up for the missions tonight? I saw Daze and the other crew chiefs removing the rocket pods off the hawk wings and stacking them along the revetment wall.

"What are guys up to, spring house cleaning?" I greeted Daze not wanting to scare him as he had his back to me.

"Hey curry, slumming again?" he answered turning around with a wrench in his hand. "You heard . . . the Air Force won?"

"Won what, I didn't know we were playing them?"

"No shithead, remember, the Army and Air Force were arguing over who should have the Mohawk. We had all agreed if the Air Force had us, at least we'd have parts to work with instead of this broken shit? Well, we lose on both counts. The Army gets to keep the Mohawk, but you guys got to fly unarmed."

"What the hell . . .?"

"If you flew with weapons, you'd be classified as close air support, and that's the domain of the Air Force," he winked.

I was speechless, what in the hell bonehead thought this was a brilliant compromise? Now when we fly out there alone, where they say we aren't flying, now we get to fight a war against someone trying very hard to kill us with absolutely nothing! When I think of the mental giant who made this ludicrous decision, it's obvious they never fought for their life, other than DC traffic on a Friday afternoon.

"I'm convinced Daze, they don't want us to come back," I uttered. "If Ho's boys don't get us, they certainly will."

They got me again; just when I thought I had this thing figured out, they pull me back in, to the insanity. Every day was a mind rape; you didn't know when or where, only that it was coming. And I was angry with myself that I was even surprised anymore. I wanted to get to that point they called the thousand-mile stare, where you were ok with death, the why of dieing, because you realized you had no control over the time or place. Because they'd be one less thing too struggle with.

The next weeks took their toll in planes and men. The good guys' invasion into Laos had finally reached Tchepone. The South Vietnamese had over twelve thousand troops on the ground in Laos, and word was that the ARVN's found huge caches of guns, ammo and supplies. Surprising, a larger then expected number of tanks and anti aircraft guns were seized or destroyed in place. The typical thought back home was we were fighting a rag tag group of peasants armed with slingshots and an AK-47 for every ten of them. The fact was we were fighting a sophisticated set place Army here with the latest in Soviet and Chinese armament. The only thing missing were the Russians and Chinese, and there were rumors of even that.

Another evening arrived to find me prepping the plane for mission twenty over the trail. I went to grab my maps and gear when I realized I was missing something.

"Shit, I forgot my helmet. I'll run down to the hootch and grab it", I yelled over to Tyrone, as he was finishing off his coffee.

"Fine with me, I'll just grab some more of this fine Brew," he answered standing behind Red's back and sticking his finger down his throat.

With that I was off, walking the dark and now quiet path down between the hootches. My mind was off daydreaming when suddenly I walked into somebody or something.

"What in the hell . . ." I muttered, looking up at what possibly could be out here at midnight. My eyes wouldn't believe what they saw. There was a row of guys on the sidewalk, starting two hootches down from mine, and winding up my stairs. And they were all quietly standing there as if waiting for their payroll checks. I walked along side them and found it led right up to my door. Now I was intrigued but remembering I lived with Moose, I was beginning to smell a rather large rat.

Excusing myself to the first guy in line, I knocked on the door. As the door swung open, I could hear Moose, "I told you buddy, wait your turn." Now fully standing in the door counting a handful of cash with a cigar in his mouth was Moose.

"Hey Bob . . . come on in," he hesitantly said, surprised because I was supposed to be flying.

"Thanks Moose, I forgot my helmet. Didn't mean to interrupt your business," I answered pushing my way around the entrepreneur. The room had been constructed out of scrap and stolen wood Moose found around the base. He was a pretty good carpenter, the beds custom built into the walls. Moose's was to the left of the door, built up about four feet off the ground. Underneath he had built in storage and book shelves. And on top of the bed was a nude Vietnamese woman. She thought I was her next customer as she smiled and held out her arms, motioning me over. Christ, four lonely months and this nude woman wasn't even turning me on. Of course, it might have been the smile with numerous missing teeth and the remaining stumps darkened by chewing on betel nuts that added that special touch. My bunk was dead center in the room, and thank god it was empty. To my right was another raised bunk with yet another naked local. This girl seemed all of fifteen years old, munching on an apple and patting the bed for me to sit down next to her.

"Well Moose, were did you get these ladies?"

"Bought them in under the wire by the control tower. I'm splitting the money with them. Hell, I could make two hundred bucks tonight," Moose answered; recounting the cash he must have counted twenty times by now.

"Just do me one favor guy," as I grabbed my helmet. "Keep them off my bed, I don't want to be cleaning up anything when I get back later."

"No problem Bob . . . sure one of these girls can't give you a quick send off?"

"Sorry, Tyrone is waiting, we're late already." With that I was out the door bushing past the line of guys waiting to spend their twenty bucks for a little boom-boom. Looking at the last guy in line, I shivered at the possibilities of infection this boy was waiting for, paying for, wow.

I was certainly pissed off walking back, now my hootch was a whorehouse, why not I guess? But Moose was the kind of guy you couldn't stay pissed off at for long. With folks leaving and coming into the unit constantly I moved over by Moose, as the guy was a wood working genius. Give him an old shipping crate and he'll build a custom bookcase in the room. Several weeks ago I flew along with McGee and several buddies in one of MASH unit Hueys over to a deserted area of Camp Eagle while the 101st was out sloshing through the paddies. That evening we made a midnight requisition of six window air conditioners. The next day Moose had cut a hole in the wall and had the small air conditioner mounted with wood trim in place. I sat there when he pulled out the longest screwdriver I'd ever seen. The power was two-hundred-twenty volts and it was live, but I figured he knew what he was doing.

The explosion caught me by surprise. My ears where ringing and I could no longer see Moose though a metal like haze that filled the hootch.

"Moose . . .?" I quietly called out certain they'd be no response. As the haze parted, I saw a blackened Moose sitting on the floor dazed with the screwdriver, all eight inches melted back to the rubber handle.

He talked only once more that day, a quiet "Fuck."

172

And tonight he had opened a whorehouse; it was nice to know the jolt of a live two-twenty power line hadn't slowed him down at all.

Back at the flight line, Tyrone must have gotten antsy, either that or Red pissed him off again. I could hear a Mohawk with engines running as I got up near the flight line. Over the top of the revetments I could see the nav lights blinking, it was my plane. I went straight to the flight line; sure enough he was strapped in, helmet on with both engines running going through his flap control surface tests with the crew chief. I always enjoyed climbing into the cockpit with the props running five feet away. One slip while climbing up and I'd have part of my anatomy removed by the props. As I threw my helmet up on the instruments and strapped in, Tyrone was already rolling out to the taxiway.

We raced west to hunt, the weather was clear and the cool night air was always a welcome relief. The action over the trail had jacked up in volume now that the South Vietnamese had withdrawn from Laos. It appeared the NVA was trying to make up for lost time and shoving every truck and bicycle it had down the trail to get the goods south before the next wet season. Often it was such a target rich environment; we couldn't find enough attack aircraft to hit all the targets.

On the eastern leg north from the Cambodian border we had a flight of F-4's engage a convoy of trucks that had been enjoying a quiet moon filled evening drive. We left them to their dirty work as we headed northwest over Tchepone to follow the trail up to the Mia Gia pass where the traffic enters from North Vietnam. Again, more truck traffic was racing south. We lost a group of seven movers, as Moonbeam had no available strike aircraft to engage. Someone's lucky day and they'd never know it.

Besides watching out the cockpit for the telltale signs of anti aircraft fire coming up at us, we could view the pockets of fire burning vividly against the blackened jungles across Laos. Pockets of trucks and their crews were baking off into the night sky. We watched a Spectre gunship with its rivers of red tracers pouring death onto some previously unsuspecting soldiers south of Tchepone.

Coming down our leg on the western side of Laos, along the Mekong River we decided to head back over Laos north of our usual mission path. With the mountains, hills and valleys deflecting radar signals differently, perhaps we could mix up our potential targets and find a route or path we didn't know of before.

Mid way across Laos heading east back to Vietnam I picked up two movers in an area that had produced nothing for us before. But we hadn't bounced our radar this direction earlier.

"Moonbeam, Spud one-seven has movers at x-ray delta four niner seven four six five."

The radio having quieted down in the last twenty minutes crackled, "Roger Spud, we got that. We'll see if Spectre three-three can head south a bit and help you with the hunting."

"Roger Moonbeam, appreciate the assistance." I responded.

We tracked a set of navigation lights head from the north and descend below and behind us as continued our run west. I lost site of the Spectre when they killed their nav lights as they descended on our target site. Now they'd be viewing the jungles below with their night vision system to visually locate the trucks or tanks we had alerted them to.

I could imagine their trails of red tracers flowing from their perch in the sky when the air behind lit up with a giant white flash.

"Hoy shit Moonbeam, give us all we got, we got an anthill here and we'll need some more feet to stomp these mothers...." came the excited broadcast from Spectre three-three.

Tyrone stared at me as if reading my mind, and turned the plane around a hundred and eighty degrees to see what all the commotion was about. Far ahead of us we could see the rivers of red death saturating the ground below the Spectre. On the ground was a huge white glow, no white fire as something huge was burning away. The radio picked up excited chatter as Moonbeam called out for every strike aircraft it could find.

Soon we watched the Spectre go black as it back off so the fighter-bombers could bring their loads in. We picked up a line east of the action and watched this fire show change as more and more fighters were brought on board and the fireball expanded its borders. What ever was cooking off was huge; the lights from the fires were dancing off the high clouds that had moved in during the evening.

We watched as long as we could until the lack of fuel gained our attention. Another thirty minutes and we were exciting Lao territory reentering Vietnam.

"Moonbeam, Spud RTB Phu Bai, thanks for the show"

"Spud one-seven, thanks for the movers, it seems you caught some stragglers heading into a truck park. I'm not sure what the final count will be, but we'll be pouring more strikes on this all night and well into tomorrow. Think we got their fuel dump too."

"Holy shit" I blurted over the intercom as Tyrone and I high-fived we all the way back to Da Nang. Then it was time to turn down the systems and head home; it had already been a long day. The moon's reflection off the ocean below shone brilliantly as we headed down the coastline. It seemed peaceful out here tonight as we rapidly dropped our altitude until we were speeding several hundred feet over the coastline.

The conversations drifted toward thoughts of home, those we left behind, and what we were missing out on. After the adrenalin attack earlier, it now seemed so peaceful out here tonight it was almost eerie as we low leveled the twinkling lights in the villages and rice paddies on our way home.

"Well, you think we can make it back before the club closes?" I asked, "My fridge is out of beer."

Pushing the throttles forward he replied, "Plenty of time, remember it takes them a half hour after closing to push all the drunks out. Besides, Taylor's in charge of the club this week, he owes me a few favors."

As I pulled out the log book to make sure the problem we had with the fuel gauges was written up, Tyrone keyed the mike raising the boys back home at the control tower "Phu Bai, Spud one-seven sixty miles out, need vector into Channel sixty-nine."

After a slight delay the radio crackled with, "Spud one-seven, Phu Bai airfield is under mortar attack, advise you to stand off. If low on fuel we advise landing at Da Nang."

Shit, my ass was sore enough from sitting on these hard seats for six hours over two missions today. Now we had to wait for some rice farmer turned part time VC to finish shooting off his weekly allotment of mortar shells.

"Bob, let's take her up a bit and head in, maybe by the time we get there the shelling will be over," Tyrone, clearly thinking that tonight was another sporadic episode of local VC harassment.

I sat back in the seat trying to unwind as Tyrone gained some altitude as we headed in to see what was going on back at Phu Bai. As we pulled up we could begin to see the intermittent flash of explosions on the horizon. They continued to light up the sky as we approached the base.

"They must have gotten an extra shipment of mortars for the holidays," Tyrone reflected. The mortaring continued as we arrived just off to the northeast of the airfield. As we circled off to the northeast we began to pick up an unusual amount of radio chatter as gunships and some Navy jet jocks were calling in as they entered the local airspace.

Now sitting up straight in my seat, Tyrone and I were realized that it was beginning to appear this was no longer the local VC fire for harassment. The mortars were falling in neat patterns off the north end of the airfield. A small number of secondary explosions occurred as they're intended targets were hit.

I was beginning to check on our fuel situation when Tyrone keyed the intercom, "Take a look at all the Christmas tree lights up here!"

The sky was now rapidly filling with the navigation lights of choppers and fighters appearing all around our airspace. Tyrone flipped through the radio channels until finding one that was beginning to first direct the fighters in on VC positions in the foothills to the northwest of the base.

We stood off in our grandstand perch for another ten minutes watching all the activities. The Navy jets were making bombing runs into the foothills, while red tracers from the helicopter gunships filled the air in the fields separating the base from the local town. All through this, the mortars continued unimpeded. It now had taken on the appearance of some heavier action, perhaps NVA regular troops. The length and accuracy of the mortars seemed beyond the capabilities of most VC units.

Numerous fires were raging both on the base and in the foothills as the light show continued to rain destruction both directions. Switching

176

through the various radio channels, I could hear a call for an Air Force C-119 gunship named Shadow. It now became a full-time job to watch all the air traffic as to not get in the way of planes flying at various angles, altitudes, and speed.

Out of the corner of my eye, I could see Tyrone's gaze fixed on something on the airfield. As I swept the air around us for traffic once more, I then attempted to follow his gaze. He appeared to be watching the string of mortars exploding in rapid succession on the north end of the airfield and off into Phu Bai.

We waited as we used up our fuel hoping we wouldn't be forced down to Da Nang. Finally the explosions seemed to stop as numerous fires, the majority off into the village burned.

"Phu Bai control, Spud One Three request permission to land," Tyrone announced over the radio.

"Negative, Spud . . . repeat, we are under mortar attack. You do not have permission to land."

"Phu Bai, we are low on fuel and need to land now, appears quiet down there," replied Tyrone. Then the argument between the tower and Tyrone continued as Tyrone placed us on final approach. The plane shuttered as Tyrone lowered the landing gear. Turning to me, he tried to explain, "Always love an argument"

"Hey, I'm with you, really have no choice," as I tugged on the straps holding me into the ejection seat.

Over the intercom came a quiet "Thanks", as Tyrone turned his attention back to the fast approaching runway. The bright moonlight bathed the runway in an eerie glow. Thank God, as we approached the runway lights that had been turned off earlier when the mortars started, as not to give the NVA a lit map of the field came on. He had won his game of chicken. I began to make sure the systems not needed for landing or taxing was shut down. I had a feeling we'd be leaving the plane rather quickly.

The jolt of the wheels squealing as they touched down on the runway brought me back to reality. My ears were filled with the immense sound of the engines screaming in reverse to fight our roll down the runway.

The plane shuttered to a stop half way down the runway, Tyrone cranked the plane left onto the first taxiway. The engines groaned as he pressed the throttles, attempting to speed into the relative safety of the revetments should the required smoke break for the NVA mortar crew end.

While these thoughts racing past us, our minds struggling to comprehend what was happening, soon we found ourselves inside the revetments. Tyrone slammed the throttles down, killing the huge turbines. I flipped off the remaining equipment, while at the same time unbuckling myself from the seat. In a single leap, I slammed onto the steel planking and heard deathly quiet. Quickly looking around, I noticed no one was to be found. I realized that the IQ level of this unit was several points higher than that of Tyrone or me at that moment, they were waiting to see if the evening rain of mortars was over.

And as fast as it began it was over. The word came later that some of the mortars had hit the town and the orphanage that night. And it ended except for the pieces of destruction that would burn itself into the memories and souls of everyone it touched. And for my friend Jess, the worst had come to be.

There was the threat of rain the next afternoon as a number of us accompanied Jess to the orphanage for what had been for too long the most frequent Vietnamese social gathering, the funeral. Standing silently in the dust we listened as the harried nuns took their children through the solemn but familiar ceremony.

Jess stood still, silent, impotent tears rolling down his face. Still shocked children stared at him, at us, wordless but with accusing eyes burning through us with the unmistakable message, "why".

But then, maybe it was all our fault? I tried to look away from them, and their withering hate filled faces. I had no answers for them, how could I even understand them or the life they lived. Hate from an adult I could have dealt with, or at least ignored. These adult eyes, trapped in children's bodies, were different; they didn't deserve to grow up this soon.

Chanting, Sister Nhi and the nuns placed the white bundles into hastily dug holes. Jess continued to weep quietly, an occasional small groan escaping from his pain. And the tears spread amongst us; it was one of the times that we, all those bold teenagers, seemed as young as we were.

178

It was one thing to fight well and kill well, and even die well, but to watch three doll-like packages put under that mean, red clay is a moment that all of us would take to our own graves.

Some sooner then anyone thought.

The funeral ended in a drizzle as the children filed silently past us, back to their damaged buildings and the rest of their damaged youth. Taking Jess by the arm Sister Nhi walked off with him, speaking softly for a short while. The rest of us stood around the jeep making small talk, watching the nun say the inadequate to the inconsolable.

A now stony Jess returned to us, his face saying it all. We all piled in the jeep leaving quickly. Driving out the gate there was no laughter, no children playing, just an eerie silence broken only by the sound of rain on fresh graves. A bit of the war the politicians back home, on both sides of the political fence, never saw.

We returned to our hootches never saying a word. Even the ungodly, anvil like heat of the afternoon never interrupted my sleep. I fought to stay asleep, in some way hoping that the real events of the morning's funeral would turn out to be a dream. Sweating, I finally stirred at around five p.m. to find mail thrown next to my bunk. Jim, who couldn't sleep, obviously had picked up our link to "the world" for both of us.

A letter from my fiancé talked about her new job back at the JC Penney's "in the new mall". The other mail was boxes of collection envelopes from my church back home, the church that I'd written to repeatedly to send any old clothes for the orphanage. They hadn't gotten around to that part of the Christian effort yet. But they knew how to reach twelve thousand miles across the pew with the collection plate.

Tossing the envelopes in the trash, I pulled on my fatigues, grabbed a Coke and headed over to the next camp to check on Jess's hootch. I wasn't flying tonight but I almost wished I had been. Flak over the trail was preferable to seeing Jess after the morning's emotional mine field. The screen door to his room creaked open and I stepped into damp darkness. As my eyes adjusted from the bright sunlight outside, I could make out Jess's figure wrapped in a sheet quietly snoring. The strong smell of incense permeated the air; we all burned the stuff to mask the fetid, humid smell of decay that lingered everywhere.

An empty bottle of Jim Beam lying on the floor next to his bed ended my internal debate on whether to wake Jess. It was time to let whiskey and mourning take their course. I quietly backed over the piles of gear strewn over the floor hoping my friend was dreaming of women and home and not the three cotton wrapped bundles.

More missions, more trucks, every night brought more kills to the list. We were all flying multiple missions a day. Some type of Asian flu had swept though the camp and taken its toll. We all took turns getting sick, as if we had planned it. The South Vietnamese were stalled inside of Laos, we were sure the brass was having a holy fit. This was to be the test of the ARVN's, that they could handle the war on their own. I often questioned why one group of Vietnamese called the north was kicking butt against the Vietnamese team called the south; maybe it had something to do with the water?

There was an invitation to celebrate Chavez's freedom flight and my assignment to the northern Lao missions later that evening. Noise and smoke filled the club, and the party was well under way by the time Lyle and I showed up. Walking through the door the aroma of stagnant water and rotting plywood combined to give the club the aroma of a baseball stadium's men's room in August.

"Ah, Uncle Jack, I'm home," Lyle yelled at me, attempting to talk over the noise of thirty drunk soldiers deep in heavy, and always significant discussions. "Good old Uncle Jack had a little cabin in the Ozarks, drank like a fish and hardly ever bathed. But when you're fifteen and the booze is free, what are a few discomforts."

We made our way to the bar noticing Ramon was slinging the drinks.

"Hey Ramon, how 'bout some beers down here?" I yelled down the bar. Ramon, motioning he had heard me, worked his way up the bar toward us refilling every glass in the bar on his way.

"This place is nuts," Ramon shouted while opening our beers. "Any excuse for a party brings this group out. Tonight, it's you guys heading out. Tomorrow they'll party over some lucky guy banging his hootch maid."

"Certainly knows how to make the occasion feel special?" I muttered to Lyle.

———

180

The drinks flowed freely as we wandered from one group of drunks to another. We were fearless tonight, jumping into the middle of any argument, cursing the Army, the gooks, and the shit deal we all shared, the depth of our profanity rising with our alcohol level.

Around midnight Jim walked in. Through the smoke, and my slightly impaired vision, I need to talk with my buddy I had started this whole army thing with; over what felt like was a hundred years ago. I grabbed a bottle of vodka, a couple of cups, and weaved my way to the first encounter group Jim had gotten sucked into. I poured him a drink; Jim nodded in acknowledgement as Turk discussed the proper method of barrel rolling a Mohawk, complete with hand gestures while attempting to balance on one foot. Finally Turk couldn't pull out of the roll and crashed into a table.

Grabbing our bottle and glasses, Jim and I made our way to a safer, empty table.

"The worst of it is, now I got a kid, we're flying planes they can't maintain, they've taken all the weapons off . . .?" Jim stammered on, clearly upset it was no longer just he in his world, that's other counted on him back home. "I can't figure out why in the fuck we've become floating targets in the sky while the politicians find the right language to bail their asses out of this mess?"

"Me fuckin' either buddy," I thought to myself as he poured more vodka, staring into the corners of his soul.

"I mean what do we do, it's all about survival, does another death mean a hill of shit in how this war plays out?"

He continued to explode over the mess we were all in as some of our buddies made their way to our table, sarcastically wishing me ill will on my new home "over the fence".

For me I was heading west to do something, it wasn't about saving the war, which was well beyond my station in life. It was about taking out the trucks rambling down the Ho Chi Minh Trail to attack our brothers in the south. Then there was the Hmong that Pop's always talked about who were being brutalized by the North Vietnamese. We heard of their stories by pilots who had been shot down in Laos. They owed their lives to these fiercely loyal people who sacrificed their own people to save our asses. It would be nice to have an solid ally, after all, what in the hell were we in Asia for?"

"The whole fuckin' thing's a waste now, Nixon's negotiating and we're still dying. This whole fuckin' country isn't worth another GI's ass, you ask me," said a soldier who was on his second tour, an admired hard charger who was respected by all.

There was some grumbled assent and then the discussion switched to the Vietnamese mortars that murdered the local villagers and children last evening.

"They don't give a fuck for their own people," said another philosopher at the end of the bar. "So, should we. What's the use of risking your ass when in the long run it won't make any difference anyway?" he asked.

Again there was grumbling from the assembled assembly soon downed out by sound of fresh beer cans being opened.

For months Jim was wondering if he should become a silent member of this "don't wanna be the last guy killed in a war" group. After all, he had a wife and kid back home that demanded a certain degree of caution. But that wasn't Jim.

"But now it's payback time. That's all, payback, that's why I'm here now."

A respectful silence came over the table. This guy had paid some big dues, they seemed to say, give him the floor. He was close to Shereck, having flown together a lot.

"Bastards got to be stopped until they call us home, but not for the ARVN's who run as soon as the shots are fired?"

I saw an opening and took it, part of me still wanted to cling to the patriotic belief we were here for some moral purpose, like life and liberty, the bullshit we all heard a million miles away. But the reality of months here had changed that.

"Jim, it's not even about whether we should be here or not," I stammered out. "It's about stopping that fuck on the other side, stopping him from carrying the mortars and rockets south that will kill one of us, or one of our brothers down south. That's what I believe when I fly those missions

182

every night over the trail. Stopping them might stop the next triple-A gun that has one of our own in their sights."

I had said it, not realizing what I said until it was out. This guy was married with a child and he didn't need to take any more chances. Jim nodded, but his face said that something inside was broken, something that all the King's horses and all the King's men with all the King's vodka couldn't put Jim together again.

Someone bought another round and we started talking about aircraft, something we could understand, touch and be sure of. It went late into the night, of course, the stories, lies, and jokes flowing with liquor until we were finally able to sleep again. It would be a lifetime before I saw Jim again.

The mid morning heat woke me before my body wanted to get up. Remembering part of last night I fell back on hard-learned lessons of a combat drinker, never, ever move your head before opening your eyes. Carefully opening mine I could see Jim's empty bunk and the fan blowing the pin-up pictures around. Thank God, the thing with that dog Toto must had been a dream. It was quiet, the only sounds were coming from the flapping Playboy calendars on the wall and muffled GI voices in the cursed sunshine outside. I slowly moved my hands up to my head, fearing a sneak attack of the spins when I tried to get up. Gingerly dropping one leg at a time over the side of the bed I was beginning to feel a glint of hope. Now the real test; I sucked in a large breath and slowly raised myself to a full sitting position up on my cot. I wasn't sure what deal I had made with the devil last night, but it seemed worth it.

The next day word came our transfer to Barrel Roll was being delayed. So we were back in the available column in flight ops as the demand for crews never abated. For the next weeks we'd find ourselves flying round the clock nightly infrared missions for the Marines down south of Da Nang. We'd fly down every night and land at Chu Lai, and pick up the missions over territory they suspected NVA units were holing up in. We'd plot the missions in their Intel shack, grab some coffee and be airborne in the night sky. Now we'd be flying alone over the jungle top out in no mans land west of Da Nang or over the border into Laos. The film required we fly straight patterns over the jungle so the film could be pieced together and plotted. It also gave the enemy a predictable target to shot at.

When we caught them unsuspecting, they knew we had picked a hot engine, cooking fire, or exhaust from a generator. Then it was open season on the Mohawk. It was better to bring her down then allow us return with their positions pin pointed for tomorrow's destruction. If they were less lucky, we'd call the positions in on the fly to a firebase perched on a mountaintop or hill near the border. There the Army or Marine guns would rain shells in quick order on an enemy attempting to rise up and move. Several times those weeks I watched these same firebases taking massive enemy fire from the outside. We'd circle the hill giving the enemy firing positions as we could see the rockets and mortars leave their tubes. But we were impotent, as the Air Force brass had made sure the Mohawks carried no weapons. So we watched impotent to do anything to stop the rain of death on our brothers on the hills. If I had a rock, we could have hit those positions, but not tonight, not any night. The rules of war made in the marble hallways a million miles away continued to kill Americans in spite of ourselves.

When you think you've seen all the twists, this insanity weaves a new tale. It makes you wonder what tomorrow holds, having given up on understanding today?

Then tomorrow awoke everyone with sheer panic; Spud two-two was down in Laos and the rumors of who was flying and what happened flew through the hootches faster then greased lightening. It had been a visual recon mission that morning that went over the fence into Laos hunting for the ever-elusive enemy. Musil wasn't supposed to fly right seat that day, hell, he wasn't supposed to be flying period. Clinton was an Intelligence Officer in charge of the Intel boys who hunted with grease pens the enemy hiding in the film of jungle, hills, and paddies we brought back. He was heading home soon and tired of listening to the stories and tales of flying the missions. So he was dead set to experience a mission himself and had spent several weeks begging everyone to fly theirs. He asked Jim and I the night before as no one was ever sure which right-seater was flying which mission given all the horse trading. I told him I had already paid off my extra missions with Turk for my pup. Now I was pretty settled in to flying mission twenty every night. Jim was assigned to yet another of a long list of missions. But not unlike the game we played as kids, missions were house traded between ourselves freely. The pilots had their own scheduling regime, but somehow this bit of the insanity seemed to work, that was until today.

But today Musil flew a mission he wasn't supposed to be on and died in a country we weren't supposed to be fighting in. And Brunson was a true adventurer; he loved to fly the daily visual missions, the ability to fly low and fast, balls to the wall. They were doing a visual and photo recon mission five to six kilometers southwest of Phou Ke Dai in Laos. This was a major section of the Ho Chi Minh Trail. Flying photo recon, like infrared meant you flew legs back and forth over a section of coordinates so you get lengths of film that would be pieced together by the intel guys to create a photo mosaic of the area. Of course flying straight lines over the tree tops gives plenty of time for the NVA triple-A gunners to get a bead on you and blast way. Brunson and Musil were on a pass when the trailing Mohawk saw them take a steep left turn and plow into the hill with a fireball erupting almost instantly.

There was no time for ejecting when hit this low, despite numerous passes, the back up Mohawk detected no movement, no radio calls. Because the NVA regulars heavily garrisoned this area there was no opportunity to put in a ground rescue unit. This was the heart of the Ho Chi Minh trail, and it was one of the most heavily defended areas in Asia. Hell, there were more anti-aircraft guns here in one place then the world had ever seen. And Jack and Clinton were flying point in the middle of no mans lands, where the chance of coming back when things went wrong were nil. And they became two of over six hundred pilots that would disappear into the jungles of Laos never to return. When Nixon and Kissinger reached their agreement with North Vietnam to end that war, they signed away the fate of these fine young men who went to war thinking their country would cover their back. North Vietnam would say they had nothing to do with Laos, despite their sixty thousand troops in place occupying this land and the US would agree knowing better. And not one pilot would ever return from Laos, and every administration in Washington would look the other way, letting whoever was alive to die by themselves in a jungle now a million miles away.

I had been sleeping as my nightly mission over Laos normally got me back before daylight. Someone ran through the hootches waking everyone up, trying to see who was here, who was flying with Brunson. Then they found Henry who many thought had gone down on the flight in his hootch? No one saw this twist, but the musical chairs had spared one and sealed the fate of another. And here it was with the unknown whether they made it or not. No one was sure what to wish for, as we all heard the stories of the treatment of captured pilots in Laos. And grief was never allowed as a company, as a unit. People just came and went through this revolving door called Vietnam. There was no ceremony morning their lose, just huddled GI's toasting a friend or acquaintance to a better life somewhere, somewhere other then this insanity where even death wasn't discussed. And when no one returned to be sent home, it was never resolved; there could be no closure. So another piece of the thousand mile stare was in place, the insanity was now becoming the norm.

It wasn't long and we were up along the DMZ flying our infrared runs in the black of the night. Here we were within range of anti-aircraft fire and Sam missiles from North Vietnam just across the river. Several of the planes carried hostile-fire detection systems that would squawk and blink yellow and red in the cockpit alerting us that radar was attempting to find us, or locking on. Then the plane would turn into a roller coaster ride as we attempted to break the radar lock, get out of the electronic cross hair, always wondering when the rocket would come up our ass and end it. The anti aircraft fire was becoming more intense as the year rolled on. There seemed to be an endless source of red tracers trying to connect the dots with every Mohawk in the skies.

My bright day came when Sally J returned; she had survived the distemper that was ravaging the dogs that found safety and friendship on the American bases. She was soon scampering to drive the rats out of the hootch each evening. By the time morning came, Sally was off guard duty usually lying exhausted at the end of the bed.

My mission assignment had switched back to flying mission twenty over the trail hunting trucks every night. With the switch came a night off, unheard of in any circles. Pops was leaving soon so I had a chance to catch up with him for dinner at the mess hall. He was still feeling sore from the bunker collapse, but I had seen him often reading in the shade of the hootch or deep in conversations with many of the Vietnamese hootch maids and workers that appeared on base every day.

We entered the mess hall, which sounds way too classy. It was actually a large room wrapped in screening and thin plywood under the heat magnifying tin roofing that appeared everywhere. Bright lights added to the ambiance as the fragrance of cleaning chemicals waffled though the evening air. Pops threw down his metal tray and started heaping everything that appeared before him. His gut was amazing, and I might add growing on him. I saw the evening treat was again mystery meat. These were thin strips of a beef jerky type meat, and I use the term meat loosely. The strips lay in a large metal serving pan soaking in dark gravy. This gravy actually gave off a rainbow of colors under the harsh mess hall lighting similar to shining a light on transmission fluid, very pretty. I gingerly pulled several pieces of mystery meat out, dumping them on my plate. We never saw vegetables here, but there was a vat of powdered something approaching mashed potatoes, well at least the gray color pointed me in that direction. Several ten-pound biscuits and we were in business. Pops and I talked for a good hour as he continually shoveled. It was a feat of Herculean effort, not his eating, but me trying to keep from vomiting. I played with the mystery meat, but just couldn't take the plunge.

It was time for his nightly reading no one could come in between so I grabbed up several strips of meat knowing there's always a new dog outside the mess hall door near death that could use this as a last resort.

Sure enough, when the door swung open there was the normal lineup of the company dogs waiting for handouts. And there was the new dog on the block. Man, he was literally a rack of bones, his skin stretched over his ribs. He had that look that if you slipped and fell he might be hungry enough to take a bite out of you. This poor guy was going to die today if he didn't get something editable in him. I proudly walked over to this new Phu Bai member and handed him the meat strips.

With the strips now in his face, I watch him sniff over the mystery meat, the transmission gravy dripping off of it forming a slick below in the sand. Then I watched him give a snort of disgust and walk away. That deserved a salute, choosing death before US Army food; here was a dog with principals.

I ended up at Turks hootch for the evening, as everyone gathered to trade gossip and word from home. By now three of the guys had gotten "Dear John" letters adding insult to their service to country stint. The word was Chavez, mom, and baby were safely in Canada. The comings and going went on through the night until everyone realized it was two am and several of the group had early missions.

My hike back to my hootch was interrupted a "whoosh", the sound of a mortar leaving a tube someplace. "Incoming," came the scream from a shadow in the distance already in a full run for a bunker. I turned and ran for the first bunker I could find. I got inside as the first of the explosions went off outside somewhere. Several more went off in quick succession as I peered in the darkness to see if I had company beyond the rats. There against the side was a huge shape shaking and sobbing uncontrollably. He took me a minute to realize it was Pops.

"Pop's, man are you ok," were the only words I could muster. I didn't know if he got hurt or what was going on.

In between the sobs and shakes he stuttered out "they're out to get me, I'm supposed to go home tomorrow, but I won't get out of here alive."

Several more mortars hit and then there was the quiet. I tried in vain to calm Pops down to no avail. He was convinced they had his name, and he would not leave in other then a body bag. His sobs slowed, but he sat there almost in a fetal position, which for a big guy was a feat, and he was not listening to any reasoning. I left him that night to return to my hootch bidding the rats and Pops farewell. Pops stayed in the bunker all night. It took a group of buddies to convince him the next morning he could leave to grab his stuff and hop a Huey south to freedom and home the next morning. I never saw Pops again, but I know the freedom we all hoped for would never come. We all left a piece of us here, a hole in our souls that would haunt us everyday for the rest of our lives. And some of us would unknowingly take pieces of this insanity home.

Evening came and my mission over the trail was to be with Koontz. Pops had kind of spooked me, so perhaps a flight with a rubber duck was what I needed. By the time I got to flight ops there was a present waiting for me, a shiny new white helmet. Man, talk about cool, not a scratch on it. This would go good with my Snoopy-flying scarf June had sent me. I was beginning to enter the weird world of strange rituals we would grab onto in an attempt to deal with this insanity. And what better way then to face it with more insanity of your own. I was hoping my "Spud" suit would show up before I went west. This was a one piece black jump suit with your call sign, the embroidered hawk of the 131st, and patches of insane humor one surrounded him self with. Patches like "Laotian Highway Patrol", "We kill so others can live", etc. And my call sign, "Killer Bob"; the reputation of my desire to fly all the Lao missions to hunt and kill trucks had taken over a large piece of me I couldn't explain.

The invasion by the ARVN's into Laos had ended days ago. We weren't sure what that would mean tonight. The NVA would certainly be attempting to get the trail back in order, trying to make up for lost time to get the men and supplies down into South Vietnam where they wanted to fight. The estimates of Lamson 719 saw fourteen thousand NVA killed, fifteen hundred trucks destroyed, seventy-four tanks, and twenty thousand pounds of supplies. The ARVN's lost over fifteen hundred men, over five thousand wounded. They left in a hurry leaving tanks and weapons all over central Laos. The pictures of ARVN's clinging to Huey skids in flight did not bold well for their reputation as a viable military force. The US flew over eight thousand missions including numerous B-52 strikes. We lost one hundred and seven choppers, eight combat aircraft, one hundred seventy six dead, and over a thousand wounded. We lost a number of planes, several more shot up, but more importantly Jim Shereck, Jack Brunson, and Clinton Musil, and they wouldn't be the last.

We took off at midnight and headed west, quickly checking in with Moonbeam as we entered Laos.

"Roger Spud, good hunting" replied Moonbeam.

The flight up the east side of Laos from the border with Cambodia was unnervingly quiet, as if everything had stayed placed that night. Then we broke northwest following the contour of Laos as we approached Tchepone.

As we settled in to our next leg, the cockpit was bathed in a red orange glow as the radar film backlit flowed in front of me. I was picking out some ground features off the film and comparing it to the map when I saw it.

The side hatches were designed largely of convex Plexiglas. This allowed both the pilot and copilot the ability to look out the sides of the aircraft seeing the ground below. While looking at the imagery in front of me, my eyes caught a flickering red reflection in the curve of the hatch. I stuck my head into the curve of my hatch to see what in the hell this was below us.

What I saw took my breath away. I was staring at a huge red bowling ball of fire vibrating in the air screaming toward us. I keyed the mike and screamed, "break left, triple-A!"

In the next pieces of seconds, I saw this ball scream close, fuckin close, then realized we were still flying straight and normal. I looked left and saw Koontz on a different radio channel oblivious to what I had screamed, to what was about to eat us.

So I swung my left arm striking him as hard as I could scream again, "break left triple-A!"

He must have seen the fear in my eyes, as he instantly banked the plane over screaming away to his left. The antiaircraft round missed us, blowing up below and to our right where we were seconds ago, seemingly the explosion buffeting us, sliding us further left, but who measuring? Koontz now knew what I was talking about, as he saw the next one, this time on his side. And we were off to the races. Larry put the Mohawk in a series of turns and dives that literally ripped hatches and panels off the plane, off the engines. We were in the fight for our life having wandered in to a radar alley. I flipped off our navigation lights to make us invisible, but to no avail. The rounds were right on us; they were tracking and firing with radar, passing us from one gun to the next as we moved west or east, or wherever. It didn't matter; we had no idea where we were. We were dodging these bowling balls of fire, and it had just started.

"Moonbeam, Spud taking heavy triple-A, vicinity of Tchepone" my voice shook through the airwaves, both from fear and the bouncing we were taking in the skies.

"Roger Spud, acknowledge," replied a business like Moonbeam. "Aircraft vicinity of Tchepone, advise heavy triple-A. Spud, we stand by to provide any assistance"

"Roger Moonbeam, will advise," was all I could say. There was nothing anyone could do; we were on our own in the fight of our life.

Upside down, inside out, it was the biggest roller coaster ride I had ever been on. One minute we were facing the ground watching the stream of tracers on its way up, and then we were peering at the stars above as we were rolling over and away from the balls of fire. Then I felt something strange, something warm and wet on my check. I brushed at it with my nomex glove and stared to see what in the hell it was. My heart stopped, it was red and warm, and figured it was fuckin blood as a panic now swept through me. I looked over at Koontz, it was all over his helmet, but he was flying, turning, reacting to the firestorm we were in.

"Larry, you ok?" I inquired.

"Fuckin no," he screamed, "are you having a fucking nice day?" puzzled by what I asked as he continued to make this plane dance and duck in the black skies filled with balls of red fire.

190

It was then I realized it was the developing fluid from the Slar system. By flying upside down and sideways the warmed thick reddish-brown developing fluid had coated everything in the cockpit. The warm red of the instruments lit it up like blood. We were still alive but barely.

It was now going on fifteen minutes, we weren't getting anywhere, away, but we were still flying and that was good, very very good. Moonbeam had put out a call to Nakhon Phanom for a team to get airborne, they knew it was a matter of very little time that we'd be dead, in chutes heading down, or if there was a God, he'd finally push us away from the guns.

Now the plane was shaking, vibrating very badly as we continued the roller coaster ride of dodging for our lives. It would go on for what we thought was eternity. And then there was quiet, calm as Koontz straightened out the bird; as the skies were now both black and quiet. We both swiveled our heads in every direction expecting more, but it never came.

As Koontz studied the instruments looking for trouble I called Moonbeam.

"Moonbeam, Spud one-four, level flight and out of trouble for the moment. We are experiencing heavy vibrations. Will RTB channel sixty-nine. Not sure of our position, will go Christmas tree?" We didn't want to get hit by another aircraft and were about to turn our navigation lights.

"Negative Spud," responded Moonbeam. "Negative Christmas tree. We have all traffic out of your sector. We are all standing by to assist. Will advise Phu Bai, good luck and God speed."

For a moment in the war, I was moved by the dozens of individuals flying tonight who stopped their piece of the war in order to give us whatever assistance they could. I would know I was never alone out here when they're were others like Moonbeam, the fighters, rescue teams, gunships, etc; who would put themselves in harms way to help each other at the drop of a hat.

Our engines were running hot, hell I was surprised they were still attached to the wings; that we were. Koontz dropped the throttles and the air speed, as we grew more and more worried about the vibrations as we slowly headed east for home. In what was an eternity, we finally saw the lights of Phu Bai and quietly glided down in the early morning darkness, when everyone was asleep including the enemy around here this evening.

As we pulled into the revetments aiming for the signal lights ahead of us, we saw a small group of people awaiting our return. Stopped, Koontz pulled back the throttles and killed the engines. I pulled off my new white helmet, now dripping with developing fluid and sweat, as the high pitch whine of the turbines made it impossible to hear anything or anybody. Several souls still awake in the early morning hours crawled under and over the Mohawk intently looking for damage. I crawled out of the cockpit, my wirily legs hitting the steel planking below barely kept me from falling to the ground. I watched Koontz drop down and kiss the ground. Then he was off to some place of solitude. We lost a number of the cowlings and hatches that weren't riveted in place. Moonbeam had called ahead of our arrival to advise Phu Bai of our problems are we were out of radio range with flight ops. Planes in our sector watching this strange ballet of anti-aircraft fire and some tremendous flying by Larry noted they saw us take over eighty rounds of the heaviest antiaircraft guns the NVA had in their inventory, the 57 and 100mm. My adrenalin wouldn't let me sleep, so I spent my next hours cleaning every ounce of red fluid from my helmet until it was the shiny white it had been five hours earlier. Not bad considering where the evening had been headed for a while. I'd never slander that rubber duck again.

Finally the day rolled around that would find us flying off to the "secret war". Only later would I learn the move was permanent. The rest of the day was spent sorting and packing. After shipping home stereo equipment from the PX, giving away warm beer, Vienna sausages, and a half case of Slim Jims, the stuff I would take west barely filled a duffel bag. The hardest part of the day came when I said my goodbye to Sally J., a clumsy pup who I'd had since shortly after her birth. I had planned on taking her home with me but a bout with distemper insured that the Army veterinarian's would never give her stateside clearance papers. I said my goodbyes to the guys and put my gear outside. I picked up Sal in my arms and gave her one last hug before handing her to Jim. This little pup had been an outlet for my most decent emotions and reminded me of that time, so long ago, when I was young. There were tears in my eyes when I left the company area, knowing I would never see her again. She was at times a furry, four legged bit of sanity in a very insane place. I gave Jim a hug, I loved this guy like a brother, and none of us knew where this thing was going.

By the time I hit the flight line, Koontz was already joking and grab-assing with the crew chiefs. He had already inspected our plane, stowed his bags and was raring to go. Red walked out from the operations building to play the "bid us goodbye" part. Not that he liked crazy Koontz or myself, but this was what the officer on duty should do, so he brought his hard-ass demeanor to the flight line. Handshakes finished, the crew chiefs bundled my bag into the Mohawk along with spare parts and mail bound for the guys in Udorn.

With that we were off, ready to taxi in the late afternoon heat. True to style, Koontz had his rubber duck stuffed in the cockpit window scanning the skies ahead of us. Koontz insisted that ducks are great at detecting antiaircraft fire. "Rubber Duck", certainly an original name, was reported to have survived many a hunting season back home.

Hatches slammed shut, seats were armed, and we rolled down the runway and into a smooth takeoff. Banking hard left we headed for Laos and the Royal Thai airbase at Udorn behind it. In brilliant sunshine our conversation approaching the Laotian border centered on our moonlit mission over North Vietnam several weeks earlier looking for a rumored POW camp that got called off at the last minute.

We had flown at least a dozen infrared missions the weeks before to insure we were checked out for any possible need in Laos. Our infrared cameras those nights had detected a number of hot spots or clues, similar to those given off by electric generators. We had wondered if anything had come from those finds, and hoped to hell something had.

Every night we flew our missions alone, but those nights was particularly spooky. Flying at tree top level in a partial moon seemed to invite disaster. But the thought of the grunts running into an ambush we might have prevented made the calculated risk seem worth it.

The missions up near the DMZ constantly set off the buzzing of our sensor equipment that picked up North Vietnamese radar attempting to lock onto us added to the nervousness. But, other then a severe case of shaken nerves, the flights had not provoked any substantial hostile fire. We both knew we too could end up being swallowed in the green and black of the jungle below.

We barely took notice as we crossed the border into Laos. The green jungles of Vietnam followed the land as it flowed into the mountains of

Laos. Climbing over the lush mountains in the afternoon sun, we were hit with the illusion of a peaceful world below us. It would be more than a decade until I would learn something of the history of a country that swallowed so many fellow flyers forever.

Laos is a slender, mountainous country that has the bad geographical luck to be sandwiched amongst Vietnam to the east, Thailand to the west, and Cambodia to the south, and the immensity of China to the north. It is essentially a green, jungle covered necklace of mountains. Between the mountains are plains with stands of elephant grass over twenty feet tall that could, and did, hide several armies.

Before the Second Indochina War, Laos was still a country teeming with elephant, black bear, and tiger. The mountainous country to the north was home to the Hmong people hidden for several centuries from the world on their mountaintop enclaves. The Hmong roamed freely through the mountains, using ancient slash and burn tactics to free farmland from the forest, moving on when the soil was exhausted, again. The Hmong, a very proud, religious, and superstitious people also attracted expansionist neighbors, especially the Vietnamese and Chinese traders who exploited the region for the cultivation of poppies. The drug trade was part of the landscape, no matter if it were grown here or injected or inhaled back home. The Hmong had used it as a medicine, the various traders over the centuries knew they could buy or steal it for great profits in a world a million miles away.

By the early 1800's a number of Hmong clans or families left the brutality of China and moved to the remote mountaintops of Northern Laos. The native Lao had remained in the lowlands harvesting the rice crop. There were wars with the Siamese to the south, but with the expansion of France's control of Indochina in the late 1800's, Laos would come under the control of yet another foreign power.

Japanese expansion during World War II sent most of the French packing. Some of the French operated a Vichy government for the Japanese, while other French fighters hid with the Vietnamese, Hmong, and Lao to fight this new invader. It was during this time that various independence movements grew in strength finding common roots in fighting the Japanese.

The United States and other Allied powers supported people such as Ho Chi Minh in fighting this common Japanese enemy, by sending supplies and training these jungle resistance movements.

The end of World War II brought Indochina back to business as usual, with the US giving tacit approval to France to reestablish colonial control. Various freedom movements who fought against the Japanese now asked the US for help in obtaining their independence. But the US was now focused on the international communist threat. Despite the guerilla's wartime help we allied again with the French taking their lead in Indochina.

France in the fifties increasingly found itself fighting a growing military threat, the Vietminh headed by Ho Chi Minh. In the past the communists had largely contained themselves to Vietnam, but now the Vietminh began expansion of the war to their neighbor to the west, Laos. The war soon involved the whole of Indochina.

The French found the Hmong could be the perfect indigenous people that could be rallied and used to fight the growing Vietminh problem. Not that the Hmong loved the French, they just hated the Vietnamese more.

By the 1950's France had over twenty thousand Hmong troops fighting for them. The battles against the Vietminh occurred largely in Northern Laos, directly west of Hanoi. The Vietminh would push west into Laos for control of the Plain of Jars.

The Hmong, who saw the mountains surrounding this plateau called the Plaines des Jares as their home, would fight back in battles that seesawed their positions every year.

During France's recruitment of the Hmong, they cultivated several Hmong for leadership positions. The most promising was a young fighter called Vang Pao. He had earlier fought the Japanese and the Chinese Nationalists in Laos. He had achieved recognition in the Lao military who often slighted the Hmong, some who viewed the Hmong as inferior mountain people.

The French sent Vang Pao to Vietnam for training, later granting him a commission in the French Army. His forceful personality had attracted the attention of the French and later the Americans. With more and more resources put under his control by the Western powers, he quickly became the most influential leader among his people. His wealth and power would grow from years of controlling French and US attention.

In 1949 Laos won its independence from France. France then quickly signed a defense pact with the newly independent Laos, offering to come to its aid if attacked. This legitimized Frances' military role in Laos, but also tied France to a military situation that would signal its end in Indochina.

The government of Laos insisted that the towns on the northern Plain of Jars be protected at all costs. It was out of a defensive concern for the ancient capital of Laos, Luang Prabang, which the French moved to cut off the most likely approach by the Vietminh. They picked the North Vietnamese town of Dien Bien Phu to make its stand; the rest is history.

Dien Binh Phu, under siege for almost two months fell with over fifteen thousand French defenders lost. Hmong soldiers were sent from the Plain of Jars to lead those few French who survived the defeat at Dien Bien Phu back to friendly forces. The French were exhausted; this defeat would end their war in Indochina while America's was just about to start. Thanks to Pop's and his appetite for reading, I had an appreciation for where I was heading.

"Spud, this is Hillsboro station. Please advise intent, over," a voice crackled over the radio reminding Koontz, the rubber duck, and me that we were still in a combat zone. It was the daytime flying Air Force command ship, which directed allied air traffic in this part of the theater. Below was the country where President Kennedy decided to make a secret stand against communism in the early sixties. His weapon was the CIA and its secret army of Hmong.

"Roger Hillsboro, Spud two-two heading two-three-three, RTB Udorn," I responded. Koontz was busy, attempting to sing along with the Temptations on Armed Forces Vietnam radio.

Poorly I might add.

"Copy Spud two-two, advise Moonbeam when you're over the fence." They would have switched their flying command posts by the time we exited Laos on the west later in the evening.

The growth of the CIA in Laos rekindled the contact with Vang Pao. Arms began to be shipped to Vang Pao's troops and the US began establishing the military logistics necessary to support the fight. The US Air Force began moving into the Royal Thai Air Force Bases beginning with the northern base at Udorn. It would be here the 7th and 13th Air

Forces would be headquartered. US Special Force units would move into the area to train the Hmong fighters and establish bases and landing strips in Laos. By 1963 over thirty thousand Hmong troops were armed by the US. The CIA brought its private airline, Air America, to Laos and Thailand. Air America would provide the supply line and transportation for the Hmong Army; a role the US military was not allowed to do. Soon we would be sharing the skies up North with the likes of Air America, Continental Air Services, Bird Air, etc.

Washington demanded a dual US role in Laos. First, stop the flow of North Vietnamese troops and materials through Laotian territory to the south, and at worst, insure the communists do not take over the country.

Unlike Vietnam, Laos' military commander was the US Ambassador in Laos. Besides his political responsibilities, the US Ambassador had the final word on all military activity. In 1964 William Sullivan was installed as the US Ambassador to Laos. Friction would develop between Sullivan and the US Military Commander in Vietnam, General Westmoreland. Westmoreland wanted full theater responsibility; Sullivan wanted to keep US troops out of Laos. He was committed a clandestine style of warfare. And he insisted on filling his ranks with volunteers, men who wanted to be there and could fight by unconventional means. He didn't like the limelight of the press poking holes all over the battlefield. He'd leave the media circus to the boys in Saigon.

But by 1965, with Vietnam heating up, Laos slipped back into obscurity.

The political bickering continued over expanding the role of US airpower in Laos. Complicated rules of engagement hampered effective support of Vang Pao's troops. The CIA and the Air Force struggled with the need to involve US pilots and technical support on the ground in Laos while avoiding direct violations of the Geneva Accords. The policy of putting these people into Laos "in the black" was established. US military people needed in this secret war were "volunteers " recruited from other units operating in Vietnam or Thailand.

In many cases they were still technically assigned to their original unit, but were gone TDY, or on temporary duty assignment. Those of us sent from the 131st were still assigned to that unit, our mail still coming and going through Vietnam. The mission had begun years earlier when Ed Paquette and Joe Lowdermilk flew into Udorn and met with the CIA planners and several Hmong leaders. The mission of the Mohawk was developed and put in place. And a small unit we referred to as the rat patrol would fly into the secret war, so secret, the 131st CO didn't know of the mission type or scope.

To those needed to be assigned on the ground in Laos, the procedure was more involved. In 1966 the CIA and the US Embassy decided they needed Air Force pilots flying out of Laotian airfields as forward air controllers or FAC's to direct the US air strikes in support of the Hmong. Experienced FAC pilots from Vietnam were recruited into the Air Forces secret Steve Canyon Program. Upon acceptance they would report to Udorn, Thailand where their personnel, payroll records, and uniforms were filed. They were put on temporary leave from the Air Force and sent on their way, in civilian clothes, to the CIA base at Long Chieng in Northern Laos. Many were given new ID's, some having their occupations listed as "Forest Rangers". To those in the know, including the communists, they would become known as the "Ravens".

But for years prior, the war had been directed by a group of "sheep dipped" Air Force enlisted men flying their forward air control command under their call sign of Butterfly. These men worked for Heine Aderholt to direct the Air Force fighters and bombers onto targets over the country they lived and worked everyday.

At the height of the conflict, the Ravens would grow to about two-dozen pilots. With a maximum speed of slightly over a hundred knots, they flew single engine Cessna O-1 Birddogs into the battlefields of Laos, coordinating air support for the CIA's hired Hmong Army. Between 1966 and 1973, when the program ended, twenty-three Butterflies and Ravens were killed or listed missing in action.

Another "in the black" program began in nineteen sixty-six. The Air Force and CIA established a forward all weather navigation station on the top of the Phou Pha Thi Mountain.

Located in the far northeastern corner of Laos, the "rock" or Lima Site eighty-five was only one hundred thirty miles west of Hanoi. This navigation station would guide the US bomber forces to their targets inside North Vietnam. The bad news was that the base was situated in the middle of communist held territory. But because it jutted fifty six hundred feet above the plains below, with sheer limestone cliffs, the CIA considered it was impossible to scale in any force. They felt a direct helicopter borne assault was the only way to take it, something the North Vietnamese were unable to mount. Over a dozen Air Force technicians operated "in the black" alongside CIA staff rotating weeks on station with a crew in Thailand that would swap on duty stations. The Hmong had long revered Phou Pha Thi as a sacred mountain.

In January of nineteen sixty-eight, the North Vietnamese tried an ill-fated air attack with three old wooden aircraft. This failed attack buoyed the CIA's opinion that the rock was impenetrable. That lasted for three months when in one evening the NVA attacked the rock, scaled the cliffs, and drove the US personnel down the hill, hiding in cliffs along its side until daylight could bring air support. The Ravens and the Air Force tried to bomb the NVA off the mountain the next morning without luck. Their only success came in pulling some CIA and Air Force personnel off the rock. But over a dozen members of the Air Force were killed or missing in action, and that number is open for debate even today.

And decades after leaving South East Asia, Washington would continue to hide the fate of these men to their families.

In 1969 after the loss of substantial US military personnel "in the black", President Nixon in a speech would note that not one US military soldier had been killed in Laos. At the end of the War in Vietnam and Indochina, over five hundred and fifty men were listed as missing in action in Laos. The figures would be much higher if the list included those working "in the black" and those working for the CIA. Additional US military men also would be shot down after the war "ended", when these US flights would have been classified as illegal. The US would have never allowed these men to be placed on any list.

To the crazy lieutenant and the idealistic eighteen year old, whipping through a clear sky, none of this was history yet. We were on our way to fight in the war "over the fence". Only years later would we learn the significance of our actions. But it was a different war. Far from the large cities of Vietnam, another war was being fought over a piece of land that had nothing to do with South Vietnam, yet it did. It was no "secret war" to us, or to the Laotians, or the North Vietnamese, or the Hmong.

It was only secret to the American public.

Crossing the border into Thailand saw the sun ahead of us to the west dip over the horizon. It was time to sign out of the Laotian territory with the evening Air Force control ship, "Moonbeam".

"Roger Spud, Moonbeam copies you. Short night for you boys?" crackled the radio.

"Negative, Moonbeam, just moving our bags to the west for the duration," answered Koontz.

"Welcome to Air Force territory and good hunting up north," Moonbeam came back.

"Roger Moonbeam, hope it lives up to the billing. We're heading RTB Udorn," Koontz radioed.

Heading now to the base at Udorn we began dropping altitude. From the moonlight I could make out a flat countryside of continuous wet rice paddies where little hamlets of stilt raised homes, rose above the klongs or streams. I had heard this was a peaceful land, but it was hard to imagine there was such a place in this war. It wasn't long before the runway at Udorn stretched in front of us.

Touching down at Udorn we stopped quickly, able to catch the first taxiway off this incredibility long runway. Koontz and I both popped open our hatches, the warm evening air rushed in, carrying small whiffs of burned JP4 aviation gas from our engines. Ground control gave us directions to the revetments that held the Mohawks. The base was immense, the runway and taxiways neatly lit with numerous permanent buildings ringing the whole field. We approached rows of large concrete revetments that seemed like a gigantic car show, only instead of corvettes and GTO's, the vehicles in this show were every aircraft the American Air Force had on its roster.

Some I knew and some I didn't.

Koontz and I were dwarfed and overwhelmed at the size of the base. We finally turned into a row of revetments filled with F-4 jets when we saw Daze standing in the generator driven floodlights directing us in.

While I shut down the radios, Koontz killed the turbines whose high-pitched whine slowed down till we could hear nothing but the loud ringing in our ears. So loud was the ringing that I found myself yelling greetings down to Daze, who stood under my hatch waiting to help us off load our gear. Now backed into the revetment, our red and green navigation lights bounced their colors off the metal revetment walls into the dark night. I backed out of the hatch, my right foot momentarily catching the extended foot ladder as I bounded, off balance, onto the tarmac below.

"Just what I need," I thought then. "Get sent to Udorn and break your neck on the ground."

"Curry, good to see you man," Daze yelled grabbing my hand as I stumbled toward him. Daze nearly shook my arm off. "Hey man, I knew you'd make it. You're going to love it here, the women and the food are both hot."

Both of us walked over to Koontz's side of the cockpit as he mumbled to himself as he finished writing in the maintenance log. Putting the log away, he grabbed his rubber duck and threw it down to the unfamiliar crew chief standing below. Not sure what was tossed at him, the surprised chief snatched it in mid flight, causing the duck to emit a long high-pitched "squeak".

The chief's years in the military had obviously not prepared him for this contingency. Disbelief spread across his reddening face as the chief stared at the duck, then at us, and then back up at Koontz who was sitting there with a shit eating grin on his face.

Turning to the guys behind him, the crew chief muttered, "Jesus Christ, we got ourselves a real fuckin' nut cake here."

Koontz, not aware of the comment, jumped down from the cockpit and hopped in the jeep along with Daze and me. Daze drove off through the darkened revetments as if were a volunteer fireman responding to a call. Close on our tail, in a three quarter ton truck, were the rest of the welcoming committee.

"Gentlemen, the flights are all in, so let's hit it," he shouted over the roar of the wind and the jeep's engine.

As we rounded the last row of revetments on two wheels, we found ourselves speeding to a halt in front of a row of large steel buildings housing flight operations for the myriad flight units based here. Koontz, Daze, and I entered the first building, walking down the long dark hallway that split the single story building in half. I followed Daze through the first set of doors nearly tripping over a ping-pong table set up right in the doorway. The room was about fifty feet long and half as wide. The ping-pong table had a set of harsh fluorescent lights over it, outlining flight gear and garbage strewn along the wall. Further down the room was an old brown vinyl couch held together in places with duct tape. At the opposite end of the room, in the glow of a small desk lamp set on a huge wooden desk, sat Pappy.

Jumping up when he realized who had walked in, Pappy bounded around the desk, hand extended.

"Larry, Curry, welcome to Udorn. The guys will be happy to see you two. Especially Harry, he's getting nervous, wants to head back so he can DEROS out of this place and get home."

"Hey, Pappy," greeted Koontz, "great to see you. We would have been over here days ago, but you know Red. He wanted to get that few last missions out of us."

"Yeah, I hear they had trouble finding volunteers for the Laos run," replied Pappy. "But it got filled this afternoon, Jim came in out of the blue and asked Red for it."

There was an anvil in my stomach when I realized that Jim was cranking up the ratchet on his own private war.

"Shit. . . Oh, hi Pappy. Good to see you again, " I choked out, extending my hand to his. I had a lot of respect for this man. A captain with about ten years experience, Pappy had more brains and balls then most of the brass back in Phu Bai. Pappy turned to me and grinned.

"Good to see you Bob. Man, I had a hard time getting you. You really pissed off the old man back there with the several congressional inquires you started." I shrugged sheepishly as Pappy continued.

"But I argued I needed a guy over here with experience working with the Air Force on these trails, and you had it. But I think what clinched it was when I explained to the Colonel that you'd be out of his hair over here."

"Thanks Pappy, appreciate the help," I said, still thinking about Jim.

"No sweat, let's just get those fuckin trucks with license plates that read North Vietnam and have some fun. That's why in the hell we're here. Not to play Mickey Mouse games like they do back in Nam. Well, you guys ready to stow your gear and get some drinks?"

"That's a definite roger, Pappy," Koontz answered. "I've been waiting for this for the past month."

Daze had already split with the others. We followed out a side door that led to an alley that extended from the flight area toward what was essentially the main street of the Udorn air base. I hopped in the back seat of the jeep behind Koontz as Pappy fired her up and spun her around to the front of the building. We came out onto "Main Street", a straight as an arrow ribbon of new asphalt, and my mouth fell open. Solid permanent buildings lined both sides of the street. Air conditioners hummed and dripped water onto the concrete sidewalks. Across the street were a restaurant, a barbershop, and a bus stop where airman and Thai civilians smoked cigarettes and looked at their watches, . . . like commuters waiting to get home. This secret war was some friggin secret.

When Pappy started down "Main Street" I realized we were driving on the left side of the road. Taking a sharp curve at speed, I saw my life about to end in the form of a huge fuel truck speeding toward us in our lane. I threw my hands over my eyes, trying to duck on the floor.

"Jesus Christ, we're going to get killed in fucking Udorn," I screamed.

The truck whizzed past us on my right and I realized we were still alive.

"Bob, they drive on the left side here in Thailand," Pappy calmly explained. "Something they learned from the British."

Embarrassed, I sat back in my seat and promised myself not to do anything that stupid again, at least until we got to the hotel. And I kept my promise. While Koontz and Pappy carried on a conversation up front, I stared at everything we were buzzing past in the darkness. We passed a large compound that had a taxiway run across our road from the runway. Steel fencing and plenty of barbed wire surrounded it.

"Spook city boys," Pappy said, jerking a thumb toward the compound. "Air America, compliments of the CIA. They doze but they never close."

They laughed, but I continued to marvel as we moved toward to the north end of the base passing blocks of barracks, flight lines filled with massive amounts of aircraft. I realized my mouth must have been hanging open for some time when a mammoth insect flew in.

War is hell.

I've known war and suffering most of my life. I was born in the Lao village of Phou La Tai on December 12th in 1943; my father always thought it was 1941. I would be named Xay Dang Xiong. A war had already begun with the Japanese in our land, and my father would tell me of the fighting and the war between the Japanese and our French friends. Three years after my birth my family would move to Phu Fa.

By 1959, at fifteen years old I was recruited as a soldier as the rumors of a new war with our neighbors to the east, the Vietnamese became true. The French were fighting them all throughout Vietnam, and now the Vietnamese were bringing the war to our mountaintops. For Hmong, this is our home; all we wanted to do was live with our families, relatives, and friends alone on this peaceful country. When the war came here, there was no choice, we had to fight or leave; and then where would we go?

The Hmong in Laos were not many in number; many of our clans still lived in China. So when war threatened, we needed all our men to fight for us, so we needed to recruit all those students that had completed the fifth grade. I had only completed forth, but felt the call of duty to serve our country and people.

The American had replaced the French in Laos by the late fifties. They had met with Vang Pao and the elders and made a plan to fight the war together. The Americans hated the communists, and they could bring the food, medicine, guns and supplies we would need to drive them back to Vietnam. As planes began to appear around the villages by the Plaines de Jares, the Americans would come to teach and train us, to fly to find the enemy, and to fight the enemy with their guns and planes.

In 1961 I was sent down to Thailand to be trained by the United States Special Forces and Thai paramilitary on the use of these new weapons, the radios to communicate, and the tactics on how to defeat the enemy. There was a lot to learn in these three months, but I need to be the best soldier I could be. I excelled so well in my training, that they kept me in Thailand to help train the next class of three hundred Hmong warriors. We would become the SGU, the Special Guerilla Units of the Secret War. Our jobs were many, as Hmong, no one knew this land, these mountains better then us. We could run the high peaks and appear behind an enemy that was confined to the roads and valleys with his heavy equipment of war before he could get there. The airplanes and helicopters of the Americans could take us quickly to a battle of our choosing, and then fly away to fight in another place.

The following year I was called to Vientiane and became a Sergeant in the Lao Army, by now Vang Pao and the military leaders had heard of my dedication and knowledge and now needed me in the war to save our Hmong, our country. I became acclimated to the way to fight this war; soon I was sent to the village of Na Khang, located near the larger town of Sam Neua up in the northeast corner of the Laos panhandle. There we would fight the communists. We would take small guerilla teams to fire at their camps in the night, to harass them and take away their sleep. We would take several of SGU soldiers and go to the top of a hill and quietly watch the enemy move in the roads and valleys below. Sometimes we carried a box given to us by the American we could click in how many tanks, trucks or soldiers that were passing us. This box would talk to the planes in the sky to bring the planes and destroy them. The Vietnamese were mad, as they knew we were out there, but couldn't find us. They forgo this was our home, we knew it well.

We would watch for the planes, if a pilot was shot down, it was our job to quickly find them, and get them back to Long Chieng. The communist Pathet Lao were even more cruel then the Vietnamese soldiers if that was possible. We would do anything to keep a pilot from these treacherous souls. Our brothers who were able to sneak away from the hidden prisoner camps and caves would tell the stories of their brutality. These communists believed the Americans and Hmong were people that lived beneath them, and they hated the airplanes and those who flew them for the destruction they could bring onto their forces. So they would take their most evil people to entertain their soldiers with brutal mistreatment. They were treated like dogs; worked till they dropped, then beaten again. They were fed gruel not befitting a pig, and if they spoke they were beaten again. An arm of leg would be broken, an ear or nose cut off. And medicine was only for their soldiers. At night they were forced in cages made of bamboo where they could not stand. They would couch and sleep in their own waste. And then the day would start over again. We would pray they would die, to end the suffering. These prisoners were highly prized by the Pathet Lao and Vietnamese, they would hide them with large forces always on the move, away even from our eyes.

After fighting these guerilla fights in the hills surrounding the Plaines des Jares, I was called upon by the American Tony Poe to train more of our fighters. The war was becoming larger, more American planes were coming, more enemy were coming, we needed more soldiers. It wasn't long and the American farmer "Pop" Buell was asking for teachers for the growing town at Sam Thong. Pop Buell had come to Laos years earlier with the USAID people to help the farmers up here in the north. He was a very caring man who loved our people dearly. When the war came, and it was harder and harder to plant and grow crops, Pops had the American planes deliver food and medicine. He set up a hospital and clinic in Sam Thong to treat our people from war and diseases and ills of our life. He also built a school in Sam Thong to again teach our children too young to go to war, even though the war often came to them. Finally he asked me to teach, and I was honored to teach our Hmong youth the classes of their first to forth grade years. To be a teacher amongst the Hmong is a high honor and profession, in the midst of war I was blessed for but a short time.

But the war would not wait, and once again I was needed, in 1964 I was called over to Long Chieng by Van Pao and the Americans at the CIA and promoted to Sergeant Major. I was assigned to Phou Ke and Phou San and assigned one hundred twenty five men. There we would report on the enemy, where they were and where they were going. We raided them, ambushed them, and killed them. We were constantly rescuing the American pilots who not only fought in our war, but also were going to or returning from bombing in North Vietnam. The war continued to build, and word of promotions in the SGU, which related to payment for the soldiers and their families, was long absent. So one day we banded together and walked for days to Long Chieng. We arrived with two hundred soldiers in Long Chieng and went to the house of General Vang Pao who heard our complaints of our SGU unit receiving no promotions. He then instructed us to return the next morning.

Zero eight hundred hours we were standing in formation in front of the General home when he appeared with several officers. The General then spoke, "if you want to be a leader, you must tell us what you know to lead others."

We were most surprised when they then took us one by one to ask us, test us on what a soldier should know. We were asked the distance of a mortar, how to fire a mortar, a carbine. How we would defend a position from the enemy, how we attack an enemy position of so many soldiers. After all two hundred of us were tested, the General then told us he had written down our names and results and he would forward them to the King for a decision on our promotion. We considered this a fair method of determining our leaders and we would return and wait the decision. It was a month and sixty-four of us received word of our promotions. And despite our promotions we would all fight against those who would take everything away from us.

In June of 1964, my father who was in charge of the soldiers guarding Long Chieng went to General Vang Pao and asked the General as he was old, could he return to his village, perhaps his son could command troops for him.

General Vang Pao asked, "Your son is Xay Dang Xiong? I did not know that, he is so young?"

So the General sent for me.

208

When I came to General Vang Pao, he looked directly at me, with apprehension, as I looked so young. He asked, "you commander? You so young, how can you control a whole company of soldiers."

I had fought well, trained many soldiers, I knew I could lead if given the chance, so I confidently replied," If you let me, I will be good commander."

He saw the confidence in my eyes, he knew I was good, I could fight, and I could lead. Shortly after this meeting, my father moved back to our village, now serving as the Provincial Governor.

I was promoted to First Lieutenant and commanded soldiers to fight the enemy and protect our base from attack. It was at a battle at Lima Site thirty-six with the enemy that I was first wounded in my knees with a grenade. I was sent down to the hospital run by Pop Buell for three days and feeling better, I needed to get back to my men, to my command. In June my SGU unit was assigned to protect our borders and our country from the Vietnamese to pick up and protect any pilots shot down. Air power was vital to our success. We also knew what the Pathet Lao would do to any pilots shot down, Hmong or American. So went call went out that pilots were down, we would focus on quickly finding and extracting them back to Long Chieng. The first pilots I rescued were two Americans in 1967 near Lima Site eighty-nine at Ban Vieng. The following year we were on patrol near the Vietnam border with the American Jerry Daniel when we were able to extract another America on his way back from bombing in North Vietnam, his plane disabled, he was forced to eject over Laos. Then in September of 1971 my units were engaging the enemy on the PDJ when we altered our mission in order to rescue another two American pilots supporting our operations. We fought as a team, the American air from above, and the Hmong SGU soldier on the ground. We both needed each other; there was no other way.

The second assignment for my unit was to protect the mountain of Phou Pha Thi. This mountain was in the valley fifteen miles west of the North Vietnamese border rising straight up from the valley floor over fifty five hundred feet. This mountain was considered scared by our people.

On top of this mountain was a secret radar and radio site run by the American CIA we called SKY and Air Force people called the "Commando Club" or Lima Site eighty-five. We were told this base held the most secret American equipment that could direct their planes in all weather to bomb Hanoi and all the country around here. We were told we must defend at all cost, that these Americans and this equipment must not be taken at any cost.

The base had several large camouflaged truck trailers on top of this mountain with radio equipment, computers, generators and about eighteen Americans running all the special radar and navigation equipment. We were positioned mid way down the mountain to protect the approach from the east the NVA would use should they attack.

On January 12, 1968 we heard strange buzzing and looked in the sky to see two old North Vietnamese aircraft in the sky above. We had never seen enemy aircraft here before as they slowly approached the mountain. Suddenly we heard and saw carbine fire come form the planes, along with grenades, and mortar shells, we were shocked, these old planes made of sticks and cloths were attacking our mountain. Everyone started shooting at these planes, they moved so slow if was not hard to hit. We fired and watched one crash into a hill nearby. Then we heard a huey helicopter nearby, suddenly a soldier on the huey opened fire from the back and the airplane seemed to stop in the air, then fall to the earth. We had four Hmong dead, the attack failed, but this was not to be a good sign of things to come. Later that month one of our patrols reported a number of enemy battalions moving into the area.

In February we destroyed an NVA Artillery company and found drawings of the mountain and plans for attack. We heard that SKY was ready to pull all of us off the mountain as the equipment was too important to get into the hands of the communists, but that day never came.

By March we could see the enemy in the distance expanding Route 602, a road into the valley to the mountain. They used a bulldozer that the pilots would try to blow up. We got word to General Vang Pao to tell the Americans, that the mountain we felt would soon be attacked.

Then on the tenth, the NVA who had been building up in the valley attacked with artillery and mortars. We immediately called for airplanes; we knew they would try to take the mountain. I don't think the Americans thought this was possible as the attack was the fiercest. The enemy had battalions of troops, but we were holding them off at the base, but we needed help. There was a pause in the shelling, and then around one am in the morning, we heard shots on the mountaintop above us and the phone lines to the top were cut. What we did not know was the enemy had special soldiers who climbed the sheer backside of the mountain, where the Americans said was too steep. During the night this enemy climbed this straight wall and entered the base from behind. They walked through the camp and killed many Americans who were technical soldiers, not used to a fire-fight or gun battle with the enemy.

We fought through darkness hoping the Lao, Hmong and American planes showed up.

At dawn we climbed the hill with the SKY commander. At the top we got in another firefight, but found a number of the Americans still alive. We needed to get the Americans off as the enemy was too strong and would take the mountain. I watched as a helicopter approached under fire from the enemy with a net hanging below it. I watched as three American's threw themselves into the net to get away, to get off the mountain. And as I watched as the helicopter swung away, and the net broke, and these three American soldiers fell to their death. My heart stopped for a minute, I was so sad, my tears were many. And then I fought again, as the enemy kept coming. We fought on for days as the enemy was above on the mountain and below us. As the American planes came and blew up what was left on the top of the mountain, we left in the jungle we knew well to return to our base, to fight another day. While the enemy lost over four hundred those days, we lost thirty-seven Hmong soldiers, over one hundred and five were wounded, and the American lost all eighteen men in their secret war no one was to know of. We lost our scared mountain to an enemy that would kill us. We did not know we would lose it forever.

After the fall of Phou Pha Thi, we returned to Long Chieng, to then quickly go to front lines. The enemy kept coming, there were more and more of them and less and less of us.

Our Army wanted to retake Lima Site fifty, so I would lead the troops to this fight. On the day of the fight, we had our planes and American jets scream in low to the ground to scare the enemy. When they were confused, we came in quickly by helicopter and attacked. The fight was brutal, with many soldiers fighting hand to hand. We fought hard and we beat these Vietnamese killing over seventy-seven and wounding two hundred sixty. We lost three Hmong soldiers that day and it still deeply hurt, these were my brothers.

The enemy regrouped in the forests to attack again. We could not retreat, it was a two or three walk to Lima Site thirty-two as the river was too strong to cross. So that night we called for Spooky the gunship. There Spooky fired at the enemy killing many. They also dropped flares to let us see the enemy in the black of night. The enemy could see our men, and in the light of a flare I was shot in the chest and stomach. I was again flown down to Pop Buell's hospital, but the wounds were too severe, so I was sent on to the American military hospital across the river in Udorn. I was there a week before I felt well enough to return to my men.

I would return to Long Chieng and find General Vang Pao wanting to attack, to take Phu King. He asked me if we could do, so VP and I flew in a helicopter and looked at how the battlefield was arranged. I told him I needed twenty top fighters with others and in three days we would take. So we attacked, we surrounded the base and called in our T-28's to bomb the enemy. A group of my finest soldiers took the top. I was on the radio with them, told them to get down, the enemy was watching them from bunkers, waiting to kill them, and then my friend was shot dead as I screamed for him to stay down.

The next day, we fought again, sending twenty up to the top, keeping eighty at the base but the enemy fought tough. We were low on equipment, Lt Marcie did not have a flak vest on, and as I talked with him on the radio he was shot dead. I was losing my friends forever and the battle was not over. Then another day of fighting, our planes came and bombed and we took the top of the hill, we had beaten the enemy on the third day. Now I was going to the top of the hill and my radioman said he would come. I told him no, it was safer down below. He argued and I let him go up with me. As I walked on the top I saw my nephew go into a bunker, I screamed that the enemy had the bunker aimed in their mortar sites. He walked into the bunker as a mortar hit. I ran into the bunker and picked up his wounded body when two rockets hits. It was very bad, as the rockets tore into my face, my chest and stomach. My radioman called for help and I was flown out. At Long Chieng I was given morphine, as the pain was too much, I felt like I would die. Once again I was sent to the American hospital in Udorn, for a while I could not see, could not walk. It was there the American airmen and soldiers there taught me about football, I made many friends the month I was there. And then when my sight returned and I could walk, I returned to Long Chieng, to rejoin the fight of my Hmong. I was promoted to Major and in 1971 I was promoted to Colonel. I would spend the dry season of 1971 retaking the Plaines de Jares for my General and my people.

We would return to our tactics of earlier years. We were fast and nimble, but they're not many of us. Each year the communists sent more and more soldiers, and their weapons were larger and there were more of them. The spring of 1971 they began shelling our headquarters at Long Chieng. Now they had large artillery they were hiding in caves that the airplanes could not bomb. We needed to take the war to them, to destroy their supplies in order to send them away. So in June we attacked the PDJ with the tactics of quick attack combined with air power. We would call out our Hmong pilots, our Chaophakaow during the day, and the American fighters and bombers. And at night we would call on Alleycat to send us gunships to take out the enemy attacking or the trucks or tanks we could hear approaching in the dark. And then we would hear distant explosions of an enemy exploding on the other side of a mountain found by a plane we couldn't see in the black of night, a plane the enemy called "whispering death", the Americans called it the Mohawk. And tomorrow would come, and the war never ended, never took a break.

The word came in mid 1971 that General Vang Pao was concerned the Americans would be cutting back the number of planes that we could call on. So we needed to take the war to the enemy, remove them from our land. So in June we attacked, and we surprised the enemy with the furiousness of our attack. We used the planes and guns in the sky. And the Thai Army moved their artillery onto the PDJ to give us power from the planes beginning to go away. We put watch teams on the mountaintops to see the enemy to find where he moved. I had men at Badman and Rocket Mobile, Ohio, and Smallman. By the end of June we retook Ban Na. And in July we attacked with a second wave. We fought a bloody battle and retook Lima Lima, finally holding on to it. By September we again took Muong Soui and there was hope we could hold onto the PDJ.

The dry season and the expected NVA counterattacks were delayed as a typhoon hit Laos bringing everything to a stop. Then the winds of autumn began drying up the waters of the monsoon. Now as the dry season came upon us, we were beginning to get an uneasy feeling, that the Americans would grow tired, like the French before them. And now the Vietnamese would come back again, with more and more troops, with larger weapons. But we had no place to go, this was our home. Our families, our parents and grandparents lived in these mountains; they too suffered from the attacks, from the mortars and artillery. Our children screamed in the bunkers from the shells, from the explosions. And they screamed in their sleep from the dreams of death of those they loved around them.

And we would fight on, as our Hmong ancestors in the years and centuries before us, in China, against the Japanese, and now again the Vietnamese, because we were the Hmong of the SGU soldiers.

So this was the hot seat of the secret war. Our jeep buzzed around the east end of the ten thousand foot plus speeding to the base's main gate passing a maze of buildings that gave no visible clue as to what secrets were hidden inside. Finally we were up at the main gate waiting for the Air Police to check the cars entering and leaving the base. These guys were snappily attired in their crisp blue uniforms, white spats around their ankles, and white helmets polished so heavily I was sure they could send signals to Mars if they caught the floodlights at the right angle.

Finally the MP's saluted Pappy and we were off and running. It was a strange feeling to be driving at night, off base without weapons. Hell, the only thing to fear seemed to be the maniac drivers who in my book were driving on the wrong side of the road. Before hitting the main highway we passed a couple blocks of Thai shops. The signs offered everything an American airman half a world from home could need; tattoos, jewelry, sharkskin leisure suits, and cold beer. But it was past midnight now and the shops were all closed and dark, the chain link gates locked. We now drove through the darkened streets of Udorn on our way to our accommodations. The older teak wood Thai buildings were shuttered, built extremely close to each other. Even at this hour, the humidity and heat had many homes darkened but with the second floor shutters wide open, hoping for a breeze. Other streets had two story cinder block buildings with darkened shops on the first floors and living areas on the second floor. Dozens of cheap white Toyotas and Datsuns buzzed around us in the streets usually filled with loud drunken Americans egging the drivers to go faster. Several samlors, the bicycle powered carts that held one or two people were quietly moving local people on to home or work.

Finally we maneuvered through several tight streets and stopped in front of a six-story building. It was a local Thai hotel, Pappy parked in the driveway behind several cabs waiting for their next fare. We grabbed our bags and walked in. Two Thai clerks were in the middle of a discussion when they noticed us come in.

Without missing a beat, the discussion stopped and in pretty good English one of them welcomed us and asked our names. We answered, but our heads were on swivels as we looked around at what to be home for us. It was strange, we were to be quartered here, not on the massive base we just left which had to have a spare bunk or two I was sure. But then again, we weren't supposed to be here, we were technically still in Phu Bai, in the war that was everything but a secret.

"Ah, yes, gentlemen, we have been waiting for you," the clerk announced preparing his paperwork. This place was definitely not bad. A small hallway with some wicker chairs and overhead fans, a small restaurant now closed was around the corner.

I was tired with no clue what I had gotten myself into when the desk clerk interrupted me.

"Mr. Curra, we have you in room three-twelve, rooming with Mr. Tim." He was holding a key for me to take. A key, I thought incredulous, even the Mohawk doesn't have a key.

"Yes, ah, thank you very much," I answered, slightly dazed. Tim was a buddy who'd left Phu Bai a couple months before. He had flown right seat on that fateful mission over Laos with Shereck when they'd lost both engines. Both punched out in their ejection seats, Shereck's chute never opened. Tim broke his shoulder and arm on the landing.

"Hey Curry and Koontz," Pappy yelled. "Throw your stuff up in the rooms, meet us outside for some beers ASAP."

For the first time in six months I stepped on an elevator. It worked. I was hoping the rats I grew used to in Phu Bai couldn't reach the floor buttons here. Stepping off I soon found my room, used my key and was soon inside off the door, two small beds, two cheap end tables and dressers and a bath.

Simple by American standards, heaven by Phu Bai standards.

Tim wasn't here, so I made out which bed was his, by the assorted magazines and old socks and threw my gear on the bed closest to the door. I took my shaving kit in the bathroom and spent a couple minutes getting cleaned up. Soon I was out the door and on my way down.

I walked out of small was instantly surrounded by wooden tables and chairs. Despite the late hour, waiters were working out of the bar on the far end, delivering drinks to tables of drunken Americans.

Next to the bar was a five piece Thai band banging out a tortured version of top ten rock. I slowly walked around the pool trying to find Koontz

216

and Pappy, but I was also afraid if I moved too fast I would wake up from this delicious dream.

Weaving my way around the tables I ogled a parade of the most beautiful Asian women I had ever seen. Alone and in pairs, these young women were dressed western, hot, as they looked longingly out at the tables where they made their living at the world's oldest trade.

"Curry, over here," Pappy's voice carried from a table set back from the edge of the pool.

I made my way over to where Koontz, Pappy, and Harry huddled around the table filled with assorted drinks; some even had little umbrellas in them.

"Well kid, welcome to the secret war," Harry asked with a drink in hand ready to toast. Koontz and Pappy were already downing theirs. "Nobody knows you're here. Hell, American doesn't know we're here. It's us, the little guys, and that strange assortment of aircraft you saw back there fighting full divisions of uncles Ho's finest."

"Little guys," I turned to Pappy, "who the hell is he talking about?"

Pappy turned serious which I was not expecting tonight; " He's talking about the mountain tribes that fight the NVA for us. Their known as the Hmong, the hill people who fought furiously along side the French when they were here. Came down from China centuries ago and have been picked on by every ethnic in Southeast Asia. We can't have forces on the ground in Laos, so the CIA essentially employs the Hmong to fight the war on the ground for us. We're here to do everything we can from the air to cover their ass and keep Ho's boys as far away from here as we can."

"Ok, but how's that different from what we were flying down south over Steel Tiger," timed in Koontz who ordered another round of ice cold San Miguel, not that the type of alcohol mattered at this point in the evening adding, "you know Ho's trail."

"Well we all know the trail is Ho's supply line to his troops in the south, cut that off and he dies. That's what our operation Steel Tiger is all about? They've pretty much taken over the eastern side of Laos; we got some Lao troops holding the western edge along the Thai border but no way in hell are they capable of attacking the trail. That's why we bomb the shit out of it from the skies. Up here we got our op called Barrel Roll, the entire focus is to protect the Hmong, the little guys. They're more then a match against the NVA man for man, that's part of the problem. The NVA don't forget, they remember the Hmong fought with the French, gave them a good bloodying. So part is vengeance, they know the Hmong will always be a thorn in their side in the future. The second, they want to take Laos with them and the Pathet Lao they got marching in line with their ideology. The Hmong are the only thing between them and Vientiane, the capital of Laos. Win that and it ensures a Lao run by the Pathet Lao that gives them an uncontested Ho Chi Minh Trail for as long as necessary."

"Welcome to the fuckin chess game called Asia mates" slurred Harry who drank away the chip on his shoulder but now was getting tired of hearing about the war he was soon departing. "Now my only target is one of those sweeties flagging their asses around these tables, so shut up or take it outside."

The Thai waiters kept the drinks coming as we talked on into the evening. Harry was heading back to Phu Bai in the morning, flying back one of the Mohawks headed home for much needed maintenance. So they had all chipped in ten bucks each and hired the band. He had one week to go before reporting to Cam Ranh Bay for his freedom flight home. Then Harry pointed to the ladies of the evening.

"We call this the parade. The hard part is picking which one you want," Harry said, his voice wistful. He was going to miss this part of the air war.

"Once you do that, you just flick a finger with one hand and have twenty baut in the other, and she's yours for the night."

Koontz raised a glass, "to the secret war." Everyone joined in the toast. The conversation and the drinks wore on. First Pappy wore out followed shortly after by a fading Koontz. The crowd outside here thinned out as GI's joined the "parade" and headed for their rooms.

Harry and I drank on and made an incongruous pair. He was about fifty years old and a "lifer" Captain. At first he avoided me, figuring we had nothing in common. He was right, not the type a nineteen-year-old enlisted man would normally have a long conversation with. But if war made strange bedfellows, massive amounts of alcohol made for some even stranger friendships.

218

Harry opened up, as he grew more tired. "Yah Bob, I'm glad my flying days are over. But this is the place to make a difference, . . . a big difference. These little people up north are solid, they need our help and we need theirs," he quietly revealed.

"Harry, what are you talking about?" I asked naively, having no idea what he was talking about or what got him on this track.

"The Hmong . . . you know . . . the little guys. The Vietnamese who have no reason to be there are slaughtering them. There's no god damn who's right and who's wrong like in Vietnam . . ." and then his mind wandered off.

"Harry, what in the hell are you saying, what or why are you telling me?"

But Harry was loaded, now starting to drift off to a special place only he could fly . . . I looked around and the "parade" was clearing out. It was close to three a.m., the band was gone and the waiters were stacking chairs.

"Hey Bob, I got to head up, . . . but before I do, I bought you a welcoming present," Harry slurred. With that he motioned to a table under a tree, and a beautiful young girl came out of the darkness and sat down next to me.

"Jesus Christ, he bought me a person," I said to myself, a little panicked.

"Bob, this is Toy . . . I think . . . shit, doesn't really matter does it? She will take care of you tonight; everything's taken care of. Stay well."

And with that Harry was gone, lurching into the night. I never saw him again. I was so nervous, I felt myself shaking a bit. I looked at Toy, if that was her name.

"Hi Toy," somehow came out. She haltingly answered me; I'm not sure what she said. God she was young, but god so was I. She was dressed in a red miniskirt that showed off killer legs. I wasn't sure what to do. I had been shot at, had experienced the exhilaration of hunting and killing other humans. But I had never been experienced with this rented woman thing, sex you know. But I sensed something else was up, after all I was the newest and youngest kid here, now I was imagining the others huddled in the darkness with Harry, seeing if I would go with her. If I didn't I'd never live that down the rest of my time here.

As everyone was leaving I motioned the waiter over. It was show time.

"No problem," the waiter said, smiled waving off my money, and explained Harry had taken care of him well along with Toy. So I got up and walked a little unsteadily to the lobby. And my shakes were not from the booze.

Toy followed politely.

The elevator buzzed and the door opened to the third floor. We entered an empty hallway and walked what seemed ten miles to my room. Fumbling for my keys, I prayed, hoping there would be a gang of my buddies waiting to yell surprise and tell me the joke was over.

"Toy, just stay here a minute," I said as I turned the key and stepped into the darkness. Nothing. Puzzled, I reached in the bathroom and flipped a light on, praying now that Harry and Pappy to pop out and give me a hard time.

But all I heard was Tim's snoring.

Panicked, I stepped back out into the hallway. Toy looked quizzical as I reached into my wallet fumbling for a five or ten.

"Toy, thanks a lot, but not tonight." I said, handing her some money while steering her back toward the elevator.

"I'm sorry, but I'm sick," motioning to my crouch, as if sign language would explain away my insecurity. You know . . . the kind that wouldn't be good for your business."

Toy's eyes widened as she got the phony message. Smiling nervously, she put the money in her dress and stepped into the elevator. I double timed back to the room, threw some water in my face and slid between the cool damp sheets. Lying there, staring at the ceiling, I tried to put the evening in perspective.

I knew overwhelmingly high moral standards hadn't prevented me from sleeping with Toy. Fear was part of the answer. I had never trusted the Vietnamese; the friendlier, the more suspicious I was. Despite this hotel,

220

despite the patio, the drinks, the band, and the "parade" of whores; Vietnam and my ghosts were only a half-day away. This learning on the run was shit.

The next morning the sounds of Tim's gargling in the bathroom woke me. It was still real; I was living in the middle of a Thai village, city, whatever they called this. Waiting for Tim, I got up and started throwing my clothes and uniforms in the empty dresser. I was a kid in a candy store.

Tim finally stepped out of the steam and I began filling him on who was doing what, to whom, back in Phu Bai. Army politics, like office politics, are something everyone loves to gossip while protesting that they could care less. We were no different. After destroying several reputations, I hit the shower.

Ten minutes later we were downstairs, strolling out into the street and wandered down a block before entering a local restaurant for lunch. Flying night missions threw one's schedule and diet off and lunch often becomes breakfast. Coupled with the late night carousing and having not eating anything since before leaving Vietnam, my stomach sounded like a highland tiger on the hunt.

The restaurant was very neat, filled with four or five tables of Air Force pilots and crew starting off their day like us. A very charming Thai lady brought coffee to our table and presented us with menus.

"My God," I said out loud, I get to chose?" as I was handed a menu. I had long forgotten most people had choices in what they ate.

"Not too shabby, eh troop?" grinned Tim.

The American version of their menu started with various egg dishes, then my eyes stopped on five different versions of hamburgers. And the prices ended at one-buck American.

I was hard pressed to make a decision, because for the last year the Army always did that for me. Big, ugly cooks in T-shirts and sprouting nose hair throwing heaving haunches of mystery meat and fourteen pound dinner rolls on a metal tray defined chow before. Life was much simpler, but infinitely duller, then.

I demolished two burgers and four cokes before Tim and I headed for the "office".

Each set of roommates had their own vehicle to get around with and Tim drove our jeep as we headed toward base, taking the long route through Udorn. The city was bustling with people speeding everywhere. The Thais, devout Buddhists, were definitely at peace with their God because they drove as if they were in a hurry to get to heaven. Samlor drivers cut off cement trucks; Toyotas passed buses on the left and right, horns were in the permanent on position. It was a beautiful, colorful anarchy here. The Thais, unlike the Vietnamese, dressed like they drove, in bright western clothes. Just above a Shell gas station was a billboard advertising a Thai Western, complete with cowboys and horses. It was hard to imagine that this close to the fear and destruction of Vietnam, an Asian city was advertising Wild West movies, and did I mention, a bowling alley?

Once on base we headed over to our operations building meeting up with Pappy, Harry, and Koontz. Harry had already flown back to Vietnam with one of the Mohawks; replaced with the bird we flew over.

"You guy's are going up tonight," Pappy informed us matter-of-factly. "You'll each be going up with an experienced pilot until you get used to flying out of Udorn."

While giving us the nickel tour of our new facilities, Pappy explained the unit had three aircrews to fly two nightly missions. Ideally this meant a schedule of two days on, one day off. That was if there was no illness, extra missions, or worse, shoot downs. We had three ships in revetments on the flight line, with access to near perfect maintenance facilities, compliments of the U.S. Air Force. Pappy had also put together a first rate crew on the flight line. Three crew chiefs and a sensor systems expert kept the up time on the planes higher then that of the ships flying in Nam. Then the Intel guys, ready with light tables, magnifying glasses, and marking pens poised ready to unravel the secrets of Ho's boys we caught on the film from all the nightly missions

"Looking good Pappy, nice digs," Koontz, said looking at the clean and spacious facilities. Well, clean according to college dorm standards.

"We got better up time here than back in Phu Bai," Pappy said, a little pride creeping into his voice.

Pappy explained that this happened while fighting for parts from competing crew chiefs back at the 131st. I asked him how we were able to get any parts sent here.

"We buy 'em if we can," Pappy laughed. "We can't afford any maintenance failure here. When we fly north to the Plain of Jars, we got to get over the mountains ringing it that rise to about ten thousand feet. If we lose an engine up there, we aren't getting out. So I take these things pretty seriously. We got great access to the Air Force PX's here in Thailand. If our boys back in Phu Bai need some of those personal items of luxury missing there, we get it for them. Of course we want first cut at needed parts, if they got em, they owe us, right?"

Koontz and I exchanged grins and spoke in unison.

"Improvise."

Piling into his jeep late that afternoon, Pappy explained that he and I were flying the first flight that night; with Koontz following with Tim later. It was a short drive over to the afternoon mission briefing at the 7th Air Force flight operations.

 The base looked even more massive and well laid out in daylight, totally unlike anything I'd seen in Nam. Moving slowly through base traffic I was particularly struck by the prim and proper look of the airmen here. They were all neatly shaven; hair cut to the same short length, uniforms properly pressed, shoes shined.

"It can't be the same war," I kept thinking to myself. In the war we had just come from, everything was chaotic, unkempt; the uniforms were crushed and faded, with a permanent red hue from the dust and clay. But more striking was the look of the troops. In "our war", the eyes were hollow and uncaring; here the bright, determined look of the airmen was at first unnerving. Because they were, and weren't, in the same war.

Passing bored Air Force guards, we entered an informal briefing room, the walls covered with maps and photos of northern Laos. Seated at a wooden desk poring over a set of reconnaissance photos was a short, intense man of perhaps thirty five, looking out of place in civilian sports clothes. Looking up, he greeted Pappy and Kyle, and then rose to shake our hands as Pappy introduced Koontz and me.

"Larry, Bob, I'd like you to meet Major Secord. He's running the show here, his people will get the intelligence from the previous evening's missions, match it up with Air Force intelligence and then establish the game plans for our missions," expounded Pappy.

Dick Secord shook our hands, joked a bit and tried to explain his role in the part of the war we were now entering. This secret war in Laos had two theatres of operation. Steel Tiger was the air operations directed against the Ho Chi Minh Trail in southern Laos. Koontz and I had flown that hairy theater out of Phu Bai for the previous four months. The Udorn operation would find us flying largely in operation Barrel Roll, the code name for air operations in Northern Laos.

"You'll be flying in support of the Royal Laotian forces fighting in an area known as the Plain of Jars," Secord explained. "These are mostly Hmong tribesmen and they are fighting experienced North Vietnamese Regular Army divisions. This is not a picnic."

Secord went on to explain that unlike their fight in South Vietnam, the NVA in Laos were using conventional tactics with large forces, artillery, tanks, and radar guided anti-aircraft guns. It was these more heavily mechanized units that we would be trying to find, and help destroy in operation Barrel Roll. He was in charge of the air operations here in Laos reporting to Ted Shackley, the CIA Station Chief. Besides the air ops he had put together the Hmong small observation teams they'd drop all over Laos to report on where the NVA was and where it was moving. The CIA boys back home kept trying to drop a wide range of electronic toys on top of Secord to help find the trucks. From devices that smelled urine to those that tired to detect engines running in the jungle, they went by public relations invented names like McNamara's Line, Igloo White, Mud River, etc. Secord was happy if they left him alone to his devices, the Hmong observation teams that used a simple counting box they created called the Hark box where they quietly tapped the number of types of trucks and vehicles into it, a plane flying by would pick up the transmissions and they'd have accurate human intelligence. Unlike the electronic urine detectors that the NVA routinely defeated by tactics like hanging sacks of elephant urine though the jungle.

The entire war was planned and run from this non descript building across the road from us. During the day the Air Force would utilize jet fighters, like the F-4 and F-105's to bomb targets called in by "Raven" FAC pilots. Additionally the Laotians and Thai's would fly T-28's and A-1's in close air support of the Hmong. Weather permitting, this air support could help guarantee at least a stalemate of the constant NVA drive to move across the Plain of Jars and threaten the secret Hmong and CIA base at Long Chieng. Growing bolder by the month, the North Vietnamese were skillfully using the cover of darkness to move men, supplies, and their tanks into position against the Laotians and the Hmong. Their forces were formidable, convoys of dozens of trucks and tanks moved along established roadways with names like Route seven or Highway seventy-one.

Our unit was known as the Night Hawks, our job was to use our radar sensor equipment to play nocturnal traffic cop to this unimpeded NVA traffic. We would fly silently in the blackness of night, like a hawk over the Plaines, hunting for our prey. Mission times would be determined at these daily briefing, staggering takeoffs and flight patterns to keep the NVA off guard. Once in Laotian air space we would report in to the airborne Air Force C-130 cargo plane, customized to house a crew operating computers and radio equipment that coordinating all air activity in their sector. Additionally they coordinated all communications from the Hmong and our forces "in the black" on the ground. Once we've located some targets, Alleycat would match up a strike aircraft to take them out. Up here we'd be working with F-4's, 105's and the C-130 Spectre gunship.

"Each night that command ship is code named Alley Cat," Secord said. "And be advised the Pathet Lao have announced cash bounties for any crew member of Ravens, Mohawks, or Spectre Gunships. Dead or alive."

Secord further explained that he and his people would review our evening's activities and kills early the next morning. Truck kills and anything suspicious would get high-speed photo recon runs by F-4's the next morning, their results ready for our afternoon briefing. Everyone was adjusting their war, trying to outplay the other side for a quick advantage.

It was highly organized, and effective, and during the briefings I found myself studying Secord, as much as what he was saying. Secord struck me as an extremely intelligent individual, razor sharp, hungry for any details that would surprise the enemy he seemed to genuinely hate.

Later after working with Secord for months. I found him an individual who thrived on the thrill of unconventional warfare. There were few rules to go by, and Secord wasn't against breaking those. He reminded

225

me of what Heine Aderholt told him, "You can always break a rule once." His style pissed off a lot of the starchier Air Force brass, but he pissed off a lot more NVA and Pathet Lao. They were used to playing against an enemy with a rulebook, that went to the sidelines every down for the next play. Secord made his plays on the go, for the NVA he had a daily, and often deadly surprise. Secord was also an accomplished pilot with over two hundred missions flown in Vietnam. It was during flight status he gained the attention of Major Harry Aderholt, who was the now the Commander of the Air Commando unit at the Air Force's secret base at Nakhon Phanom on the eastern side of Thailand, on the Mekong River bordering Laos. Some say far enough away from the stuffed shirt brass to keep them at bay.

Aderholt was a believer in a different kind of Air Force to fight this war. He wanted slower moving attack aircraft that could stay on station to keep the war on the enemy, not swooping in and dumping dumb bombs on a moving target at five hundred plus miles per hour. He wanted to sit on the NVA's back and keep shooting till he called uncle, or better yet, stopped saying anything. So his Air Force looked like the mothballed veterans of the Arizona desert had been given a second chance here in the jungles of Southeast Asia. We had O-1 birddogs, A-1's and T-28's from the 50's, and A-26 bombers re-enlisted from World War II. He took some Army star-scopes off rifles that let them see in the night and strapped them in his planes to hunt trucks on the Ho Chi Minh trail at night.

Heine had been responsible since the beginning of the American war in Laos to get weapons to Vang Pao's men and with Bill Lair to open up small landing strips called Lima Sites throughout Laos. He was also responsible for support of CIA operations in Asia and needed someone to organize and run the secret Air Force missions into Laos at night. After service in Laos, Secord would continue on the black ops side of the Air Force rising to Major General before retiring. His name would dot the history books of the last part of the twentieth century as his and Heine's brand of military fighting would finally be recognized in how America would fight the new conflicts of the 21st century. Close work with indigenous forces, advantages of night fighting, and the value of the flying gunship were all methods proven in the secret war decades earlier.

Secord was part of a nebulous group of military men who traded in their uniforms to fight the war "in the black." They became part of an unlikely, clandestine stew that included US Embassy political officials, career CIA operatives, out and out adventurers, Air America and the often over used indigenous Hmong army to fight this war.

This new breed of military man was developed who had to learn to fight a war in with special ops, to operate whole armies under an alias, to learn how to bring the war to the enemy in the dark of night when we had the advantage. And to do it without committing a half a million men to a war many had no choice. Many of these principals would get their feet wet in Laos, commit their body and soul to a cause and a people who felt allied with us. And many watched a government sell both out when it was time to shift gears.

Secord finished his welcoming speech and Pappy and I stopped off on the way back to the Air Force map room so I could get the detailed coordinate maps of Laos, North Vietnam, and southern China. If we were hunting trucks on my first mission up in the PDJ, I wanted to study every river, road, and hilltop these maps would show me before I got there. I was already used to Southern Laos with the spread of the Ho Chi Minh trail, I knew it like the back of my hand. I knew every river bend, every hilltop and sensed where the roads were. Now I knew where these trucks were headed up here, and this time it included families and children. The stakes were bigger here, and I couldn't waste time up there figuring out where I was. I couldn't let a truck get through now if I could help it.

The first set of maps broke Laos into segments or pieces. They had details of mountains, hilltops, valleys, rivers; everything I would need to plot the black dots. These were the movers that represented the trucks and tanks full of death headed against the little guys up here. The radar imagery that would scroll in front of me on every mission displaying its own topographic map of these same rivers, bends and hilltops. The black dots or movers would appear, many times along the known roadways up here. Names like Colonial Route Seven or Route Seventy-Four; they were basically rutted dusty or muddy routes that ran along the contours of the land up here that could handle trucks without spilling them over a crest or into the deep jungle. Once the movers or dots showed up, I took a set of protractors scaled to my map. I would then find three distinctive landmarks, a hilltop, a river bend, etc and retrace these paths of the protractor on my map with grease pencil. Where the paths converged was where I'd find my trucks or tanks. More then often, they would be on one of these dirt routes heading as fast as the roadway allowed. The hunt part done, I passed the coordinates on to Alleycat, and they would bring in the strike aircraft or gunship to take them on and out. This strange partnership of Army and Air Force worked in total harmony over the battlefield unlike those of in the hallways and conference rooms of a headquarters a million miles away. The C-130 and C-119 gunships were accounting for over fifty per cent of the truck kills over Laos. When flown in combination with the OV-1, these truck kills increased over sixty per cent.

Back at our Ops, Pappy stuck his face in the maps while Kyle and I got involved in a high stakes game of ping-pong, a game that became a tension relieving ritual before each mission, distracting our keyed up senses while waiting for takeoff. After being soundly whipped in Ping Pong, Pappy was satisfied with his mission preparations and we decided to eat again. We had an hour before our mission took off, so we walked across the street to a restaurant with more pretty Thai waitresses. He promised me they had meat that hadn't first come out of a tin and that was marinated in transmission fluid for several days. Oh, you could cut it with a knife he said. Hell, a grenade wouldn't even have phased some of the mystery meat in Phu Bai. With it I inhaled a garden salad, this was a first, in Nam anything this green and leafy would have been first rolled and then smoked.

Six o'clock rolled around and as Pappy and I strapped ourselves into the cockpit, the sudden exposure to the good life at Udorn was forgotten. This was a combat mission, and twenty minutes after takeoff the territory would be as hostile and more deadly then any mission over Vietnam. Maps in place, equipment checked out, we taxied in rush hour traffic and jockeyed for takeoff position. It was the evening mission rush hour at Udorn, with all traffic heading in the same direction . . . north across the Mekong, some would call it "the fence" into Laos.

Here another kind of "parade" began with every imaginable plane in the American inventory out there. The jet jocks sat in their muscle car F-4's, revving engines, ready to punch the envelope after takeoff. The large truck like four engine C-130 Alley Cat was out there ready to send its daytime counterpart home for a rest. Two small Thai T-28 fighters straight out of a World War II movie taxied behind several unmarked Air America STOL cargo planes. And then there was us, the bastard child of the US Army, waiting for an anxious fifteen minutes before our turn came for takeoff.

Finally, with a short takeoff we were free of earth and buzzing north toward the Mekong River. As we banked, I watched the traffic in Udorn scurrying through the town like a group of gas-powered ants hurrying toward a candy bar before dark closed in. Roads running north out of Udorn entered a flat land of never ending rice paddies occasionally separated with small groups of huts. This was the Midwest of Southeast Asia where rice was king and very little changed, no matter what foreigners arrived.

Traffic thinned to almost nothing as we approached the winding Mekong River. The first town across the river in Laos was Vientiane, its modern day capital. Vientiane was a movie set for a modern spy movie with the accredited political missions of the competing powers, communist, the west, and those in between, courting the world's journalists and each other. Factions that planned deadly war tactics against the others by day drank tables apart in the old French cafes at night.

You couldn't see that from a Mohawk, but at night the lights of Vientiane blazed unmolested, protected by an unofficial truce that kept the town off limits to combatants on all sides. Only miles away, hidden in the blackness, the dying continued.

The landscape changed dramatically as we headed north from Vientiane. The paddy field countryside rose sharply into cloud piercing mountains, with verdant jungle following the sheer slopes of the mountains to the top. The mountains became islands in a stream to us, the stream being the densely forested valleys that fell away to invisible floors. Since crossing the Mekong we had been climbing steadily, gaining altitude to get over the range. After avoiding the peak of the tallest mountain, Phou Bia at ninety-two hundred feet, we descended into the menacing Plain of Jars.

I was glad I was along for the ride; well at least until now, as I watched the incredible landscape changes. Shortly before entering the Plain of Jars or the PDJ, we flew over the secret CIA and Hmong base camp of Long Chieng also known as the Alternate. Even after the war, the "town" was not even listed on maps. It was here General Vang Pao commanded his Hmong fighters; Air America based their operations for Laos, and the "off duty" Air Force FAC pilots and Forward Observers known as Ravens or Butterflies worked from. From here in any direction was unfriendly territory. Control and allegiance of other towns on the Plain depended on the season; one day run by friendlies, but subject to new management overnight.

Our job in the Plain of Jars was to find the troop and supply trucks, tanks, and artillery pieces heading from North Vietnam.

Our first run on the plains that evening was done in the fading sunlight. The flat plains ran about forty miles square before the mountains shot skyward from the earth again. Beyond those mountains, to the north and east, was patient, deadly North Vietnam. Further to the north lay the vastness of China, and the all weather highway they were building through Laos toward the Thai border.

Our first run picked up "movers", trucks or tanks moving on Highway Seven near what American aviators called the "Roadrunner Lake."

"Alleycat, this is Spud two-three with movers," I radioed on my first find of the new war.

"Roger, copy Spud. Can you give us coordinates and number" Alleycat responded.

Comparing the imagery on the sensor screen to my map I radioed, "Roger Alleycat, four movers at Victor Lima eight two six seven niner two."

"Copy Spud two-three, we'll see if we can round up some guns up here, looks like the night's starting early."

Win some, lose some; my first "movers" won the race down Highway Seven, as Alleycat did not have any gunships on station yet. Night was fully upon us now as I listened to the radio traffic from Alleycat to the air traffic heading in and out of the area. We flew "Christmas Tree" up here, all our navigation lights on until the shooting started, as the air traffic did get tight at times.

Another forty-five minutes passed before we picked up moving ground traffic again.

"Alleycat, Spud two-three, we got six plus movers north on seven one" I stuttered excitedly into the radio.

"Roger Spud, hold please. Spectre three-three, Spud has movers north on the plain, six plus, can you move." The conversation crackled in and out before Alleycat came back.

"Spud, we got Spectre three-three heading north now, please give us those coordinates."

I excitedly double checked my measurements, then keyed the mike, "Alleycat, Spud two three, six plus movers at Victor Lima four five two six seven seven, copy?"

"We copy Spud, Spectre three-three, you got that?"

"Roger Alleycat, Spectre three-three copies, on station in three minutes."

We sped east, hunting for more traffic, waiting and hoping to catch a glimpse of the C-130 Spectre gunship, which was a truly awesome weapon. We had grown to love these gunships while hunting over the Trail in southern Laos. Each Spectre had four 7.62mm miniguns hanging out the left side along with four 20mm gatling cannons. Located forward of the guns was a starlight scope that could "see" in the darkness to locate the target. The Spectre advantage was its ability to circle in slow orbit over the target, virtually sitting on top of it, ready to rain death. And it had the fuel and ammo to sit out the most tenacious enemy.

We never saw the Spectre until its tracers poured from a black hole in the sky toward the inky land below. Since they flew low and slow, they never flew Christmas tree, not wanting to be a better target for the antiaircraft guns on the ground.

When operating with fighter support, a beacon on the top, invisible from the ground, alerted the jet jocks above to Spectre's location.

"Jesus Christ Bob, look," Pappy roared over the intercom. I looked to Pappy's side and saw a river of red tracers pour out of the sky, melting into the ground below. Suddenly, the ground exploded into first one, then three, then more hard burning fires. The Spectre was ruining some NVA's cruise over the plains this evening.

"Alleycat, Spectre three-three, we got a convoy down here. Hit four trucks, the rest are scattering, we will stay on target."

Pappy and I screamed so loud, I was sure those ass whipped NVA on the ground below could hear us. My first mission up here and we were stopping traffic. We continued for hours before the adrenalin was replaced by a cautious kind of fatigue. We were doing our job, but I understood now why the NVA hated our pilots so much.

Getting low on fuel, we signed out with Alleycat and headed home after another day in a very strange office. By the time we flew south over Long Chieng, Koontz and Kyle were on station to replace us. As we left, Spectre three-three had finished the first contact with nine confirmed truck kills. We had reported more traffic, but were off station before we heard the results of our find.

We arrived back at Udorn, finding the runway busy with flights returning, and being replaced by a seemingly limitless pool of aircraft disappearing north or east into the war.

Pappy and I made the shutdown second nature. Climbing into the damp evening air we were back in the peaceful unreality of Udorn. I wished my Phu Bai buddies were here to share this part of the war. At least in Thailand, you could eat and sleep in peace. I made a mental note to drop Jim a line. After quickly returning our flight gear to the Ops building we headed to the club to await Koontz and Tim.

In the club we ran into Daze, and Herman, our sensor repair tech. Nursing beers time passes quickly. Finally the time until Koontz and Tim showed up, walking the walk and talking the talk.

"Got us a gang of movers," Tim boasted, ending the never mentioned tension over whether your buddies would get real unlucky that night.

They had followed our successful night, with a Spectre gunship and several flights of F-4's working over their "movers." We naturally disparaged their success and they ours. Off by ourselves at a table, I found myself staring at the neatly uniformed airmen, half of whom wore civilian clothes now. Staring back at our group I realized Koontz and I were still in our flight suits, forever stained from Vietnam's endless reddish clay. Our hair was now obviously a month past a reasonable cut, and those of us who shaved could have used one. I seemed to imagine some airman returning my stare, trying to figure us out.

"Rat Patrol" Tim offered. I looked at him now realizing he was following my gaze.

"They call us the Rat Patrol," continued Tim. "Most aren't sure where we fly or what we do. And our appearance rankles some of the brass. But, they're not sure how to handle us, who outranks who. So they call us the Rat Patrol. Believe me, stranger dudes then us find their way through here. Especially the Air America crews."

Within a week, Koontz and I were flying together again. It didn't take Koontz and I long to get into the swing of things here. There was a lot more radio traffic up here, as we now had to take into account Vang Pao's troops on the ground. There was also an increasing amount of Spectre gunships and F-4's available for our targets. Vang Pao's troops were in constant trouble, and it was felt that if air power had saved him before, it could do it again. But from the volume of the missions over the Plains, even we could figure out that they must be running short of the Hmong soldiers to do the dirty work on the ground.

Several weeks after we arrived, Josh Winter showed up to replace another short timer heading back to Nam. Now at least I wasn't the FNG, or the fucking new guy designated catcher for all the ribbing. He brought with him rumors the 131st Aviation Company would soon move down to Da Nang. Maybe Nixon's talk of reducing the troops would soon affect the air units, we could only hope. 1970 had been a "successful" year for Vang Pao and the CIA in Northern Laos. Operation Leapfrog began in August, with Pao's troops helicoptered across the Plain of Jars by Air America. Battle after battle went successful for Pao.

But not without some of the heaviest air support of the war, Vang Pao, who had seen the devastating power of B-52 saturation bombing, continued to demand more. And America, bent on turning the war back over to the Asians, turned up the heat. The Raven FAC's, flying their 0-1 Birddogs, were flown ragged during Pao's attacks, trying to control and direct the massive air attack.

By the end of 1970 the CIA became concerned Pao was stretching himself too thin, with his front spread across too much of the Plain. It had happened too many times before with the Hmong advancing in hard fighting before the North Vietnamese diverted new divisions to drive Pao's men back across the plains. The CIA finally delivered an ultimatum, no more air support if Pao continued his wide run across the plain.

Pao stalled, knowing he was the only game in town for the Americans. The inevitable happened, Royal Laotian Regular Forces holding Muong Soui; the critical town protecting the plains, retreated toward Vientiane again at the first sign of the NVA equipped Pathet Lao. Vang Pao's irregulars, holding positions to the north and east, were cut off again. A sea-saw battle began raging across the Plain, swinging inexorably in Hanoi's favor.

Spring of 1971 saw the NVA sweep across the Plain, attacking both Royal Thai Artillery positions and the Vang Pao's Hmong at the Raven's base camp at Long Chieng. A steel noose was closing in on the forward bastion of the "little guys." In previous years civilian refuges from the war of devastation were moved to camps south of Long Chieng. But the scale of the latest offensive, and ten years of war, found close to two hundred thousand men, women, and children faced with running again. Only by the spring of 1971 they were out of running room.

It was this grim phase of the war that Koontz and I entered, with the North Vietnamese holding chunks of the Plain of Jars that put them within shelling range of Long Chieng.

While holding those forward positions, the NVA continued moving massive amounts of supplies and materials into the Plains. Not a night went by that some of our "movers" didn't turn out to be Russian built NVA tanks or 175mm artillery pieces being towed into position. And with the stepped up offensive our Mohawks began taking massive amounts of antiaircraft fire nightly.

Even the formidable Spectre gunships, circling in their low orbits, were regularly taking hits. American fighters were routinely on station to take out the antiaircraft guns, with F-4's or 105's following the river of red tracers down to their NVA source.

On a scorching May morning Koontz and I had left the hotel early to jawbone with Secord about traffic we were picking up moving off the main roads. Alleycat and the gunships had not found these movers, and I was concerned similar sightings would be ignored as faulty readings or equipment. When we entered Secord's domain, we found him bent over, looking at a filmstrip of F-4 photos of someplace on the edge of the plains.

"Good afternoon Major," I uttered to get his attention.

"Afternoon Bob, Larry," Secord responded, rising up with the photos still in hand.

"Take a look at these guys, what do ya make out," handing the strip to Koontz.

Koontz put it on the table as we both strained our eyes at the clear black and white photos. The F-4's cameras would continuously shoot pictures as they streaked low across the terrain.

The motor driven photos were taken so close together, I had often been tempted to put them in a stack, holding one side steady with my thumb, then quickly riffling them, creating that cheap movie effect I had seen years ago in a Boy's Life magazine years earlier. That morning the picture's showed a stand of trees just off the plains with what seemed to be stacks of boxes underneath.

"Boxes of something, I'm not sure what," I mumbled, still looking at the photos.

"Here, try these", Secord grinned, handing us a high-powered magnifying glass.

Still no luck, Koontz reluctantly agreed to figure out what was captivating Secord; after several more minutes, we still hadn't got a clue of what we were looking at.

"Toilet paper, it's fuckin' toilet paper! The entire toilet paper supply for the NVA Army for the entire wet season," Secord reported triumphantly. A gleam in his eye said he felt a miracle had just been handed to him.

"I going to lay an Arc light on those woods. I'll have a flight of B-52's blow up their whole fuckin' supply of toilet paper," Secord laughed, hitting stride. I looked to Koontz and then laughed along.

"Why not, I thought, the whole war's a load of shit anyway."

"Those jerks will be wiping their asses with wet leaves for the entire wet season," Secord continued.

God, it'd be beautiful, the whole fuckin' North Vietnamese army pissed off and shitty every day of their war up here."

Koontz and I looked at each other again and laughed with Secord. It was brilliant in a perverse way, I wasn't sure it required B-52's, but what the hell.

The subject turned serious again, to our off the beaten path readings. I had been picking up a large amount of traffic moving south of Route seven on every pass now seemingly in the middle of the jungle along a cliff line. But the Spectre's couldn't find anything but the heavy tree line leading south from Route seven to a cliff. Secord looked intrigued and said he'd look into it; maybe send in a photo recon ASAP.

Our job there done, Koontz and I returned to the war that evening, finding a column of tanks moving across the middle of the Plains. Alleycat had several flights of F-4's digging in the column's metallic ass as we headed for home. We were excited about the kills, but disturbed about the increasing NVA traffic. They seem to have more vehicles than we had planes to destroy them, and it was getting worse.

The next day's briefing had Pappy and I back to Secord's briefing room. He had been up in Vientiane that morning in a huddle with our "in the black" military team coordinating air action.

"You guys were right, Curry," Secord, said as he handed me a set of photos. "The NVA had put a road under the tree cover just south of Route seven. I had an F-4 photo run in at daybreak. He saw the goddamn trucks on his first pass. There was a Raven FAC in the area who got in some Thai T-28's who finished these guys off."

I looked at a series of very clear photos showing at least ten burned out truck hulks. The jungle cover had been burned away, clearly showing a rutted dirt road that had gotten a lot of use.

"The Raven took some hits and put it in the dirt north of Route Seven, Secord continued. "Luckily we had an Air America chopper in the area that pulled them out. We got eleven trucks . . . burned all morning. They were combination gas and ammo trucks. We'll have to add this to our maps, once they get these trucks pushed out of the way."

Pappy was now staring at the photos while I thanked my lucky stars they found something there. It didn't help to fly the trail if people thought you were seeing or hearing things.

Secord began to fill us in on the changing game plan. General Vang Pao would soon be launching a counter attack. They've been getting shelled every night since early in the year. The plan was to launch a counterattack, hoping to drive the NVA off the Plains.

"So be careful when looking for traffic. Pao's boys are going to leapfrog by helicopter again," he warned. "From one mission to the next, territory may have changed hands at least once.

Pappy and I flew together that night, with takeoff at twenty three hundred hours. We reached the Mekong quickly and heard Alleycat inform us all air traffic was to hold at the Mekong and not proceed north. Of course no reason was given.

"Arc light . . . they're putting in B-52 strikes on some unlucky fucker," Pappy explained. "They always do this, don't want us flying underneath when the bombs are released."

We flew in circles for about twenty minutes, thinking about the lights of Vientiane below, wondering who was planning to do what to whom, over cocktails.

Then the sky to the north lit up as the air rumbled with the sound of a hundred trains passing. The mountains on the south edge of the plains lit up in a red blue glow. The strike appeared to be going in about a hundred miles north of us. It was awesome to feel the explosions this far away. It ended with the all clear from Alleycat to proceed north.

"I wonder what they hit, had to be something big?" Pappy questioned.

"Toilet paper I'd presume," I answered and then stopped, to catch his reaction. I then explained the previous days conversation with Secord as we flew north on our evening hunting trip.

"You think that's funny," Pappy challenged. "Secord and Heine got ordered up a mission to drop soapy dishwater on the Ho Chi Minh trail near Tchepone. Someone delivered him and Heine over one hundred fifty thousand pounds of the detergent in steel drums. They broke them down into brown bags and filled the back of several C-130's for drops on three separate nights. The idea was to dump them on hairpin turns or tight spaces to cause accidents; the last drop plane got shot up pretty good. Thought they'd make the trail too slippery to use."

We both laughed, but figured maybe it threw the NVA off guard for a day. If we couldn't stop them, at least make their life miserable, or their trucks cleaner. And a shiny clean truck blazing down a jungle road would be easier to pick out.

Years later Heine Aderholt would tell me of the operation where he bought out all the beer at Nakhon Phanom, and sent folks down the road to buy out all the beer at Udorn. He had everyone at the base drink all the beer and load the empty cans on a C-130's that he then bombed the trail with. Bizarre was an important ingredient of the cat and mouse war effort.

Traffic picked up later that evening, but more appeared to be heading north and east, away from Long Chieng and Sam Thong.

Part of the spring was taken up breaking in the FNG. Josh was like a kid in a candy store. Every night he'd rush back to his room, change quickly and hit the bars. Many nights I'd plain join him. But god forbid if my flight came back late, Josh was on a constant, one-man mission to spend each evening with a pretty lady.

Getting dressed for an afternoon briefing with Secord, I kidded Josh about his exploits. The former virgin from Minnesota was making up for all those lonely nights he had spent shivering back home.

"You know Josh, knowing your luck, you're going to find the one with clap that makes your parts fall off. You been lucky so far, but how do you go home and explain that one?"

With a grunt and a wave off from Josh we headed out into the heat. We had time before the briefing to head "downtown" and stop at a couple shops. The price for gold jewelry was incredibly low. Some of the older guys had already bought several gold chains with huge medals hanging from it. Worn with their black evening party suits, they seemed impressive, at least to themselves.

Josh and I walked around several blocks visiting the local jewelry stores, filled with every imaginable ring, chain, and necklace. Strangely, to us, all these shops were run by Indians, who we'd sense later, was fueling a growing resentment and jealousy of the Thai working class.

On our way back to the jeep we walked thru an outdoor bazaar, roofed with colorful sheets of silk. Each tightly packed booth, under the breezy roof, had sets of tables piled high with every imaginable item; cheap clothes, Japanese radios, ivory jewelry, and knock off Omega watches. The bazaar was also home to the "local pharmacy" with pot, hashish, and opium, all neatly packaged in UPS brown paper. The dope sales pitch was invariably by an older Thai, who, minus most of his teeth, explained the products, were flown in fresh from Laos.

"Quality you can't find anywhere else," he promised. It was interesting that even with the NVA now controlling most of the Plain of Jars, the opium poppies still got through.

I was reminded it was lunchtime when we passed the popcorn style chicken booth; where plucked chickens that had been dipped in bright green, red, or yellow solutions were hanging from a rope by their still intact head.

The buzzing flies they attracted convinced us to find lunch elsewhere.

That afternoon at the briefing, Koontz and I got the word we'd be flying up further north to get intelligence on China's all-weather highway running out of southern China into Laos known as the Chi-Com. Intelligence put the number of engineers and troops protecting it at twenty five to thirty thousand troops with heavy antiaircraft protection. The road originally thought to innocently link two Chinese provinces together over a slender area of Laos, now broke off and headed due south through the Khouang Province toward the Plain of Jars and some feared on to Thailand.

Secord's people had intelligence it was bringing in NVA troops who first traveled across southern China to enter Laos at this western point. It was a roundabout route but kept the NVA out of range of our air strikes.

Koontz and I took off at zero-one hundred hours, sobered by the knowledge that we would have no company on this flight. Koontz had his rubber duck along; I was hoping he was right about that luck thing. A half hour later I checked in with Alleycat, advising him that we were passing through his control sector. We got a short "roger" as traffic was heavy in the plains that evening and they had all they could handle.

Koontz flipped off our navigation lights now, no air traffic where we were going.

We turned on the radar mapping systems over Long Chieng as Koontz broke off to the northwest. We were on our own now as the loss of the mountaintop base of Phou Pha Thi years ago meant we had no additional navigation information as we neared China. We'd have to read the radar imagery and plot our position onto maps whose accuracy we were leery of.

Instead of talk about home, we talked about the war up here.

"Shit, we could be flying possibly against Chinese antiaircraft guns," I said.

Koontz said he heard that Pao's men might make a move on the Phou Pha Thi Mountain again. "It's a sacred mountain for the Hmong. The CIA spooks may go along with it 'cause they got intelligence some of the Air Force men captured there in '68 are still being held in caves there."

The mention of prisoners ended that conversation.

About fifty miles northwest of Luang Prabang we started picking up movers, a shit load of traffic along a north to south roadway. This was the Chinese highway, the traffic splitting off toward the ancient capital.

We were nervous enough on other missions, when we had plenty of friendly company. But we were now on our own and had to take the film, find our way in and out of here, while hopefully not pissing off some antiaircraft gun unit below us. We flew north for another hundred and fifty miles tracking more movers then I had seen in one place since over-flying the coastal highways of North Vietnam.

I tried to plot our movement north, but our maps were turning out to be as inaccurate as we'd feared. Koontz was attempting to plot distance by time and compass, but it was educated guesswork. We sure wanted to get all of the film, because I didn't want to come back anytime soon.

"Jesus Christ Larry, I think we're here," I yelled into the intercom pointing to our map.

I had picked up on our radar film a couple of unique bends in the Mekong River to the west.

If I was right that put us almost a hundred and twenty miles into China.

"Son of a bitch," was Koontz's response as he compared the picture on the radar film to the map of the Mekong. The map didn't show the blanket of jungle too well, but every river bend and island matched.

240

It was clear we should have turned a half an hour ago.

Koontz put the plane on its side as we headed south at great speed. We had our film and would continue to map again as we headed home.

It was quiet now, with the drone of the engines and our fast beating hearts the only sound we would hear for a while.

Awhile lasted ten minutes, and then our sensor unit began buzzing and flashing yellow and red lights, indicating Chinese radar units were attempting to lock onto us.

Koontz and I were frantic as we peered outside waiting for the telltale sign of red tracers heading toward us. We weren't scared yet, that would come later.

Now we were busy searching into the darkness waiting for the rising fire balls that had tried to engulf us before. Koontz had the throttles to the wall heading south, southeast. The further south we flew, the more the radios crackled as we began to get back into range of our planes over the Plains.

The antiaircraft fire never came, but someone down there was keeping pretty good track of where we were. It was time to attempt to check in with Alleycat.

"Alleycat, Spud two-two checking in, position somewhere northwest of the PDJ," I spilled into the airwaves.

Then came a garbled, " Spud two . . . bandits . . . advise . . .Angels 2 minu. . . , then silence.

"What in the hell was that?" Koontz asked as we waited for more information. There was none.

"Bandits, great," I said. "Now we'll get shot down by some gook MIG."

"Alleycat, Spud two-two, please repeat, coming in garbled," I asked.

Still garbled, the words hit home.

"Spud identify your position, we have bandits out of China, heading one five four to the Plains. Angels in position."

"Jesus Christ Koontz, that's us, they're going to blow our fuckin' asses away," I yelled, watching the reality set into Koontz's face in the warm red glow of the instrument lights.

"Alleycat, that's us god dammit," Koontz said frantically, keying the mike. "Call them off . . . here listen to rubber duck . . ."

Koontz frantically squeezed his rubber duck letting out his high pitched 'squeak'.

The radio was silent except for one very clear word from Alleycat,

"Fuck . . ."

Seconds seemed like days, and then the radio crackled.

"Spud, go Christmas tree immediately, think I got Angel Flight ready to blow your ass away."

Koontz's hand never moved faster as our navigation lights instantly came on. Then to our right two sets of navigation lights went on and off as American fighters streaked over our heads.

My heart was pumping so hard; I thought the veins in my neck would burst.

"Shit, we were that fuckin close to becoming a kill for some jet jock," Koontz nervously said over the intercom.

"Spud two-two, you guys almost bought it. We picked you up fifteen minutes ago, as no friendly traffic was listed as heading out of China, we assumed you were bandits and scrambled fighters out of Udorn."

"Alleycat, we will be RTB Udorn to clean out our pants, have a good night." I now calmly radioed.

The trip to Udorn went quickly, we were on the ground and quickly shut down in our revetment. I took my sweaty helmet off, gathered my maps and gear when Daze appeared under my hatch.

"Pappy wants to see us ASAP," he yelled up as the turbines wound down.

Koontz was already down and in the truck as I hopped down and joined them. We figured Pappy had heard about the excitement tonight. But it was four a.m. so surely an ass chewing could wait until tomorrow, couldn't it?

The three of us walked into the darkened Op room with Pappy sitting sternly at his desk.

"I have some bad news for you gentlemen, "Pappy began as he rose out of his chair. " No day off tomorrow or for a while, so I want you guys to get back and go directly to bed. I want everyone's ass back down here at fourteen hundred sharp, got it"

"What's up sir," asked a confused and tired Koontz.

"I've been with Secord's people since we got back earlier. Genera Pao's launched his summer offensive to take back the Plaines," Pappy answered as he headed toward the door. "They can't afford to lose men like they have in the past years, they got an entire generation that's almost been wiped out. We got several Thai artillery units ready to be inserted on the west side of the Plaines to support him and Dick's trying to get all the strike aircraft we all can handle. Some F-4 recon film has detected a group of Ho's tanks near Ban Ban heading west. We got a lot at stake, see you both tomorrow."

With that Pappy was gone and Koontz and I stared at each other across the darkened room with the now quiet ping-pong table. "Well shit, that was my ride to a nice soft bed that just walked out that door," complained a still puzzled Koontz.

"Well, I'm grabbing a ride back with Daze when he's done with the plane," I answered. "Ping pong anyone?" as I picked up a paddle and threw it at Larry.

So we whiled some time away playing ping pong in some deserted warehouse early one morning while the shells fell not far away on Long Chieng, south over a ring of ridges surrounding the Plain of Jars. The NVA this spring has introduced the new 105-millimeter artillery they hid in a number of caves surrounding the PDJ. On rollers they could be fired at will and rolled back in the cave to hide from our attack aircraft.

Now the city of Long Chieng was home to a bizarre collection of the forces fighting the communist forces. First this was the base of General Vang Pao's Hmong army forces known as the SGU, or Special Guerilla Units. These army units consisted of Hmong men from the ages of ten to those over fifty still alive. These units moved in guerilla attacks against NVA or Pathet Lao forces. They also were dropped in small groups as forward seeing eyes looking for enemy movements or depots. And there were units dispersed to the various towns and Lima sites that would hold ground and protect the Hmong homes and villages.

Part of Vang Pao's forces included the Hmong pilots for the Lao Air Force who flew the CIA provided T-28's in support of their Hmong troops on the ground, or against communist targets throughout Laos. These slow flying aircraft were fearlessly flown over the treetops in order to drop their ordinance directly on the target.

Then throw in the American Special Forces units that worked the ground with the Hmong, trained their troops or consulted with their leaders. Add some CIA case officers always moving in and out of Pao's units planning, cajoling, or paying the forces needed to get the end result.

Now toss in the sheep dipped pilots that were known as Ravens, or earlier in the war as the Butterflies. These were Air Force pilots and enlisted men who became part of the Air Commando operations that took them through a process of sheep dipping, that of removing their connection to the US Air Force and setting them up with new ID's so they would fly in Laos as civilians in order not to violate the Geneva Accords on Lao's neutrality. These FAC's would fly slow moving O-1 Birddogs, or sometimes the T-28's in order to direct in the fast moving fighter bombers on the proper targets. They were up at the crack of dawn and teamed up to be airborne until the sun went down. That's when we went into business. At night our sensor equipment would see through the black of night and locate the trucks or tanks moving against the Hmong forces. Once we located the target, we passed on the coordinates to Alleycat who determined priority in targets and assigned the proper strike aircraft to take them out. To the Hmong, the OV-1 was a set of flashing navigation lights in the night sky over the Plains or mountains, followed by the sweet sound and smell of burning armor and the crackling of ammo or supplies being burned off in the night that signaled another NVA unit they avoid fighting.

Now consider the families of these Hmong soldiers who lived with them. They suffered from the same shelling and attacks of the NVA. They tried to manage a home however mobile, raise children, and daily find food so they all could survive. Many of these women, children, and elders also called Long Chieng their home. One of many homes in a consist life of moving as the enemy attacked or retreated, as family members died or were wounded. Tonight they were hiding from the NVA artillery fire, hoping stay alive to face another day. Another day that only offered the certainty of more of the same.

Daze walked back the in the HQ as Koontz announced to no one who gave a shit that he had trounced me in our early morning set of table tennis. The excitement has wakened him up now and he bored us all the way into the city on his new found skills in ball rotation and spin control. Daze just gave me a threatening stare all the way back I'm sure blaming me for creating this monster. Christ it was always my fringing fault for everything that went wrong around here lately.

The ringing was getting louder until it finally invaded my dream. I was trying to understand why my girlfriend's head in my dream was obnoxiously beeping until my hand reached out and knocked the alarm clock off the stand. Now I'd have to suffer the routine of laying there for a minute trying to figure out where I was, who I was, and what in the hell was I getting woken up for. It didn't help finally figuring it out; as there was no other plan, no calling in sick, or just saying I quit, send me home. So my routine continued like every day, shower, flight suit on, and out the door to find my buddies for much needed food and the commute to the office.

The weather was clearly getting worse as we drove in the early afternoon heat to the base. The land was almost flat here just south of the Mekong, so you could watch different weather cells moving across the horizon for a fairly long distance. On clear days you could watch individual clouds with its own thunderstorm moving through the city or on the other side of the base. Today was gray skies with the sound of huge thunder in the distance, but that was the monsoon season in Asia.

Not sooner did we get to the flight line than Pappy had all of us flying tonight on our way to the CIA headquarters, or its official name, the 4802 Joint Liaison Detachment just down the road.

When we got there the place was crowded with numerous people tripping over each other transferring phone calls, pulling out maps, or shuffling papers. On the other side of the room, Secord waved us over. We went into an over sized office with a number of folks I hadn't met. And most I wouldn't as he quickly wound into a discussion of what was going on.

"Gentlemen, things are going to get real interesting for awhile. You know our advantage is the wet season and the NVA is going to dig in as supplies and reinforcements are screwed for him till he gets the weather and roads back. General Vang Pao will launch his offensive tomorrow at sunrise to take back as much of the PDJ and surrounding territory he can grab. Pappy, any thoughts on recent traffic, movers?" Secord asked.

"Well Dick, there's been a lot of activity around Roadrunner Lake out by Ban Ban. Gotta think they're hiding a lot of shit, might try moving it if they sense something?" replied Pappy. Sitting behind Secord was Hugh Tovar, the CIA Station Chief.

"Is that where you found the hidden road along the ledge?" asked Hugh.

"Yah, we recently picked up movers back there, but no one ever found traffic there before. No clue how long they had it?" responded Pappy.

"Makes sense, you know Ho's boys are going to swing resources already up here to counter attack anything the little guys try. I'm grabbing as many sorties as we can, so you should have gunships as soon as you are on station. Let's start out east and see what we scare up. Good hunting folks" and with that Secord and Tovar were quickly out the door immediately sucked up by a line of guys clamoring for their attention.

Back to the flight line with the first crew grabbing a bite across the road before they were off rolling and heading north to the PDJ. Pappy was off with Daze trying to bribe the Air force for some parts or supplies.

Given we were the second flight out, I was alone with no place to go, so I decided a catnap would be in order. I dimmed the lights and crashed shortly on the duct-taped couch. Somewhere around nine my attempts at sleep were interrupted when Daze walked through the door. "Pappy's ready to roll" as he turned the lights on. I rubbed the sleep out of my eyes, grabbed my survival vest, helmet, gloves, and ejection seat harness and followed Daze outside.

246

I loved this part of the day as we walked in the darkness to the flight line. We strolled past the dream machines of a youth in love with planes. Directly across from us was the B-66's that flew up to meet the flights of B-52's coming up from the south. This bird's new mission in life was to jam the various radar and communication systems of the NVA in the path of this flying destruction. Then the slender bullets of the F-105 who flew to protect the B-52's and direct their own weapons and bombs on the plentiful targets in Laos and North Vietnam. Our Mohawks were housed in revetments next to the Waterpump project. Another "in the black" project that trained the Lao, Hmong, and Thai to fly and bomb with the old US T-28 prop plane, originally designed as a trainer. Now with beefier engines and various weapon systems it was quite the force over the hills and jungles of Laos. The T-28 truly found its mission here in Laos. All the time, the smell of JP-4, the aviation fuel served as a great perfume and backdrop to this collection of performance and weaponry. The quiet was only broken by the sound of tire squealing from planes floating back in from their night of missions.

Then rounding the corner I could hear the roar of a generator and the harshness of several floodlights drowning the plane in white light as the yellow safety pins were being pulled to ready for flight. Pappy was doing his preflight check as I looked at the green maintenance books for signs of trouble. There were a number of notes talking of upgrading some of the SLAR radar system; Daze must have worked on the plane constantly since our return.

Shortly thereafter Pappy gave the thumbs up, and we jumped up on the extended foot pedal to boost ourselves though the open hatch. Several minutes of strapping ourselves to the ejection seat and we were ready to fire up the engines. Pappy looked for Dazes hand signal and then started up first number one, then the number two engine. As he went through his control surface check with Daze, I set all the radio frequencies to be ready for tonight's show. The engines quickly ran up to a high pitch buffeting the cool night air through the open hatch. The floodlights were extinguished and moved out of our way. Pappy flipped the navigation lights on as flashes of them bounced off the revetment wall.

A quick call to the control tower and we were soon on our way traveling the taxiways past the various revetments of fighters and bombers, many now empty as they were already in the war somewhere over Laos tonight. As we exited our revetment, we passed the Waterpump planes. We were parked next to the 1st Air Commando team that trained the Lao pilots before sending them straight to war up north. Tonight the flight line was down to four T-28's. They're pilots served until they were shot down, killed or captured. I was thankful we had an alternative exit plan.

With little traffic at this hour we sped down the taxiways, at times momentary becoming airborne as we hit bumps. We waited for several F-4's to take off, and then we were soon racing north in the black sky to join the battle over the fence. As we crossed the Mekong River that separated Thailand from Laos, the lightening became more animated up ahead.

"Time we gained some altitude." Pappy spoke breaking the silence. I cleared us in with Alleycat as we flew north we quickly gained altitude, finally hitting ten thousand feet as we cleared Phou Bai Mountain on the south edge of the Plain of Jars.

"Spud one-four, we have Spectre up ready to continue the hunt, advise with movers", barked Alleycat from the radio. Wow, they said the Air Force was dedicating more gunships, we just weren't used to having them waiting for us.

"Roger Alleycat, we will see what we can dig up tonight, take some pressure off the little guys," Pappy replied. Man, everyone was on the edge of their seats tonight.

It didn't take us long; there had been a lot of activity on the east side of the plain. Pappy and I were heading over to the hidden road we had found near a cliff by Roadrunner Lake. As soon as we started mapping we picked up a set of five to seven dots or movers indicating the number of trucks was much higher, as if they ran close to each other we wouldn't pick up everyone."

As I keyed the mike I announced, "Alleycat, Spud's got seven plus movers at x-ray delta niner seven six three niner two" figuring the plus was just artistic freedom.

"Spud one-four, we got Spectre three-one heading your way, good hunting"

So the show was starting early for us, but that's what we get paid the big bucks for. Suddenly at my two o'clock position I watched a ribbon of red streak out of the sky impacting in puddles of red in the ground. The tracer rounds were so intense I could make out individual trees in what had been the sheer blackness of the jungle below us. It wasn't long before white secondary white explosions on the ground began setting things on fire, more explosions bursting as the river of red moved further along a predetermined path.

Up in that Spectre gunship was a team of gunslingers that was proving the most deadly prescription for providing massive and precise gun power. A pilot, copilot, navigator, and flight engineer flew the C-130. In the main cargo bay was the targeting control group consisting of a fire control officer, ECM systems operator, and the infrared and LLTV sensor operators. Then they'd have the gun crew consisting of an illumination operator, righter scanner and three to four gunners. We'd serve as the long eyes for this Hunter killer team with our side looking radar looking out and locating movers from a distance of up to fifty miles. Once we located the coordinates, the Spectre would cruise to the location, there the fire control team would operate their close-in infrared to pick up the trucks or tanks we had detected. Once located the LLTV operators could visually see the trucks on their TV screens, determine if real or decoy, types, etc. Once they opened fire, the unsuspecting truck drivers and crew could be seen reacting, bailing out, or dieing in place from the gunfire so intense a bullet would fill every square inch of a football field of fire that had erupted in seconds. And the C-130 could stay in this low orbit so the guns never gave up until everything was dead or dieing. The other alternative had always been fighter jets dropping a load of bombs on a target and streaking away. The NVA soldier could always hope there weren't more jets, but with the Spectre, this bird was flat out not going away.

The red rain continued to fall as Spectre alerted Alleycat it had found a number of T-76 tanks and assorted trucks and were still pouring it on. We were still mapping but staying in a wider orbit in an attempt to see what else was moving out in this target fertile area. Then Pappy saw the muzzle bursts from about ten miles out.

"Spectre three-one, triple A on your nine o'clock" he quickly broadcast. We watched the Spectre continue firing for a few seconds as a number of anti aircraft bursts exploded close to where the Spectre was poring out its tracers. Then all went black as we wondered.

"Spud, thanks for the call, that was close," replied Spectre three-one as it switched gears, "Alleycat, we got some 37mm triple-A, you got some fighters covering for us?"

Up here the NVA had all the tools a modern military force only the scope of a superpower would have to call on. Their tanks, artillery and anti aircraft guns were the latest available in the Soviet or Chinese inventory. And the triple-A, or anti-aircraft artillery was fearsome. Unlike the jets that could streak through at five to seven hundred miles an hour and be gone, this OV-1 and the Spectre were doing several hundred plus. Slow and low was great for giving fire, but also deadly when caught in their sites from a fast firing 37mm, 55mm or larger.

Alleycat called, "Spectre three-one, we got some phantom's in orbit, appreciate some coordinates."

Pappy and I had been guess-timating off our map boards where the gun flashes first occurred since we saw the firsts burst head up.

"Spectre, Alleycat, we have an estimate of x-ray delta seven three-three niner two two," offered Pappy.

"Spud one-four, roger; Alleycat, we'll do a low pass on Spuds coordinates and do an infrared and camera pass and see if we can get a fix," responded Spectre.

"Roger Spectre, will hold Killer flight till confirm"

Several minutes of no chatter and a blackened sky seemed like eternity.

"Nice call Spud one-four, Alleycat, we got a pair of thirty sevens at x-ray delta niner four three niner four zero, we'll put some rounds in to highlight, and then Killer flight can do the nasty" radioed Spectre.

"Roger Spectre, Killer Flight on the way"

I laughed, how appropriate, my call sign given to me back in Vietnam when I started the Lao missions was 'killer." In a minute we watched a short squirt of red rain leave the black sky and impact on a spot on the black below. It was soon followed by a massive barrage of triple-A streaking back up into the sky in an angry response. What these pissed off gunners didn't realize was they were broadcasting to a flight of F-4 Phantom fighters already streaking down their throat from above exactly where they were. Within seconds the whole hilltop where these triple-A batteries were poised on blew up in massive multiple explosions as the five hundred pounders found their target. The ammos started cooking off as we could watch individual explosions lighting up the tree line.

"There you go, delivered on time and hot from the oven", cracked the Phantom jocks as they shot off for a refuel and rearm, "it's your show now."

"Roger Killer two-two, thanks for the hammer, we'll take care of the rest" responded Spectre.

And as to add insult to the occasion, the Spectre opened up all its guns on the hilltop. Whatever soldier survived the F-4 bombs perhaps wished he hadn't as the Spectre raked the hill tops with thousands of rounds to insure they'd be peace and quiet that evening.

"Ok, Spud, ready to go back to work" inquired a now satisfied Spectre. "Rockin and rolling, we got more movers if you still got the appetite?" I replied as my note pad strapped to my left leg was filling with coordinates and number of movers. We both blasted our way through the evening, as it seemed the whole of the NVA on the Plains was moving somewhere tonight. Another two hours and Spectre three-one was RTB back to Ubon having exhausted its ammo and getting low on fuel. We headed north to at least map any traffic for the Intel guys, or at least allow Alleycat to notify a Hmong firebase or Lima team for some hostile fire.

By the time we finished and were ready to head south for home the bad weather we had forgotten about since getting here had started moving in over the plains. The bad news was major thunderstorms had entirely filled the skies we'd have to fly through to get to Udorn. We had no forward looking weather radar, all the Udorn tower could tell us was the storms cells were rising well over twenty thousand feet and climbing. We'd have to take a straight line and punch through as we were now flying blind.

"Let's shut down the Slar now and hope we don't get bounced out of this thing," Pappy advised as our cockpit bubbled in glass was dark except for the red glow from the instruments was being buffeted by gail like winds and rain that was unending. As lightening lit up the sky, it lit up the gray clouds streaming outside our bubble of glass. It was as if we were riding a bucking bronco in the middle of a huge wet cotton ball. The sound was deafening as we bucked our way south to safety. These monsoons were enormous with the power to rip apart anything in its path. Pappy and my eyes scanned all the gauges. Where we right side up, was the oil pressure ok, what about the temperature? We had ten thousand foot mountains in our way and we needed both engines to get over them. I was beginning to sweat in the cold; I had forgotten we could die this way. Did it make a difference, somehow by gunfire was not welcomed but almost expected, but this; I could die like this back home?

In the corner of my eye I saw Pappy struggle, he had the stick forward all the way to the instrument panel, as if putting us in a dive to death. Then I saw the altimeter; it was spinning, but up, not down.

"We've caught in an updraft," he screamed over the intercom, I stared at the altimeter and realized we were streaking up over fourteen thousand feet and it wasn't stopping.

"Pappy, look at the altitude, we got no oxygen..." I cried out. We both stared at each other for a second, Pappy then concentrated to push the stick forward, now applying more power hoping we'd break out of this before...

Before we lost consciousness; once we were over twelve thousand feet we should have on board oxygen, the higher we went the more our brains starved from the lack of it. Somewhere real soon we'd black out and that would be it. The Mohawk could carry the oxygen, but we'd need bottles, masks, equipment the Army never thought of ordering. Now we were passing sixteen thousand, somehow it seemed quiet now, I saw Pappy's silhouette bouncing against the straps of the ejection seat, fighting the stick, but it was quiet now, not a sound, was this how it started, or ended?

"Jesus Christ..." Pappy's voice broke through my trance. I quickly looked back at him, he was still fighting, but something was different, but what? It was upside down, inside out, but what?

252

The stick was back now, in his chest, not against the instruments, he had pushed the throttles forward as I looked at the instruments to figure out what in the hell was going on. The rain, wind and darkness were still slamming us. Then I saw it, the spinning, the altimeter, it was going the other way, and faster then greased shit. Christ, now we headed toward the earth like a leaf or twig and still we had nothing to say about it. Where was the mountain, when will we hit, we were passing through eight thousand feet, did we make it past Phou Bai sticking up straight at ninety two hundred?

"Got no fuckin control, we're caught in the middle of one of these god damned cells" Pappy tried to explain. I watched Pappy fight and struggle with the controls, I could only watch, helpless in keeping us airborne. Now we were fighting to stay up above the ground. What in the hell else could go wrong, there was no logic here, we would toss up, down, sideways, the engines would roar as they fought the gail winds outside as we were trying to claw our way south, south to safety. There were no radio calls up here, this mother of a storm had us all to herself, and only she would decide when it was over. That was unless the Mohawk couldn't stay together anymore. In the glow of the lightening strikes I watched the wings flex up, then down, the strain was unbearable as if I was watching my own arm trying not to break under the pressure.

We broke out of it somewhere south of the Mekong River when we suddenly came out the clouds into black and rain. Now we could see lights of the villages and huts below us, and below us was a good thing. The radio suddenly worked, people were talking, guiding us in, and it was if something, someone had finally let us go, to fly away for another day.

As we rolled to a stop part of the way down the runway at Udorn, Pappy and I both popped our hatches, for air, but also perhaps to assure ourselves that we knew we were down and were getting out. The sweet smell of burned JP4 fuel waffled into the hatch as the turbines buffeted the cool and wet outside air. We chatted as if nothing much had happened that evening, after all it was over for at least today.

As we turned into the taxiway for our revetments, there was Daze standing in the downpour with his signal lights directing us to the front of our parking stall. Pappy pulled both throttles back and shut down the turbines. As I pulled my helmet off, I shook my head hoping my ears would pop and I'd be able to hear what ever Daze was yelling up to me standing under my hatch.

"I hear you guys broke some altitude records out there," I made out Daze yelling. Unable to respond with anything approaching smart-ass, I threw down my helmet and maps catching Daze off guard. Then I quickly swung my ass out the hatch as my foot searched for the footstep. Hitting it, it was then a hop to the ground, the beautiful ground. "Always a smart ass" I feebly responded in kind.

It was now going on two am; we had made it back with ten minutes worth of fuel left and both wings, not a bad night considering. But we had also confirmed over twenty-seven truck kills that night, including two T-76 tanks. That was definitely going to make a dent in what the little guys would be facing in their fight kicking off tomorrow to take back the Plain of Jars. As we spoke, crews were reading the helicopters, O-1's and T-28's that would kick off the ground assault against an NVA who didn't get a lot of quality sleep this past night.

That felt good.

Hmoob Saum Qaum Huab/Hmong Over the Clouds
Chapter Cuaj

The first Lao pilots of the secret war began with France's attempt to help the newly independent Lao Neutralist government fight off the communists by forming the Royal Laotian Air Force or RLAF. The French military trained the first group of Lao pilots in Algiers and Morocco while the United States delivered ten T-6 aircraft to the capital in Vientiane Laos. The T-6 was felt to be a simple airplane to train, fly, and maintain, as it had been designed in the 1930's as a trainer for the American Army. When the French withdrew from Southeast Asia, the Americans increased their military and economic aid to Laos and soon determined that a larger Air Force with better planes was needed. So the US Air Force Air Commandos were sent to Udorn Thailand along with the stronger T-28 aircraft in the early sixties. The Thai airbase at Udorn south of us was growing fast, and soon Lao pilots and student were being sent to the Commandos who named their secret operation "Waterpump" to train the Lao to fly the new T-28's.

The early days of the war saw the American Butterflies who were now living with us in Laos flying each day to find the enemy and direct the fighters and bombers into the target. Before the large number of American aircraft showed up, the Lao or Thai Air Force did the majority of the air attacks. Soon over thirty of these T-28's were in Udorn, with many students busy learning how to fly and bomb targets.

Each Lao student spent over two hundred hours learning how to fly and fight with the T-28. They learned instruments, formation flying, rocket firing and direction, bombing angles, how to drop napalm, and how to strafe enemy positions with the .50 caliber machine guns. Soon hundreds of Lao pilots were flying these T-28 airplanes out of Vientiane for battle in the north and in the south toward the Ho Chi Minh trail.

As the war grew, General Vang Pao went to the US Ambassador repeatedly in Vientiane and to Colonel Billy asking for the approval to send his Hmong to fly and fight their war from the skies. Who better to fight then soldiers who knew the ground and where the enemy was? But the Americans where afraid of the capacity of the Hmong to fly, that we would not be able to understand the airplane. We had no written language and not too long ago had only been farmers raising families in the remote mountaintops. But they did not understand how fast we could be to learn, to understand. The French knew, that's why they picked the Hmong to fight alongside them. We were the fierce warriors the enemy feared, and we wanted them to fear us from the sky.

We all walked in the shadow of Lee Lue, a Hmong warrior of immeasurable stature. He was born around 1935 in Xieng Khouang Province to Chong Ger Lee. His mother Pa Vang would not live to see her son become revered to the whole of the Hmong people. He was quite young when selected with several other young Hmong to attend school, which he grew to love. During his schooling he married Jou, but was unable to be with her often because of his schooling and the distance to her village. The war had touched Lee Lue and all the Hmong during his years of growing up and schooling. In 1953 after another Vietnamese invasion of Laos, Lee's family moved them to the village of Xieng Khouang to get away from the war, the killing. Lee Lue's love for teaching endeared him to continue on to Teacher College where upon completion in 1958 he returned to teach school in Lat Houng. Teachers to the Hmong are the most respected people after the King.

Shortly after he began teaching, the war in northern Laos began in earnest. It was 1960 when General Vang Pao met the Americans in his village and bound the future of the Hmong people to the Americans who promised to defeat the communists that killed our people, took our homes. Young men from all the villages joined with Vang Pao to fight for our people. But teachers were needed for our children, to show them the journey to responsibility, spiritually, and a good life.

The war shook the world around us; the ongoing battles found our people many times unable to grow crops, to feed ourselves. So the planes came to give us food, and medicine, and hope. To the soldiers the American fighter planes destroyed the enemy, they set their trucks on fire, stopped the tanks that rolled over our homes and people. We learned quickly the new tools of war the Americans brought us. We knew the land, the mountains, and we were fleet of foot in the high altitudes. With these new tools, we could fight the Vietnamese who came to drive us out of our land. And we watched the airplanes above us and wanted their power, their force for the Hmong. We had respected the French before for their knowledge, for their love of education, and their strength. And now we saw the same things in the Americans. Their air machines took your breath away. They were flying guns that could outrun the enemy, hunt him down and kill him. And we longed to be able to fly these machines, to chase the enemy from the sky and send him home forever.

Most of our American friends fought from the sky. The Butterflies and Ravens lived with us at Long Chieng. They flew everyday to find the enemy in the forests and on the roads. Then they would call for the fighters in the sky, to rain bombs and fire on an enemy who was only in Laos to kill us, to take our land. They knew our wives and children like their own, they were a part of our family, of our clan. They became our friends, our brothers; they fought with us, died with us.

Then there were the fighters who came from across the great river. Their planes would drop the bombs or bullets that saved our lives, our homes. They too died, or were dragged off to caves by the Pathet Lao, and like the French who suffered before them, the communists would cut off their ears, beat them, break their bones, starve them, make them less then human. Like our Hmong brothers and women held prisoner the enemy gave them a death much worse then a bullet. Let them think about their loved ones, their home far, far away until they went mad, knowing it was never to be.

At night we waited for the planes in the blackness we could never see. The Nighthawks, and Spooky, and Stinger and Spectre. They hunted up in the black, and with their magic eyes they could see the enemy, and then we would watch the rivers of red bullets, like liquid fire pour from the sky onto the enemy sneaking in this same blackness to find us. And then we would watch the enemy with his red fire reach into the sky, to find Nighthawk, or Spectre or Stinger. And then we might hear the explosion, see the fireball in the sky, we would know that our American friends would be raining on the Plaines that night alone and dieing in this same blackness. What a horrible way to die, alone, without friends.

The Lao and Thai soldiers began flying first, they were sent south to Udorn to learn how to fly the T-28's that the Americans brought. And they flew from Thailand and Vientiane to fight the war from the sky against the Vietnamese. But General Vang Pao wanted the Hmong to fly, to fight the battles that took his people. Several Americans fought to let us fly, and finally in 1967 the word came, they wanted to see if the Hmong could learn to fly the T-28's and they asked for volunteers. Six months of intensive flight training later the first class with Hmong pilots graduated, and Lee Lue the teacher, was the leader of group.

Flying was hard for the Lao and Hmong. Our languages did not allow for numbers and math that we needed to read the instruments. We learned to fly by example, watch the pilot and do what he did, over and over. Then we would graduate and go north, to fly to fight. We learned by a baptism of fire, how to dodge the triple-A from the ground, what angle could we bomb at and not get shot at too much. We also flew too much, but there was no choice, our people were dieing and they called for us. The weather in Laos was many times rainy or cloudy, or the fires of clearing and planting below us made it hard to see the ground, or the mountains hidden behind it. But we fought on, now we could fly.

The Hmong pilots excelled, and Lee Lue stood out above everyone. His missions became legendary; his dedication was an inspiration to all the Hmong. It wasn't long and he was promoted by Vang Pao to lead the Chaophakaow, the Hmong pilots. He was a choice of the American Ravens, who directed the air strikes, and soon American pilots far and wide heard of his exploits; he had become a legend to Hmong and Americans throughout the skies, beyond the secret war. He flew from when the sun rose in the east to when the sun went down in the western sky. He returned only to get more fuel, more bombs. After all, Lee Lue told us, ""They'll never get me. " He was fighting for his people and at the end of the day we needed to help him climb out of his plane, as he no longer had the strength to walk to his home, until the next morning when he was ready to do it all again. He knew the struggle of the infantryman on the ground, having been one. We Hmong never flew for records or medals; we were fighting for our homes, our villages and our people.

The Americans estimated Lee Lu must have flown over five thousand missions before July of 1969 rolled around. This was the wet season up here in the north, when the Vietnamese were holed up in their camps and bunkers as their trucks and tanks were unable to move. Now we were facing the NVA at Muong Soui, a vital airfield and village in early July. The rain had cleared from the night before when the call went out again for pilots to take out an enemy gun emplacement. Lee Lue and a flight of four T-28's were quickly in the air and took the call made by Vang Pao himself. There were two twin enemy ZPU anti-aircraft guns playing havoc with any plane in the vicinity. These guns could fire almost two thousand rounds per minute and were very accurate. They also said there was enemy bunkers filled with important enemy officers.

After confirming the target, Lee Lue and his flight rolled in with the proper angle for his bomb drop. We could watch him from the ground, fearless as he drove on to destroy the guns that were blazing away at him, at the bunkers that held our enemy. Then, as he released his bombs we all saw it, as he hit the first target, tracers from the second gun still firing reached up into the air and struck his aircraft from the nose to its tail. We watched him go up, up, trailing smoke, waiting for him to break left, left as he always did.

Vang Pao was on the radio screaming for him to bail out, but he continued to climb, until he couldn't and then his plane fell to the right still trailing smoke, now picking up speed, diving still to the right.

Everyone was screaming at him over the radio, trying to get his attention, trying to get him to climb again. It was then his plane hit the ridge several hundred yards in front of Vang Pao who was still screaming to his flight leader, his Lee Lue.

A hush fell over everyone; it wasn't possible what we had all seen. We lost Lee Lue, and that could not happen, it did not happen? We all stood silent, when we heard the sounds of aircraft driving on, coming back around. And then we saw his brothers in the sky as they lined up on the gun that brought down our hero. Vang Pao again screamed into the radio, begging the pilots to be careful, he could not take another crash, another death, not now.

But these Hmong pilots had a score to settle, for this is what Lee Lue would have done. And they drove on the target, taking intense fire again as they fired their guns and dropped their load of fire, and death, and revenge. And then the gun went silent.

Vang Pao ordered his soldiers to Lee Lue's plane in hopes it was not true. And we watched them pull the limp bodies of both pilots from the wreckage and carry them back as everyone wept, Vang Pao crying, "Lee Lue's dead, my Lee Lue's dead...."

And a nation and a war came to a stop that day. The word spread quickly through Laos and Thailand, the Hmong fighter hero had died for his country. This kind fearless Lee Lue always with a giant smile on his face had left us. How could we go on without him? He took a small piece of each of our spirits that day, and we long to see his face, his smile. When they pulled him from the plane, we all saw he was not in his flight suit, but his dress khaki's with all his medals. He had been on his way to take photos as he was up for promotion to Captain. When the call from Vang Pao came over the radio asking for the Chaophakaow, the Hmong pilots to take out a target, Lee Lue dropped everything and flew to the battle.

Even in his death Lee Lue brought the respect the Hmong they had been fighting for all their years. The next morning every major officer of the Lao military flew into Long Chieng for the funeral of this nations flying hero. For so long the Lao people had looked down on the Hmong as less then they. Now they all saluted the greatest pilot the Lao nation had ever seen. In addition to the Lao, the Americans flooded to his funeral. They knew all how great of a warrior and a pilot this teacher from the mountains was, and what he had become to everyone fighting in this secret war. The funeral ceremony lasted three days as this nation came to a standstill. The Hmong followed tradition in folding their hands in front of themselves holding three sticks of incense and on their knees crawled to the coffin offering their endearing respect. In a solemn tribute to his greatness and his humanity the American Ravens, these pilots from far, far away, knelt on the ground and did likewise. It was truly a great movement as an American Colonel laid their Distinguished Flying Cross medal on his coffin.

First numbed, then filled with anger over the loss of Lee Lue, Vang Pao decided it was time to get even, to get more then even. He studied the maps and enemy positions of the NVA and determined he would gamble big with an operation he called his About Face Campaign to take back the Plain of Jars, and as the Americans would say, " kick some ass." This time we surprised the communists with our combination of air power and fearless soldiers on the ground. We soon captured tanks, guns, and food as the Vietnamese ran from the Plains, when they could, when they weren't surrounded or chased from the sky. It was truly a masterful move; General Vang Pao was now chasing the enemy from the ground and the air.

Not everyone that flew was a pilot. Many Hmong flew with American and Hmong pilots as "backseaters," the men who knew the war on the ground, where the enemy was, where the friendlies were, and ran the radios coordinating the war from the sky. While the pilot flew, these backseaters communicated with the Hmong and Thai units on the ground determining the battle situation, and then directed the bombers and fighters in on the exact location of the enemy with devastating ferocity. This combination was lethal to many an enemy unit who did not know the countryside as well as those who lived here. Flying low and slow, they like the American Butterflies and Ravens took heavy, heavy fire every day from the ground. Many were wounded or killed taking the war to the enemy. And a bond developed between the pilot and backseater where trust in each other was essential to coming back alive. And then there were those times when a backseater inexperienced with flying would bring the plane back with their wounded or dead pilot and then fly again tomorrow, because there was still a war, still Hmong on the ground needing his help, still fighters in the sky with bombs to be dropped.

Many Hmong died flying in battle, from the guns, the weather, the haze, the bloodshot eyes, or a slow reaction after days of battle. But we knew our Hmong brothers and sisters were dieing on the ground, they needed us and we them; after all, we are the Hmong Over the Clouds.

Fight Over Oz
Chapter 10

Some referred to the war in northern of Laos as the Land of Oz, a war that was becoming increasingly complicated. Several of the original architects of the US version had moved on wondering if what had transpired perhaps had gone out of control? The CIA and Embassy was finding itself increasingly at odds with the US military back in Vietnam who could pull air power at will, often in attempts to wrestle control of a battlefield they little understood. Then there are the politicians back in Washington far removed from the reality that occurred here getting ready to walk away from the mess they made called Vietnam and abandon a people called the Hmong.

By the late sixties the devastation of the seesaw war up here had virtually depleted the ranks of the Hmong warriors. Hell, an entire generation of men had virtually disappeared. Many families were down to one male, and many times he was barely a teenager, many as young as ten to twelve years. But like their fathers and brothers they took up the weapons of war, many times the rifle being taller then they were. You see here there was no end of tour, no counting down the days before returning home to shopping centers and outdoor movies. They are home, their sisters and mothers and aunts are here, dodging the same mortars, eating the same gruel, drinking the same tainted water. But they have hope, that of the Americans who like the French before them promised to stand by their goals of peace and freedom. They heard the stories of many an American who told of the freedoms their ancestors had fought for a century and a half before, against tremendous odds just like them.

And if the Hmong had one source of strength, it was family. An extended family for sure, reaching all the way out to the clans they each belonged to. It was only a century and a half before that a number of these clans, no longer able to take the brutality of the Chinese struck out on their own, fleeing their home in China to the relative obscurity of the remote mountains up here in northern Laos that apparently no one else wanted. The quiet was not long lived as first the Vietnamese reached out, then the French arrived, followed by the Japanese. It wasn't long before the French returned now bringing their battle with the communist Vietnamese with them.

But over their century in Indochina the French grew tired, and were replaced in one way or another by the Americans. And now the rumors of an America growing tired were in the news. And to some, they saw it creep in the door here, as talk of a decreased air sorties became reality. The word was by July 1st the number of sorties available in Barrel Roll would drop by fifty per cent.

It was this, the air power that Vang Pao saw as the great equalizer. He couldn't face the militarily strong and sophisticated NVA Army in set military action. But he could dazzle them with lightening quick guerilla strikes relying on air power to deliver the blow necessary to take out the enemy once he found them and corralled them.

King Savang Vatthana and Prime Minister Souvanna Phouma worried of their precarious position argued with Vang Pao to takes as much ground as possible before the American air power was cut back. Apprehensive of the increasing toll on his remaining troops, Pao finally agreed to take the war back to the NVA as he had done numerous times before. But unlike his About Face campaign of 1969, his strategy was to again deploy the guerrilla tactics combined with air power he had so effectively used before. He knew he had to strike fast while he still had American air power. And perhaps a success would convince the Americans to continue the support he knew was necessary to survive. He was used to juggling resources from wherever he could gather them to save the certain onslaught his people would suffer should he fail. By June Pao operated from only two bases Long Chieng and Bouam Loung, so the plans were laid, on June 11th he helicoptered nine thousand troops to bottom of PDJ to face over twenty thousand NVA troops in place.

By the time I reported in, Pappy had been at his desk all morning on the phone. Somehow this guy had sworn, threatened, and upset enough people between here and Vietnam to find full sets of oxygen bottles and masks for all his Mohawks. They were to be installed before the evening flights went up. More impressive was the fact he had oxygen to put in the bottles, shit, this guy was good.

It didn't hurt to threaten that no Mohawk was flying until he had equipment necessary so the friggin weather wouldn't kill us. It also didn't hurt that a major offensive had launched that morning and every plane was critical. In the end, it was a blue Air Force pickup that dropped off the required gear. Somehow I figured an Army supply sergeant back in Vietnam would not consider stocking oxygen in a bottle when they figured nature provided it for free, along with the assorted scents of Vietnam, including blood, sweat, and burning shit.

With time to spare, a little fresh air sounded good. It was now a beautiful sunny afternoon as I strolled outside our HQ warehouse for that fresh air and a cold coke from our Thai coke lady who was always perched outside with cold soda, cigarettes and candy. A coke in hand I strolled aimlessly outside staring at everything around me with no set purpose in mind. My eyes fixed on the gated compound of Air America that was constantly causing traffic to stop on the roadway in front of me as their myriad of airplanes rolled across the roadway from the runway on one side of the road to enter their secret world on the other side. By now I had heard the stories, having met a number of their "civilian" pilots, loaders, crew chiefs, etc., in the assorted clubs and bars on and off base. In Laos they moved everything necessary to conduct a war in this remote mountainous section of the world. They also saved the ass of many an aviator unlucky enough to be shot down in Laos, far from any friendly force.

Secrets, there were a lot more then meets the eye. Take Air America, a private airline that was actually owned by the CIA. With the role of running covert missions all over Asia, the CIA in 1950 had secretly bought out the air assets of Civil Air Transport (CAT), an airline that had been started in China after World War II by the famous Gen. Claire L. Chennault. While still flying commercial flights, it began its clandestine operations during the Korean War by dropping agents and supplies into China. During the French involvement of the 50's in Vietnam the French were continually short of aviation assets to move troops, guns, and supplies around an ever-evolving battlefield. CAT flew many missions for the French, a number even under the tri-colored roundels of the French Air Force.

With the fall of the French in Asia, America saw Laos as the first of the potential dominos to fall in Asia given its central location to a Communist China, North Vietnam and its close proximity to Thailand. While attempting to honor the neutrality in Laos the US opened the United States Operations Mission (USOM) in Vientiane to deliver and administer economic assistance. By 1955 large-scale rice failures were threatening Laos and USOM called on CAT to deliver much needed food supplies into the unreachable mountain villages of Laos. By the late fifties CAT had changed its name to Air America and was involved all through Asia by the US to move food, supplies and shortly the weapons of war again. By 1959 things were beginning to change quickly with US Special Forces arriving in Laos to begin operations with the Lao government increasingly uneasy with the thousands of Vietnamese soldiers inside its borders. The Air Force had Major Harry "Heine" Aderholt in place in Thailand laying the groundwork for a soon to be burgeoning US air presence in this theater of the war. Aderholt was intimately familiar with the needs of running air operations in Laos and how to run clandestine operations. He and Bill Lair were sure a number of small dirt runways later called Lima Sites, located all over Laos would be necessary to support the war. And that would require special aircraft that could handle the short runways and high altitudes. Among a wide cast of aircraft that would fly this war, Heine also introduced the Helio Courier STOL aircraft to the war that could supply and move troops to and from many an obscure landing strips in this forbidding landscape.

In 1960, a strange sets of events brought the US and Soviet military staring down each other in northern Laos. A political split in the Laotian government found neutralist and right wing forces facing each other militarily. The Soviets quickly mounted a huge airlift of supplies to the Pathet Lao forces in the north of Laos virtually turning the Plain of Jars into a Soviet airbase. The US scrambled forces from throughout Asia now facing the prospects of the cold war erupting in this remote country called Laos. The headlines were flooded with dispatches from Laos, for the time being Vietnam was clearly future news. As Eisenhower sent ships north from the Philippines in a show of force, he noted the limited American assets available and readily agreed to a proposal by the CIA to support and arm the Hmong forces in Laos whom had similarly reached an accord with the French decades earlier.

So ten years before my time here, the pieces had rapidly fallen in place for our involvement in the "secret war". A war that while geographically paralleling Vietnam, its operation was dramatically different. Unlike Vietnam, the North Vietnamese were the large in place fixed army defending vital depots and roadways. The US and its indigenous forces were the guerillas that could quickly attack and disappear. Unlike Vietnam, there was no large scale American Army suffering thousands of causalities weekly year after year. And because of those differences, Vietnam would soon overshadow this war, and in the end seal its fate.

Looking for solutions the CIA called on their paramilitary specialist Bill Lair to began to devise options for US military strategy for Laos. Lair had already had prior success in Thailand helping their military control their remote border posts from attacks by Communist insurgents. He was familiar with the Hmong military leader named Vang Pao. Pao had worked successfully with the French, was respected by the Lao military leaders, and was concerned the now nearby communists would quickly seek revenge on his mountain people living remotely in northern Laos. Bill thought he'd go up into Laos and meet Vang Pao. In the meeting Pao told him the Hmong people could not live with the communists, that they'd have to fight or leave Laos. It didn't take long before Lair and Pao decided they both needed each other. Pao could raise an army to fight the communists if Lair and the Americans could support them; it seemed a fair trade for both sides. A Washington not even knowing whom Vang Pao was, but distraught with the pending conflict and little recourse quickly signalled approval and Air America was soon dropping weapons and supplies to the Hmong south of the Plain of Jars.

With US military training of the Hmong occurring, Lair and Aderholt quickly set upon a plan of bulldozing small landing strips called Lima sites throughout Laos. They knew US air support would be vital to the Hmong fighters and they wanted to be able to get in and out of the remote areas as needed. Air America quickly expanded their aircraft and operations as the demand for more transport exploded. Their inventory included STOL aircraft, caribous, helicopters of assorted sizes, and larger transports including C-130's, C-123's etc.

Both fearing an outbreak of war, Russia and the US turned to a hastily created Geneva Conference on the situation in Laos. In mid 1962 the United States announced support of the Geneva Declaration on the Neutrality of Laos accord and for a while Air American and Hmong military operations ceased. But by 1963 it was determined that communist support of the accord was a ruse, that over eight thousand NVA troops were still in Laos, so operations quickly came back on line. The Hmong now over twenty five thousand strong were employed blowing up trucks, depots and roadways now funnelling troops and supplies into South Vietnam with Air America providing the transport and the necessary supplies. By 1964 NVA and Pathet Lao forces attempted to overrun the Plain of Jars in order to drive and destroy the Hmong on their home ground. The war in Vietnam was now kicking into high gear with vast numbers of men and materials being moved into Vietnam. Often the military command in Vietnam will attempt to hijack the management of the war in Laos. As with the political bickering that saw the weapons removed from our Mohawks that resulted in needless deaths, games often occurred granting or withholding needed air assets in asinine attempts to wangle control from a theater of war that was showing more success at less cost then the conflict in Vietnam.

By 1965 the secret war was in full force, run by the CIA and the Air Force Air Commando special ops boys, but effective control rested with the US Ambassador in Laos. So the CIA set up their command center at the Royal Thai Air Force base in Udorn across the Mekong from the US Laotian Embassy in Vientiane. They called it the 4802nd Joint Liaison Detachment headquarters physically located next to Air America and across from the 131st Mohawk group that we affectionately called the rat patrol. Lair headed this group until 1968 when Pat Laundry took over. The Thai military also located their out of country operations group known as the Headquarters 333 in Udorn next door to these other secret ops.

Besides getting supplies and troops around the battlefield in the mid sixties, Air America was now called upon to rescue the growing number of US pilots being shot down throughout Laos. Each year watched control of the strategic Plain of Jars seesaw between the communists and the Hmong. While the NVA called on more and more troops from their homeland to the battle, the Hmong were being bloodied every year, losing more and more troops they couldn't replace. So the Americans in order to maintain the balance upped the number of fighter sorties from twenty to over four hundred a day.

In 1969, Vang Pao caught the enemy by surprise when he launched Operation About Face. Not hit and run guerrilla tactics, but a major offensive that sent the communists running from the Plaines for the first time in over ten years. Massive supply depots were captured including over twenty-five Soviet PT-76 tanks, two thousand tons of foods, thousands of guns, twenty five hundred tons of ammo and almost a thousand heavy guns including artillery and anti aircraft guns.

The following dry season saw a major North Vietnamese effort once and for all attempt to crush the opposition in Laos. NVA troops in country were now estimated by intelligence sources at around eighty thousand troops. Not bad for a country that agreed to honor the neutrality of its neighbor by withdrawing all troops. So the control of the Plain now swung back to the communists in 1970, and they were now shelling the Hmong and CIA base at Long Chieng from the ridges surrounding it. The dry season had brought more NVA divisions to the north of Laos. They were hell bent on smashing the Hmong once and for all. February saw the shelling of the Hmong headquarters at Long Chieng. The dreaded 130mm artillery had arrived in the PDJ, and the communists had placed them in caves and pushed them out on rollers to blast away at the Hmong bases. These guns could quickly be rolled back into the caves to protect themselves from US and Lao air power.

The dry season had also seen the NVA and Pathet Lao forces again drive across the Plain of Jars. They were again able to inflict sapper attacks and artillery on the Hmong and CIA base city of Long Chieng. The war down south in Laos had also gone badly, the NVA clearly held the upper hand following the capture of Paksong, twenty-five miles east of the Mekong River town of Pakse. On April 15th, Vang Pao attacked positions on Skyline ridge and mountains around Long Chieng to put an end to the constant artillery raining down on them. In May there were reports that the communists were now using helicopters at night in the north. The NVA was becoming increasing bold as secret talks with Kissinger assured them America wanted out. The more the communists grabbed, the more bargaining power they'd have at the end.

Koontz and I arrived in Northern Laos at the start of the monsoon season here. The war revolved around the weather. The dry season, that period from October to April of each year saw the North Vietnamese mount their large attacks to gain ground. In the south of Laos this was the season to drive as much supplies to South Vietnam before the monsoon rains washed out their roads. With no capability to move troops or supplies by air unless the rumors of helicopters during the night were true, Mother Nature pretty much dictated their war.

Just last month intelligence showed the NVA planned to take Bouam Loung, Lima Site thirty-two. Then in mid May the Hmong SGU defending the position found tunnels, the signs were all there, an attack was imminent.

On May 20th, the NVA launched their attack with hundreds of troops and Pathet Lao forces with fierce fighting lasting all day. The communists knew that while the bad weather held on, the Hmong could not call in the air strikes that had often given them the upper edge; the NVA were confident they were poised to take Bouam Loung. Little did they know the cat and mouse game each side played up here allowed an American FAC to drop the newly designed and portable Mobile Beacon that transmitted a position silently through the overcast sky above Lima Site thirty-two. That evening with the skies deeply overcast, the NVA commander ordered a final assault on Bouam Loung with orders to wipe out anyone alive. As the human wave approached the perimeter, the Hmong commander radioed Alleycat with the coordinates of the enemy, offset from the mobile beacon. A Lao Air Force Spooky gunship waiting on station high above the cloud cover dropped their rivers of red fire at the exact coordinates off of the beacon and the NVA army sneaking to the fence line never saw the fire storm arrive. The entire wave and subsequent ones were destroyed by air power the enemy never saw coming.

Sunrise saw the hundreds of bodies stretched out in front of the perimeter from a new weapon that the enemy had never encountered before. They left four Pathet Lao battalions around Bouam Loung to prevent a breakout and the NVA army retreated into the jungles. The Hmong commander left the dead enemy bodies stretched and rotting in front of the barbed wire as a warning sign of what is in store for an enemy with second thoughts.

Now it was June and Vang Pao's turn, the reports had started coming in that afternoon about Vang Pao's initial success on the PDJ. His SGU, or Special Guerrilla Units used familiar hit & run tactics where they'd helicopter troops and attack targeted outposts. The Hmong would force or bait them into the open or by firing to give away their positions, where waiting air strikes were called in to clean them out. While Pao's troops were keeping the NVA busy, Forward Air guides were inserted among the NVA at spots we know them by their call signs like Hotel Echo, to report on new movements or counter attacks where air power again could take them on. Our job would be to take the war to the enemy in the darkness, when we could see them, and hoping they wouldn't find us.

I grabbed some supper across the street and put in some serious ping-pong action until the early team took off about nine pm. The empty CO's chair called out to me, with my feet on his desk I stretched out for a cap nap. A dim light cast an eerie yellowish shadow across the ping-pong table at the far end of this large room. Sharp pains in my back from this uncomfortable position woke me up every half hour. The only sounds came from the lone ticking clock in the room and the moans as I frequently readjusted my sleeping position.

Somewhere around midnight my attempts at sleep were interrupted when Pappy strolled through the door. "Ready to go son?" he questioned as he turned the lights on.

Groggily I answered, "Yah sure, lets go." I rolled out of the chair squinting in the now bright light to find my way to the chair that held my flight gear. Pappy grabbed some notes from his desk and we were on our way.

We strolled out to our flight line in the cool, dark evening air. There was hardly any activity out here at this hour. I watched the navigation lights of the returning planes float down to the runway. The only sound came when the tires squealed on touchdown, and the engines roared to life as the pilot threw them in reverse to stop their roll down the runway.

We didn't talk on the way out. I had a thousand thoughts running through my mind, I'm sure Pappy did also. Rounding the corner to our row I could hear the roar of a generator. Sure enough, Daze had the portable floodlights on the plane as he busily ran around getting her ready. This was the Mohawk I had flown this previous evening when all hell broke lose on our return. As I walked up to the cockpit Daze waved as he finished pulling the yellow warning flags that pinned the external fuel tanks in place. Pappy began his preflight check of the plane as I hopped up into the cockpit window and pulled the green maintenance book. The only new note was the problem we had had earlier with one of our radios. Dazes pen scratching noted that he had pulled the offending radio and replaced it.

I jumped back down and talked with Daze for a few minutes as Pappy finished his inspection. It was hard to talk over the noise of the generator, but I tried to thank Daze for his help that evening. He grabbed me by the shoulder and yelled into my ear, "We're hearing things are pretty hot out their tonight, ... try to bring this back in one piece ok?" I nodded and then slapped him in the back of his head, "yah, I'll be ok too."

Pappy snapping on his gear strolled up, "Well Daze, she's looks good, lets get her out of here."

Quickly we hopped into the cockpit and strapped ourselves in. Pappy had the engines roaring as I flipped on the radios. The engines quickly ran up to a high pitch buffeting the cool night air through the open hatch. I could hear surges through the earphones as various system powered up. Pappy flipped the navigation lights on as flashes of red and green light bounced off the revetment wall.

Daze had moved the generator and lights out of the way and now directed Pappy through a series of tests to make sure the planes control surfaces were all working. I checked to make sure the various radios were set to the proper frequencies for the operations up in Barrel Roll.

Soon we were taxing out of our revetment to head north and join the fight. Our call to the control tower quickly gave us our instructions on taxiways and runway to use. With little traffic at this hour we sped down the taxiways, at times momentary becoming airborne as we hit bumps. We had a short wait while two Air America C-130's landed, and then the turn was ours. We wasted no time in becoming airborne and climbed around to head north. Heading low and fast we glazed off the rice fields of northern Thailand with the water glimmering back whatever light was available. Occasionally we could make out slivers of light or fires in the farmers hootches.

The night was eerie in its silence. I wondered what hell the little guys were enduring ahead of us on the PDJ. The communists waited for the familiar cover of darkness to regroup and move troops, supplies, and guns to counter the Hong advances of the previous day. We began to gain altitude as I switched the radio frequencies to check into the airspace with Alleycat.

"Alleycat, Spud two-three entering airspace at this time."

"Roger Spud two-three, Gunships ETA one seven minutes. Good hunting."

"Thanks", crackled out, everything was feeling pretty ominous now. I wasn't feeling so good as I wasn't sure how this would play out. Pappy fed the engines more fuel as we climbed to ten thousand feet attempting to get over the ring of mountains that surrounded the Plain of Jars.

Once over we could see fires burning across the plateau called the PDJ. It was evident the Hmong had leapfrogged across a wide spanse of territory causing a great deal of havoc. The radio traffic was intense as the Hmong were calling in air strikes to take more territory or avert counter attacks. As we trekked west hunting for movers, we watched new fireballs erupted below us as sortie after sortie were taking the offensive. It wasn't long as we found movers again.

"Alleycat, Spud two-three has multiple movers at x-ray delta eight two two eight zero zero," I rattled off into the deluge of radio chatter everywhere up here.

"Roger Spud, Spectre three-one ETA zero five, will advise" fired back an Alleycat who obviously had their coffee pots going full throttle. We'd have to wait for our gunship so we cruised east to the North Vietnamese border, turned one-eighty and headed back west noting over twenty movers in our first leg. The little guys have stirred up a hornet's nest today. The weather was good tonight, good for the enemy to drive and not get stuck or washed out on rain soaked roads, and good enough for us to attempt to detour their trip into a flaming wreck. It was a race to see who would win and who would die.

"Spud two-three, this is Spectre three-one on station and orbiting. Here you got some fish in the barrel for us?"

We had just mapped the same movers we'd picked up on our jaunt eastbound and now could tell they were heading west obviously delivering supplies, troops, or guns to their remote outposts.

"Roger Spectre, Spuds got zero-niner movers heading westbound on Route seven, coordinates x-ray delta eight four three niner zero three."

"Roger Spud, acknowledge x-ray delta eight four three niner zero three, could be a long busy night," Spectre signed off going into action.

We continued west back across the Plaines, Long Chieng now off to our left and south as the radios continued to buzz with new flights of fighter and bombers coming on station to await new targets. We turned north and were on the westbound side of the PDJ when Spectre called Alleycat announcing success.

"Alleycat, this is Spectre three-one leaving twelve trucks burning south on the PDJ, any other targets for us?" Targets didn't seem to be a problem tonight, Alleycat had gotten calls from Hotel Echo, a remote Hmong listening post on the upper plain that heard trucks moving in the night air to their south and soon Spectre was racing north for more action.

Now far north of the Plain, we began heading east toward the North Vietnam border near the town of Dien Bein Phu where the French were roundly defeated decades ago that signaled their final withdrawal from Southeast Asia. As Spectre took out the trucks Hotel Echo had heard in the darkness we started picking up movers in a hurry heading north off the Plains. We began to pick up more movers by x-ray delta five niner six four four zero when the plane shook from a series of bright flashes and explosions to our left rear.

"What the . . ." as Pappy put the Mohawk on its side turning hard right and diving, the ground now coming at us through the Plexiglas above our heads.

"Alleycat, Spud taking heavy triple-A south of Khang Khay," I broadcast over the radio hoping someone with big guns could return fire. Pappy tried to level out and now we could watch new lines of red tracers curving and rising from the ground toward us, it was almost as if they were floating up to meet us. Pappy again put her on its' side breaking hard left, trying to turn inside the arch fast approaching.

"Spud two three, have fighters enroute, and kill the god damn Christmas tree," a heavy voice from the orbiting Alleycat thundered through the headsets.

273

"Shit . . . " as I reached for the toggle switch to kill the rotating beacons providing the bull eyes for these gunners to aim at. Air traffic had been so intense we had been seriously worried about running into each other out here so we had been flying with nav lights on, or "Christmas Tree". As one Mohawk pilot explained in a Stars & Stripes newspaper article several months ago, you can return with some holes in you from triple-a, but it's hard to fly with an F-4 stuck in your side. Pappy kept weaving, diving, and turning as more guns came on line, we could see at least six lines of red tracers arching into the black sky searching for us out here somewhere. They were getting close, as the lines of red fire had turned into red and white vibrating bowling balls whizzing past our cockpit. I was braced for the impact, my body one minute pressed against the ejection seat from the g's we were pulling, then seemingly floating against the straps holding me to the seat. Pappy was intently putting the Mohawk over its performance edge; they weren't giving us any choice.

"Spud two-three, we have Killer flight one-seven on station. They got you're triple-A positions, proceed zero-five to exit area," Alleycat came back instantly to choreograph our exit and put a flight of F-4's in on the offending anti-aircraft guns that were hunting us in the sky. Pappy leveled enough to get a compass bearing for a split second, then head as close to north as he could to get the hell out of the way. Alleycat had the Phantoms coming in on a west to east run to make sure they didn't climb up our ass after they dropped their load and hit the afterburners.

"Alleycat, Spud two-three heading zero five." I announced over the radio as I guessed Pappy had us heading north as fast as we could go, when not diving for the deck to dodge the shit still heading our way.

"Roger Spud, Killer one-seven enroute to target," as Alleycat released the three F-4's to seek revenge.

Thirty seconds later we heard and felt massive explosions form behind us, Pappy chanced it and turned one-eighty to view the battlefield. A hilltop was silhouetted in the bright explosions from the five hundred and seven hundred fifty-pound bombs the F-4's had dropped on the gun positions. Now more flashes lit up the sky as numerous secondary explosions went off from the ammo cooking off.

"Spud, hope that keeps them off your cute triple tail ass for awhile," the Phantom leader radioed now heading south to refuel and rearm.

_____

"Most-appreciative of the fireworks Killer, we owe you some beers down south," Pappy responded as we both scanned all the gauges, heat, rpms, oil pressure; anything to see signs of trouble. We needed both engines working to get the altitude to get us back over the mountains to get home. If we lost an engine, we'd have to leave the plane and punch out over the PDJ. The guys who saved our ass were from the Triple Nickel Squadron back at Udorn; they wouldn't be hard to track down.

"We'll look for you Spud, good luck," as the Phantoms signed off.

"Spud two-three, I got Spectre three-three on station, are you able to continue hunt" inquired Alleycat.

"Roger that Alleycat, we got some payback," Pappy yelled into the mike now visually pissed off. Then there was silence as he stared through me. I took a second to get the hint, and started ruffling my maps in an attempt to refocus on hunting for trucks; everyone's appetite had grown appreciatively in the last twenty minutes.

The night was long and fruitful, by the time we were entering final approach at Udorn, we got a call from Spectre three-two returning themselves from the PDJ. They informed us the triple-A up at Khang Khay was covering for the movers we detected before and after the aerial fire show. They got six T-76 tanks moving south along Highway Seven in addition to fourteen trucks. Seems everyone was able to stop a counter attack on the Hmong sitting at Hunter and Badman near Lima Site 32. At least we were able to help these guys get some sleep tonight.

The next days and nights saw intense fighting as the Hmong jumped around the Plaines in lightening moves that saw the NVA on the run. Every evening was exhausting as we destroyed hundred and trucks and tanks attempting to re-supply, attack, or just run. The traffic in the skies were heavy, as targets were dislodged from their dug in positions and scrambling for new cover.

Within days Vang Pao's men had captured over eight hundred tons of supplies, over twelve hundred rounds of 82mm mortars, and numerous large artillery and antiaircraft pieces. One gun he placed in front of his house in Long Chieng as a trophy of the latest success.

But while he had success to the north on the PDJ, the enemy continued to hunker down in the caves along the Skyline Ridge to the north of Long Chieng that kept hammering away with their artillery. On June 15th NVA sappers attacked Long Chieng under the cover of mortars and artillery fire. So Vang Pao attacked Skyline Ridge to drive the constant enemy pressure away from his home base. Besides the military force at Long Chieng, down the road at Ban Sorn, also known as Lima Site 272 there was fifty thousand Hmong, families of his soldiers along with their schools and the hospital. By the end of June Vang Pao captured the hilltop of Ban Na with the support of several Thai battalions. Hotel Echo found itself under attack again and the Hmong road watchers withdrew in the night to have air power blast away the enemy now standing in their position.

Between missions, we had heard the protests back home were hot and heavy, we could see the political pressure over here as more and more military units packed bags to head back. The war wasn't leaving, only the Americans. On June 22 the Mansfield Amendment passed the Senate calling for the US to withdraw within ninety days after Hanoi released our POW's. We knew that handed the enemy the message the US was ready to leave. Washington had blinked and was looking for a way out.

An undeterred Vang Pao ordered Phase Two of his offense on July 1, now forcing the US to deal with how they were going to support him after they had previously announced they were reducing air power. He airlifted a strike force to assault Lima Lima and the US Embassy quickly reacted by airlifting Thai 105mm artillery teams onto the south end of the Plain of Jars to support the Hmong General who was calling his own shots. While the US sent the artillery to replace the air power Pao had lost, it also handicapped him as now Pao had to place his Hmong soldiers in static defensive positions to guard the artillery. His Army worked well when they were on the attack, not guarding fixed positions.

In early July the Hmong took Lima Lima, only to lose it three days later. More weeks of fierce fighting finally saw the Hmong take back Lima Lima on the seventeenth, but for how long? US air power was now cut by fifty per cent as Vang Pao watched the growing devastation on his people this seesaw war was having. An entire generation of men was wiped out by ten years of fighting, and a new generation of women raising their children on their own with little income if any was causing a refugee crisis. The fear in the Embassy and CIA circles was the Hmong leaders would finally call for all their families to retreat to western Laos and their men would follow devastating the ranks of the army.

Then the rules of war changed yet again, a Washington removed from reality years ago now dictated that any request for American support here in the battle for the Land of Oz would require a ten day advance notice, most likely in typed in triplicate. Vang Pao and the US military fighting with him were incensed. How does one fight a constantly changing field of battle that requires ten-day notices, on most days ten minutes is pressing the issue? Now the Lao and the Hmong were facing another enemy, those in Washington who were already packing the US bags to get out of Southeast Asia. In the daily routine of war and death, all that was obvious to those flying and fighting was that there were more pressing issues here today, like seeing tomorrow.

Randy flew in about noon on one of the Phu Bai birds bringing over mail and parts. He was heading back to the states in a couple weeks and connived someone of importance to steal a couple days in Udorn. I had the night off, so Phil and I picked him up and took him into town to grab a hotel room and get his evening started with several San Miguel's. We had found a cool darkened bar in town where they kept the San Miguel so cold it frosted the glass when they poured it. Three of those and then take a person outside into the blinding sun and incredible heat and you literally watch them melt right down to the sidewalk. Perfectly cruel, but cheap entertainment was so lacking lately.

After scrapping Randy from the sidewalk we were off to some great food at one of the local restaurants where they had two versions of hot, Thai hot and the ever-mild Yankee hot. We got caught up on all the gossip on what was going on back in Phu Bai. He confirmed the rumor that the 131st was packing up in a month and moving down to Da Nang. As the number of troops left in Vietnam dwindled, those units left were staging back to larger cities before the final trip back to the states. It looked like our unit here would be passed off to the 225th Aviation Company down in Tuay Hoa. We'd never go there except on our way home, but we needed to be on someone's roster in Vietnam, as we weren't supposed to be here. Then I heard Hump was still alive causing havoc. He had devised a new weapons delivery system consisting of a grenade with the pin pulled inserted into a glass jar. There was a small slide by door in the floor on the pilot's side of the Mohawk that he'd drop this improvised bomb through to hit targets on the ground. My first thought was what happened if you broke the glass jar inside the cockpit? The insanity was never ending; the only certainty was more of it.

After dinner we hit the never-ending set of bars in Udorn flush with airmen off duty from a day of getting bombs loaded, planes refueled, memos in triplicate, intelligence gathered and ignored. We made our way into the Thai Lady, where several incredible looking dancers were gyrating up in bamboo cages hanging over the stage. On stage was a Philipino band that mimicked the hits and groups playing back home, an American Bandstand meets Asia. The noise was deafening as every table was filled with drunken Americans yelling at each other over the music they came here for. We stumbled through the club and ran into Lyle, Tyrone, and Sal who where already back from the early missions. Still in their Army flight suits and jungle fatigues they were already arguing with some air force jocks several tables away, something about size and virility. We pulled up some chairs and jumped into the middle of several ongoing mindless conversations. As the evening wound on, we were constantly interrupted by the parade of ladies of the evening plying their wares around the bar. Thai women were the perfect mélange of beauty and everything Asian. An evening with a beautiful lady cost one hundred baht or five dollars American. Now even a lowly enlisted man could afford to join the ranks of the ugly American who turned the daughters of third world counties into whores.

Someone in green bumped someone in blue, or vice versa, and the fists and chairs started flying. I hit the floor ducking the bottles and flying bodies and saw Randy on the floor alongside me, I motioned in the general direction of the door, and soon our contingent of army rats who started the fight crawled to the relative safety of the streets. Dusting ourselves off, we looked into the bar windows seeing the entire place involved in a brawl that now only pitted Air Force against Air Force. Ever proud we were able to handoff our place in this fight we grabbed cabs back to the hotel to continue the drinking.

As the evening wore down there was only Randy, Daze and myself left. We ended up taking the party upstairs so Randy could sample the Thai weed he was bringing back to the gang in Phu Bai. Without warning Randy changed the discussion to war, he had been waiting for the right time and place all evening.

"Several of us are concerned about you," as he stared into my eyes. "We all know this war is wrong? We want to know why can't you just wait out your time, fly the missions up in North Vietnam where there is a bombing halt, where we aren't killing everyone?"

I never saw the ambush; I was speechless as I tired to make my mind work. The evening had been bullshit discussions that we'd never remember the next day, but I saw the look in Randy's eyes and the hate. He wasted no time and took his second shot, "we all know this war is wrong, so what in the hell is the sick fascination you obliviously have in killing every night?"

Which war do we argue, Vietnam where nothing made sense, Laos where I can see the Hmong getting hunted from their homes everyday? But that war, this secret war wasn't known in Vietnam. How do I start that lesson here, and maybe he was right, the insanity may have gotten to me, to everyone? I did like the killing, the adrenalin rush when we watched the trucks explode. The only thing that made sense in this moment was the ever-present thought that the other side wasn't having this discussion; they were plotting our destruction.

"You know Randy, none of us really know what in the hell is going on. I know its different here then Phu Bai, the people here; the Hmong don't run or try to kill us in the night. They're being hunted by the same NVA that doesn't look so wholesome from this angle, he's got no business here, this isn't his country." Searching for a way out, I stammered, " But I think we'd agree on one thing, that every truck that is stopped from going south is a rocket or mortar that doesn't kill one of us waiting to leave this insanity?"

We both stared at each other waiting for more, I knew he disagreed violently with what I was doing here and I'd never convince him of anything else.

"Well, we can agree these Thai sticks are the best weed ever," as he packed the pipe. The evening went back to where it had been heading before the train wreck. Somewhere in the hours ahead Daze and I headed off to our rooms. The next day Randy flew back to Phu Bai, and I would never see him again.

The missions continued in its intensity as air power was constantly trying to keep up with Vang Pao, and ahead of him to find the NVA trucks and tanks before they found Vang Pao. Somewhere in there I became a two digit midget, which meant I had less then one hundred days left on my tour, there was a light at the end of my tunnel. Celebrations included buying a one hundred tablet bottle of One-A-Day aspirin so I could watch the days disappear before me as I shoved each one down my throat. It was a constant battle as each night the enemy would try to shove anti-aircraft fire up the other direction. There was more good news when the Udorn airbase burger palace began serving pizza; the only complication being it was made with Swiss cheese. But beggars can't be choosers; after all it wasn't powdered cheese.

Weather started improving in August, which was always a double-edged sword. Better to hunt trucks and tanks as they were moving, but given enough good weather the NVA could bring troops and supplies to counter the Hmong offensives.

The word came through that the 131st back in Vietnam was on it's way to Da Nang. We were now officially part of the 225th Aviation Company. So I'd be spending the rest of my tour flying up here in the Land of Oz.

Then more news, we'd be taking an infrared mission out tonight? Given we've been hunting trucks everyone wondered what was so important we'd divert a crew for this. There were no days off from flying since Vang Pao started his offensive, the spare crew idea was history, there was too much to do.

In 1970 intel had showed two possible POW camps twenty miles west of Hanoi at Ap Lo and Son Tay. The Son Tay camp was thought to have held fifty American prisoners. Plans had been developed to send Special Forces into one of these camps and rescue the POW's that were being abused and tortured every day. In the beginning Secord was involved to hold onto the vital Hmong Lima Sites on the far-east side of the PDJ. The helicopters would need to land there going in and out to refuel. But as the decision to go, and where continued to change, the technology had improved to where the team could fly in straight from Thailand. Anything that could cut down on the number of steps necessary in any mission decreased the complications of things going wrong immensely.

Finally on November 30th 1970 a team of Special Forces left Udorn for the suspected POW camp at Son Tay. The mission went off brilliantly except for the fact our intel didn't know the POW's had been secretly moved in July to another camp. The boldness of this brazen attack deep within North Vietnam shocked the communists. They rethought the entire prisoner picture and in short time moved the POW's they held up to the prison in or near Hanoi.

Laos was a different picture; here the Pathet Lao held the prisoners. This way they could play separate hands at the negotiations table. Hanoi could deal on the POW's they held, and the communists in Laos could bargain for another concession if they so choose.

The latest rumors and intel showed the Pathet Lao might be holding Hmong and possibly American POW's and MIA's in several caves along the Lao border with North Vietnam east and north of Sam Neua. They needed several infrared missions over several sites to first confirm the reports, and to confuse the enemy over what exactly we were looking for. If we picked up clues or heat sources in our target area, they would try to insert a Hmong SGU unit to scope out the site visually. A Special Forces extraction team was ready to go in if we got a confirmation quickly, before they had time to move them.

Lyle and Tracy spent the afternoon at the 4802nd Detachment with the CIA team and a Hmong Colonel to plan out the mission. They wanted to bypass any known NVA or Pathet Lao site in order not to tip anyone off of thier presence as long as possible. If we headed east from the PDJ, they would have easily alerted everyone before the Mohawk got to where it was needed. So the plan was they'd head south and east passing over Nankhon Phanom just as entering Laos. They'd fly over Laos entering North Vietnam below the Mu Gia pass and actually fly up through central North Vietnam and reenter Laos from the east. The guess was they wouldn't be waiting for the crew to be entering from the east. It was a gamble, but what the hell wasn't here.

The Mohawk took off at sunset, wanting to reach the area in early night sky when any fires, generators or trucks might be operating, and at a time when the NVA was in full disarray getting their trucks moving down the trails as they wanted to use every minute of darkness to hide their activity. If one waited too late, the battlefield would start slowing down as the NVA usually stopped their trucks from moving an hour or two before sunlight in order to hide them from the daylight eyes of all our planes and satellites.

They breezed over the border and entering Laos among the numerous flights of American planes beginning their night time hunter killer missions over the trail. The Mohawk signed in with Moonbeam with a different call sign, not wanting anyone on the ground to know there was a strange Spud in the theatre. Before leaving Udorn everyone insisted that someone be physically sent over to the Alleycat ship before they took off to let them know they'd be re-entering from North Vietnam about midnight with a strange call sign. Remembering our mission coming back down from the Chinese Highway to the north, they didn't want to be marked as bandits and blown from the sky by our own guys. We all got lucky once; no one was feeling lucky again.

After entering unfamiliar territory of central North Vietnam they turned north. Flying low and fast hoping a strange turboprop plane was at best confusing for anyone on the ground. They were out of range of any guidance radar and had to fly visually off of landmarks in the partially lit moonlight sky. They looked for several river bends to confirm the route. No one talked much, as if someone on the ground would hear them up here. It was eerie and spooky at the same time. Lyle said he felt like an amateur thief breaking in to a country at night, with no idea how this was going to end up.

Finally the turn west was made and thankfully the night was still eerily quiet. Both were quietly shaking waiting for massive shit to start flying up at us at any minute. It felt as if they were flying on four pots of caffeine perhaps wishing they had some to give have a cup to at least fidget with.

"We coming up on target," Lyle announced quietly over the intercom. Tracy fired up the infrared system, hearing the power surge though the headsets as it took its load on the Mohawk generators. All the status lights came on line, they were ready. Across the border and they were soon filming. The next twenty minutes were busy with lining up the runs to insure the Mohawk had filmed the entire target area. Every minute up here over the trees was tipping off anyone below they were being watched. It also gave any gunners enough time to line up their sites and gauge the hawks speed and position.

Suddenly a string of red tracers appeared directly in the Mohawk's path, snaking out of a tree line. There was no time or room to evade so they drove on straight through. Lyle stared at the gauges to see if anything changed, if the oil went to zero on an engine letting us know they hit something critical. They flew a bit north to make sure everything was still in one piece. Lyle and Tracy both thought the tracers appeared slow and lower then usual, but there were two more passes to complete. No one was trilled with the idea of flying back through gunfire now alerted to their presence, on the other hand they certainly didn't want to re-fly this mission anytime soon. So the plane banked round and screamed back through to the south of where they had just gotten fired on. Both were shocked as they were met with quiet skies. The Mohawk circled again and this time came back north for the final pass. This time they were ready as the Mohawk flew though small arms and rockets aimed airborne lighting up the sky and buffeting the plane as it shuttered through the erupting sky on the last pass. Tracy puckered his butt hoping it would hold him to the seat and make a skinner target. Lyle banked hard left and quickly left the scene of the crime as fast as these two engines would could. They signed back in and out with Alleycat on the PDJ with the bogus call sign flying south to get the film back for analysis.

The hawk landed in Udorn and the intel guys scooped up the film and raced off to develop it and hand it over to the CIA guys at the 4802nd Detachment. I was sitting in the HQ trying to down a cold coke trying to cool my parched throat after hunting trucks over the PDJ when I was greeted with more good news. The door swung open, and Daze strolled in wiping his greasy hands nervously in a rag.

283

"Bob, we got some more bad news about Phu Bai," Daze reluctantly offered.

"What, they all went home and we're the only ones left here," I asked still sipping on my coke.

"No man, they left, and, and they left every last dog alone," Daze now left dangling.

Questioning what he was saying I stumbled, "what, they left our dogs . . .why . . . how could they? Then impact hit me, "They left Sally . . .they left her alone to die?"

"They left everyone man, something about they, the dogs weren't issued equipment so there was to be no room, anyone caught sneaking a pup was threatened with a court martial," came the explanation I didn't want to believe.

I was half listening. Sally was gone, she was certainly dead by now like all the rest of the pups that had been the small bit of sanity that kept us all human, or as close as one could get over here. Then my anger turned to Daze yelling, "You knew about this before we took off, why in the hell didn't you say anything."

Now I was quietly crying, sobbing as Daze tried to explain, "and what good was that, you guys had enough to think about. We couldn't do anything."

I was having trouble breathing; I needed to get air, to get out of here and think. So I spun around and ran out of the room, out of the building toward the flight line. I sat under Spud two-twos wings, up against the landing gear thinking, remembering her, and quietly weeping alone in the darkness.

Sometime later Lyle appeared out of the darkness, "lets go Bob, this is not good out here, you'll get yourself shot by some nervous MP . . .lets get us a couple hours shut eye."

We walked quietly back to Pappy's broken chair and a taped up couch for a little sleep. The war had taken a lot this evening; it took Sally and forever a piece of my soul. I finally found my million mile stare; all I gave a shit about from here out was seeking revenge on the sons of bitches that caused enough shit that someone thought it important enough to send thousands of men, women, boys and girls to this insanity half a word away.

The flying continued unabated in the days and weeks ahead. The Hmong were doing well on the PDJ, although the new installed long range artillery hidden in the caves continued to play havoc with their rear base areas. We were waiting on replacement planes as the planes we were flying were over the limit before the required inspections that tore down the engines and vital systems to look for problems or errors that remained hidden from the normal daily maintenance.

Pappy and I took off for another hunt for some elusive tanks the Hmong had seen approaching Muong Soui early the morning before. As we approached the PDJ we both smelled heat, electrical heat. Hunt as we did, we couldn't locate the source, but my stomach was growling from a growing nervousness. It seemed to go away, then every once in a while we'd both get a strong whiff. We headed near Muong Soui and made several passes attempting to pick up anything moving in the darkness. We were so engrossed in finding these tanks when the electrical panels between us and to the rear starting crackling as smoke started pouring out form between the cracks of the panels bolted in place.

"Alleycat, Spud one-six is declaring an emergency and is RTB Udorn," Pappy quickly alerted the orbiting control ship and banked us south to head for safety. The smell was back stronger then ever as the smoke continued to pour from behind us.

Pappy instructed me, "Lets start shutting down everything not critical for flight. Let's kill all the radios except what I need to get us down." I had been shutting down the SLAR radar and was now focused on the radio panel between us. I unstrapped myself from the ejection seat momentarily so I could reach around my seat to unhook the fire extinguisher on my right.

The electrical fire continued to burn behind us, we had no idea where it was coming from or how large or small it was, our focus to get this thing on the ground as quick as possible. The smoke was beginning to fill the cockpit as we were given priority for final approach at Udorn. Floating down toward the runway I could see the flashing red lights of all the emergency vehicles and fire trucks waiting our touch down. The rescue group here had their double bladed helicopter airborne that could literally sit over a crippled airplane and dispense foam to put down the fire before the trucks were able to approach.

We touched down and quickly rolled off the main onto an adjoining taxiway. Both of us popped the hatch to release the smoke and get some fresh air in. As soon as we were on the taxiway, Pappy was directed by the tower to kill the engines, shut her down and both of us get out as quickly as possible. As the props wound down the fire trucks were surrounding us. We took a little time to flip on the ejection seat safety handles so we didn't snag the ring with our gear climbing out and eject us before we got out. Several firefighters in the space suit looking aluminum suits and hoods were next to the cockpit helping us climb out. As soon as we were out they sprayed the electrical panels where the smoke was still bellowing.

Behind the fire trucks were Daze and several crew chiefs were sitting in their trucks. Pappy went ahead of me and was screaming for a good spell as I decided to hold back and watch the action around the Mohawk. Soon Daze walked up after Pappy simmered down and drove a jeep back to our ops building.

"I've been telling everyone, this shit is getting old, we got no parts coming in and I can stretch duck tape only so far," Daze explained to me. "If it was up to me I'd ground all these birds."

"You know, every night is something new," I complained. "I feel I'm running out of luck and I'm going to get killed by something stupid I never anticipated." Daze just nodded as we watched the fire trucks slowly take off assured the fire was out. Daze backed up the quarter ton truck with the hitch and attached it to the front gear of the Mohawk. I hopped in and we slowly towed the crippled bird back to the flight line. Another day, another dollar in the Land of Oz.

With the stand down of more and more US forces throughout Vietnam, the parts to keep the Mohawks flying were becoming impossible to get. The parts problem was never good, hell most people never knew what a Mohawk was, much less the supply sergeants in the supply depots far from our airstrips. The Mohawk we had the electrical fire in was now sitting in an Air Force hanger, looking like a defrocked prehistoric bird, as the crew chiefs were forced to strip more and more parts off of her to keep the other birds flying. We took bets on when we'd have to report this plane as missing in action when the last bolt fell to the hanger floor. Even among the Mohawk units the first priority went to the units in Vietnam who got the parts delivered there first for everyone. Lately, if there was anything left, we got the junk. We had heard Spud one-three has lost an engine on three separate missions up north. While losing an engine was never good, with the flat coastal areas they could return to Da Nang on one engine and make it. The rumors were they'd try and pawn off Spud one-three on us. If we lost an engine up in the PDJ it was all over, as one engine would never get us enough altitude to get over the mountains that ringed the PDJ. We'd have to eject or punch out into the night sky and hope the Hmong got to us first after daylight. And losing three engines meant this plane was jinxed, no one wanted to fly it, that's why we were sure we'd see it show up in our revetment one morning.

Two days later everyone was summoned, well ordered to the flight line by Pappy. None of us had any clue what was up, but that wasn't unusual here.

"Gentlemen, we got a problem here," Pappy began. "We got word they're getting ready to rotate aircraft, and Spud one-three is set to join us in a couple days."

Several "shits" and "fucks" rolled though the collective group as Pappy continued, "I argued as much as I could but I was overruled. We all know what will happen if we lose an engine up north, and this birds lost three in two weeks. I'm going to propose something that requires we all agree or I drop it; that we all refuse to fly if they send us one-three. They'll threaten us all with a court martial, and the fact is they could do it. So I want you all to think individually and give me your answers. If we do this, we all agree unanimously or we don't do it, got it?

"Got it Sir," replied Koontz for all of us.

That night we flew our missions and came back to gather in the bars downtown in the early morning hours. The discussion was all about the choice and the threat we faced. Fly and die, or stand firm and perhaps find ourselves in the brig. But hell, they had already sent us to Vietnam, hadn't they?

The next day the answer to Pappy was a collective yes; we'd all stand together and refuse to fly if they sent us one-three. For the next week we all flew our missions with no word on our fate. No one wanted to think about it, we were fighting the enemy and the army; there was no safe place.

Then returning to the hotel in the village one night we found everyone partying hardy, so we joined the noise and obvious celebration. It didn't take too long to realize we had won, the brass back in Vietnam backed down and they'd be sending a different plane to join our Mohawks here. It was a small victory in a sea of shit, but we'd take it.

With our daily briefings at the CIA ops, the growing concern was the amount of activity increasing in the PDJ now that the weather was improving. By the beginning of September the Hmong took Muong Soui and thought the PDJ could be held. Ho's boys were trucking in troops and supplies to route the Hmong. Their large guns continued to hammer away at the Thai artillery bases on the south and west edge of the Plaines. On September 21st the enemy made their first push of the fall. Upon our return in the early morning hours we were told to grab some quick sleep and report to 7/13 Air Force headquarters in the morning.

We were directed to a gray trailer out of the tarmac behind the air ops building where air force officers with large sticks moved aircraft names over large Plexiglas boards that lined the walls. In the ops center up several steps were some large easy chairs where ranking officers watched the air ops and made decisions on what forces to send where depending on the threat. It reminded me of an old World War II movies where the English commanders were marshaling their air forces in a secret room, moving model airplanes across a map of the English Channel during the Battle of Britain. Here we were fighting the war in the Land of Oz, and this was a secret to everyone in the world except those dying in Oz.

In this nondescript trailer Koontz and I waited in a small room while a meeting continued in the adjoining space. Shortly the door opened and we were directed into the large conference room. Here was the top command staff of the 7th/13th Air Force who had flown from around Southeast Asia to meet on the growing action up north in Laos. We spent the next forty-five minutes around maps and photos describing the trucks and tanks we were taking on every night on the PDJ to people with more stars on their collars then I had seen on the Hollywood walk of fame. We talked about the increasing antiaircraft fire and what we thought the enemy was up to. We left with their giving us a commitment to give us gunships every night to press the attack forward and a renewed hope that maybe the Hmong would get the air sorties they desperately needed.

288

For the next week we flew every plane every night around the clock with gunships in tow. We found dozens of trucks on each run, and the Spectre crews were blasting away as fast as gattling guns could fire. And every night we continued to take heavy anti aircraft fire, I was hoping our rein of terror would continue as we were pissing off a lot of people down there and that was what I wanted to do, because nothing else mattered. My life revolved around what we did up here every night. I no longer had anything here, Sally was gone and if I made it to go home, well, that was not of worry today.

Koontz and I flew over the fence the evening of September 30th ready for another night of setting trucks on fire on the Plaines. We flew over the twinkling lights of Vientiane where men and women dined and drank in the safety of the capital while war raged not far to the north. The first indication that tonight would be different was when we tried to check in with Alleycat. Alleycat was still on the ground in Udorn with mechanical problems, so we continued our flight north and soon was over the PDJ. We made our run east to the North Vietnamese border and were updated on the status of Alleycat; it was still battling mechanical problems but hope to be up soon.

Alleycat was the nighttime flying command ship for the northern region. A trailer with electronics and radio communications of every type was slid into the cargo area of a C-130. Loaded with a crew of intelligence, radio operators, interpreters, and command officers entrusted with directing a wide range of aircraft and ground forces to fight an ever-changing war beneath them. This was the first time in the war I was flying over Laos without an Alleycat or Moonbeam. Soon we were receiving calls from down south asking us to attempt to reach ground units to gain intel on what was going on the various Lima Sites and listening posts on the ground. The added problem was the Plaines was surrounded by a massive range of high mountains, so radio calls needed a high flying plane to receive and send signals and messages from the war in the north, down to the various CIA, Lao, and US military ops centers in the south. We were soon relaying message from Hmong units located at locations known as Hill Billy, Smallman, and Yellow Dog. It wasn't too much longer then we were requesting fire from the Thai artillery at Mustang and Lion for some frantic Hmong taking fire at Hotel Yankee and Blue Boy. The radio dial spun as I flipped to different frequencies to take requests for info on what was happening on the ground up here from the Plexiglas boys down south. Soon we were directing air strikes for the Hmong near Xieng Khouang and at Hunter and Badman.

We continued our mission routes as the radar system mapped the PDJ and beyond, we reported movers but our mission was changed, that night we would become Alleycat. The radio calls were non stop, now I could hear the panic as the small guys at Hill Billy and Fox Echo were taking fire, so when I couldn't get artillery online I'd scream until we could hunt up an air strikes. I could hear them on the ground yelling over the mortars, I thought I could feel their earth move, hear them die. And the only help they ever had was from the sky, and tonight we were all they got, and they'd get every piece of hope we could give them. We plowed back and forth through the skies of Oz that night trying to interpret the Hmong on the ground taking fire and forced to think in English because we were all they had. Then Muong Soui was under attack and the attention focused here quickly as families living with the Hmong fighters were sharing in the barrage of mortars, rockets, and artillery. Enough stops around the radio dial and we were able to scare or piss off enough people to get the Lao in Vientiane to get a Spooky gunship airborne to help out those men, women, and children huddled in the bunkers at Muong Soui.

At this point we were informed that Alleycat would not be airborne that night, they'd try to get Cricket, the daytime command center launched earlier in the morning, but could we continue and for how long could we stay up? There was only one answer to the first and that was yes, the how long question had Koontz do some quick math on our remaining fuel and consumption and we advised Udorn we could give them short of three more hours and then we'd fall out of the sky from lack of fuel. So our mission now involved on the job training, trying to figure out the various Hmong bases, their call signs and frequencies and match them up with available strike or support aircraft and artillery firebases, to understand their version of English under the pressure of them taking fire and returning it.

We continued to fly and coordinate for another two and a half hours. We had brief breaks when Koontz took drastic maneuvers to dodge the constant antiaircraft fire floating up from the Plaines and hilltops below us. I had long ignored the radar film creeping up the screen in front of me. I wasn't looking for targets, I now had more targets then anyone could deal with. I was out of paper, so I began writing call signs, radio frequencies and coordinates with my grease pen on my maps, the radar screen, and finally my hatch window. I could soon almost tell if the call was coming from Stringbean or Badman based on the Hmong accent. I was now familiar with what Thai artillery bass to call in, like Rossini or Tom Tom depending on their firing position in relation to who needed the help. As the fighting subsided in the early morning hours there was work to arrange what wounded needed to get flown out at first light, or if Red Hat or Tonto needed a rearm or supply drop asap.

As I began to stare at Koontz's gleaming white helmet as a possible new writing space, he finally informed me we were almost out of fuel and we'd have to RTB, or return to base. As we turned back to fuel and sleep we got a call from a now airborne Cricket speeding north out of Udorn. The timing could not have been better. The activity on the PDJ had actually calmed down and we were headed home. Soon Cricket would be over the Plaines back in control of someone's secret war.

"Roger Spud, this is Cricket, acknowledge you are RTB," came that welcome sound over the radio.

"You got that right, RTB to some warm food and a warm bed," replied an exhausted Koontz.

"Spud, on behalf of all of us and 7th Air Force, we would like to acknowledge and thank you for the tremendous job you performed tonight in taking on a mission that was critical in maintaining continued and critical support throughout the night to our allies. We are indebted to your crew."

"Roger Cricket, our pleasure," replied a shocked Koontz who quickly followed by a signature squawk from his rubber duck over the airwaves.

"And to your duck," replied Cricket.

We were both speechless, there had been no thought of what we could or couldn't do that evening. Anyone would have done it, you don't question picking up the pieces necessary in survive to another day. It was a night we would remember forever.

We were able to sponge a night off and decided to try the swiss cheese pizza and the outdoor movie on the Thai Airbase. Sitting in the beautiful night sky without thinking about flying, it was a perfect evening. We enjoyed ourselves on the on base clubs waiting for the others to return from their flights. Then the rat patrol was having a group outing with an evening at the bowling alley in the village of Udorn. This strange mix of west meets east was always a mind teaser; hell, they promoted Thai shoot-em up western movies on huge billboards along the highways.

As US forces continued to leave Vietnam and the surrounding theater, the North Vietnamese never lost an opportunity to test the waters and insert forces where we had left. By fall the Air Force was no longer keeping fighters on station above the battlefield to protect all us slow movers from the communist Mig fighters some hundred miles to the east in Hanoi. Speed, hell we hoped for two hundred fifty knots to fly away from ground fire and anti-aircraft much less a screaming jet. We had no capability for air to air action; our weapons systems, thanks to the army wigs back home now consisted of our two thirty-eight pistols we both carried on our sides. That created quite the threat to a thug in the sky screaming toward us at six hundred knots armed to his teeth.

The North Vietnamese were given Mig-21 fighter jets from the Soviets and the Chinese. They were armed with the infrared air-to-air missiles and with speeds of over six hundred knots that could easily overtake any of the slow moving aircraft prosecuting the war up here like the OV-1. Located in bases around Hanoi, they were protected from bombing by American forces thanks to the continued brilliant wisdom of the politicians playing army in the basement of the White House.

With their Air Force being dismantled and sent home, the US commanders put a group of Phantoms on ready alert at Udorn. We'd pass them in our jeeps every day coming and going to the base as the F-4 pilots sat in their flight suits in a shack on the east end of the runway. Their planes were armed and fueled and if the call came that Migs were on their way, they race to their fighter, strap in, and fire up the engines while the crew chiefs pulled the yellow caution pins from their fuel tanks and missile racks and quickly put the pilot through a safety check, then duck while the planes streaked north.

The only problem with that was the NVA by now had done the math. They could take off and streak across the border and play havoc over the PDJ before the Phantoms arrived on station. They could pass go, collect two hundred dollars, and return safely to their bases where again, we weren't allowed to touch them. All they had to do was test the equation, and today was their day.

Sanders and I took off early and headed north for our night of truck hunting to the east of the PDJ. There was a lot of activity in the area where the valleys and roads coming into Laos from North Vietnam wound. It was time for the communists to start building the troops for the coming dry season. It was their turn to move their pieces across the Plaines. And we'd use every opportunity to turn their trucks winding in a single line over the narrow roads into a burning roadblock.

We had gotten north and east early and were mapping movers already over our target area. All we could do now was track and count, as the gunships hadn't arrived yet. We cruised alone for another ten minutes when the radio crackled.

"Spud two-two, this is Alleycat, be advised we got bandits out of Bulls-eye, heading two-six-three, zero-eight to your position, angels unknown."

Sanders stared directly at me and through me as he swung the Mohawk on its side turning south, southwest as we pushed the throttles to the wall. We were off to the races and bringing up tail to every plane that was flying this far north.

What Alleycat had told us was US radar had detected bandits or Mig fighters, heading out of Bull's-eye, code name for Hanoi; heading at a bearing of two hundred seventy three degrees or direct to the west, eight minutes to our position. The clock had started, we could now get a play by play to our shoot down, and we could wait for death and we couldn't do a fucking thing.

And help, well that was the Phantoms loaded for air-to-air combat on the ready; the troubling part of the call was no word on fighters heading to save us.

"Spud, bandits at a heading of two-six-three, zero-six to your position, angels unknown."

Sanders and I said nothing as we headed south as fast as this Mohawk would fly, we were running with our back to the enemy who was screaming at us at over three times our speed. He was being directed by radar, when he got close, his nose radar would take over, find us and lock on. Then he'd launch his air-to-air missiles and if he didn't have time to take pleasure in watching our destruction was free to retreat to the safety of Hanoi. After all, the missiles would lock onto us with their infrared systems seeing the heat from our engines leading them directly up our butt.

"Spud, bandits at a heading of two-seven-one, zero-five to your position, angels unknown."

Five minutes more to live, this was a feeling I had never experienced before, when the anti-aircraft fire had come, or when the Sam's had exploded we reacted, we could turn, dive, we could do something. I was now scared shitless, all we could do was watch the airspeed and wait for the inevitable. The ground was fogged in; so we couldn't dive low, or hug the mountains and valleys to make his job of finding us harder. Dropping low below the clouds insured we'd plaster ourselves on the side of a mountain, here we could pray for a group of cocky fighter jocks.

"Spud, bandits at a heading of two-five-seven, zero-four to your position, we got a Killer flight at zero-nine."

Hope! Or was I hearing things, fighters nine minutes to our position, bandits four; we needed distance and time. I looked at Sanders, he heard it too, I saw a smile briefly, then we both went back to thinking; The F-4's were screaming north to engage the Migs. It was unlikely the Migs wanted to engage the F-4's, they wanted an easy target, like us.
Time, I flipped the cover back from the radar imagery painting in front of me and looked at the film coming up. I wanted to know where we were. We could only see clouds outside the cockpit glass, but the radar was mapping the ground below us, it could see through the weather. I could see the southern part of the PDJ, there, there was Skyline Ridge, I grabbed for the maps trying to see how far Phou Bia Mountain was. Sanders instantly saw what I was up to.

"Spud, bandits now at a heading of two-two-three, zero-three to your position, F-4's zero-seven."

"Fuck" Sanders snapped, I didn't need the intercom to hear that. The Migs heading had changing to a southerly position, they were directly behind us now, heading south like us. The F-4's had picked up some time on the Migs, but not enough.

With my finger poking at the radar screen for impact I keyed my microphone, "if I can see that the film shows us over Phou Bia Mountain, we can drop down into the valley, cut the line of sight the Mig radar was painting us with?" I was guessing, looking for a buy in, or an argument with my reasoning. "The problem is there's a three minute delay when I see the terrain on the film up here. That means I'd have to guess we're past Phou Bia Mountain before we see it here. I could guess wrong, but if I was right we might buy a couple minutes till the F-4's get here?"

"Spud, bandits now at a heading of one-niner-seven, zero-two to your position, Killer flight zero-six." They were climbing up our ass, they hadn't been scared off by the F-4's they certainly knew of at this point.

Sanders put his right hand on the throttles and calmly said, "let's do it, tell me when."

I stared at the film comparing it quickly to the map I had embedded in my mind from flying up here every night. Now I had to guess, how much film was three minutes, too little and we bought the side of Phou Bia. "Think, think" I found myself talking to myself.

"Now" I yelled, hoping like hell I was right.

He pushed the stick forward and dumped off the throttles, we were screaming toward the ground. The plane shock and shuttered as we now picked up speed in our descent, I watched the altimeter needle wind down through the numbers, it went passed nine thousand, we were lower then Phou Bia Mountain, but what side? More seconds screamed by, all we could see were solid clouds, but we were still flying, we were still alive.

"Spud, bandits now heading away at a heading of zero-six-five, Killer flight zero-four." They were heading back to Hanoi with the Phantoms in hot pursuit.

"Yah-whoo" we both screamed through the intercom. Sanders pulled back on the stick feeding power as we leveled out and continued south to safety across the fence. The F-4's chased the Migs all the way back to Hanoi where they were advised to break off contact. The rules of war allowed the Migs to land safely to wait for another day, another opportunity. Apparently their radar lost us when we took the plunge below the mountain range cutting the line of site his radar needed to get a lock-on so he could release his missiles. It was true they had no desire to mingle with the F-4's. When they lost us on radar momentarily, they didn't have time to chase and re-target us, the F-4's were screaming north and the Migs withdrew to try again another day.

We touched down lightly in the slow drizzle of rain reflecting the colored lights of the runway and taxiways. We both released our latches and both hatches sprung open to let the fresh air rush in. I took a deep breath I never thought I'd experience again.

The war had taken a strange new twist tonight, and another piece of insanity would etch itself forever in our soul.

The Migs caused quite the uproar throughout the Barrel Roll region, and its implications on the politics of Hanoi reverberated across the ocean. It was the talk of everyone who flew, and then you could almost watch the river of rumor to fact spread throughout the base, clubs, restaurants and bars.

To the CIA and the 7th Air Force this was a bold new move in the poker game called the secret war. The plan of battle called for a wide range of slow moving aircraft to fight the war over the heads of the Hmong who counted on these flying artillery, troop transport, and supply trains. But every one of these planes were sitting ducks for the fast flying Migs who sat just across the border ready to pounce again. Was it a fluke, a one-time event that would be forgotten in the months ahead?

Everyone knew it heralded a new boldness on behalf of Hanoi that was being influenced by the hands they were holding and playing in secret negotiations with Henry Kissinger that no one knew of yet. While the outcome of this war was being decided elsewhere, everywhere here was fighting merely for survival and focused on the fight at hand. The Air Force with stretched resources pushed the F-4's on the alert pad ready to cut the time to get launched. Then they randomly put an air-to-air Phantom in the skies over Laos, to at least make the Migs contemplate a dogfight should be fortunate enough to choose the wrong time. The bad news was the F-4's drank fuel like a drunken sailor and their time on station orbiting over a battlefield is limited forcing them south to find a flying tanker.

Fall approached finding the Hmong had taken and held a number of positions on and around the PDJ. Now as September was ending we were trying to keep the NVA tanks and trucks from reinforcing their troops that had pinned down six Hmong SGU companies at Lima Site 276, in addition to blunting any new adventures.

By October we could see signs the communists were preparing for their dry season offensive, the daily photo recon was now showing NVA tanks on Route Nine. The communist 130mm artillery pieces were moved within range of the Thai artillery bases and began shelling them. Air power tried to hunt these guns, as they were outside the range of the Thai artillery. The communists could reach the Thai guns, and now the Thai needed the air power they had been sent to replace. It was all part of the magical mystery tour in the Land of Oz.

For a while it appeared the command staff was in agreement on the prosecution of the war up north, they had committed fighters and gunships to take on the targets we were finding. It was open season now, too many times before we had flown mission without gunships. We could watch the enemy move, but were impotent in doing anything about it. Now we were leaving the Plaines every night with trucks and tanks burning into the night. My promise I had made the night I heard of Sally's abandonment was unfolding and now we had the big guns to even the score.

Revenge for our onslaught was just as swift as the Migs returned to the Plaines. They knew we needed to scramble fighters from Udorn, and that gave them time to hunt for the sheep that wandered too far from the herd. If the Migs arrived and the weather was good, we'd drop down into the valleys and crevices of the mountains attempting to stay below the radar, to be the mouse that scampered from behind one hill to another. The Migs one night decided to take out a Mohawk when the Air Force had a fighter in orbit. A broken Mig later, and the communists were gun shy to stay up here too long. They'd go for the easy kill, but now when they got warning that the Phantoms were enroute, they quickly turned tail and ran. They were no match for the American fighter pilots, and they were smart enough to realize it. If the weather was bad, we prayed the F-4's made it up; even from a distance to intimidate the Migs into thinking maybe tomorrow was a better day.

Even if they didn't get anyone, they drove the us and the flying gunships off the PDJ for awhile, to give their forces on the ground a breather. It was three-dimensional chess, and sometimes a new move was created, sometimes a piece fell off the board. Every move was countered by another one, one that was equally outside of the box.

The war on the ground was equally as complicated. Now the NVA 312th Division was on the PDJ striking jabs at the Thai artillery and at the base at Long Chieng. Several Lima Sites were surrounded with enemy anti-aircraft guns that resulted in bringing down the Air America planes that were critical to supplying the necessary food and ammo. Many of the supplies at Bouam Loung were now being dropped from the sky by Chinook helicopters. The decision was made to land only to pick up the dead or wounded.

Vang Pao and the Hmong once again hoped to hold on to the Plaines, to stop the see saw battle that had seen the PDJ taken from them too many times before. But the communists were ready to throw more divisions into the battle. As before, the Hmong had taken crack NVA troops and guns away from the war going on in South Vietnam. Many an American in South Vietnam would owe their life to a Hmong warrior for taking the soldier or gun away that had their name written on it. And the secret is, they'd never realize it, that's how it was in the Land of Oz. For the North Vietnamese, they wanted to press the battle and tie up as much real estate as possible before they reached any agreement with the US, and the Hmong were in their way.

The winds had changed over the Plaines, literally as Typhoon Hester rolled thought Laos. We battled through the storms every night to find an enemy that was hunkered down in their bunkers and caves. Nothing was moving up here, and it was becoming apparent that Mother Nature could do what no army could, bring the war to a halt. The Hmong had a reprieve from what they knew all too well the dry season would bring them, more NVA.

By the beginning of November the skies again cleared and now the NVA was on the move. We spend a great deal of time keeping the tanks and trucks away from the small Hmong road watch teams on hilltops with names like Rocket Mobile, Ohio, and Smallman. We could hear them by radio, listen to Alleycat talking with them, perhaps to see if they could hear the truck or tank approaching that we had picked up. Or to have Alleycat fire up the Thai artillery when Spectre was finishing off a convoy on the other side of the PDJ.

Now into November the war was winding down for me; I had long passed my Phu Bai day, which meant there were sixty-nine days left in my tour. At a bar one night we ran into some Air America guys who were befuddled by our Spud call sign until they realized we were the nighthawks who directed fire up north in the skies after the sun set. They told us that several Hmong up in Long Chieng were looking for the crew who became Alleycat one night in the sky, when the remote sites of Muong Soui and Xieng Khouang where under fire and needed artillery and air strikes. After a night of rebellious behavior that occurred every night at the Thai lady, they told us to meet them at the Air America gate at fourteen hundred hours, they'd catch us a ride north.

"And wear civvies; no wallets, ids, you won't need them there, " were the final words Shad yelled as we all headed out from the bars that evening.

Koontz had already headed back home to the stated weeks ago, so I asked Lyle if he was interested in visiting the boonies. He agreed and we showed up at the gate at the requested fourteen hundred hours expecting no one else to show given the haze everyone was in the evening before. We were shocked when Shad showed up and took us on a long trek through the maze of storage building until we rounded a corner and saw a gray C-119 being loaded with pallets of food and supplies.

"Ok guys, next stop Alternate," Shad directed us on board up the loading ramp, the cargo master pointed out some swinging web seats on the side we strapped ourselves into. In little time the gate closed and we were taxing for position to take off and head north. Sitting back here in the darkness of day heading north to where we had gone every night. I realized this was going to be strange, I just didn't know how strange.

The flight lumbered north, once airborne we unstrapped ourselves and climbed around the cargo bay to look out the few windows or portholes we could find as we flew low over the fence into Laos. We flew up the valleys; the beauty of the hills in the daylight was overwhelming. It was a contrast of incredible magnitude, Lao farmers working in flat rice paddies next to a sheer mountain of rock or stark karsts that magically reached into the sky.

Somewhere in this geography field trip the plane began to weave between the stands of karsts that stood between it and the runway ay Long Chieng. We quickly made our way back to the webbed seat and were bouncing on the runway before we could strap in. The props were thrown in reverse as soon as the wheels hit and we were thrown to the floor. Trying to maintain a sense of coolness, I ignored the sharp pain in my ass and tried to act like I've done this a thousand times.

We taxied off to a quick stop and the loading ramp quickly came down. Before it hit the ground outside a half a dozen Hmong jumped in to undo the tie downs and get the goods to wherever or whoever was in dire need of them. We walked out the ramp and looked around this place called Long Chieng.

Strange white guys with our befuddled look attracted attention immediately. As a large number of Hmong children engulfed us, a soldier quickly appeared and asked if we were from the hawks that flew at night. We shook our heads yes and were escorted off up the dirt roads to several building that housed the Americans, the guys from Air America, the Forward Air Controllers known as the Ravens and the assorted CIA or Embassy types.

The history of the FAC's, known as the Ravens and Butterflies is long and as varied as everything else in this strange secret war. When the United Stated aligned with the Lao Government, Vang Pao and his Hmong soldiers, air power was an essential component of war that the US could bring to the table. The fighters, bombers, command and intel planes could not be stationed in Laos in order not to violate the various Geneva Accords. These planes would come from bases in Vietnam, off Navy carriers, or from numerous Royal Thai Air forces bases built with American money. Close air support required FAC's or forward air controllers in low and slow flying aircraft that could easy see the battlefield, verify the enemy positions, and mark the targets for the strike aircraft. In order to do this effectively, these FAC's needed to be close to the action, and this meant they'd have to base in forward areas of Laos. The Air Force called upon the Air Commandos to perform theses functions but they'd first have to be "sheep dipped." These Butterflies and Ravens were flown to Udorn where they'd turn in their ids, uniforms, and all evidence of employment in the military. Many times they were "sold" their aircraft to take into Laos, and then assigned to private companies or aid agencies operating inside Laos.

In the early years these "unassigned" Air Commandos, or Butterflies flew as non rated or enlisted officers flying with pilots, many times Air American planes where they located and marked targets for the fighters coming into Laos. Names we had heard of, like Charlie Jones and Jim Stanford.

When the 7th Air Force Commander General Momyer found out enlisted airmen and not qualified pilots were directing his strike aircraft he hit the ceiling. The result was the creation of the Ravens that would replace the role of the Butterfly FAC's. The rules called for successful Vietnam tested pilots that would volunteer for the Steve Canyon Program. One approved they proceeded to Udorn, where again they were processed or sheep dipped to operate in the black in Laos. These pilots were a select few, never totaling fewer then two hundred pilots in the entire war. They flew O-1's, O-2's, and T-28's to direct the vast array of allied air power during the daylight over Laos. Those up north with us called Long Chieng their home. Names we heard of in the briefings or in the stories of combat, like Larry Sanborn, call sign Sandy, Fred Platt aka Magnet Ass, Ron Rinehart aka Papa Fax, etc.

Five minutes into the introductions, we started compared the planes, missions, who flew what, what we ran into at night versus their war in the day. We got a tour of the ramp as the T-28's and 0-1's were American and Hmong pilots were returning at the end of the day. It looked like an old World War II movie was happening in front of my eyes. We got to hear about Lee Lue, the revered Hmong teacher who became an Ace, whose reputation I had heard about in Udorn. His death had certainly dealt a blow to the Hmong collective soul. Someone pointed out the Kings house across the way with a Thai 105 artillery piece set up in its front yard.

More Americans flew in and we were trying to keep everyone's names and stories straight. We were invited to the bar up on the second level of one of the raven hootches. The beers were flowing and the conversations picked up speed and tempo. One of the guys heard my tail of Sally J. and tried to talk me into one of the pups from a Princess Hamburger for fifty bucks, later thirty. I was almost considering the insanity of doing it to myself twice when word came we were invited to dinner with the Hmong SGU and several of the soldiers who were returning off the PDJ and being honored. We walked over to one of the Hmong officer's house, a concrete block type building someone rumored was Vang Pao's. The dinner spread consisted of a lot of rice, sauces, and vegetables. Then General Vang Pao arrived with one of his Colonels, Colonel Xay Dang Xiong. Colonel Xay Dang Xiong was in charge of Vang Pao's summer campaign to take back the PDJ. It was his men from Xieng Khouang and Hunter. Several of these fighters were here, being honored this evening. Soon glasses of White Horse Whiskey were being passed around and talk replaced dinner as the major event.

Then there was a call for attention to celebrate the victory of these Hmong warriors. Several cooked and de-feathered chickens were brought out for Vang Pao and Colonel Xay Dang Xiong to read the future of the battles ahead. The position of the feet told a story of their future versus those of the forces around them including those who battled them.

302

Following came the Hmong Baci (ba-sii) a string tie celebration, pieces of white flax or string were passed around to everyone as each of us tied the string around the soldiers just back from battle around their wrist. The string above the knot was cut off to remove the bad spirits; they were set on fire and quickly extinguished in cold water. Each person then told of the warrior's feats, and best wishes for heath, victory and family.

The evening was quite moving; these gentle people had fought the best of the NVA to standstill so they could live the way they wanted, free. A million miles away a country professed these same ideals, and the Hmong trusted their promise of brotherhood would be honored. These soldiers talked excitingly about their feats, how they bloodied the enemy, and soon they could go back to their families. Several had plans of school down south in Vientiane after the war, or in France if they could. The White Horse whiskey continued to pour and the evening wore on. Somewhere we managed to limp back to the bar and see who would stand last. I never knew who that was, as I awoke with a massive hangover when I heard the T-28's fire up in the morning. I wasn't a Whiskey drinker and my body was reminding me of it.

Several hours latter and some coffee later, Lyle and I were up and about, now we needed to arrange a ride down south as tonight we'd be flying north of here to do what we do best, burn trucks.

We flew out of Long Chieng on a C-123 headed down to Vientiane then on to Udorn. I left Long Chieng for the last time. I didn't know that it wouldn't be too many years and the Hmong would follow with the enemy in hot pursuit. I couldn't see the future; I was like everyone only thinking of today.

The day came in November for my last mission and then several days off to get my affairs in order before flying back to Vietnam to return home. I didn't have much in the way of affairs to straighten out, but no one wanted anyone flying days before returning back home, it was bad karma.

By the time we got back, we raced the jeep to get over to our rat patrol HQ. I ran to quickly throw on my flight gear and yelled to Sanders I'd meet him on the flight line. He must have gotten antsy, either that or Daze pissed him off again I surmised. I could hear a Mohawk with engines running as I got up near the flight line. Over the top of the revetments I could see the nav lights blinking, it was my plane. I went straight to the flight line; sure enough Sanders was strapped in helmet on with both engines running going through his flap control surface tests with the crew chief. I always enjoyed climbing into the cockpit with the props running five feet away. One slip while climbing up the side of the plane to crawl through the hatch and I'd have part of my anatomy removed by the props. As I threw my helmet up on the instruments and strapped in, Sanders was already rolling out to the taxiway.

"Problem with your watch Mr. Curry," the intercom broke the silence.

"Ouch," I thought to myself. Picking my words carefully I responded, "Sorry about that, it won't happen again."

"Good, glad to hear that."

Now I knew he forgot, this was my last mission, I was heading back to Vietnam in days and then back to the real world in a week. I took the opportunity to fire up the radar systems early, I wasn't sure what crawled up his butt, but I thought it'd be best if he had some "one on one" time with himself.

The Typhoon had left weeks ago and the PDJ was enjoying dry weather. Any other decade that might be good news for the Hmong, unfortunately now it meant more communist troops and guns would attempt to make their pilgrimage across the Plain of Jars. As we crossed the fence near Vientiane, the Mekong River was running well over its banks as the rains from Typhoon Hester made its way from China to the sea. The jungle was shimmering in the bright sunset as we began our climb up over the sheer mountains to the Plaines. We checked in with Alleycat about the same time as Spectre three-three did. If the enemy was moving tonight, we had the team in place up north here to take care of them.

"Shit Bob, it's your last mission . . .almost forgot," the intercom interrupted the silence. "Any special requests?"

Surprised I replied, "Well maybe one, lets try not to get shot down?"

"No shit, hey sorry about before, got a letter full of problems from back home, life shit you know."

We cruised north as we talked about life shit. It's pretty hard finding out problems from home a week or more after it happened, by the time you wrote back it was usually resolved for better or worse. Family was learning to deal us out of the equation. I was heading back soon and scared of what to expect. Somehow my reality was here in this bizarre land called Oz. That life I struggled to remember was pretty foreign to me now. How would I fit in because what I thought was important back then seemed so petty now?

Our self-help meeting in the sky meeting was abruptly interrupted with a radio call, "Spud, Spectre, this is Alleycat, be advised we got bandits out of Bulls-eye, heading two-eight-eight, zero-eight to your position, angels unknown."

The words weren't complete and Sanders had spun the Mohawk on its tail and we were dropping altitude and heading west in a hurry.

"Shit Curry, you gonna give me bad luck tonight with your last mission shit."

"Great, pin this on me, I got enough issues," I replied as we both quietly wondered if tonight was the night. And where in the hell was our cover?

"Spud, Spectre, bandits now at a heading of two-six-two, zero-seven to your position."

Ok, now we had a fair fight, all we needed to do was hide in the tall grass long enough for them to realize they got some F-4's climbing up their butts. Unfortunately we had started our mission well north of the PDJ, so the Migs once they hit the Plaines would be between the F-4's and us. Just then Sanders turned us into a valley heading northwest. With a full moon we could go low and stay below the peaks. If we kept that up their radar wouldn't track us, and hopefully they thought we were heading south out of the PDJ, not north.

"Spud, Spectre, bandits now at a heading of two-six-six, zero-five to your position, fighters zero-seven."

Well, the Migs were heading toward the south, southwest so that was good. The bad news was they hadn't turned yet, and they must know the Phantoms were on the way.

"They're heading for the Spectre," Sanders said across the intercom just as I thought it. Shit, of course they wanted the gunship, an incredible trophy and there was nothing we could do. Now I prayed to a god I had left somewhere back in Vietnam for these guys waiting to die, listening to Alleycat doing their final play by play.

We continued north and west; even Alleycat knew the game, leaving us out of the play by play with, "Spectre, bandits now at a heading of one-niner-eight, zero-four to your position, fighters zero-six."

Man, they wanted him bad, they normally would have turned and run by now. We listened to the deadly silence tick by until, "Spectre, bandits now at a heading AWAY at zero-six-two, fighters zero-three."

"Shit, they must have running on afterburners," I yelled, referring to the F-4's that must have kicked in their afterburners to close on the Migs this fast. It also meant they were burning precious fuel, a gamble that might limit their time up here for a dogfight. But there was a Spectre hanging in the balance and that took a whole lot of extra risk on everyone's part. But at least the Migs were heading back and we hadn't heard of them venturing out this way twice in one day . . . I hoped.

We continued north for another several minutes until Sanders banked and turned us south back to the Plaines. I got my heart rate down and turned my attention back to the radar film that had been recording for the last ten to fifteen minutes while I was preoccupied.

"Holly Shit!"

That instantly got Sander's attention, "What, what?"

I franticly pointed to the screen, we had picked up a trail of movers so thick it looks like a line of ants walking down the screen; so thick Sanders could see it from his seat.

"Holly shit is right," was his overwhelmed response.

"Alleycat, we need Spectre here real quick if he's still up," I radioed.

"Roger Spud two-three, Spectre three-three back enroute to the PDJ," replied Alleycat.

Our mission legs had normally gone around the Plain of Jars, other then our flight several months ago to map the Chi-Com Highway, the Chinese road coming over the border from China into the northwest corner of Laos. Now we knew the rumors were true, the North Vietnamese had been sending troops and supplies up into China well away from any allied guns. Then they traveled west across China and took the Chi-Com highway down from China into Laos bypassing all our flying guns hunting for them coming west directly from Vietnam.

"Alleycat this is Spud two-three, we have fifty plus movers in a line from x-ray delta five niner six four four zero to x-ray bravo niner seven six two zero three."

I could have heard a shoe drop as the silence was deafening.

"Spud, confirm five-zero plus movers?"

"Roger Alleycat, five-zero plus movers."

I think I heard the only airborne "fuck" from Alleycat in this war.

In fast order Spectre was on target and destroying trucks, tanks, bikes; hell, shopping carts for all I know. We were now re-flying to the west of this one forbidden and forgotten road as we saw of river of red fire burning in the bottom of this long valley. The red rain from Spectre's guns continued to pour death on the mix. We didn't need to give any more coordinates; the enemy had lit themselves up, but we keep filming. We flew in awe until fuel became a concern, but not before Alleycat was directing several flights of F-4's, and 105's in on the action.

"I got this one" I looked at Sanders, then waiting for the nod as we broke south to home, for me literally.

"Alleycat, this is Spud two-three, RTB Udorn, alpha mike-foxtrot" as I was in fact telling Alleycat "adios motherfucker," a small formality everyone had grown to use as their last signoff before heading stateside.

"Roger Spud two-three, thanks for the invite to the roast up north, god specd."

And we returned to party into the night with everyone in the rat patrol, and anyone who happened by. It was an insane end to my secret war; at least that's what I believed tonight.

I woke the next morning and reality hit me that after three hundred plus missions, I now had three free days left in Udorn before returning to my unit, now the 225th Aviation Unit in Thuay Hoa. Another week there and I finally report into Cam Ranh Bay for this Army thing called DERO's. I only knew it as that magic carpet ride back to the states.

I awoke late that morning after a night out closing the bars after my last flight out. Steve and I decided to grab the jeep and head into town. The streets were buzzing with people going about their business of everyday existence.

When we got to the center of the city, we parked our jeep and walked over to the central marketplace. Teaming with people buying and selling about anything imaginable, it was a colorful place. Built in-between several narrow streets, it consisted of tables and booths under bright colored sheets of flag like material rippling in the slight breeze. We moved through the narrow passageways as our eyes took in all the sights. One booth had racks and racks of colorful clothes. Another had assortments of fans, TV sets, and radios. Directly across the aisle was a booth filled with Asian pharmaceuticals of every type imaginable.

"Bob, how bout something for lunch?" Steve asked as we came up on a food cart.

Swinging on hooks by their heads were a half dozen chickens on display. They dazzled your appetite as they hung there each painted a brilliant red, or orange or green. I think it was the flies buzzing around these meaty delights that brought thoughts of an afternoon of dry heaving. After several trips around the market purchasing gifts to take back home to everyone, we hopped into the jeep we stole for the day and headed out into the country, into no mans land.

It didn't take long and we found ourselves outside of town cruising north through the countryside busy with farmer's carts and huge lumber trucks heading to the mills. The farther we drove north, the more we saw the puzzled looks of the Thai wondering what these white men were doing out here this far. I watched a group of uniformed school children heading home. The water buffalo were plentiful in the rice paddies that were endless in this flat countryside next to the Mekong.

Finally we hit the end of the road, the town of Nong Khai that had the ferryboats over to Vientiane. That had been our plan that day. We stood on the dock waiting while watching the Mekong swirl with such power and force. From the air, it was hard to miss the massive strength this river had. From here, Vientiane seemed a million miles away. It was hard to imagine that those escaping from Laos would attempt to cross this river of certain death on a flimsy raft or by attempting to swim. For whatever reason the ferry still had not returned and we decided to turn our jeep east and head out. Little did we realize that if we had continued our journey to Vientiane, given we had only our military id's we would have caused turmoil at the checkpoint given the rule on no foreign forces.

About twenty minutes east out of Nong Khai we jumped off on a small side road to explore what we came here for. Both of us were certain we must be the first foreign explorers that made their way to this part of Asia that ended on a remote bank of the Mekong. We had to drive about five miles an hour as the road was skinny and curved around the fields and houses high up on stilts given the flooding that occurred regularly. Kids and women peered from behind fences, houses, and trees trying to figure out who we were, and where we came form, and why, or more importantly, what we were looking for. Finally we knew it, felt it, we had driven where no one had, and we had found that remote corner our civilization. And as we rounded the next curve it was confirmed, we saw it; the Coke O'Cola sign hanging from the roof of a small outdoor market, the friggin coke man had beat us to the end of the world?

The day came to fly the Mohawk back to Vietnam for the first part of the journey home. Ten am was always quiet on the flight line, things didn't get exciting here till the crews began showing up to get ready for the night missions. We had all said our good byes at a party that lasted a good part of the night at the Paradise Hotel. Today it was Pappy and Daze seeing us off, wishing us well in our lives we were to return to in the real world a million miles away.

We flew southeast dead over the Ho Chi Minh trail on our way back, checking in with flying command ship Hillsboro on a trip that for the first time didn't involve a day on the job hunting for humans under the dense jungle. We arrived on the coast of Vietnam tired from the long flight, the anticipation and anxiety of the unknown before us.

We touched down in the afternoon heat of Thuay Hoa and I realized what I had been missing from my diet these last months; sand. It was everywhere, between the runways, taxiways, hootches, and I was betting soon up my ass. As we taxied off to find the 225th, we passed massive rows of empty bunkers, or concrete shells for what at one time must have been a large Air Force contingent. They were all but empty now; it looked like a ghost town in the old west. Then I noticed the infamous triple-tail of several Mohawks peering over a revetment wall in the distance. So there was life here? Soon the engines were winding down and I was hauling my gear to the HQ building to check in before I checked out. Nobody here could give two shits for the longest time who I was, or what I wanted. But I had done this before, I could play this game. People kept shuffling in and out, all more important then the next. Finally a lull, and I must have been spooking the company clerk with my presence, my silence.

"What could I help you with," came his question with his back toward me.

"Curry, back from Laos, looking to get out of here?" I was now thinking of the world awaiting me after the next seven days and a wake up.

More stamping of forms, slamming of file cabinets and then a short discussion instructing me that I should check here every morning to see if they could find me transit down to Cam Ranh Bay. Meanwhile, I could bunk in the fourth hootch down the first row.

I threw my bag on another empty bunk in the fourth hootch as directed, another large screened shed that held about a dozen others. All these guys came and went in the next days trying to ignore the strange new guy that never brought good luck anywhere in Vietnam. Every morning I made the pilgrimage to flight ops to learn today, as was yesterday, there were no flights to Cam Ranh Bay. I was beginning to think I was destined not to leave here, ever.

The day before I was due to report into Cam Ranh Bay, I decided it was time to cause some havoc here, no more Mr. invisible guy. The plan I needed was to make it a priority they get rid of me rather then keep this pain in the ass around here. So I asked to go up the chain of command after every answer involving "not today." Finally I met the CO who was mildly annoyed with my problem, told me he'd look into it and that I should stop by flight ops late afternoon.

Well, that wasn't bad at all I thought.

Late afternoon and it was time to bring this thing to a close, I made sure all my items were packed in anticipation for the good news and walked over to flight ops to find another group of guys all scurrying with important things to do. I waited for the next lull and introduced myself.

"Oh ya, Curry," he drawled. I was excited, as he knew my name; this was going to be good news, finally.

"Well, no cargo flights or slicks heading to Cam Ranh Bay anytime this week we know of. But the CO said to find a way to accommodate you. We'll need you to fly an infrared run tonight outside Saigon, and we'll have the pilot drop you off on the way back," the words dropped through my ears straight to my gut.

"Ah shit sir, I don't want to fly a mission on my last night before heading home," I weakly answered as my mind raced for ideas, "bad luck you know."

"Only way to get you there Curry," came the automatic response, and then I made the fateful decision to hesitate. "Be here at twenty one hundred hours with all your gear and you can map out your mission then" as he quickly turned and involved himself in another conversation.

"Crap," I said to myself and I wandered back to the hootch. My mind was racing in a thousand directions. Superstition had become almost route over here, and this was definitely a bad sign that I was never to go home, at least not alive. Then I thought of Pop's last day back in Phu Bai were he cried all night in the bunker certain the NVA had a mortar with his name on it. And my mind wandered afar, everything bad was coming to be, now I was pissed at that god again who was having his last laugh, that he let me survive this whole tour, and then he'd pull it away just when I thought I was out, when I had made it. But somehow that made sense, in all this insanity that was the perfect poetry to this whole fucked up mess.

Twenty one hundred hours I was at flight ops with my bags and met Duncan who I was flying with. I was still sick to my stomach and found little comfort Duncan had been flying down here a good long time. The mission was to find an NVA unit thought to be in a heavily wooded area northeast of Saigon. I laid out the maps of this unfamiliar geography and mapped out the mission to and from the target area. Then in detail I mapped out the multiple paths we'd need to fly to overlap everything they were looking for. I was on autopilot as my mind raced to a thousand different places.

And as we lifted off from Thuay Hoa my heart sank. We raced to Saigon and I was sure of my death. As we flew west I remembered the missions when the Migs chased us, when we waited for the end. It had been a while since I felt that acceptance of destiny.

We reached the target area to begin our mapping and then I saw heavy ground fog all over the target area, maybe God had given me a break here? We continued to fly around waiting for the large fog patch to move. Duncan wanted to get this done, not wanting to fly another mission again. So the war of nerves went on for over a half hour and this lonely path of fog refused to budge, move, or dissipate. I was getting hopeful I might actually get the hell out of this mess in one piece. For what seemed forever, Duncan finally made the call to cancel the mission due to weather. I wanted to reach over and kiss him, but that might have complicated my goal of having him drop me off at Cam Ranh Bay, and nothing was more important than that today.

And then this fiasco called a war was over, or so I thought as we flew on to Cam Ranh Bay.

The wheels touched down and I felt a sigh of relief as I was nearing an end. I was on the final stretch of my journey. Duncan taxied over to the ramp, as I looked around me to make sure I didn't leave anything in the Mohawk. As Duncan said good-bye, he shut down the right engine so I could hop down, shut and lock my hatch, and pull my bag out of a rear storage area.

I walked away from the Mohawk with my duffle bag in the dark of the morning as Duncan restarted the second turbine. I could hear the high pitch of its engines increase as Duncan released the brakes and taxied back out to the runway, to return what we had found that night in the rice paddies outside Saigon.

I went into the shack next to the runway and saw the sign as to where to stand for the bus trip to the DERO's unit. I'd have to sleep on the bench here for three to four hours until the first shuttle showed up. Then I'd be off to another way station where forms were stamped, papers shuffled and abuse meant out to one and all. Hours napping on the bench and I heard a van pull up and the door wench open. Wiping the sand from my eyes, I dragged my bag to the waiting van. The door slammed and we were careening through the maze of warehouses and past numerous green vehicles on their way to somewhere important. Twenty minutes later and the van stopped by some shack building next to what appeared to be a swamp. More papers were stamped and filed, and I was told to find hootch fourteen. Like Bein Hoa, this was the trademark screen porch with a hot tin roof built with plenty of headroom for the rats to traverse underneath.

I threw my bag on the stained mattress of the only available bunk around. I introduced myself to a dozen other guys who had wandered in from every corner of this mans jungle. Here's where we'd enjoy rumors of when we'd be leaving, after all, in this mans army you'd only get the truth after it happened. The days now consisted of talk; insistent sleep, grabbing sodas and snacks to stave off the temptation of going to the funeral buffet at the mess hall and this eternal game called hurry up and wait.

Talk also revolved around how to sneak things home, drugs, souvenirs from dead NVA or Vietcong, and guns of every size and shape. Franklin was intrigued on figuring out how to get some Thai weed and hashish back to the states. He had some buddies back home he wanted to amaze with the quality and strength. He was sold on putting it in a large plastic bottle of Menin bath talc, with the small holes on the top he was sure it would fly through customs. I watched, amazed that one would risk finally getting home with sneaking anything past the MP's who had probably seen it a thousand times before.

The days seemed endless and the waiting was eternal. Finally the call came to fall out, the rumored magic day had finally arrived, and we'd soon be on that freedom bird leaving this insanity behind. I just wanted to forget what happened, get back to where I left off, it seemed like a simple request.

"All right assholes, lets go. Grab a piss cup and proceed to the shitter," yelled a Sergeant who did not want to be here, there seemed to be a lot of that going around here.

So the fifty of us grabbed a plastic cup with our name on it and followed him into a long brick building where a long steel trough stretched along the wall. We were directed to stand up against the trough and unzip. Suddenly standing behind every two of us was an MP who was intent on making sure the piss in the cup was coming from our individual penis. Just when I thought I had seen degrading, they surprised me again.

My problem is my penis is shy, it doesn't like anyone watching, and in fact I usually stare straight ahead at the wall. As I strained, physically and mentally the line of soldiers slowly departed leaving the cup, an MP, my penis, and me alone. The MP started yelling that I was going to miss my flight home, that perhaps I was afraid the test would show drugs, that I'd be hauled off to the brig. I strained so hard I could see yellow, I could see the freedom bird take off and I'd still be here.

Then I heard it, a trickle, the MP heard it too, as he was filled with hope and excitement, the possibility of leaving this bunker of smells. A higher power released me that morning; there indeed was a god.

I ran to the last bus sitting there; everyone on board was screaming hateful and disgusting things at me, as they had feared they'd all miss the bird home. The door slammed behind me as the bus lurched off and I fell down the passageway to find a seat.

We drove around this huge base back to the airstrip I had come in on days earlier. As we wound the last corner, we all saw it at the same time, the most beautiful woman in the world we had ever seen, the incredible white and red DC-8, our Freedom Bird. Everyone screamed and slapped anyone in reach, the fevered pitch reached insanity and this time it felt great.

All of us fell out of the bus, ran into a straight line with our papers and duffel bag at the ready. We stood there staring at the sleek passenger jet poised in front of us that would take us home. And then in the doorway poised a stewardess with the pillbox hat and legs that went forever up under her skirt. Another thunderous round of screams and cat calls. She smiled and disappeared back into the plane. It didn't get any better; it was too much for our minds to handle.

And then the waiting began, the war of nerves. Something was holding us up and soon the rumors began. Mechanical problems with the plane, bad results on the piss tests, you name it, we thought it.

"You don't think they fuck with us like this and take us back, do you," an idea floated up from behind us.

"Fucking cruel, that's what this is, playing with us one more time," floated over from a brother on the right. The mood turned to somber, disgust, then on to hopelessness.

And about the time the razor blades of despair would appear, the call came to board and pandemonium broke out. We bounced up the steel gangway to the plane, and as I entered the doorway, I turned around to see that I was leaving, I was really leaving. We tripped our way down the darkened aisle to find a seat. Once there in our seats, everyone was screaming, slapping each other, we had almost made it out.

And this great insanity continued, everyone yelled at the slightest sign of finality. When the door closed we screamed, when the call came to fasten seat belts came we screamed, and when we heard the engines begin to wind up we screamed.

And then we started taxing down the taxiway and a hush came over the collective group. Everyone stared outside the window one last time, to try and imprint what we were leaving, as if our soul hadn't already snapped enough shots. And then the white strips of the runway appeared below our wings and wheels as we turned onto the end of the runway and the engine ran up, the sounds deafening our very thoughts. I thought I felt the brakes come lose, yes; we were rolling at first oh so slow, then faster, faster. We all felt it; we all strained up, upward as if we could pull this beast off the ground, out of this shit forever. And then the plane lurched into the air, we were free at last, and we all screamed again. We were finally rid of this place of horror; we truly believed it that day.

It didn't take long for the exhaustion of the day to roll through the cabin. Quiet ensued as the vast majority of this sea of faded green dozed off and slept for the hours until we reached our first refueling stop in Japan. Some excitement returned as we stepped off into another country that actually was not shooting at us this day, which merited a high five by itself. I remembered the milk shakes at this airfield on my way over, and told several buddies who would help provide cover on our run for the snack counter. It wasn't long and we were all sucking chocolate malts with real milk, man life didn't get any better then this. A stomachache later we meandered though the airport reminding ourselves of where we were going, what it would look like; the anticipation silenced us as we allowed our mind to travel ahead, clear the path.

After boarding, a somberness seemed to flow through the plane, it felt like warm water that came up through the feet, up my legs and over my body. I felt an exhaustion that sapped my mind, that let me feel empty, and I didn't know why. I know I wanted to get someplace, the place where it was all-better again. I was hoping it was home, waiting for me.

We landed again in Alaska for fuel, these twenty some hours became a blur, the excitement of leaving had left. Now as we lifted off from Anchorage, the fear of what was waiting for us in Seattle stalked our minds. The fear I thought I had left came back, my mind was racing, and my heart was again beating outside my chest.

And then we were there, back in the USA. We walked off the plane and found ourselves into another line, Grab you duffle bag and get your asses over here," came the sweet voice of welcome. Now we waited to pull open our duffel bags as MP's with no sense of humor tore through everything we owned. They would eagerly decide a certain item wasn't coming into the country and tossed it into a large bin behind them. I then watched the MP across from me pull a Menin bath powder container out of some ones bags, twist the top and insert a long rod into it hoping to hit something solid. My stomach hit the floor. After everything I owned was ripped apart, they were pushed off to a table where other MP's were screaming to get it packed, now, and get our asses through the next door awaiting us.

As I pushed the door open, I entered the twilight zone, there was more yelling as we were told to put down our bag and strip down to our socks. Now standing there naked once again, I heard the most horrendous sound I had ever remembered behind me, the snapping of a glove as we were ordered to bend over. I groaned from the invasion while thanking god I had decided at the last minute not to stuff those NVA souvenirs up my ass.

This part of our welcome home complete, we walked with a bit of a limp out into the dark night in Seattle, rain slowly pelting us as we quietly walked to a darkened green bus waiting there for us. We had left in the dark of night, and now we came back home in the same blackness. It felt like the country really needed to sneak us out, and then back in, quietly, silently as if we had done something very wrong. I'd later realize that for many, we had.

The bus wound though the darkened streets and passageways of a country that had grown tired of this trip, of those of us who came before. It reminded me of the silent bus trip in Long Bien taking us to our new homes after we had arrived in Vietnam. We drove in the dark lest we be seen, lest someone open fire on us, lest we attract hostile-fire. And then I remembered this same panic was in my gut right now, only I was home.

The gates of Ft Lewis opened and we were driven to an old building on the base off the beaten path. The doors slammed open and several Sergeants were screaming at us to get out, now, quickly. It was basic training all over, remove their humanity, process them quickly and get them on their way.

The screaming continued for the next twenty-four hours as we filled in enough forms to make a dent in the forest surrounding this place. We went into a large cold auditorium where we were ordered to strip naked again, throw our jungle fatigues in large trashcans and then off to take a group shower. They were intent on making sure the sand and red clay from Vietnam would not enter the country if they had anything to say about it. Then another naked line of combat vets snaked though cold buildings to get a new set of clothes thrown at us by soldiers behind the supply counters pissed they were here today, of course it could have been us.

If anyone dared to argue, ask a question, or mutter a word, the threat of staying here for a long time was used without impunity. One guy dared to ask about the steak dinner and milk rumor that we had talked and dreamed about back in Cam Ranh Bay. The Army's salute and thanks to those who served in combat in that hole called Vietnam.

"Steak dinner, you think the Army's made of money? You want steak or you want to get home, your choice?" came the angry response.

"Just get us the fuck out of here," came the whisper.

We all climbed into our new ill-fitting clothes, Army dress greens, green shirt, tie; it had been awhile, this was all too unfamiliar and uncomfortable. More papers in triplicate, more abuse, but my mind was elsewhere, on cruise control awaiting a sign that this piece of the journey was over.

And then it was, we had our airplane tickets in hand, our new duffel bag filled with the shit from Vietnam they hadn't taken and tossed. And then another green Army school bus was waiting for us again in the black of night. But I was getting used to this, I was beginning to feel like a target again, and I was home.

We pulled up in the Army school bus to the front of the Seattle Airport. It was now a little after ten PM. My ticket was sweaty in my hand, I had two hours to wait on I'd be on my way home. Well, at least to the O'Hara Airport, with a couple hours delay there. Then around eight am, I'd be home, back in the real world where I had left it a lifetime ago.

Then as the door opened, the bus driver calmly announced, "be prepared, hostile-fire."

"What?"

The door opened and we could hear chanting of some sort off in the distance. Everyone jumped up and grabbed their duffel bag, now waiting for those ahead of us to move out. The shuffling began as one by one the fifty odd service men made it off the bus into the damp evening air. We all sauntered now toward the door as I could make out a ruckus up ahead at the main doorway. The line slowed slightly; then I could make out a group of about a dozen demonstrators. It wasn't until I got closer that the anti-war slogans became clear. I had seen these groups on TV before I left, I had read about it while I was gone. And now here they were, they seemed older this time, then I remembered. I watched a group of middle age women violently screaming and yelling at the soldiers ahead. I could see the hate in her eyes, god what in the hell is going on now, ever since landing in the states this has been a nightmare?

Then something wet splattered on the side of my face, then again something hit my chest. I wiped my face with my hand and realized it was a raw egg, and then I saw Franklin in front of me splattered in blood and something like guts, chicken guts? "What the hell?" as I turned to see this screaming group of fanatics throwing eggs and some mixture of blood and animal parts at any soldier they could see. The screaming was now mixed with the sound of police whistles arriving in the front of the line.

"Pigs, . . .murderers, . . .baby killers, . . ." I could make out in the barrage of sounds that were attacking us along with the tossed eggs, blood and guts. My thought was to get inside as quickly as I could, as if I was looking for that bunker I thought I had left a million miles behind.

Finally I got to the door, but the screaming and yelling continued, a Police officer was arguing with one of the male protesters as he tried to peel him off the back of a soldier in front of me. I shuffled in as fast as I could follow those ahead of us. The words continued to ring out, a small

318

shoving match occurred behind us as several black GI's decided to return some verbiage. A small cheer went up from the rest of us.

"Pigs, . . .murderers, . . .baby killers, . . ." echoed through the doorway as we all stumbled inside. Once inside the airport I realized we had become a spectacle. The business people and families on their way home or to a flight east for business had stopped to see what the noise was all about. I could feel the stares, the cold looks, and not a word was uttered in here. Then they saw the blood and eggs smeared all over the previous pressed army green uniforms. They quickly ran off, several picking up children and looking for the relative safety of a far corner of the airport. So this was home, the wrath of a war gone mad was now clearly our fault.

As everyone got into the airport the police sealed the doors keeping the protesters outside. We all stared at each other, stunned from what had just happened. There was no one in authority to explain what happened, or what we should do. The military was done with us, we had our tickets and as far as they were concerned the faster we headed out of town the better it was for everyone. They had waited till the black of the night to sneak us in here, after all, they had warned us of the hostile-fire. We had mistakenly thought we had left it for the last time forty-eight hours and a million miles ago, we would be forever wrong.

Then several of us had the same idea, we quickly strolled through the ticketing area in search of the men's room. Once there the duffel backs were ripped open and I grabbed out some "civie's", a regular shirt, jeans and shoes. My only desire was to blend in, to forget where I had been. Reaching down, I picked up my new uniform and pushed it piece by piece into the trashcan. I no longer had a use for these anymore; I no longer wanted to be a target.

The next stop was to the ticket counter to check my duffel bag, and remove the last bit of evidence about my sorted past from these people. Once this was completed I felt a sense of relief. I was now one of them, those normal people who daily went about their business unaware or uncaring that so many were dieing or starving or being raped a half a world away.

The time was now spent in small groups at the gates waiting for the boarding call. Some of the groups still had their uniforms on; the demonstrators were kept outside the airport. We munched on heavenly bags of chips and soda from the concourse machines in place of the steak dinner with real milk the Army had promised upon our return. Having time to think, I knew the words Army and a great meal shouldn't be used in the same sentence, how many times did I need to repeat that lesson? By now the airport had pretty much shut down, except for these red eye flights heading east.

Then the call came, ticket in hand I soon found myself picking out my seat on a huge 747, settling into a seat next to the window. The plane slowly filled, it looked like a light load back to Chicago. The day's events were tiring, it didn't take me but a second to curl up and doze off.

Then I was awoken as a lady slid into the aisle seat. "Hello, . . . oh I'm sorry to wake you up."

"That's OK," I answered as I shook off my dreaming. I looked over to her, Christ, for a second she looked like one of the women who had been protesting, yelling, and spiting. She looked so white, so middle class, so proper; she looked so dangerous.

"Where are you coming from, heading home?" she quietly asked.

I choked, " Veit..., (cough), ah, . . . vacation, I'm heading home from vacation."

We had idle talk on the way back; she must have seen I was famished when I gobbled down the airline food, so she offered me her sandwich, which I eagerly thanked her for. Several naps later and I arrived to a still quiet O'Hara airport to await my final flight home. I watched the traffic pick up in the airport as the early morning business travelers finally arrived to began the invasion of the chairs and passageways as they hurried off to making money in some distant city. As I watched them, my mind traveled back to the red dusty shacks at the airfields in Vietnam where men or boys with the million-mile stare slugged through on their way to a war on some hilltop or rice paddy. There was no excitement there, no excited chatter between people running to catch a plane like here. There was only that stare, and a million miles of pain.

The call came for the hour trip north, to home, to whatever I left a year ago. I boarded the plane with so much intrepidation, if was as if I was flying somewhere for the first time. As we flew north I was able to stare out the windows as the sun rose from the east. My flight from Seattle was in the dark of night; the twinkling of the lights below could have been anywhere. But now I could see neat little Midwest farm fields lay bare, ready for the cold and snow of the coming winter. No carpet of jungle foliage, no steam of the water rising off the rice paddies, no mountains that jutted straight up out of nowhere? It was changing too fast, I was sure I had left the insanity back in Vietnam, that's what I wanted so very much.

Smoke stacks were disgorging huge billows of white clouds into the cold sky. I stared at the little cars and truck scurrying along highways and freeways below. The last time I saw them from this angle I was trying to direct in a flight of F-4's to put them on fire, ruin their day. The anti-aircraft fire, the flying telephone pole, or the Sam missile was not to be here today. But sitting behind the closed cockpit door was starting to freak me out. Not seeing where I was going or what was coming at us was troubling, and now I was trying to second-guess the sound of the turbines out the window. We finally touched down and the plane taxied to the gate as my heart pounded hard, so hard it was soon outside my chest, I was nervous as hell, I was home.

Coming up the stairs, I saw her in the crowd, the most beautiful thing I had laid eyes on. All the people and sounds were unimportant; I was focused on getting to June who I left a year ago, a lifetime ago. And then I was in her arms, her in mine. Small short kisses and a giant hug, this was all so unfamiliar. Then so many things to say, too many as I was as awkward as the first time I tried to talk to her, date her. We talked as we left the airport into the frigid cold I had forgotten about, I chattered and shook from this insistent cold all the way home.

As we drove through the city, I stared at everything I had left before, but through the car window the feeling was so removed. I was back, but it wasn't as I had left it. I couldn't describe why, but this feeling would never change. I would from here on view life as if it was on the other side of that pane of glass. As life went on, I so much wanted to be part of it, but I couldn't find my way to the other side of the glass. I had learned a world away to never get too close to anyone, to always look for a way out of anywhere. I learned to survive today; otherwise nothing else mattered.

No one else was at home when we got there, as it was a weekday morning with everyone away at work. Somehow I had expected the world to come to a stop for a minute, hell I'd been gone a year. I'd forgotten how no one really gave a shit. Too many sixty-second flashes of a distant war on TV every night became boring and yesterdays news. I was now old news, I was boring, and worse yet, I made it. Now it was expected I'd pick up my life where I had left it, get on and get over it.

June wanted to take me to the new shopping mall where she worked and meet her friend and coworkers that only knew me by a photograph or the ramblings of a strange man writing home in letters stained with the dust of the endless red clay and sand. I entered the blocks long two-story mall with every shiny storefront staring at me. Fountains with streams of water falling and gurgling as shoppers quickly walked past with bags of every gadget and fashion imaginable. As I walked down the mall, I was nervous with who was coming up behind me, and then there were people above on the second level all moving too quick. June was talking excitingly about everything I missed when I was gone. I heard her, but everything for periods seemed to be in slow motion, then I stared into a store window at people excitingly pushing through racks of clothes and my next vision was that of Highway One in Phu Bai, the dust, the red fuckin dust, the dingy shacks, the cardboard containers they lived in, the movement of excited people screaming, moving quickly to get out of the way, to find cover. I saw Jack and Clinton and the others standing there in their stained fatigues staring at me, wondering why I left; and then my mind took me back to the mall. And now, like a million miles before, my heart was pounding outside my chest, the sweat was pouring down my forehead. It was then I realized I never left the war, the insanity. Those bastards had sent it home with me, those evil fucking bastards.

But I had learned well; back in Phu Bai or over the Plain of Jars, feelings got you in trouble. It blurred your judgment for what you needed to do that instant, or there was no next time. And if it bothered one too much, the ever-present flight psychiatrists were ready to ground you and send you to join the ground pounders in the rice paddies. I called it mental camouflage, it had worked there, and maybe it would work here.

I had the advantage here; no one wanted to hear about it.

I was born Xia Vue Yang in Phavene, Nong Het, Xieng Khouang, Laos. When I asked my mother when I was born, she replied: The 15th day of the 10th month. What year was that? She also replied with a smile, " The year we just finished harvesting our rice field." And now, you know the rest. In our family tradition, and maybe most likely in Hmong culture, the time of birth and death was not kept in any public records. When you are to be born, you are born, when you die, you die. Life goes on.

My father was fortunate enough to receive a few years of elementary school, and then went on serving in the French Indochina war, and then the "secret war" in Laos. I remembered that we never had "real" peacetime during my youth. We were always on the run, surviving the best we can, and fought against all natural elements on earth. The tough ones and maybe the "lucky ones" usually survived. I also remembered that during a few of my summer breaks, I used to fly with my friends in their T-28 fighter planes and doing some "funny" sight seeing while they were dropping bombs in enemy territories. Shots were fired towards us, and I was amazed to experience first hand the "theory of relativity" when two objects are moving at the same time, a straight line becomes a virtual curve. My pilot friends told me that those "virtual curves" were bullets from the communists' 12.6 mm AA guns.

This chapter is dedicated to my father, former SGU colonel Yong Chue Yang. I could have been drafted to join the "secret war" and fought along side my T-28 pilot friends or among countless young Hmong boys who died during the war. I also express my deep gratitude towards my fellow Lao-Hmong and American Veterans who have lost so much and so little to be recognized by the society nowadays.

By the fall of 1971 and the delayed start of the dry season thanks to Typhoon Hester, the war heated up with the anticipated attacks of the Vietnamese to retake the Plaines. The NVA 130mm artillery guns were blasting away at the Thai artillery units on the PDJ who were unable to touch them with their smaller range guns. More of our SGU soldiers were needed to protect the in-place artillery. More soldiers from our Army who had already suffered greatly from our decade long fight. Our strength was not guarding fixed bases; it was small unit guerilla attacks. Long Chieng was constantly under attack, if not by the large NVA artillery, it was the sappers sneaking under the wire or the mortars and rockets.

Migs fighters continued to attack the PDJ, now even bombing our villages and Lima Sites positions. In mid December the Thai artillery bases were under direct attack by ground forces. The Americans had cut down the number of sorties during the day like Vang Pao had heard. With over twenty North Vietnamese battalions they were wreaking wanton destruction everywhere. And unlike the smaller battles of prior years over this northern mass of Laos, the Vietnamese were hell bent on gaining as much territory as they could.

Our Hmong and Thai sites on the Plaines were seeing communist anti-aircraft batteries and guns being put in place forcing the re-supply to many bases by air-dropping, as landing was too dangerous. By the end of December the Thai artillery bases were overrun or withdrew from the PDJ. The captured guns were now turned on Long Chieng and the numerous mountaintop positions we still held.

By the end of December, the Americans believed Alternate (Long Chieng) would be run over any day. Vang Pao wanted the B-52's to bomb the enemy, calling out for "air". On New Years Eve, Long Chieng is attacked and held siege. The communist forces held the south end of the airstrip as the shelling and attacks continued into the New Year.

We heard by the end of January in 1972 that President Nixon told the world press there had been secret discussions with the North Vietnamese over an end to the war. He stated the US had agreed to withdraw from Vietnam and that the American POW's were to be released within six months of reaching an acceptable agreement. The US President supported the resignations of the South Vietnamese President and Vice President and democratic elections in the south within six months. There was no talk of the North Vietnamese withdrawing?

I wondered if this didn't sound familiar to the conditions when the French left years earlier. Now the Americans had grown tired and we worried about our people. But we all remembered the earlier promises of the Americans, that they would standby us. Maybe it didn't matter, the North Vietnamese rejected the American proposals days later?

In February Vang Pao flew to Udorn and the Americans promised Thai battalions to join us and offered more B-52 strikes in the north. Our immediate fears were reduced. For the next eight weeks we fought the NVA hill back down off skyline ridge and soon Long Chieng could breathe again.

By June of 72, the Hmong T-28's attacked the guns at Sam Thong and Phou Pha Xai once again destroying the enemy. We hear the trucks being hit in the night; we watch the rivers of fire come from the sky as Alleycat, Spectre and the Hawk continue their hunt.

More of the Thai came to join us in the battle as we have lost a generation of Hmong men. Now many of our youth armed the planes, guarded the villages, and joined in the attack. But the Vietnamese keep coming, and the guns were bigger and there were more of them.

By fall Long Chieng is back under attack and now many of our SKY friends and Ravens fly down to Vientiane every night to sleep, returning to fight in the morning. Then word comes that President Nixon announced a peace accord had been reached with the North Vietnamese. The Americans will halt bombing above the twentieth parallel. There is fear that the "air" would leave us Hmong, but as the days continue, the Americans still support us, fly with us, bomb for us. They tell us it is still our secret war. So they are keeping their promise they made to Vang Pao and our leaders, there is hope and fear amongst the death and destruction.

Word comes that President Nixon was re-elected in the US, perhaps now he has the power to fight the communists. Soon there is word of a cease-fire in Vietnam for the end of January in 1973. The word from Vientiane is the Royal Lao government will need to make their own peace with the communists. And what does the mean of the Americans; can they leave Vietnam and still support us?

The Americans fighting with us here are now upset over a movie star named Jane Fonda traveling to Hanoi and praising the communists. They showed us a newspaper with her sitting on an anti aircraft gun that shot down our Hmong brothers and our American allies. She talked of the good treatment the North Vietnamese are giving the American prisoners, the pilots who deserve no such treatment, as they are the aggressors? How is this true? We know how the communists treat their prisoners, worse then an animal before slaughter. And is this what the Americans think back in their country, where is this all going?

The war is now more deadly; the Ravens are spending their days going after the monstrous guns and new viscous weapons the enemy is bringing into the Plaines. The enemy now has smaller Sam missiles that can shot more of our planes down. The Hawks and Spectre still hunt at night for the trucks and tanks. And many of our troops carry the beacon, the small box that tells Spooky and the jets where we are even in the clouds or rain. The enemy called this plane "silent death"; the American called it the F-111. The enemy is still confused how the Americans could bomb them through the clouds and bad weather. We also hear the Americans are using a new bomb that looks for a light beam to help it aim, that can go into a cave and blow up the guns hidden until they come out to fire at us, but is it too late?

Word comes from the Lao government in Vientiane that there is pressure from the American Embassy to concede some issues to the Pathet Lao, that they want us to follow the agreement in Vietnam quickly to end the war all over Asia. Then President Thieu in South Vietnam openly balks at what the Americans are agreeing to without his consultation, or that of his government.

The confusion is more now; if the American are doing this to an ally in a war everyone talks about, what about us? We are a secret war in a tiny country the world cannot find on a map. And we are Hmong from the mountaintops; can anyone hear the cries and tears of our people?

The response to the Americans from the communists was immediate, they would cancel the negotiations. In mid December we felt the American response when waves of B-52's bombed Hanoi and Haiphong around the clock. Our people on the east side of the PDJ were a hundred miles from Hanoi, they could feel the bombs, and from the mountaintops they could see the fires. For weeks the bombing continued, there was hope the Americans would hold firm, that they would not abandon us to leave a war that now tired them as the French before them.

And in early 1973 the bombing over Hanoi ended and the politicians in Vietnam and America and Laos were talking, and arguing, and threatening. The Pathet Lao now called themselves the Patriotic Force, the games of war was entering a new phase. And while that happened, the war continued to kill and maim, and we wondered when it would end, and what would that mean to us.

Then on January 23rd 1973 the Americans and North Vietnamese signed an agreement to end their war. The Americans would withdraw completely from South Vietnam, but the enemy could stay in South Vietnam? There was fierce pressure now on our government to reach an agreement with the communists in Laos. Many times air drops of supplies or food would not occur, our government said the Americans wanted this agreement quickly and this was their tool, to show us they were serious.

Early in February we heard Hanoi released the American POW's, but not the Hmong they were holding. Nor were any prisoners released from Laos, even though the North Vietnamese were holding Americans and Hmong inside Laos. They'd say the Pathet Lao held the title to these POW's, a tool to hold over the Americans in order to increase pressure on the Lao government to give in.

Finally in late February our government reached an agreement with the communists, there would be a coalition government in Laos. Everyone was to hold their positions, all foreign powers were to remove their troops in ninety days, all special forces were to be disbanded, The old royal capital of Luang Prabang and the capital of Vientiane were to be neutral cities. Vang Pao said the agreement was certain death to Lao and the Hmong.

The Lao troops, which included the Hmong, were to hold their ground, and like the Pathet Lao forces, plant flags to show the territory they held for a neutral observer force to note. While many of our outposts planted their flag and held to the cease-fire, the Pathet Lao took it as an opportunity gain more ground. Soon the Russians flew several thousand Pathet Lao into Vientiane to act as "Police Officers". The communists did have a well-planned program unfolding. For years the Americans trained us to fight a war and kill. But the communists had trained people to run a village, work with the people to build a political structure. And now they had troops trained to take over the government from within. First they installed their own Police under the guise of instilling order, then they would move onto the other government agencies, and soon the political cadre would instill fervor in the masses of citizens fighting simply to eat and stay alive. They would point to the foreigners, the Americans as those who caused all the trouble. And then they'd point to those who fought with the foreigners, the Hmong. And soon the Americans would leave just us, to incur the collective wrath of an Asia looking for revenge.

And then on June 3rd the Ravens left us, the American air power in Thailand closed down their bases, and now only a couple Embassy people would stay on with us. And like before, the North Vietnamese would keep over forty thousand troops in our country. The Americans in Washington knew only too well this would happen, the Vietnamese signed two Geneva Accords in the fifties and sixties that called for them to pull their troops out, they never did. The communists used the agreement to take over a country; the Americans used it to flee.

The end was coming, Vang Pao sent his Hmong soldiers home as required by the agreement, maintaining only those Hmong soldiers that were also registered as soldiers in the Lao Army and therefore a legal force of the current neutralist government. The communists continued to move their army's and weapons throughout the country as their political forces worked within the Lao government on a game plan long ago coordinated with the North Vietnamese plans to eliminate South Vietnam.

We heard the Americans had brought back Heine Aderholt, now an Air Force General to oversea the dismantlement of US forces in Southeast Asia. And the Americans at the Embassy in Vientiane were set on dissolving everything we had collectively agreed upon over a decade ago. Then in early February of 1975 the communists attacked the government in Vientiane as Vang Pao sent his T-28's south to fight for his country of Laos. He asked the failing Lao government to give him the planes and guns they had, to fight the war from Long Chieng. But those left in the Lao government had long been compromised, tired, and bullied by the enemy.

In April war flourished in Asia once again. The Khmer Rouge took over Cambodia with the backing of China. In the same month North Vietnam troops and tanks rolled into South Vietnam. The Americans would no longer provide the South Vietnamese government with the fuel and ammunition needed to fight the battalions of troops flooding south. The NVA waited to commit more troops until US President Ford announced the American war in Asia was over. It was now a disaster in South Vietnam as the country collapsed as fast as the communists could drive south to victory. And now we knew who would be next.

On May 6th the Pathet Lao announced they would "wipe out the Hmong". Our leaders all met at Long Chieng to decide our future. Military, political and spiritual leaders debated what we could do, was it a time to fight or leave? Vang Pao had earlier released twenty thousand of his troops to comply with the agreement, now it would be impossible to recall them. We had weapons for maybe a year, but no air power, no food, no supplies, only unfulfilled American promises. The American Embassy coldly advised Vang Pao to leave, they could do nothing more for him. He refused to leave his people, so the Americans argued on how few they would get out of the way of certain death. They finally promised they get out five thousand of a people. Five thousand when there was over three hundred thousand facing retribution.

Only then did the CIA contact General Aderholt to grab some planes and get several hundred Hmong out of Long Chieng. Our friend General Aderholt called around what was left of the US airplanes and crews still in Thailand. He found one C-130 ready to go back to the Philippines that had been allocated recently for use to get Americans out of Cambodia as the Khmer Rouge slaughter swept through that country. Heine called the Chairman of the American Joint Chiefs of Staff to get permission to use the plane. He then called for aircrews and found out the last American pilots and crews had been released and were on their way to Bangkok to fly home. He was furious the American politicians back in Washington had made no plans to rescue their allies, the Hmong. The General called the Thai police in Bangkok and asked them to arrest the American pilots at the airport. Then he waited for the phone to ring.

"Heine, what in the hell are you . . ." the call would come from some very surprised and angry pilots.

Heine told them the Hmong were trapped in Long Chieng, the Embassy had hung them out to die, and he needed their help. We needed their help.

So the Americans who knew us, who shared our secret war, turned around that day and flew back into Long Chieng to grab as many Hmong as they could fly out. It was an exodus of humanity fearing certain slaughter in the days ahead. They grabbed up General Vang Pao and his family and flew them out to Thailand, followed by Europe, then America, as he was a certain dead man now. Many of our Hmong pilots grabbed every Lao plane they could steal to fly us out. The Lao Air Force now under control of the communists was told to shoot down any plane carrying refugees out of Laos.

And then the airstrip at Long Chieng was silent, as thousands of Hmong understood the fate before them. They would have to walk out, swim out or die. The journey of tears had begun.

The communists swiftly took over the government that year and the hunt to destroy the Hmong had begun in earnest. Lao leaders who we had served next to us were now told us to move our families to certain villages or valleys to insure our safety. Then the trucks of troops would appear and mow our people down. We lost thousands in a trap at the Hin Heup Bridge where they told our people to cross to reach safety, then they mortared, shot and bayoneted our men; our families.

330

*We fled to the Mekong, to get to Thailand if we could. My friend Neng
Lee would wake his family in the early dawn hours, pray to God, and
travel the jungles silently, crossing the Mekong River for safety in a
refugee camp. We fled into the hills on the run now from the Lao and the
Vietnamese army who rode with them, who killed with them. The secret
war had entered a new phase. The only people this secret war protected
was the American politicians a million miles away.*

*Those hundreds, then thousands that made the perilous journey across
the deadly Mekong River to Thailand were sent to the first of the refugee
camps that would soon hold thousands. Our friend Heine sent cots and
any supplies he could muster from the American equipment shipping out
of Thailand.*

*My friend Colonel Xay Dang Xiong, as one of General Vang Pao's staff
was flown to Thailand to travel on to Guam and the United States. But
thousands of his Hmong people in the Thai refugee camp fearing
retribution, begged the Colonel to stay on. The Colonel with a
guaranteed flight to safety instead stayed with his people in Thailand for
over three years to insure their safety. But the American government
continued to ignore the plight of a people who fought by their side, who
sacrificed their own sons to protect their fallen pilots. Many died those
years needlessly, many more lost hope as America turned it's attention
elsewhere.*

*The new Lao government, known as the Lao Peoples Democratic
Republic quickly established Seminar Camps, different from re-
education camps that the foreign press heard about. These camps like
the POW camps that held the American pilots they refused to return
were mobile, moving every few weeks. Any soldier or official and his
family could be sent off to a Seminar Camp. They were forced into hard
labor with little food. The babies soon died, as their mother's breasts
were unable to give milk. They would cut muscle from our men, cook it
in front of their screams and force the others to eat it. The women were
raped by the government soldiers in front of everyone; a form of
entertainment, belittlement, and torture. To those in the villages, the
Vietnamese soldiers moved into the beds of the Hmong wives. If the
husband resisted, they would be killed or sent off. The communists
would again show their total distain for the Hmong.*

The Lao Royal family was sent off to this seminar, this torture camp. This King and his family, who had once dined at the American White House, would die alone of starvation, of torture while the American political leaders were a million miles away, their secret safe.

The Hmong left in Laos were being hunted every day. Our people would hide in the jungles from the roving troops. On the run, a sound could give them away, many a mother or father would give their crying starving babies our medicine, the opium to silence them, to save their brothers and sisters. We cried in silence for what had become of us, the tears of the Hmong falling on the leaves that hid us.

Then came the rains of poison. Vietnamese planes would now appear in the sky dropping rain colored red, black, yellow, blue on our people. And our people would drop over and die, or become hideously sick. Those who didn't make it to Thailand found their way to the ten thousand foot mountain of Phou Bia south of the Plain of Jars. We crawled to the top, to the rain and cold. We drank the water from the leaves until the poisons tainted that. Then in December of 1978 the communists began their final assault, firing artillery mortars and dropping poison. We lost over fifty thousand of our people on the mountain from the communists in those days, and the world never heard a shot, a cry.

For many, their war of survival had moved south to Thailand. There in camps like Ban Vinai they herded us into huts with simple roofs, some built over graveyards to contain us. The Americans ignored us; we were still a secret they didn't need in America. The United Nations moved in, but became a puppet of everything wrong. We had to buy food with meager earning from our art that sold for scandalous prices to the foreigners. There was no milk for the babies, and soon the Thai began stealing from those Hmong who still made it over the Mekong. To many without money or goods, they were often returned to the Lao who would shot them on the spot.

Several European and American reporters told of our fate, they told of the poison still being dropped on us. In 1979 the press confirmed a Russian control team was in Lao taking notes and statistics on the success of each chemical application. We were now a live experiment for the use of chemical warfare. The Americans Presidents; Nixon, Ford, and Carter ignored our pleas. Laos was not even listed on the American annual report of Nations that tortured their own people. The US government and UN admitted they found that Soviet nerve agents had been used in Laos and Cambodia as well as Afghanistan.

Some of our people began leaving to France, Australia and America. The squalid camps had become too big of an embarrassment to the world, to the Americans. To those who did make it to America, we were split up and sent to the large urban areas of a country that was completely foreign to us. A country whose laws, cities, climate, education, and social structure were as alien as if they had put us on the moon. To many Americans, we were Asians or Vietnamese fleeing to take their jobs, their home, and values. And to the US government we were still a secret.

In 1991 the United Nations announced they would forcibly return the Hmong from to Laos, to certain death. Never in the history of the UN have a people at gunpoint been forced back to a totalitarian communist government who had vowed to "wipe us out." The Americans who did not have one American POW returned from Laos now stood silent as the killing continued. They had new battles in other parts of the war that held their attention now.

As the Hmong entered the new century we still hear reports of our Hmong being hunted down in the jungles of Laos. And new generations of our people are born far from the mountaintops of our people. We live in a land of Americans who do not know the secret; the secret of an American government that needed us to fight a war and then left us to die alone in the quiet jungles and mountains of a beautiful country a million miles away, in the streets and slums of their country.

We are your people of the Secret War America; we are the Tears of the Hmong.

Betrayal
Chapter Thirteen

The end of a war makes for a perfect photo opportunity, a centuries old conference table in a stately European palace, or floating on a huge battleship at sea. Add a dozen heads of state scurrying about, looking somber, important. Then with a sweep of the pen, it's over.
All the horror, brutality, and insanity of war had officially ended.

For the politician, the world is now portrayed as full of promise, a world or region has been set back on its pedestal. Time to refocus the nation on a new direction, dictator, enemy, or target. After all, old news doesn't get you re-elected, that's what the signing of the paper was for.

It's a time for rebuilding the physical damage of conflict. There are buildings and bridges that need to rebuilt; planes, tanks, ships, and trucks to replace those lost by war. The math is simple; besides it will be good for the economy. War has always increased economic demand, created jobs, provided overtime and income to the American home. It's a time of celebration, peace and prosperity is always fleeting, lets enjoy it while we can.

For some, it's a time for revenge; to move the war undercover and now hunt those who dared to fight you, dared to disagree, or dared to defend their home and family. The war is over, the attention is directed elsewhere, so do it quietly, swiftly.

To the poor and weak, it's a time to run, to hide. You're on your own, those who allied with you have totaled their loses, moved their pieces elsewhere. You can rely on no one to help you, no time to pray or rely on promises made to you in the heat of conflict. Go quickly, you've already squandered precious time.

It's also a time to get on with it, get over it, move forward; a PR firm's dream for small catchy phases, sound bytes.

For many who fought or who stood in its path, now the war is it's most insidious. It's a guerrilla war of the mind and the body. It's time to mend the physical wounds that came home with you. But it's also time to think, to remember the unthinkable, and then to stuff all those memories as far as one can.

———

When a nation goes to war, the true costs are never anticipated, there are no detailed cost benefit analyses prepared. After all, there appears to be a life and death struggle that has so shaken our country to its bone, that it now fears for its own existence. There appears to be no other choice, even now a bold willingness to send its men and women to fight and kill, to go into harms way.

And we watch pieces of its effects, the body bags that come home to one's family, the wounded hobbling off a plane or ship, pictures of destroyed planes, trucks, ships. And in the end, that is the perceived totality of that.

Vietnam changed all that, a war that became the most debated foreign policy venture in America's history. Only the debate played out while the war was fought, stretching across four Presidents and both parties. For Washington a million miles away from the insanity it set in motion, the war was an extension of failed diplomacy. And with the sweep of a pen Washington walked away from a war that would keep on killing and destroying. And that by itself is the most insidious.

The POW/MIA's

The communists skillfully split the responsibility and title to the American POW/MIA's in Southeast Asia. To those captured in Vietnam, Hanoi transferred the prisoners north to prisons in the relative safety of Hanoi, in order to maintain control and exert the most political advantage it could in the world press.

The largest military force positioned in Laos was the North Vietnamese. At one time their force was estimated to have over eighty thousand seasoned troops moving supplies to South Vietnam, or attempting to control the northern Plain of Jars. The Pathet Lao took directions from its Vietnamese brothers who also provided all the tools of war. When Americans were shot down, it was most often by North Vietnamese anti aircraft batteries or Sam missiles in Laos. Once captured, they were hidden in caves in the north of Laos near the Vietnamese border and moved frequently to avoid detection.

To the American public, there was only the war in Vietnam as the conflict in Laos was confined to special ops, the CIA and various commando/special force actions. Air power did not violate the Geneva Agreement on the Neutrality of Laos as these planes and crews flew over Laos, not in it. This wasn't completely true as American military pilots lived and flew in Laos as Butterflies or Ravens, having been "sheep dipped" or removed from official Air Force rosters and serving "voluntarily" on their own in Laos. Then there are the many contract airlines and crews flying directly for the CIA.

Unfortunately in war, these planes did get shot down, and over the years the number of POW/MIA's in Laos alone were estimated at over five hundred and fifty Americans. YET NOT ONE WAS EVER RETURNED ALIVE. The mathematical odds are beyond comprehension here. Not one out of five hundred and fifty was returned alive? Even though at wars end, the communist Pathet Lao forces claimed to hold US prisoners. Even though pilots who ejected, crashed, or parachuted were heard radioing their position and condition before communist troops captured them. Even though the Hmong would report sightings of Americans for years after Washington's war ended.

But an American government had a mission to bring American troops home from the quagmire in Vietnam and quickly end the political turmoil in the streets of the US. They needed to be reelected and a negotiated peace was as close to a victory as they could achieve. They had hidden the secret war in Laos, so the public focus needed to be on a speedy and honorable withdrawal from Vietnam. If Washington could keep the focus on the war American knew about, then the rest could die away on its own. If America saw the POW's return from North Vietnam that would be the closure everyone wanted.

But the communists saw the peace accord as a way to remove the US military from Asia forever. They knew the American government would agree to most anything to put an end to this chapter. So they split the bargaining chip of the POW/MIA issue into two, those in their control inside Vietnam, and those in their control in Laos. They would argue their troops were not in Laos; therefore any American POW/MIA's had to be held by the Pathet Lao. Now all they needed to do was to bargain with the Americans for the POW's in North Vietnam, the Lao POW's could be bargained separately down the road.

The chief US negotiator was Henry Kissinger who would claim the premise was fully understood all POWs held anywhere would be released. A skilled negotiator as Kissinger would know, that's what the writing in the agreements is for, the "premise", not a handshake, nod, or understanding. And the agreement is only as strong as the country that signs it. Every agreement signed in the previous years in Geneva had been broken by these same North Vietnamese, not that the US hadn't done their fair share. So ignorance, misunderstandings, and assurances would be the cover for a failed attempt to exit Southeast Asia under false assumptions, premises, hope, and prayers. Sadly the American public would buy it.

The North Vietnamese did finally release their POW's, even though the full accounting of POW's and MIA's is still open to debate. As the Laos agreement was negotiated separately, there was no like agreement on release of POW's held in Laos. And what signatory authority was indeed the proper authority, was it the Lao Neutralists, the Pathet Lao, the Coalition government or the forty thousand Vietnamese troops still guarding the POW's? The Pathet Lao would bait the Americans to put pressure on the Royal Lao government for concessions in order to release small numbers of POW's or a list of those held. In fact in late March of 1975 the Pathet Lao representative Soth Petrasy told the US that eight POWs held by Laos would be released within days in Hanoi if the Americans would push for concessions from the Lao government. The Americans desperate to leave Asia quickly obliged, now withholding supplies and payroll for their secret army in Laos to obtain the concessions. The concessions would be granted, the POW's would never be released, and the money for hostage game would occur all over again.

A new American team was now in place in Laos to shut down operations as quickly as possible. A team only concerned with closing down the secret war was at best oblivious or at worst treasonous in ignoring the agreements the Americans before them had made with the Lao and Hmong. In the end, the final cost to America in Laos was another five hundred and fifty American soldiers and airmen sent to a war hidden from the country, and then abandoned to die in the caves and jungles on their own. The American public saw the POW's return from Hanoi, they had no idea where the hell Laos was, much less a secret war. Every American Administration would similarly ignore the facts, as they did not want to make the decision on their call to potentially send US troops back into Asia to rescue Americans everyone had skillfully ignored before.

And since 1975 the Lao government would state each year that they held no US prisoners, they knew nothing of any POW's or MIA's. Even though American intelligence would continue to receive reports on sightings of Americans throughout these years. And like the Seminar Camps where the Hmong were kept and tortured, the POW camps continually moved to avoid detection or lengthily confirmation procedures that rendered potential American attempts futile.

In 1985 the first joint Lao-American teams searching for remains of US soldiers and airmen occurred in Laos resulting in the return of thirteen to their families in the US. These exercises have continued over the years, in 2004 the body of Clinton Musil was identified from the crash site of his Mohawk in Laos. The only small hope to families and friends today is to bring them home for burial, and that hope in itself is fading.

But for five hundred and fifty American POW's, their fate was forever sealed when the United States with the sweep of the pen, sold them out, denied their existence. Only the rest of the world was ready to move on. After all, they saw the pen, heard the news, the war was over, wasn't it?

The Veterans

The veterans returning from Vietnam, Laos, Cambodia, and other corners of Asia came back one by one, slipping back in the middle of the night into the country that sent them to fight their war. Servicemen anywhere in this era knew, were ordered, not to wear their uniform or let others know they were in the military. The abuse was most rampant in the streets of America, where they were daily abused, violated, spit on, told to go away.

A country, whose elected leaders across both parties and under multiple administrations had decided once again to send a generation of soldiers to war in a foreign land. And when this decision was suspect, when the morality of a nation was called into question, the nation found its scapegoat. It now directed its hate at the returning soldier on the plane or bus, the man or woman in uniform on the street, or the vet looking for a job. The Vietnam veteran found hatred at the very VA Hospitals that were to care for their wounds of war.

With the shock of the brutality and insanity of war fresh in their minds, the veteran now had to duck and run for cover from a new enemy, the very people who sent him or her to the insanity. One instinct that becomes heightened and honed during their tour in war is survival. So the tactics of avoid and evade became a part of this new troublesome civilian life. One learned quickly they could not find safety even in the nations veterans groups such as the VFW or DAV. They, like the rest of the nation saw the veteran of Vietnam as the cause of everything wrong in the social fiber and politics of the country. Besides, the Vietnam Vet had lost that war, which could only bring perceived dishonor to all veterans.

338

To survive, the Vietnam veteran went underground. He or she hid any association with a war the country was attempting to exorcize from its soul. They hid so well, many did not dare to reach out and find others who shared their pain and questions. The statistics on veterans of this conflict displays the tip of the iceberg on the problems wrought on this group. The rates of divorce, alcohol and drug abuse, homelessness, legal troubles, are all multiples of those of their same generation who did not go off to war. And a government would further distance itself from anything to do with this war in order to move on. They wished the problem would go away, and for a while it appeared to. For decades the VA, with the help of Administration cutbacks, continued to ignore the travesty this war wrought on the Vietnam Veteran. PTSD, or Post Traumatic Stress Disorder was acknowledged a decade after Vietnam as a defined mental diagnosis by the American Psychiatric Association. That continued shock to an individual by traumatic events such as war, would have profound impact on the ability of many veterans to function in society. But it was subtle, it masked itself well as doctors and society attempted to treat the symptoms; alcohol or drug abuse, relationship problems, anger, isolation and suicide. And for every veteran suffering from PTSD, the effects multiplied itself through society by everyone this vet touched, his family, friends, employers, and the community. Finally when the problem was acknowledged, the vet was well under ground. They had learned skillfully, hiding the connection to a war he/she was attempting to stuff. And now trying to deal alone with a demon he/she little understood, or by this point even realize?

And then there was Agent Orange, the defoliant sprayed across Asia during the war to destroy the jungle that hid the enemy. While corporate giants made massive profits selling war materials to the government, there were products like Agent Orange that had known destructive medical effects on anyone who came in contact with it. But the barrels rolled through Vietnam denuding the jungle, and tainting a generation of soldiers and Vietnamese civilians with a time bomb within their body. A time bomb that destroyed their bodies and lives from within, and many times caused birth defects and disease in their children. And when the medical community and experts on the deadly chemicals finally acknowledged the results, the nations corporations and government denied and delayed while these same men and women suffered and died an ugly death. While they watched their children suffer in so many ways, while their families lost everything watching their veteran suffered alone in agony, while their government stonewalled treatment or justice.

When the same government that brutalized the veteran once in the war, who then assisted in directing the rage and hate of a nation against to those who returned, who then denied the existence of their brothers still imprisoned in Asia, and now protected the corporate barons who made millions willingly, off chemical warfare products that ravaged a mans body and family? When in the hell exactly is the war over?

For the veterans of the wars of Southeast Asia, their fate was forever sealed when the United States with the sweep of the pen, sold them out, ignored their existence, and abandoned them to suffer or die alone.

After all, the rest of a tired country saw the sweep of the pen, heard the news, the war was over, wasn't it?

The Hmong

To most Americans, a Hmong standing on the street appears to be another recent Asian immigrant that made their way to this country in order to avoid economic chaos elsewhere. And as with every immigrant group in our history of accepting differing ethnic cultures, they would incur these same time honored American traditions of racial hatred and suspicion. They would be seen as another gook, slope, or chink attempting to take jobs and benefits away from those slightly above their station in life. Their culture would be misunderstood at best, scorned and held as high examples of another pagan religion infiltrating our schools and neighborhoods at worst. The Hmong would serve well as the next target for a new crop of ethnic joke and slurs that everyone could use entertain themselves with. After all, ignorance is many times a preferred alternative to knowledge and understanding.

And no one would know the secret, understand their story, care of their plight. They would never know that like many of our forefathers and mothers before us, the Hmong too had fled from religious and ethnic persecution, death, and torture. They would not know that Hmong stands for free people; they held many of the same ideals we hold dearly in our own nations constitution. Only the Hmong practiced it on the quiet mountaintops of a beautiful country a million miles away. And like America today, the freedom of the Hmong was a threat to everyone and everything bent on power, expansion, and enslavement of the human soul. In Asia the Hmong and their ideals were a threat to the existence of those who sought to conquer and enslave. Their destiny could only be extinction. The Hmong had been persecuted for centuries in China for the very ideals we embrace in this country, the power and beauty of ethnic diversity, the right to be free within themselves. Two hundred years ago they picked up their families and moved to the quiet mountaintops of Laos, to live alone, to threaten no one; except to those around them, their very lifestyle would.

First the French would approach them, offering to ally together against their common enemies. To the Hmong it was a way to stay alive from those who sought their destruction. Soon the French would leave Asia, replaced by an America that saw communism as a collection of similar worldwide movements that threatened the west in a place called Cuba, a city called Berlin, a region called Asia.

Laos was suddenly thrust into the situation room of the Eisenhower White House as the Soviets massed a major unexpected airlift in the Plaines of Jares in northern Laos in the late fifties to support a communist movement to replace the neutralist government. Now faced with threats in every corner of the globe a group of Americans trained in the new emerging warfare and tactics of post World War II guerilla people's movements went to work to develop options other then sending massive troops into another war in Asia. Korea was too fresh on this countries mind.

So a strategy of commando and guerilla warfare melded with American air power became a low level response to checkmate the Soviets intentions in Laos. The French would tell us of a people called the Hmong who themselves were fighting for their own survival from the Chinese, Vietnamese, and decades earlier the Lowland Lao and the Thai. They were the minority ethic group of Southeast Asia that became the target of anyone looking for expansion and enslavement.

The Americans would meet the Hmong leaders at the base camp of Vang Pao in 1960 and agree to fight the communists together. We would supply the Hmong with arms to fight, and the air power to counter the massive amounts of sophisticated Vietnamese weapons and thousands of troops entering their country to do battle in the Hmong homes and villages. The White House would embrace this new Secret War, and for almost ten years it was fought without the world or the American press exposing it. Several Presidents would directly deny our role in it, deny Americans had been killed in Laos, and later deny we had any responsibility for setting the Hmong on a course of destruction.

And when the larger war in Vietnam would be fought in the American streets, universities, living rooms and the hallways of Congress, this same government would, with full knowledge leave the Hmong to die on the mountains and in the jungles alone a million miles away. They would let these allies who fought alongside with their families, be hunted each day like animals for slaughter. They would knowingly let them be sprayed with poisons from the air and ground for decades. They would let them live and die in the squallier of refugee camps in Thailand that ended up brutalizing them. And when the American government grew more tired of this untidy mess, quietly agreed to let the United Nations at gunpoint force these poor weakened people back into Laos to be summarily shot, tortured, and killed.

And to those few who made it to this country, we treat them with the same deep disrespect America pulled together for its soldiers returning from this same insanity. We would also deny them any medical benefits for the wounds of war the Hmong soldiers incurred fighting our war. An Army who used our weapons, whose paychecks came from the American government. To the politicians in Washington, their hope was it would all go away, perhaps soon the Hmong veterans would all be dead and the story of their troubled journey with them.

To those in this country that continue to profess that America protects the huddled masses; know we left these Hmong who were still alive, like our POW's, to huddle alone in the darkness of the jungles praying only not to be left alone to die. But we were too tired to hear their cries, their pleas, their babies dying in their arms. Today, we are still too cynical to even understand their journey, to respect them for the sacrifice, for the destruction of over one third of their people. The sacrifice they made for this same America that would leave them alone in the end. It is estimated that the Hmong forces tied up over one hundred thousand communist troops that could not be deployed against American forces in Vietnam. That it destroyed over fifteen billion dollars in enemy equipment and supplies. And in this secret, many Americans are alive today solely for the efforts of these courageous people.

For a nation of Hmong men, women, and children, their fate was forever sealed when the United States with the sweep of the pen, sold them out, denied their existence. Only the rest of the world was ready to move on. After all, they saw the pen, heard the news, the war was over, wasn't it?

———

Laos –Timeline

1373 - The country of "Lan Xang" known as the land of a million elephants was officially recognized as a nation. Its territory included the lands of current days Laos stretching south to include parts of Siam (Thailand) and Cambodia.

1480 – Vietnamese invasion of Laos is repulsed.

1700 – Infighting of the Royal Family splits the country of Laos into two, then three kingdoms where the fighting continues for over a century.

1830 – A war with Siam (current day Thailand) forces thousands of Laotians back over the Mekong River to live as the war moves back north into Vientiane and beyond.

1872 – France defeats Vietnamese troops and imposes the Protectorate of Hue assuming control over the whole of Vietnam.

1889 – France assumes control over Laos and declares Vientiane it's capital.

1940 – Japan occupies the whole of Southeast Asia in its World War II expansion gamble. It was then that Vietnam's Vo Nguyen Giap forms the Vietminh Army.

1946 – Laos and Vietnam declare independence in the waning days of the Japanese empire. The British retake Saigon for the Allies and turn it back over to the French.

1949 – Mao and his Chinese Communists take over final control of China. Lao joins United Nations.

1950 – Korean War breaks out. United Nations and United States send troops into South Korea.

1953 – Vietminh forces invade Laos. The French and Lao sign a defense agreement obligating French to protect the fragile Lao government.

1954 – France occupies Diem Bien Phu in the north of Vietnam to protect the northeastern approaches to Laos. The battle wages three months and the French are defeated. Vietnam divided into North and South by Geneva Accord.

1955 – US Military advisors arrive in Laos.

1959 – Group 559 is formally created by the North Vietnamese. Their function is to expand and protect the growing systems of roads in Laos known as the Ho Chi Minh Trail. These roads were used to transport troops and supplies into battle in South Vietnam.

1960 –Lao's Sovvanna Phouma is returned to power in a coup by Lao Army Captain Kong Lee.

1961 – Laos is seen by the American Government as the first "domino" at risk of falling in Asia. Eisenhower and Kennedy both confer over possible action. The Soviets begin airlifting massive amounts of military material into Laos. The little landlocked country of Laos is heating up as a potential battleground for the Americans and Soviets. The CIA begins support of General Vang Pao, both an admired Lao military officer and Hmong leader. The US delivers of first six T-6 aircraft to the Lao military. A hastily designed conference is put together in Geneva to ward off the potential of a superpower conflict.

1962 – The Geneva Agreement on Laos is reached, calling for the removal of all foreign military forces from Laos, and calling for protection of its neutrality. North Vietnam denies it's thousands of troops on the ground inside Laos. American commits itself to the first twelve thousand troops in South Vietnam.

1964 – Project "Waterpump" is begun by the US in Udorn Thailand at the request of the Lao Prime Minister to train Lao pilots in preparation for action against increasing Communist forces operating in Laos. The Pathet Lao along with the North Vietnamese occupy the Plain of Jars in addition to the Ho Chi Minh Trail complex in southern Laos. US Air Commandos are authorized to fly in Laos as forward air controllers. The Lao government authorizes US Recon flights over Laos and the Barrel Roll bombing campaign over northern Laos is authorized. William Sullivan replaces Leo Unger as US Ambassador to Laos.

1965 – The secret war in Laos rolls into full gear as Operation Steel Tiger focuses hundred of US bombing sorties targeting the expansive Ho Chi Minh Trail complex in southern Laos. Special Forces teams are dropped on the trail to report enemy movements. Udorn Thailand now serves as Air Force headquarters for the war in Laos. US troop strength in South Vietnam now passes two hundred thousand men.

1966 – The Air Commandos known as Butterfly acting as forward air control missions in Laos are replaced by Air Force pilots known as the Ravens. The US installs a top-secret radar station far in Northern Laos near the North Vietnam border called "The Rock". It was placed on a sheer mountaintop called Phou Pha Thi in northwestern Laos near the Vietnam border. This mountain was a scared mountain for the Hmong. These Air Force officers and enlisted men are "sanitized" to become civilian operators manning the highly classified navigation system needed by the US bombers and fighters flying on to targets in northern Laos and North Vietnam. The number of bombing sorties continues to grow over the Ho Chi Minh Trail. American troop strength in Vietnam is now over four hundred thousand troops.

1967 – The top-secret navigation equipment operating in the black on a high mountaintop is upgraded that allows navigation for US bombers around the clock and in all weather. American troop strength in South Vietnam now exceeds a half a million men. The North Vietnamese begin a program of building all weather roads both in Southern and northern Laos.

1968 – The North Vietnamese attacks the US top-secret base at the Rock. It is abandoned after attempts to repulse the attack. Hmong forces under General Vang Pao briefly recapture it. American troop strength peaks at five hundred forty thousand men in South Vietnam. President Nixon replaces Lyndon Johnson in the White House. The North Koreans capture the USS Pueblo with its crew and electronics equipment.

1969 – The North Vietnamese increase their pressure in Northern Laos as they take Lima Site 36, the town of Muong Soui on the Plain of Jars and threaten the secret based at Long Chieng. In July the beloved Hmong Flying Ace Lee Lue was killed. In Fall Vang Pao launches Operation About Face that successfully route the enemy. Testimony over the secret war in Laos begins in the US Congress, as US Ambassador to Laos Sullivan is replaces by McMurtrie Godley III. Henry Kissinger is secretly meeting in Paris with the North Vietnamese and US troop strength in Vietnam dips below a half a million men.

1970 – The air war over northern Lao intensifies as the US brings in B-52's into northern Laos in response to a vastly increased North Vietnam effort to seize the Plain of Jars. The US and South Vietnamese troops invade Cambodia in an attempt to destroy the North Vietnamese sanctuaries across the border used to continue the fight in South Vietnam. Kissinger and North Vietnam in secret negotiations. US troop strength in South Vietnam falls dramatically to two hundred and eighty thousand troops.

1971 – The South Vietnamese invade the Ho Chi Minh trail areas of central Laos in an operation called Lamson 719, an attempt to sever the trail. North Vietnam dramatically increases troops in northern Laos in attempt to destroy the Hmong. US troop strength in South Vietnam continues to fall to one hundred and forty thousand troops.

1972 – In Laos, the Government and the Pathet Lao begin Peace talks. Nixon travels to China and wins re-election.

1973 – The Peace agreement in Vietnam becomes official on January 27th. The Lao Peace Agreement is signed on February 21st calling for a halt of all bombing and fighting with the advent of a new coalition government. The last American troops leave Vietnam.

1974 – The new coalition government is formed in Laos. US reconnaissance flights monitoring the build up of communist forces against Laos and South Vietnam are halted. Air America and all US forces leave Laos as North Vietnam maintains over fifty thousand troops in Laos. Nixon resigns as US President.

1975 – Early in the year the North Vietnamese forces attack the Hmong forces in Laos, seizing Vientiane in April, the same month their invasion of South Vietnam results in it's overthrow. The Communist Pathet Lao launch a chemical warfare program in an effort to exterminate the Hmong from Lao forever. The Lao government falls and the People's Republic of Laos is installed. US troops leave Thailand as Lao border closed. The royal family and those captured in Laos in Laos are thrown in "seminar camps". Jimmy Cater elected President.

1977 – The last Hmong holdout on Phu Bai Mountain is attacked by communist forces with heavy artillery, napalm and chemical weapons. Those who can flee attempt to make it south to the Mekong river, where the relative safety of reaching Thailand across this large fast moving river is their only hope.

1978 – Vietnam invades Cambodia.

1979 – China attacks Vietnam as Russia moves into Afghanistan.

1980 - China provides limited sanctuary, military training, and equipment to various resistance elements including Kong Le's Neutralists after their escalating conflict with the Vietnamese government. Iran takes US hostages, Cater defeated by Ronald Reagan as US President.

1981 – Western scientists confirm poisons being used by the Vietnamese in Laos and Cambodia came from Soviet Union.

1985 – Laos government begins some limited joint searches with the United States of known wartime crash sites of United States aircraft. Thailand begins forcibly sending refugees to Laos.

1989 – Berlin wall falls. Lao government links POW/MIA issue with narcotics as Lao remains a major opium producing state.

1990 - Laos receives a national interest certification on the issue of cooperation in counter narcotics activities.

1991 – The Supreme People's Assembly (SPA), the country's highest legislative body, adopts a new constitution legally establishes a set of authorities that resemble the traditional differentiation among executive, legislative, and judicial branches of government reaffirming Marxist commitment. Soviet Union collapse, aid to Laos ends.

1992- Relations between the US and Laos changed as Embassy's were upgraded to Ambassador status in the summer. US offer helicopters and aid to combat drug production. Thailand continues forces return of refuges to Laos.

1993- United States Senate Select Committee on Prisoner of War/MIA Affairs concluded in January that: "The current leaders of Laos, who are the successors to the Pathet Lao forces that contended for power during the war, almost certainly have some information concerning missing Americans that they have not yet shared."

1997 – The ASEAN Association of Southeast Asian Nations (ASEAN) admitted Laos to its membership. The currency (kip) plunges to half its value, with the average Lao income at $400 per capita.

1999 – 2001 – Three American Hmong disappear after entering Laos on visits.

2003 – An American pastor and two European journalists are sentenced to fifteen years in jail for the death of a village official. After international pressure they are released.

2003 – Several incidents of insurgency are blamed on Lao rebels for attacking buses and killing civilians

2003 – The United States and the Lao PDR sign the Bilateral Trade Agreement on September 23rd, it now awaits Congressional ratification.

56ᵗʰ Air Commando Wing – The Air Commando Wing created to respond to the war in Laos, headquartered at Nakhon Phanom Royal Air Force Base.

ABCCC – Known as "AB Triple C", these units provided the airborne command ships that flew in northern Laos as Alleycat and Cricket, and in southern Laos as Moonbeam and Hillsboro. These aircraft coordinated all air and ground activity in their sector of Lao's matching strike aircraft to targets and coordinating rescue operations

Aderholt, Heine – Brigadier General United States Air Force, known as the father of the Air Commandos. Heine served in developing and managing the air war and the aerial support of the Lao and Hmong forces in the Secret War in Laos. Retired, he still works today relentlessly on behalf of his Air Commandos, their families, and the Hmong.

Across the Fence – The fence being the Mekong River, used to describe going into Laos as going across the fence.

Air America – The private airlines owned by the CIA providing air transportation of food, weapons, soldiers and people throughout Asia. The major action was in the secret war in Laos.

Alleycat – Call sign for the Airborne Command & Control Center C-130 command and control aircraft that stayed on station in northern Laos at night. Replaced by the ABCCC Command Ship call sign Cricket during the day.

AAA (Triple A) – Anti-Aircraft Artillery. Artillery guns that fired shells of various sizes into the sky to shoot down US aircraft. These guns were visually aimed or locked on with radar and could shoot at up to four hundred rounds per minute per gun barrel.

Arc Light – Air Force B-52 bomber strikes in southern & northern Vietnam & Laos.

ARVN – Army of the Republic of Vietnam, the South Vietnamese Army.

BAHT – The Thai unit of currency.

Barrel Roll – Area of operations interdiction in northern Laos.

Battalion – An Army unit that has around 900 men.

Bird Dog- Nick name for the O-1 aircraft flown by FAC's.

Body Bags – Plastic bags used for removal of bodies on the battlefield.

Boom Boom – Vietnamese slang for sex with a prostitute.

Butterfly – Call sign for original enlisted Forward Air Controller (FAC) in Laos. They located targets and directed the air strikes to hit. The Butterflies were replaced in 1967 by commissioned pilots using the call sign Raven.

Candlestick – Call sign for the C-123 forward air control/flare aircraft in Laos.

CAS – Controlled American Source, the code name for the CIA operating out of bases in northern Laos.

CBU – Cluster Bomb Unit (anti-personnel weapons).

Chaophakaow – Call sign for the Hmong pilots of the T-28's referring to "Lord or White Buddha".

Chopper – helicopter.

CIA – US Central Intelligence Agency, the agency.

Close Air Support – air strikes against enemy targets that are close to friendly forces, requiring tight control from FAC's monitoring the fire and movement of those forces.

CO – Commanding officer.

Commando Club – Code name for a radar system operated from Site 85 on Phou Pha Thi Mountains in northern Laos.

Continental Air Services – The private airlines flying cargo and transport for the CIA and USAID in Laos.

Crew Chief – Mohawk member who maintains the aircraft.

Cricket – Call sign for the C-130 Airborne Command & Control Center also called AB Triple C flew in northern Laos in daytime as "Cricket." Replaced by "Alleycat" at night.

DEROS – date eligible for return from overseas; the date a person's tour in Vietnam was estimated to end.

Di Di Mau – Vietnamese term for move quickly.

Dinky Dau – Vietnamese term for "crazy" or "You're crazy."

DMZ – demilitarized zone, the dividing line between North and South Vietnam established in 1954 at the Geneva Convention.

Ejection Seats – The seats in many Air Force and Navy combat aircraft in addition to the Army's OV-1 that had an explosive charge built into the seat. When the plane was crippled, unable to fly, the pilot or copilot who was strapped into this seat would pull an ejection handle that would trigger the explosive charge and send the pilot through the canopy away from the failing aircraft, then deploying a chute.

FAC – (pronounced Fack) A Forward Air Controller that locates, confirms, and marks enemy locations on the ground from an aircraft or on the ground and then directs air strikes on them.

Fast Mover – Jet; usually the F-4.

Feather – A propeller adjusted in pitch so that it will neither pull nor push air.

Fire Base – A temporary artillery firing position usually were comprised of four howitzers with crews and a company of Infantry.

Firefight – A battle with the enemy.

FNG – A slang name for a newly arrived person in Vietnam translated to a "Fuckin' new guy."

Freedom Bird – Any aircraft that took you back to the "world" (U.S.A.), the aircraft on which you left Vietnam.

General Vang Pao (VP) – Leader of the Hmong units opposing North Vietnamese in Laos. Educated in the 1950s at the French Police Academy in Luang Prabang as the only Hmong graduating first in his class. Pao is a feared warrior and the revered leader of the Hmong who fought all his life against Communism. Respected by the CIA and US military leadership. Presently he lives in Southern California.

Gooks – A derogatory slang term for an Asian; derived from Korean slang for "person" and passed down by Korean War.

Grunt – Slang for an infantryman in Vietnam; supposedly derived from the sound one made from lifting up his rucksack. Also called Ground Pounder.

Gunship – An armed helicopter or fixed-wing aircraft whose purpose is to act like a flying gun platform for close air support or destroying the enemy.

Helio Courier – A STOL (short takeoff and landing) aircraft used by Air America to supply remotes bases in Laos.

Hillsboro – The C-130 Airborne Battlefield Command & Control Center (ABCCC) controlling southern Laos during the day.

Hmong – Stood for "Free People" these are the mountain people of Laos who cooperated with the US in resistance to the North Vietnamese. Their army was known as the SGU led by Gen Vang Pao. They entered Laos in the early 1800's fleeing persecution in China. Some Americans referred to the Hmong as Meo, which is considered derogatory by the Hmong.

Ho Chi Minh Trail – The primary North Vietnamese supply route of trails, pipelines, and roads through Laos into South Vietnam.

Hootch – A house or living quarters or a native hut.

Hue – Hue was the imperial capital of Vietnam between 1802 and 1945. It was isolated by the Annamese mountain chain and bordered by Laos to the west and the Demilitarized Zone to the north and the scene of a major fight during TET.

Huey – A nickname for the UH-series helicopters: "utility helicopter."

Igloo White – A surveillance system consisting of hand-implementation and air delivered sensors, relay aircraft and infiltration surveillance center at NKP RTAFB, Thailand. These air supported anti-vehicular and antipersonnel system using acoustics and seismic sensors. Started in late 1967, Igloo White was formerly Muscle Shoals.

in-country – Slang for serving physically in Vietnam during the Vietnam War.

Intel – Slang for intelligence information.

Infrared – An electronic surveillance system used in the Armies OV-1 Mohawk that would film a target area and display the terrain based on heat signature, allowing to see trucks, generators, gun's etc in the darkness of night.

Karst – Limestone formations or mountains that rise in irregular formations in Laos.

KIA – Killed in Action.

Klick – Slang term for a kilometer.

Luang Prabang – The ancient capital of Laos.

Lamplighter – Nickname of C-130 aircraft operating in northern Laos, eventually Blindbat became the nickname for all AC-130 flare missions.

LIMA-LIMA – Low level, as in aircraft altitude.

Lima Site – Aircraft landing site (dirt strips) in Laos used as re-supply landing sites.
Given numbers to identify individually.

Long Chieng – Known as Lima Site 20A or 20 Alternate or simply as Alternate. It was a formal staging area used by the CIA (also called the CIA secret operating base in Laos) and Headquarter for the Hmong SGU soldiers led by Vang Pao.

M-16 – The standard U.S. military rifle used in Vietnam from 1966 on, the successor to the M-14.

MACV – Military Assistance Command / Vietnam. The main American military command unit that had responsibility for and authority over all U.S. military activities in Vietnam. Based at Tân Sơn Nhất.

MASH – Mobile Army Surgical Hospital.

Medevac – Term for medical evacuation, usually with a Huey. Also called Dust Off.

Meo – A derogatory word describing the Hmong people.

MIA – A person missing in action.

MIG – Principal Soviet fighter planes used by the North Vietnamese.

Mohawk – The Grumman OV-1 Mohawk aircraft.

Moonbeam – C-130 ABCCC Command Ship operating over Southern Laos during the night.

MR – Military regions in Laos, regions one through five.

NKP – Nakhon Phanom Royal Thai AFB, Thailand. Home for various electronic warfare operations in the Ho Chi Minh trail as well as the wide and varied aircraft hunting the NVA in Laos.

Pathet Lao – The communist resistance government and army in Laos aligned strongly with the North Vietnamese.

PDJ – Slang for Plain of Jars, an area in northern Laos distinguished by large pot-shaped burial urns left by earlier inhabitants. The PDJ was also a desired fertile plateau surrounded by mountains on northern Laos is considered by the Hmong as part of their homeland. It was the site of many blooded battles during the Secret War.

Phou Pha Thi – Secret radar site in Laos, 25 kilometers from North Vietnam border that directed air strikes against the enemy in North Vietnam until captured by the NVA in 1968. Phou Pha Thi is also a scared mountain of the Hmong.

Plain of Jars (Plaines des Jares) – Known as the PDJ an area in northern Laos distinguished by large pot-shaped burial urns left by earlier inhabitants. The PDJ was also a desired fertile plateau surrounded by mountains on northern Laos is considered by the Hmong as part of their homeland. It was the site of many blooded battles during the Secret War.

Post-traumatic stress disorder – Symptoms after the experiencing of a psychologically traumatic event or events outside the range of human experience usually considered being normal. These symptoms involve re-experiencing the traumatic event, numbing of responsiveness to, or involvement with, the external world, exaggerated startle response, difficulty in concentrating, memory impairment, guilt feelings, and sleep difficulties.

POW – Prisoner of War.

Prairie Fire – Consisted of air supported ground reconnaissance teams sent into enemy territory to select targets for air strikes and to make post strike assessment of damage.

Project 404/Palace Dog – A secret USAF unit that controlled much of the Air War in Laos in the 1960s and 1970s. Airmen and soldiers were "released" from military service temporarily and assigned to work for non-military government programs or private contractors in order to prosecute the war inside Laos.

PSP – Perforated steel plates used as for runways or aircraft parking area.

PX – The Post Exchange or military store.

Raven – Call signs for a small group of USAF Forward Air Controllers (FACs) in Laos flying O-1 Bird Dog U-17, U-10 and the T-28.

Re-education or Seminar Camps – Intended to reform drug addicts, prostitutes and used as concentration or retraining camps of those who had fought against the Pathet Lao after the war. They used torture, starvation and execution.

Rolling Thunder – Name for the air strikes against selected targets and lines of communications in North Vietnam.

RLAF – Royal Lao Air Force.

RTAF – Royal Thai Air Force.

RTAFB – Royal Thai Air Force Base.

SAM Missile – The NVA ground to air missile fired and locked onto US aircraft until detonation. Known as the flying telephone pole, if sighted, the only way to evade was to turn within the SAM's turn radius.

Sandy – Call sign for the A-1's flying the search and rescue missions in Vietnam and Laos.

SGU– Special Guerilla Unit, the Hmong Army led by General Vang Pao.

Secord, Richard – Air Force Major Secord served for the CIA in Laos directing air activity in the secret war in addition to covert operations including the Hmong Road watch teams. He rose to rank of Major General in the Air Force and was involved in other actions in the mid-east, covert ops, etc.

Shadow – Call sign of the AC-119G gunship.

SKY – Hmong term for their American CIA advisors.

SLAR – Side Looking Airborne Radar, the electronic sensor system flown on the Army's OV-1 Mohawk that would map terrain to either side of the aircraft and identify vehicles moving on the ground below the jungle canopy displaying the location in the cockpit for immediate identification and assignment to strike aircraft teamed with the Mohawk.

Slow Mover – An aircraft that flies slow as compared to jet fighters, usually a propeller driven aircraft.

Spectre – Call sign of the AC-130 gunship.

Spooky – Call sign of the AC-47 gunships.

Sortie – One aircraft making one takeoff and landing to conduct the mission for which it was scheduled.

Spud – Call sign of the Mohawks flying for the 131st Aviation Company in Vietnam and Laos.

Steel Tiger – The geographic area in Southern Laos designated by 7th AF to facilitate planning & operations, the term also referred to strikes in Southern Laos & against personnel & equipment from North Vietnam utilizing the Ho Chi Minh trail.

Stinger/Shadow – Call signs of the AC-119K gunship with 7.62 and 20mm mini guns mounted in side windows.

Task Force Alpha – Code name assigned to the organization in 1967 that built and operated an infiltration and surveillance center for receiving and analyzing acoustics& seismic sensor information on enemy activities in order to pinpoint their location for an air or ground attack. Referred to as the McNamara Line after the Secretary of Defense who promoted it. Located at NKP RTAFB, Thailand.

TDY – Temporary Duty assignment, the method of sending airmen or soldiers to duty in Laos while officially still assigned in Vietnam.

TET – The Vietnamese News Years celebrated at the end of January each year.

Udorn – Thai Air Force Base for Air Commandos operating in Laos from Thailand.

Up Country – Being in country in Laos.

USAID – The US Agency for International Development. Used to distribute food and humanitarian aid to countries. Also used a cover for the military working clandestinely in Laos.

Viet Cong (VC) – The Communist-led local forces fighting the South Vietnamese government.

Vientiane – Capital of Laos.

Visual Recon (VR) – Looking for the enemy on the ground visually from the air. Many times complemented with taking photo film of the search areas.

VVA – Vietnam Veterans of America. The Vietnam Veterans organization created by an Act of Congress.

Wake-up – The last day of a soldier's Vietnam tour. Used as in "13 and a wake-up".

Wasted – Slang for killed.

Water Pump – Code name for Detachment 6, 1stACW(USAF), which deployed to Udorn RTAFB for the purpose of training and support for Thailand and Laos Air Force including T-28 pilot training.

(The) World – Slang for the United States.

White Star – One of General Vang Pao's code names.

Yankee Team – Tactical reconnaissance program that in northern & southern Laos.

Zapped – Slang for killed.

The Grumman Mohawk

Photo from Grumman

The Army's OV-1 Mohawk answered a call for battlefield surveillance; recon, and close air support. Only three hundred and eighty planes were built and served the Army in the wars of Southeast Asia in Vietnam, Laos, Cambodia, and China. Its missions were highly classified; even today the plane is rarely mentioned in military history or aviation books.

The Mohawk initially was a joint design effort by the Army and the Marines who wanted a battlefield reconnaissance and close support aircraft that could give them immediate information on location and movement of enemy forces. The design called for a pilot and copilot configuration with a cockpit that offered an unobstructed view of the terrain around and below them. Speed was important, as the plane would be flying alone over enemy territory. It would be the only Army aircraft that utilized ejection seats, allowing for the type of missions and territory this plane was designed for. By the late fifties when the first prototypes began flying, the Marines had dropped out of the project due to funding limitations. So the Mohawk would fly as the Army's first fixed wing aircraft specifically designed for it since the Air Force was formed after World War II.

The first Mohawk model was the A model, whose role was visual recon of suspected enemy areas while serving as a photo platform flying just over the tree tops. The nose and belly mounted cameras took high quality continuous photos that formed a photo mosaic that the intelligence team could quickly put together offering an "instant" photo of everything going on in the targeted area. The bulging side cockpit windows gave it an almost insect appearance allowing the pilot and co-pilot the ability to look directly down onto the terrain below, giving an unobstructed view of the battlefield. With the silent turboprop engine, many a Mohawk was able to completely sneak up on an enemy going about his or her normal daily routine. That was until the Mohawk passed directly overhead with the enemy now exposed to its crew and the rolling film camera.

The A model was dual control, offering the pilot and co-pilot complete control of the aircraft. In Vietnam, the majority of these dangerous tree top missions were flown in teams of Mohawks. Many of these planes were armed with a variety of ordinance including fifty caliber machine guns and 2.75 rockets. This allowed them to quickly take out an enemy caught in the open who had the innate ability to quickly meld into the harsh jungle terrain. The arming of the Mohawks always provoked high-level arguments with the Air Force brass that argued close air support was strictly the role of the Air Force. Needless to say, in spite of agreements to disarm the Mohawks, many continued carrying weapons to the end of the Vietnam War. In 1966, an armed Mohawk flying as a recon team with another Mohawk successfully downed a North Vietnamese Mig fighter with its air to ground 2.75 rockets. The Mig fighter was going after the lead Mohawk over the northern end of the Ho Chi Minh trail. Blinded by his desire to pounce on the lead Mohawk, the Mig was blown from the sky by the quick thinking pilot of the second Mohawk in the flight.

Quickly following the A model was the B model Mohawk, whose appearance is easily discernable with its large cigar shaped radar pod protruding from the right side of the cockpit out past its nose. This pod emitted radar signals out to each side, mapping a strip of terrain that detected moving vehicles many times hidden underneath the jungle canopy of Southeast Asia. To carry this large system, the wings were extended, engines beefed up, and the radar monitoring systems that allowed him or her to immediately detect potential targets in the cockpit and coordinate would replace the copilot's controls. The radar film (later LCD display) was displayed in the cockpit where the vehicles could be quickly plotted and handed off to a gunship or fighter to take out the target. This would prove deadly to the enemy in Laos.

In the late sixties the D Model Mohawk was introduced. It embodied the various design upgrades and enhancements the rigors of the battlefield demanded, but more importantly offered one model that could switch easily between missions. It could fly a visual recon mission in the afternoon and be ready to fly an infrared or radar mission in the evening. This now gave the aviation unit increased flexibility in the types of mission it was able to fly.

Beside Vietnam, the Mohawk gave the battlefield commander instant intelligence on where the enemy was moving. In Korea since the mid fifties, for over thirty years the Mohawk operated around the clock mapping the DMZ and beyond, gathering vital information on what the enemy was up to. In Europe the Mohawk routinely flew the borders of Eastern Europe plotting troop movements and positions, allowing a birds-eye view to battlefield commander on what was going on that instant.

The enemy alone in the jungle often used the cover of darkness to move about their supplies, or reposition their troops for action. The darkness often gave an elusive air of safety to the enemy who feared less our attack at night. This gave the C Model or the Infrared Mohawk its opening. Again, the copilot's dual control was replaced with the controls that managed the sensitive infrared systems that allowed the Mohawk to see in total darkness. Belly mounted IR cameras would film the terrain at night, painting the differences in heat detected in the terrain below. Rivers ran cooler than the fields that surrounding it; fields of different crops gave up different temperatures or heat signatures. It was a photo camera without the flash, but deadly accurate. What we hunted for was the clues of enemies cooking fires, hot truck engines, or generators running. These were easily detected and their positions quickly plotted. Fire from aircraft or artillery could be directed to the coordinates. The enemy, or what remained of it after the incoming artillery or ordinance, would find darkness was no longer a place of safety. The Vietnamese called the Mohawk "whispering death." The Mohawk was bringing the war to the enemy in the middle of the night.

The electronic surveillance systems were constantly upgraded, increasing detection, distance, and now providing real time transmission of detection to allied ground and air units.

A new model of surveillance was added to the Mohawk, the Quick Look I and II ECM sensor system. This pod carried on the outer store station of the Mohawk wing would detect signals from enemy radar units. Once located, available strike aircraft could be directed to take out the enemy target.

In the early nineties, Mohawks were again deployed for war, this time the deserts of the Middle East in the Gulf War. There again, away from the press and cameras, the Mohawk flew their mission around the clock silently over the desert hunting an enemy that rarely knew the Mohawk was there. From hunting Iraq radar sites, to detecting Iraq truck and tank movement, to hunting the mobile scuds, or finding a hidden Iraq location, the Mohawk successfully completed its missions and returned home after serving its last war in the American Military lineup.

Beside the US Army, the Mohawk served numerous government agencies and foreign governments during its lifetime. The US Customs Service used Mohawks for its drug interdiction programs beginning in the seventies. Following the suspect plane easily with its speed, it carried a forward-looking radar system to detect aircraft flying in under ground radar, and then coordinated interdiction by enforcement agencies. The US Forestry department used the OV-1C's to help detect fires underneath the rugged forests. The US Geological Services used the various systems of the Mohawk in providing far ranging studies of the US geography, including exploration and later monitoring of the Alaska pipeline. Separately, the Navy Test Pilot School and NASA used the Mohawk for various flight-testing and research experiments. The EPA used the Mohawk to monitor for slight temperature changes on discharges from the nation's nuclear power plants.

The Mohawk was not limited to US Military operations. In 1975, two Mohawks were delivered to the Israeli Air Force for use in monitoring military movements across the borders. While highly classified, the D model was capable of flying infrared over enemy locations, and the Quick Look system, which pin pointed locations of radar or enemy radio sources.

Beginning in 1992 the Argentina Army began taking delivery of over twenty D model Mohawks in an effort to upgrade their Army Aviation. Today they fly the full array of military missions the US performed, and have constantly upgraded their electronic surveillance systems. They also fill an offensive role with the addition of various weapons systems that greatly increases their mission scope.

The Mohawk was retired from active military service in the US in September 1996.

Planes of the Secret War

A-1 Skyraider –Douglas A1-H aircraft, single propeller aircraft used for Close Air Support. This workhorse carried an unbelievable load of ordinance to provide close air support. Known as call sign Sandy was responsible for covering fire on pilot extractions from Laos and Vietnam.

A-26 Invader – The Douglas A26 Invader was a twin-engine attack bomber that started combat in World War II. In 1966, these workhorse Invaders were deployed to Nakhon Phanom to perform hunter-killer missions against truck convoys in southern Laos.

A-37 Cessna Dragonfly – A dual-seat, twinjet light attack aircraft used for close air support.

AC-47 Spooky – A twin-engine, propeller-driven gunship armed with four 7.62mm mini-guns and illumination, providing direct gunfire support for many units and firebases in the middle of a firefight.

AC-119 Gunship (Stinger) – The third development in gunship technology built for hunting trucks and tanks in Laos and the Ho Chi Minh Trail as there were not enough C-130's to convert. It was a twin-engine, propeller-driven gunship armed with two 20mm M61A1 cannons, a forward-looking AN/APN-147 Doppler terrain avoidance radar, a AN/AAD-4 Forward-Looking Infrared Radar (FLIR) system, and an AN/APQ-136 search radar.

AC-130 Gunship (Spectre) – The most feared weapon in Laos it had was a four-engine, turboprop gunship armed with four 7.62mm General Electric XMU-470 Miniguns, four 20mm General Electric M61 Vulcan cannons, an analog fire control computer, a Night Observation Device (NOD) or Starlite Scope, AN/AAD-4 Forward-Looking Infrared Radar (FLIR), a Singer-General Precision fire control computer, a TI Moving Target Indicator (MTI), and a 20kW searchlight. Several had a 105mm Howitzer cannon.

B-52 Bomber – The veteran Air force high-altitude strategic bomber converted for tactical bombing in Vietnam and after. Each B-52 used in Vietnam could carry eighty-four five hundred-pound bombs internally and twenty-four seven hundred fifty pound bombs on wing racks, with a three thousand mile nonstop range. It devised the term carpet-bombing with the wholesale destruction a flight of these would have on a target.

C-7 Caribou – A smaller twin-engine, propeller-driven transport aircraft which had the ability to operate from extremely short unimproved landing sites which were not within the capability of US Air Force C-123 and C-130's.

C-47-Douglas Skytrain – A Twin-engine, propeller-driven transport aircraft. In Vietnam, the C-47 served again as a transport, but it was also used for a variety of other missions, which included flying ground attack, reconnaissance, and psychological warfare missions. The AC-47 "Spooky", a heavily armed gunship version of the C-47, was equipped with three side-firing 7.62mm Miniguns and was nicknamed "Puff the Magic Dragon."

C-123-Fairchild Provider – A twin-engine, propeller-driven transport aircraft that carried troops and supplies through the war theater. It could carry 24,000 pounds or 60 troops, also served as a gun platform.

C-130 Hercules – The workhorse of the military used primarily for troop and supply transport but convert to dozens of specialized models including flying command centers, gunships, etc.

F-4 Phantom II – The principal US twin-engine, all-weather, tactical fighter-bomber was capable of operating at speeds of more than 1,600 miles per hour and at altitudes approaching 60,000 feet. A multiple purpose fighter that served roles in air-to-air combat, close air support with payloads of over 16,000 lbs, and reconnaissance missions.

F-105 Thud – From 1965 to 1970, the Thunderchief did most of the Air Force's bombing in Vietnam, typically carrying a cargo of eight 750-pound bombs. Though primarily an attack aircraft over Vietnam, the F-105 was able to shoot down several MiG-17s and MiG-21s.

F-111 Aardvark – The Air Force jet designed with swept weeks to enable long-range, low-altitude, and high-speed weapons delivery. It used the new radar return bombing technique that allowed for precision bombing offset from mobile beacons on the ground.

HH3-C Jolly Green Helicopter – Used for combat rescue missions with armor, defensive armament, self-sealing fuel tanks, a rescue hoist, and in-flight refueling capability. Operating out of Udorn, Thailand, and Da Nang, South Vietnam, this helicopter could reach any point in North Vietnam and return to its home base.

Mig-21 – This Soviet built fighter was flown by the North Vietnamese Air Force as a short-range interceptor to do battle with the American Air force. It had a range of over a thousand miles, cruised at 500mph with a top speed of 1,300 miles per hour. It was extremely light and maneuverable with exceptional reliability, sortie-rate, and low cost of operation.

O-1 Birddog – Cessna single engine aircraft used for forward air control or FAC duties in Vietnam and Laos. Held a pilot and observer with air to ground and air-to-air radio equipment to control air strikes.

O-2 – Twin engine Cessna Skymaster (also called "push me, pull me") that replaced the O-1 Birddog in forward air control or FAC duties

OV-10 Bronco – A FAC aircraft that began replacing the O-1's and 2's later in the war by the Air Force and Marines. Confused by many with the Army's OV-1.

OV-1 Mohawk – The Grumman twin-engine turboprop aircraft designed for the Army's reconnaissance, electronic surveillance, and close air support. Flew a crew of two in ejection seats on visual, photo recon, infrared detection, side looking airborne radar (SLAR) and later communication and radar site detection.

Pilatus Porter – Single engine STOL aircraft used by Air America, Continental, Bird and others to get supplies and people into the remote landing strips of Laos.

T-6 – Designed as a military trainer in 1936, it was provided to the Thai and Lao Air Force as a bomber in the war in Laos. It could be outfitted with bomb racks, fixed and flexible guns, recon cameras, which made it an extremely flexible plane for small Air Forces.

T-28D – Designed as a military trainer in 1948, it was rebuilt as the T-28A's with more store stations to carry additional armament in addition to a more powerful engine. This ingenious aircraft proved to be an effective, combat proven, gun and bomb platform. It was flown by the Royal Thai and Lao Air Forces, in addition to the US Ravens.

U-10 – Single engine four passenger STOL aircraft with side-by-side controls, also known as the Super Courier.

U-17A – Military version of the Cessna 185 that allowed four passengers with a single engine.

UH-1 Huey Helicopter – The workhorse of Asia, responsible for carrying troops, supplies, wounded and dead from battle, and duty as Gunships this helicopter revolutionized warfare forever. If there is one aircraft linked forever to the Vietnam and the Asian wars it is the Huey.

Anti-Aircraft Artillery (AAA) and SAM Weapons

SAM Missiles – Known as flying telephone poles, these ground to air missiles played havoc with US aircraft in North Vietnam and later Laos. Aimed manually or directed by radar these missiles would lock on an aircraft and follow it till explosion.

Anti-Aircraft Artillery (AAA) – Known as triple-A to pilots, these guns were the AK-47 equivalent of the ground to air war in Laos, North and South Vietnam. These guns ranged from trailer-mounted guns to self-driven artillery platforms. They could be aimed through gun sites or directed by radar. The size ranged from 37mm to 57mm, to the large 100mm and 122mm guns. Laos had more AAA guns then any theater of war the world has seen.

37mm AAA gun, two barrel 400 firing off rounds at 400 per barrel per minute, 57mm AAA gun, firing off rounds at 120 per minute, 100mm AAA gun, firing off rounds at 10-15 per minute

My buddy Sally J and the School/Orphanage in Hue

Bob Curry and Jim Eichelberger in Phu Bai Vietnam 1971

OV-1 Mohawk on Rocket Run in Vietnam and Laos

Secret Waterpump Project at Udorn and flight of OV-1's Mohawks over the Fence

Mohawk Infrared Sensor System (L) and SLAR, Side Looking Airborne Radar (R) (courtesy Grumman Aircraft)

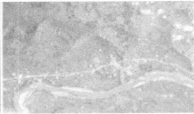

AC-130 Spectre Gunship and a piece of the Ho Chi Minh Trail

General Vang Pao and captured NVA weapons on PDJ in 1971

General Van Pao and Colonel Xiong at Long Chieng 1971

US Colonel O'Dell and Lao Colonel Xiong on PDJ in 1971

Major General Richard Secord and Brigadier General Heine Aderholt

Neng Lee (top row 2nd from right) and students at Vientiane University Laos 1969 and in 2003.

Colonel Yong Chue Yang, his son Xia Vue Yang in 1967 in Laos and 2004 in America

Hmong Ace Lee Lue (on right) and an NVA Mig 21

Bill Lair, Robert Curry, and Brigadier General Heine Aderholt

2003 Lao-Hmong American National Celebration. From left, Yang Chee (President Lao Hmong American Coalition), Robert Curry, Larry Sanborn (Raven FAC), Van Pao (Hmong POW), Air Force Lt. Col Bob Riesling Vietnam & Laos Veteran and Arnold Zaharia Navy CBY Vietnam Veteran.

Colonel Xay Dang Xiong, Yang Chee (President Lao-Hmong American Coalition) Captain Mary X.Yang , and Colonel Lee Lao

About the Author

Robert Curry is a veteran of the Vietnam and Laos wars having flown in over two hundred and fifty combat missions in the Mohawk. Pictured with his wife June, she was engaged to him before his journey to Vietnam, and watched a much different person return home. It is only through the treatment for his disability at the VA; his family, friends, and the Hmong people was he able to complete this book. Since the printing of this book, the suthor founded Dryhootch.org, a veterans nonprofit organization that "helps the veteran and his family who survived the war, survive the peace." Dryhootch has gone on to multiple locations, partnerships with government agencies, Medical Colleges, Veterans Organizations, community groups, and mental helath agencies. In 2012 Robert was honored at the White House as a Champion of Courage in his work on helping our nations veterans.

He has gone on to publish "Dryhootch, an Owners Manual on Combat PTSD" and is a speaker at national events on combat PTSD.

His work can be seen at www.Hostilefire.org